THE ETHICAL BASIS OF
POLITICAL AUTHORITY

By
WESTEL W. WILLOUGHBY

Social Justice

Examination of the Nature of the State

The Fundamental Concepts of Public Law

The Ethical Basis of Political Authority

THE ETHICAL BASIS
OF
POLITICAL AUTHORITY

BY

WESTEL W. WILLOUGHBY

PROFESSOR OF POLITICAL SCIENCE, JOHNS HOPKINS UNIVERSITY

New York
THE MACMILLAN COMPANY
1930

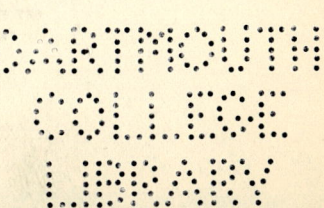

Copyright, 1930,
By THE MACMILLAN COMPANY.

Published April, 1930.

All rights reserved—no part of this book may be reproduced in any form without permission in writing from the publisher.

SET UP AND ELECTROTYPED BY J. J. LITTLE & IVES
PRINTED IN THE UNITED STATES OF AMERICA

PREFACE

In another work, entitled *Fundamental Concepts of Public Law,* the author has considered the nature of the State and its powers as they are regarded by the jurist. In the present work the aim is to examine political authority as it is viewed by the moralist. The two works are thus complementary and together set forth a system of Political Philosophy. In the earlier volume the State was viewed as the creator and enforcer of law, and the effort was made to determine juristic concepts without regard to their ethical validity. That is, the inquiry was formalistic in character, and had no other purpose than the construction of an apparatus of thought by means of which coherence and logical consistency might be given to accepted doctrines of Public Law. In the present volume the inquiry is teleological, the purpose being the establishment of the ethical rightfulness of political authority as determined by the results which are, or may be, obtained by its exercise. This problem, it will be found, requires not only that an answer be given to the abstract question as to ethical propriety of political coercion in any form, but that criteria be stated for testing the right of particular States or Governments to exist, or of particular individuals to possess political power, and for determining the ethical character of State policies, whether municipal or international.

To some extent these matters have been dealt with by the author in two volumes published some twenty-five years ago, entitled, respectively, *The Nature of the State,* and *Social Justice*. From these volumes some thoughts and occasional paragraphs have been borrowed.

W. W. W.

BALTIMORE, MD.
  March, 1930

CONTENTS

PART I

ETHICAL THEORIES

CHAPTER		PAGE
I.	FINAL POLITICAL PHILOSOPHY AND ITS RELATION TO OTHER SPECULATIVE INQUIRIES	3
II.	THEORIES WHICH EVADE OR DENY THE REALITY OF THE PROBLEM OF POLITICAL COERCION	18
III.	THEORIES OF ANARCHY	42
IV.	THE NATURE AND FUNCTIONS OF THE STATE AS ENVISAGED BY SOCIALISTS AND COMMUNISTS	59
V.	DIVINE RIGHT THEORIES	83
VI.	THE PATRIMONIAL THEORY	110
VII.	MYSTICAL OR TRANSCENDENTAL THEORIES	114
VIII.	FASCISM	131
IX.	THE CONTRACT THEORY	149
X.	HOBBES	166
XI.	SPINOZA AND LOCKE	186
XII.	ROUSSEAU	199
XIII.	VIEWS OF HOBBES, LOCKE AND ROUSSEAU COMPARED, AND THE CONTRACT THEORY CRITICIZED	219
XIV.	THE TRUE BASIS OF THE RIGHT OF POLITICAL COERCION	236
XV.	THE LEGITIMATE ENDS OF POLITICAL COERCION	270
XVI.	THE LEGITIMATE SPHERE OF POLITICAL AUTHORITY	281
XVII.	GOVERNMENT	304
XVIII.	INTERNATIONAL RELATIONS: NATIONAL STATES AND NATIONALITY	325
XIX.	THE RIGHTS ACCORDED TO STATES BY INTERNATIONAL LAW	356

PART II

ETHICO-JURISTIC THEORIES

CHAPTER		PAGE
XX.	Introduction to Part II	381
XXI.	The Theories of Duguit	385
XXII.	The Theories of Krabbe	410
XXIII.	Political Pluralism	427
	Index	457

PART I
ETHICAL THEORIES

CHAPTER I

FINAL POLITICAL PHILOSOPHY AND ITS RELATION TO OTHER SPECULATIVE INQUIRIES

Juristic and Final Political Philosophy Distinguished. Political inquiries become philosophical when they seek to determine the essential qualities of political life. The speculative domain thus marked out is divisible into two clearly defined fields. In the one, the attempt is to state with precision the nature of the State as viewed by the jurist, and thus to present the fundamental concepts which Public Law employs. In the other, the effort is to reach a satisfactory conclusion as to the grounds upon which the exercise of political coercion may be morally justified, and the criteria in accordance with which its specific manifestations may, from the viewpoint of ethical right, be criticized. In the one, the State is regarded as the creator and enforcer of law, and the aim is to obtain an apparatus of juristic thought, a series of premises and propositions by means of which logical coherence may be given to international and constitutional jurisprudence. In the other, the State is studied as a means for satisfying the spiritual and material needs of men. This means that inquiry must be made as to the State's ethical right to exist, as to the ethical legitimacy of the different governmental forms in which it may be organized, and as to the justification for its specific policies, national or international.

The ground which thus needs to be covered can be more fully indicated by considering the relations which

Political Philosophy, as thus defined, bears to other speculative and normative inquiries.

Final Political Philosophy and Ethics. Aristotle speaks of Ethics as a part or subdivision of Politics. This is understandable when it is remembered that he does not sharply distinguish between the concepts of Society and the State, and that he regards the latter as the all-comprehensive agency through which man's highest good may be realized. Thus, his *Politics* has a scope broad enough to cover matters social, as well as political, in the narrower sense of the word, and to include questions of ethics as well as of constitutional right or of governmental expediency.

If, however, following modern usage, the concept of the State is distinguished from that of Society, and is held to denote only that particular type or phase of social life in which the individuals composing the social group are viewed as composed of two classes of persons, the rulers and the ruled, and with more or less definitely determined organs and laws through which this rulership is exercised, the domain of Politics or of Political Science becomes restricted to the study or examination of those matters which are directly concerned with, or arise out of, this type or phase of social life, and, as thus restricted, must be content to take its place, by the side of the other social sciences which deal respectively with the various phases and problems of communal human life.

These several social sciences, among which that of Ethics is included, may, and usually do, deal, to a considerable extent, with the same phenomena, but they do so from different points of view. Thus, Ethics has to deal with the moral aspects of all the acts of men, political as well as non-political, and, therefore, Political Ethics may very properly be regarded as but one of the subdivisions of the general science of Ethics. It is in this sense that Plato speaks of it. At the same time, Political

Ethics may, with equal right, be spoken of as but one of the topics of the general science of Politics.

Upon its theoretical side, Ethics necessarily depends upon inquiries into the distinctive nature of man and of the moral order of the universe, and is therefore more or less metaphysical in character. Upon its practical side, however, its union with Politics is close. When the character of moral obligations or sanctions, or the nature of the highest good is dealt with, one is in the realm of theoretical or abstract Ethics. When the establishment of proper norms for human conduct is essayed, the domain of practical Ethics is entered. Practical Ethics is essentially a social science in that it has for its aim the determination of just rules for the guidance of men in their dealings with one another. The solitary individual may be, in fact, a moral being, but, until he is brought into association with others of his kind, there can occur to him few, if any, obligations of a moral nature. In other words, though the feeling of moral obligation may be an original datum of human consciousness, and man, as a partaker in a divine or absolute reason, may be regarded as potentially a moral being, the possibility of his coming to a self-recognition of this fact, as well as the opportunity of realizing it in practice, is rendered possible only in a state of society. The concrete facts which condition the formation and exercise of ethical ideals are thus preponderantly political in character. The influence exerted by the commands of the State in creating and molding current conceptions of right and justice is necessarily enormous. The true and desirable relation between Law and Ethics obtains when Ethics dictates the principles and distinctions which the laws embody. As a matter of fact, however, legal determinations are often the source whence men derive their ethical distinctions. In so far, then, as ethical speculation is devoted to a search for a justification of the existence, and the manner of existence, of the authority of a political institution, its inquiries are as much political as ethical. Conversely, in so far as the political philosopher seeks a moral basis for institutions and authorities, his speculations are as much ethical as political. It is true that political institutions and laws are necessarily limited to the control of external acts, and that men cannot be made moral by act of parliament; but the ultimate aim which should be sought by all political powers is that, through their influence, and assisted by the environment which they create, the highest possible moral life may be lived. In final purpose, then, Ethics and Politics agree. Only in the instrumentalities through which they operate do they differ. The one seeks to control human conduct by direct appeal to the individual's reason and conscience; the other, to render these appeals effective by the educational influence of the institutions which it establishes, and the order and formal justice which it maintains.[1]

Final Political Philosophy and Metaphysics. In so far as metaphysical inquiries are concerned with the essential attributes of men as rational, moral beings, their relation to final political philosophy is direct, and, indeed, fundamental, for, until these attributes are ascertained, it is not possible to discuss the nature of political authority as determined by the actual results reached, or possibly to be reached, by its exercise. Few there are who do not regard the State as one of the most important, if not the most important, of the agencies through which the possible perfections of men may be secured. It is, therefore, not a matter for surprise that so many metaphysicians should have sought to carry over their speculations into the political field in order to suggest the mode in which the State should be organized,

---

[1] So close is the relation between Political Science and Ethics, that one of the best histories that we have of political speculations—that of Janet—bears the title, *Histoire de la Science Politique dans ses Rapports avec la Morale.*

and to indicate the policies it should pursue in order that men may find the fullest possible play for their potentialities, and thus attain that *summum bonum* which, as metaphysically determined, is properly due them. Hence it is, that we find that the world's greatest metaphysicians have been also political philosophers. This has been as true of Plato and Aristotle in early days, as it has been of Aquinas and Occam in medieval times, and of Spinoza, Hobbes, Locke, Mill, Kant, Fichte and Hegel of more recent date.

At times, purely ontological conceptions have influenced political conclusions. Thus, to give but a single example, Plato, in his notion of the State, treats it as, in a sense, a universal,—the universal of man,—and, since, in his general philosophical system, he considers the universal as more real, more important than the particular, so the body politic is regarded as a higher type of humanity than are the particular individuals whom it comprehends. As a result, in his political scheme the welfare of these individuals is ruthlessly subordinated to that of the civic whole, and the citizen treated as having no rights, indeed no ends, that may be realized apart from the State. Aristotle, upon the other hand, while not denying reality to ideas as universals, holds that they do not exist apart from the particulars included within them, and to these particulars are therefore given a certain significance if not an independent existence of their own. In other words they are not regarded as wholly swallowed up by, or absorbed into, their universals. The reflex of this in Aristotle's political thought is seen in the rights and claims which are conceded by him to the individual citizens, *quâ* individuals, as against the State. So, similarly, in the Middle Ages the doctrines of nominalism and realism exerted an influence upon theories of the State and of the Church. And, in general, the special view which each philosopher has held as to the metaphysical nature of moral or intellectual freedom has been reflected in his political conclusions.

Political Philosophy and Theology. No necessary relation exists between political principles and theological doctrines. As a matter of historical fact, however, they have been closely associated. As soon as the Church and State were regarded as distinct institutions, speculation began as to their relation to each other. Thus, throughout the Middle Ages, the distinction between matters temporal and matters spiritual, between powers political and powers ecclesiastical, occupied the attention of scholars and statesmen. This controversy was saturated with doctrines of natural and of divine law, and with the rights and obligations created or imposed by "right reason." To a very considerable extent this meant that tradition, intuition, faith, and an application of the precepts of Holy Scripture, took the place of rationalistic thinking. It also meant that political speculation was almost wholly concerned with moral obligations. The ethical right of the State to exist, its ethically legitimate sphere of authority, the content of its law, the character and extent of the arbitrary or personal power properly exercisable by rulers, and the reciprocal rights and duties of their subjects,— these, rather than the examination of the ideas of sovereignty and law as positive legal concepts, were the topics that were over and over again discussed, and the answers sought, not in utilitarian considerations growing out of existing needs and conditions, but in a priori examinations of the essential nature of man and the content and character of divine or natural law.

Thus, during all this time, political philosophy was metaphysical, where it was not frankly theological, in character. Its inquiries extended little beyond the realms of *Naturrecht* or *Naturrechtlehre* and of biblical exegesis. The existence of natural or purely rational or divine laws, absolutely binding in their force, being assumed, speculators, one after another, essayed the elaboration of codes of conduct that should govern rulers and ruled in the establishment, organization, and maintenance of political relations. Absoluteness was the one characteristic of the systems that were constructed; principles of law absolutely binding *in foro interno* upon every one were the results almost uniformly reached. Being subjective in character, the freest possible play to the speculative abilities and prejudices of their authors was permitted, and thus, as one writer has remarked, the science or philosophy of natural law while preventing the creation of a true and useful science of politics, was the apotheosis of political philosophy.

In modern times the absolute has largely given way to the relative in both ethical and political speculation. We no longer have a naïve belief in our ability to ascertain the truth of all things by a process of a priori excogitation; tradition, at most, is given only a mildly persuasive value; the binding force of scriptural precepts or the dicta of the Church Fathers outside the field of dogmatic theology is repudiated; and, as a result, the State has been brought down from the clouds and subjected to the utilitarian tests of human needs as determined by conditions of time and place and people.[2] This, of course, has introduced the element of relativity, and it is now a truism to say that the form of government and the code of laws best for one people are not necessarily the best for another people, nor, indeed, for the same people at different times if their circumstances have changed.

The acceptance of the relativity of ethical obligations in general, or of political obligations in particular, has not, of course, meant that abstract moralizing or final political philosophizing no longer has a sufficient reason

---

[2] This statement needs qualification so far as certain mystical, if not theological, conceptions of the State have persisted. These conceptions will be later treated.

for being pursued. It is still requisite that the essential character of political obligation be determined, and the abstract criteria of rightness and wrongness ascertained. And, applying these conclusions in the political field, it is still imperative that an ethical *quo warranto* be established for the State, and standards of political conduct erected for testing the ethical propriety of its acts. These inquiries have their value, even though we no longer believe that it is possible to construct a scheme of government and of laws which, without regard to time or place or people, can be declared to be the best possible or ideal one. In other words, there is, and always will be, need for clear thinking regarding the fundamental grounds upon which political coercion may be ethically justified,—a justification which will reveal the source of the citizen's obligations to the State and his right to claim a participation in the determination of its form of governmental organization, and in the formulation and execution of its policies. Implicit in such a final political philosophy will also be the relations which States should bear to one another, and the grounds upon which particular communities may properly claim a right to determine the sovereignty to which they are to yield obedience, that is, to assert a right to national self-determination.

By way of summary of our statement of the relation which political philosophy bears to other fields of speculative inquiry, it may, then, be said that metaphysics, ethical philosophy, and political philosophy constitute the three divisions into which any general philosophical system is logically divisible. By metaphysics is determined the nature and essential attributes of men as rational, moral beings. Upon its conclusions are based the principles which the moralist declares. The results reached by the moralist are, in turn, those which it should be the aim of political life to realize. Thus, to state the sequence in other words, metaphysics determines the nature of human freedom; ethics lays down the principles by which it should be regulated; and politics ascertains certain of the means through which those principles can receive recognition and enforcement. In this way the final aim of philosophy is fulfilled. Without ethics and politics, metaphysics is reduced to useless imaginings; without metaphysics, ethics is largely deprived of its premises, and, without politics, is largely denied the means of securing a realization of the aims which it declares desirable. Without metaphysics and ethics, politics is unable either to determine the relative ethical values of different possible lines of public policy, or to establish grounds upon which political obedience may rightly be demanded.

The Importance of Final Political Philosophy. Philosophy is the search for what is essentially true, and alone is able to satisfy the mind's insatiable demand for ultimate causes and for the determination of the ethical validity of the various motives which influence or figure in human conduct. The pure intellectual delight to be obtained from speculative inquiry is, to most minds, a sufficient recompense for its pursuit. Its results are, therefore, satisfying quite apart from their practical value in determining the conduct of men. But, leaving this conviction aside, no argument is needed to show the value of determining, by relentless logic, the general principles in accordance with which the ethical validity of political authority in all its forms and phases is to be tested. Only when such general principles have been determined does it become possible to fix logically, and therefore convincingly, the obligations of political loyalty and allegiance, as well as the rights of the governed to participate, either directly or through their chosen representatives, in the conduct of their own public affairs.

A collateral, but none the less important, function of political philosophy, especially upon its final or teleological side, is the aid which it affords in the interpretation of historical events. Political theories have ever been dependent upon, and have been evoked by, particular objective conditions; and they therefore reflect the thoughts, and serve to interpret the actuating motives at the basis of important political movements. In the history of political theories, the student is able at once to enter into a knowledge of what men in the past have really striven for, —what have been their ideals. Who, for instance, could hope to understand the Puritan movement, either in England or in our own country, without a knowledge of its political theories, or expect to appreciate the history of the middle and early modern ages without a comprehension of the various medieval views regarding the relation between Church and State? How is one to explain the long-continued and widespread acceptance of the doctrine of the divine right of kings, which to-day seems so essentially absurd, without knowing what that theory really meant to its believers, and what were its relations to such other antagonistic theories as those of papal supremacy and popular sovereignty?

Not only have political speculations been largely influenced by practical contemporaneous problems, they have also been, to an almost equal extent, though less directly, controlled by what has been called the "intellectual climate" of their times. This is a point which Lecky, in his *History of the Development of Rationalism in Europe,* has strongly emphasized and amply sustained by facts and reasoning. Beliefs which at one time have had almost universal currency have, at other times, been declared absurd, the reason for the change being, not so much that specific evidence or exact logic has overthrown the old ideas, as that the intellectual trend of the later time has been towards a skepticism as regards the particular class of facts involved. Witchcraft, for example, is now relegated by all enlightened minds to the limbo of superstition and fraud; yet, as Lecky says, "for more than fifteen hundred years it was universally believed that the Bible established, in the clearest manner, the reality of the crime, and that an amount of evidence, so varied and so ample as to preclude the very possibility of doubt, attested its continuance and its prevalence. The clergy denounced it with all the emphasis of authority. The legislators of almost every land enacted laws for its punishment. Acute judges, whose lives were spent in sifting evidence, investigated the question on countless occasions and condemned the accused." All this occurred, not because humanity was wanting, not because ignorance was universal, but because acceptance of the miraculous was a characteristic of the thought of the age; and the belief in witchcraft died out only when, through the advance of science, the idea gradually gained ground that uniform law holds sway throughout the phenomenal world.

Exactly the same phenomenon is to be observed in tracing the development of political theories. Dominant political systems have lost support and been supplanted by others, as the chief thought of the time has changed from matters military to matters industrial, or from belief in the beneficence of authority to confidence in the inherent goodness of freedom. Arguments which at one time were deemed abundantly sufficient to sustain the divine right of kings, or the religious duty of absolute obedience, have been, at another time, spurned as not even worthy of examination. We wonder now that men of the learning of Locke or Sidney should have considered it worth while to expend so much effort in the refutation of the absurdities of Filmer's system. So, too, doctrines of political persecution and of natural rights have had their heyday of prosperity, only to become blasted as the general intellectual climate assumed towards them a wintry aspect.

Sir Frederick Pollock, in his *History of the Science of Politics*, mentions still another advantage to be derived from political speculation; namely, that of exposing the falsity of incorrect theories. Thus he says: "To the persons who deny the necessity or possibility of philosophy, it is a sufficient answer that at all events critical philosophy is needed for the exposure of philosophies falsely so called; and in the same way political science must and does exist, if it were only for the refutation of absurd political theories and projects." In illustration of this he points to the declaration of the rights of man by the French constituent assembly. "This consists of general statements of what men, as men, are entitled to, and may justly demand. If true, the statements are of the utmost importance to politicians and legislators; if false, they are highly mischievous."

That there still persist and find considerable acceptance conceptions of the State and theories as to the nature of political obligation that are essentially false and pernicious if attempted to be applied will, it is believed, abundantly appear in the pages which follow.

Alleged Dangers of Political Philosophy. A misunderstanding of its methods and purposes has led, in certain quarters, to a distrust of political theorizing, especially upon its teleological side. Thus the statement has been made by writers of no little distinction that, to use Bacon's simile, like the virgin consecrated to God, political philosophy is barren in its results. Other writers have, upon the other hand, gone so far as to declare that, like the imp devoted to the evil one, it is fertile with disaster. Bishop Berkeley alleged, as a reproach to philosophical thinkers generally, that they first kick up a dust and then complain that they cannot see; and Burke describes the discussions of abstract political questions as "the Great Serbonian Bog twixt Damiata and Mt. Cassius old, where armies whole have sunk"; and, in another place he says: "One sure symptom of an ill-conducted state is the propensity of the people to resort to theories." To the same effect is Leslie Stephen when he declares that: "Happy is the nation that has no political philosophy; for such a philosophy is generally the offspring of a recent, or the symptom of an approaching revolution." So, also, we have one of the most eminent of our own political scholars, Professor W. A. Dunning of Columbia University, saying, after a review of certain historical instances which he thinks support him in his conclusions: "It seems as if the exaltation of the principles of a particular system into doctrines of universal philosophy only sounds the knell of the system." "If this be true," he continues, "we may have as good grounds for rejoicing as for regret that no distinctively American political philosophy has yet appeared." These statements, it is to be observed, carry with them an indictment not of political philosophy in general, but only of the attempt to elevate the principles of a particular polity into a universal system. It is apparent, however, that a distrust of abstract political thinking was present in the mind of Professor Dunning.

Finally, we have the view voiced by Lecky, which appears in his *History of Rationalism in Europe,* where he says that the habit of philosophizing in politics is subversive of that mental balance which enables one rationally to judge of practical matters. He says: "Another consequence of the intellectual influence of political life is the tendency to sacrifice general principles to practical results. It has often been remarked that the English constitution, which is commonly regarded as the most perfect realization of political freedom, is beyond all others the most illogical, and that a very large proportion of those measures which have proved most beneficial have involved the grossest logical inconsistencies, the most partial and unequal application of some general principle. The object of the politician is expediency, and his duty is to adapt his measures to the often crude, undeveloped and vacillating conceptions of the nation. The object, on the other hand, of the philosopher is truth, and his duty is to push every principle which he believes to be true to its legitimate consequences, regardless of the results which may follow. Nothing can be more fatal in politics than a preponderance of the philosophical, or in philosophy than a preponderance of the political spirit. In the first case, the ruler will find himself totally incapable of adapting his measures to the exigencies of exceptional circumstances; he will become involved in inextricable difficulties by the complexity of the phenomena he endeavors to reduce to order; and he will be in perpetual collision with public opinion. In the second case, the thinker will be continually harrassed by considerations of expediency which introduce the bias of the will into what should be a purely intellectual process, and impart a timidity and a disingenuousness to the whole tone of his thoughts. It is probable that the capacity for pursuing abstract truth for its own sake, which has given German thinkers so great an ascendancy in Europe, is in no slight degree to be attributed to the political languor of their nation."

The work from which this quotation is taken was published in 1865, and the last sentence in which he hazards the suggestion that there may be a causal connection between the aptitude of the Germans to pursue abstract truth, and their political languor, has been most strikingly refuted by events of later years. The real objection, however, to Lecky's reasoning, as well as to that of the other writers who have been quoted, rests in the fact that they have misconceived the proper purpose and province of political theorizing. In general they have identified political philosophy with the formulation of canons of political conduct by which the statesman is to be absolutely guided in his conduct of public affairs, or the elaboration of ideally perfect forms of government for the immediate establishment of which every effort should be made. Practical guidance in the administration of the state may certainly be obtained from the scientific study of political phenomena. But the provision of these guiding rules is the task of the art of politics rather than of its philosophy, and no claim of absoluteness is made for these maxims. It is, indeed, as will later be seen, well within the proper province of political philosophy to deduce from the essential needs and ends of men as rational, moral beings ideal systems of social and political life,—ideals which set the goals to be striven for, and erect the standards by which the utility and ethical worth of existing institutions are to be judged. But this is a result far different from the elaboration of Utopias, the immediate establishment of which is urged without reference to the special conditions of the time, place and peoples to be affected by them. Janet, in his *Histoire de la Science Politique*, when summing up his estimate of Plato's *Republic*, makes this point so clear that his words deserve quotation. He says: "A distinction must be drawn between Utopian politics and ideal politics. The first consists in combining artificially, and by means of the imagination, the elements of which all society is composed, and thus creating an arbitrary mechanism which has no life, no reality, no possible application, either present or future. . . . Ideal politics, on the contrary, consist in forming a true idea of the State, in conceiving it in its perfection (as much so, of course, as the limits of the human mind permit), and, lastly, in presenting to societies a model, as ethics presents one to individuals. No State will ever reach that perfection, any more than any hero or saint has ever attained or ever will attain moral perfection. But if we do not forbid ethics to propose an ideal to men, why should we forbid politics to present one to peoples and to governments?"

CHAPTER II

THEORIES WHICH EVADE OR DENY THE REALITY OF THE PROBLEM OF POLITICAL COERCION

The Problem. The most conspicuous fact about every Government, whatever its special form or its specific activities, is that it is an instrumentality through which coercive control is exercised by those who operate it over other individuals,—a coercion resistance to which is punished by the severest penalties, including, in many States, the most extreme of all, shameful death. This coercion, though supported and made possible by a preponderance of physical might, is not ordinarily one of mere force, for, in general, its essential rightfulness, as well as its utility, is recognized, and its exercise acquiesced in by those whose lives and actions are controlled. It nevertheless remains true that the coercion thus employed, is, *per se*, that is, when detached from its ultimate results and viewed in its immediate effect upon the individuals subjected to it, an evil; for, to the extent that this control is coercive, its exercise, or threat of exercise, is necessarily irksome or painful to the ones controlled. It is, therefore, not strange that the question of determining what ultimate good, if any, may be held to justify the infliction of this immediate evil, should have agitated the minds of men since the time when first they began to be conscious of themselves as rational beings, to glimpse the meaning of human existence, and to form the conviction that they are not the helpless victims of whatever forces that may happen to play upon them.

It might seem that such a quest as this, so persistently

pursued, would long ago have been crowned with success, and its conclusions accepted by all thinking men. As a matter of fact, however, this is not the case. Men still dispute as the grounds upon which political coercion may be justified, and not a few deny that it can be ethically justified upon any grounds. And, even when there is agreement as the fundamental basis upon which the State's right of coercion rests, there is diversity of opinion as to the deductions that may properly be drawn as to the legitimate sphere of political authority, and the modes of its exercise. New conditions and requirements of community life constantly present this central problem in altered aspects and raise novel questions as to the propriety of the applications to be made of the conclusions reached. It would seem, therefore, that there will always be need for clear and systematic, if not of original, thinking in the field of final political philosophy.

Analysis of the Problem of Political Coercion. The inquiry as to the ethical validity of the exercise of political authority resolves itself into four distinct problems. First, the abstract question as to the right of the State to exist, that is, as to the ethical legitimacy of political coercion in any form or under any conditions; Second, the question as to the justification for the existence and maintenance of particular forms of governmental organization through, and by means of, which the State, the political entity, exerts its authority; Third, the determination of the principles in accordance with which the right of particular persons to occupy the seats of political power may be determined; and, Fourth, the statement of the criteria for estimating the ethical character of political policies. The first, it is clear, is the fundamental question, and the answer given to it will determine, in no small measure, the tests to be applied in answering the other questions. Nevertheless, these four questions are distinct, for one can admit the legitimacy of political coercion without committing himself as to the ethical propriety of a particular form of government under given conditions, or as to the right of particular individuals to control that government, or as to the moral merits of the policies pursued by them. However, because more fundamental, and as preparing the way for the solution of the other problems of political ethics, especial attention will be devoted in the present volume to the determination of the grounds upon which political authority in general, that is, however manifested, may be ethically defended. Before proceeding, however, to a consideration of the various theories that have sought to give an affirmative answer to this question, it will be worth while, if only for the purpose of simplifying and clarifying the discussion, to examine certain other theories which, while purporting to give an answer to the problem, have, in fact, either evaded it or denied its reality.

The Historical Theory. It would appear that there are some persons who are willing to accept the doctrine that, because the political State, as we now have it, is the result of an historical growth, its existence is therefore justified. Some, as, for example, Bossuet, have held that this is so because there is a divine providence that directs the destinies of men, and, therefore, that political as well as all the other established institutions of men are to be regarded as agencies sanctioned and justified by this divine will. This view, it is seen, is but a ruder application of the Divine Right theory which, as applied specifically to matters political will, later on, be more particularly discussed. Some philosophers, as, for example, Hegel, see in human history the gradual and progressive realization of certain eternal and metaphysically determinable principles of right. Thus, though, at any one time, the State or any other human institution, is not wholly rational, it is justified as representing one of the phases of human development and as one of the means whereby humanity is progressing towards that goal which is metaphysically marked out for it. Thus, while Hegel does not say that whatever is, is right, he does assert that the rational is the real and that the real is the rational. We shall have more to say of this theory when we come to deal with those theories which see in the State a mystical or transcendental entity or being.

Professor John W. Burgess seems to accept this Hegelian doctrine, though, according to him, the ideal towards which mankind is moving is not that perfect realization of that freedom of the will of which Hegel speaks, but the establishment of a world State. It is not perfectly clear that Professor Burgess is concerned with the ethical right of the State to exist, as distinguished from the determination of its origin, but the fact that he urges the historical explanation as an answer to the problem which, according to him, the theological and social compact theories were unable to solve, would make it appear that he is attempting to justify, as well as to explain, the existence of the State. After pointing out that publicists and jurists differ widely as to the origin of the State, he says:

"I think, however, that these divergences of opinion may be so classified as to reduce the apparently numerous shades of difference to three propositions. I will call the first of these the theological theory, the second the social, and the third the historical. The first claims that the State is founded by God, the second that it is founded by human agreement, and the third that it is the product of history. I think the latter is the true view, and that, when correctly comprehended, it will be seen to do full justice to the other two, and to reconcile all three. The proposition that the State is the product of history means that it is the gradual and continuous development of human society, out of a grossly imperfect beginning, through crude but improving forms of manifestation, towards a perfect and universal organization of mankind. It means, to go a little deeper into the psychology of the subject, that it is the gradual realization, in legal institutions, of the universal principles of human nature, and the gradual subordination of the individual side of that nature to the universal side. . . . If the theologian means, by his doctrine of the divine origin of the State, simply that the Creator of man implanted the substance of the State in the nature of man, the historian will surely be under no necessity to contradict him. . . . The principle of the historical genesis of the State does not, then, stand opposed to the doctrine of the divine origin of the State, when that doctrine is rationally construed: it includes it, and makes it the starting point in the evolution."[1]

As for the theory that finds the origin of political institutions in agreements between the governed or between them and their rulers, Burgess points out that it is inherently false since it presupposes upon the part of the contracting parties, ideas and motives that could only have come into existence as a result of an already highly developed state life. "It presupposes," he says, "that the idea of the State, with all its attributes, is consciously present in the minds of the individuals proposing to constitute the State, and that the disposition to obey the law is already universally established. Now we know that these conditions never exist in the beginning of the political development of a people, but are attained only after the State has made several periods of its history."

A little later on, he says: "The historical development of the State . . . takes for its basis and point of departure human nature: it distinguishes in that nature a universal side and a particular side; it accepts the principle that the creator of that nature is, therefore the

[1] *Political Science and Comparative Constitutional Law*, Vol. I, pp. 59-62.

originator of the subjective State, i.e., the political idea. But the political scientist is looking for the State made objective in institutions and laws, and this is the product of history." [2]

In the paragraphs which have been quoted it is apparent that Professor Burgess is under the impression that the chief purpose of the divine right and social compact theories is to explain the origin in time of the State, whereas, in truth, this is not what they seek to do. The theological theory may assert that men have been impelled by an impulse divinely implanted in them, or by the pressure of needs resulting from their natures as divinely determined, but it does not deny that, as an historical fact, States have been the handiwork of men and their development an historical process. So, too, those who have supported the social compact theories, have not claimed, except possibly in a very few instances, that States have actually come into existence as a result of formal agreements between the governed or between them and their rulers, and not as a product of war, of an arbitrary assumption of authority by particular individuals, or as the more gradual result of historical processes. What both theories have sought to provide has been an ethical basis for existing States, however they may have come into existence. In other words, the theological theory has said that the existence of political authority is ethically justified, and obedience to it is a moral obligation, because it is divinely sanctioned. The social contract theory has said that political authority, whatever its historical origin, can be ethically justified only if it be regarded as founded upon the consent of the governed; not that, in any particular case, this consent has actually been given in any formal or overt manner, but that the continuance of that authority, the modes of its exercise, its governmental structure, and the persons by whom operated, can be

[2] *Op. cit.*, Vol. I., p. 63.

legitimized only in so far as it can be reasonably assumed that the governed have given or are continuing to give their assent thereto.

The Natural or Instinctive Theory. By some thinkers it has been deemed a sufficient answer to the question of the right of the politically coercive State to exist to say that men are by nature, that is, instinctively, political beings. Thus, as we have seen, Professor Burgess speaks of the State as but the objective manifestation of principles that are subjective in men and the product of their very nature.

Of course, the State is natural in the same sense that everything which exists is natural. But, unless one asserts that existence is proof of a right to existence, no progress is made in the search for an ethical basis for political authority by asserting that men are by very nature political beings, or that, as a result of an instinctive psychological urge, they group themselves into political units. Granting this, the questions are still insistent: What is it that makes just the coercion of the individual by the political unit of which he is a member? What reason is there why the phenomena which result from man's instinctive politicality are to be pronounced ethically good? By what test is to be determined the right of a particular State or Government to exist, or of particular individuals to occupy the seats of political power? And, by what criteria is to be measured the morality of the public policies which they pursue? In short, the instinctive political urge in men (granting it to exist), or the need for the State which men have in order to satisfy desires that result from their very natures, may explain, as a matter of practical fact, why political authority has been created and continues to be maintained, but it does not furnish an ethical justification for that authority. First, it must be shown that those desires are such that it is ethically desirable that they should be satisfied, and that the politically coercive State is the only, or, at any rate, the best, instrumentality for securing this satisfaction.

In support of the natural theory is often quoted the assertion of Aristotle that man is by nature a political being. It scarcely needs be said that Aristotle makes this statement, not as a premise, but as a conclusion. As is well known, he holds that the real nature of a being is to be determined by the possible perfection to which that being can be brought. When, then, Aristotle says that man is, by nature, a political being, he means that his metaphysical and ethical speculations have led him to form an estimate of man's *summum bonum,* of his ideally best life, which, as a practical proposition, it is impossible for him to realize except in social and political association with others of his kind.

The Organismic Theory. Allied to the "naturalistic" conception of the State is the doctrine that it may be regarded as an "Organism" in the sense in which that word is used by biologists, and, therefore, that it has immutable laws of growth, decay, and death, of health and sickness, and the like, and that, from its organic character, legitimate deductions can be drawn as to the relation that exists between the whole and its part, between the public welfare and that of its constituent cells, the individual citizens.

Here we must draw a distinction between the positing of an analogy, or the use of the biological conception simply as a means for explaining or illustrating a point, and the affirmance of an identity and the deducing of conclusions therefrom. Writers too numerous to mention, in discussing the nature of political society, have referred to the State as a biological organism in one or the other of these two ways, and one or two of the most striking of these instances are worth quoting or describing.[3]

[3] For a detailed examination of this phase of political theory see Coker, *Organismic Theories of the State.* (Vol. 38, No. 2, Columbia University Studies in History, Economics and Public Law.)

Hobbes, in the very first paragraph of his Introduction to the *Leviathan*, says:

"Nature, the art whereby God hath made and governs the world, is by the 'art' of man, as in many other things, so in this also imitated, that it can make an artificial animal. For seeing life is but a motion of limbs, the beginning whereof is in some principal part within; why may we not say, that all 'automata' (engines that move themselves by springs and wheels as doth a watch) have an artificial life? For what is the 'heart,' but a 'spring'; and the 'nerves,' but so many 'strings'; and the 'joints,' but so many 'wheels,' giving motion to the whole body, such as was intended by the artificer? 'Art' goes yet further, imitating that rational and most excellent work of nature, 'man.' For by art is created that great 'Leviathan' called a 'Commonwealth,' or 'State,' in Latin *Civitas*, which is but an artificial man; though of greater stature and strength than the natural, for whose protection and defence it was intended; and in which the 'sovereignty' is an artificial 'soul,' as giving life and motion to the whole body; the 'magistrates,' and other 'officers' of judicature and execution, artificial 'joints'; 'reward' and 'punishment,' by which fastened to the seat of the sovereignty every joint and member is moved to perform his duty, are the 'nerves,' that do the same in the body natural; the 'wealth' and 'riches' of all the particular members, are the 'strength'; *salus populi*, the 'people's safety,' its 'business'; counsellors, by whom all things needful for it to know are suggested unto it, are the 'memory'; 'equity,' and 'laws,' an artificial 'reason' and 'will'; 'concord,' 'health,' 'sedition,' sickness; and 'civil war,' 'death.' Lastly, the 'pacts' and 'covenants,' by which the parts of this body-politic were at first made, set together, and united, resemble that 'fiat,' or 'let us make man,' pronounced by God in the creation."

It is clear here that only resemblances and analogies are in the mind of Hobbes. In fact, the State and man are conceived of rather as mechanisms than as organisms, as artificial rather than as natural or spontaneously created and living beings. And we may, with considerable confidence, conjecture that Hobbes introduces and emphasizes this artificial and mechanistic conception of the State in order to free it from the mystical and divine attributes which, during the Stuart period in England, were so generally ascribed to it.

In the writings of Herbert Spencer we come much nearer to the assertion that political society is an organism in substantially the same sense that beings of the biological world are so regarded.[4]

Spencer is primarily concerned with Society rather than with the State, but a State is a social group politically organized; indeed, a State is a Society in its most developed form. Spencer has a chapter which bears the unequivocal title "A Society is an Organism," but, in closing the preceding chapter, he had said: "that the permanent relations among the parts of a Society are *analogous*[5] to the permanent relations among the parts of a living body, we have now to consider."

Space will not permit us to follow Spencer in the many resemblances which he finds between socially and politically organized groups of human beings and the living organism: but one striking difference he is forced to admit. "The parts of an animal form a concrete whole; but the parts of a society form a whole that is discrete. While the living units composing the one are bound together in close contact, the living units composing the other are free, not in contact, and more or less widely dispersed." However, he asserts that this admission is consistent with

---
[4] Spencer's views upon this point are especially to be found in his Part II, "The Inductions of Sociology," of his *Principles of Sociology.*
[5] Italics not in the original.

the maintenance of the alleged "analogy." [6] "Though coherence among its parts is a prerequisite to that coöperation by which the life of an individual organism is carried on; and though the members of a social organism, not forming a concrete whole, cannot maintain coöperation by means of physical influences directly propagated from part to part; yet they can and do maintain coöperation by another agency. Not in contact, they nevertheless affect one another through intervening spaces, both by emotional language, and by the language, oral and written, of the intellect."

Another cardinal feature, says Spencer, which distinguishes the biological organism from the social unit is the following: "In the one, consciousness is concentrated in a small part of the aggregate. In the other, it is diffused throughout the aggregate: all the units possess the capacities for happiness and misery, if not in equal degrees, still in degrees that approximate. As, then, there is no social sensorium, it results that the welfare of the aggregate, considered apart from that of the units, is not an end to be sought. The society exists for the benefit of its members, not its members for the benefit of that society." [7]

These being the facts, it is clear that when Spencer asserts that Society is an organism, as he does in the very title to his chapter, he gives to the term a meaning broad enough to include such widely different units that confusion of thought must necessarily result from giving to them the same descriptive title.

Bluntschli is also one of the writers who have emphasized the likeness between political societies and liv-

---

[6] Here again it will be observed that only an analogy is spoken of.
[7] Thus, Spencer, while so strongly emphasizing the similarities between living organisms and social aggregates, is yet able to protest vehemently against anything more than a minimum control of the individual by the State. This phase of this political philosophy we shall consider later on when we come to the discussion of the legitimate sphere or scope of political authority.

ing organisms. Indeed, he carries not merely the analogy but the actual identity, so far as to ascribe a gender to the State. "The State," he says, "is in no way a lifeless instrument, a dead machine: it is a living and therefore organized being. . . . This conception refutes both the mathematical and mechanical view of the State, and the atomistic way of treating it, which forgets the whole in the individuals." But, though a true living organism, the State is not a "natural" organism. "The State indeed is not a product of nature, and therefore it is not a natural organism; it is indirectly [but only indirectly, be it observed] the work of man. The tendency to political life is to be found in human nature [here the naturalistic theory emerges], and so far the State has a natural basis; but the realization of this political tendency has been left to human labor, and human arrangement, and so far the State is a product of human activity, and its organism is a copy of a natural organism." [8]

Bluntschli then continues:

"In calling the State an organism we are not thinking of the activities by which plants and animals seek, consume and assimilate nourishment, and reproduce their species. We are thinking of the following characteristics of natural organisms:

(a) Every organism is a union of soul and body, i.e., of material elements and vital forces.

(b) Although an organism is and remains a whole, yet in its parts it has members, which are animated by special motives and capacities in order to satisfy in various ways the varying needs of the whole self.

(c) The organism develops itself from within outwards, and has an external growth.

In all three respects the organic nature of the State is evident."

[8] *The Theory of the State* (English transl.), Bk. I, Chap. I.

Bluntschli then goes on to assert that the State has a will of its own as distinguished from the wills of its individual citizens; it has organs for the expression and execution of this will; its functions have a spiritual character, and it is animated by a soul; it has a development and a growth of its own,—a childhood and a maturity,—but with this to distinguish it from plants and animals: its development is not as regular as theirs. "The influence of human free will or of external fate frequently produces considerable deviations, hastening, sometimes reversing the normal movement, according as it is broken in upon by great and strong individuals, or by the mild passions of the nation itself." In result, we find that it is "a moral and spiritual organism, a great body which is capable of taking up unto itself the feelings and thoughts of the nation, of uttering them in laws, and realizing them in acts. . . . History ascribes to the State a personality which, having spirit and body, possesses and manifests a will of its own." Thus, the State is more than a living organism, it is a person. More than this, it is a masculine person. "This becomes first apparent in contrast with the feminine character of the Church. A religious community may have all the other characteristics of a political community, yet she does not wish to be a State, and is not a State, just because she does not consciously rule herself like a man, and act freely in her external life, but wishes only to serve God and perform her religious duties." [9]

It is not necessary further to describe the manner in which political writers have developed what has appeared to them the organismic characteristics of the State. They are of significance to ethical political theory only in so far as they purport to give to the State a basis that not only explains, but justifies, its existence,—justifies it by making its creation, if not its specific forms of organiza-

---

[9] In his *Gesammelte Schriften*, Bluntschli develops further this alleged essential masculinity of the State.

tions and policies, a spontaneous act and independent of the free will of the individuals composing it; or by ascribing to it a real will and ends of its own, and a moral or spiritual personality, and thus endowing it with such a transcendental character that it does not need to defend itself against ethical criticism or examination upon the part of its individual citizens or subjects,—which puts it, indeed, upon a plane where it is not appropriate that the individuals, from the standpoint of their own interests and judgments, should question its right to be.

This transcendental conception of the State we shall have occasion later on to consider with some degree of care, but it may here be said that the conception of a moral or spiritual, as distinguished from a natural or living organism, is, if the words have any definite meaning at all, an impossible one. A living or natural organism is a substantive or concrete biological or physiological subject. Morality or spirituality are attributes that can attach themselves only to abstract entities known as persons. Such an entity is spoken of as a spiritual or moral person when it is conceived of as the possible possessor of ethical rights which others should respect, and obligated by ethical duties towards others or towards a Supreme Being. Such a personality as this is ascribable only to rational beings such as human individuals. It may, indeed, be impossible to conceive of such a person as existing except as incarnate in a living organism, but the individual *quâ* person, is a wholly distinct conception from the individual *quâ* an organism. A man, regarded as a person, is a moral being, but to his physical organic frame no such attribute can be attached. It is true that, in law, personality is attributed sometimes to inanimate objects, and sometimes to mere abstract entities, but the personality thus spoken of is a purely juristic one, and a conception wholly distinct from the personality that is posited by the psychologist or moralist. It is also true that it is proper to speak of the "will" of a social or political aggregate,—a will that is not identical with that of any of the particular individuals composing the aggregate or even of the arithmetical sum of the wills of those individuals, but, when such a will is spoken of, it is in either a figurative or a purely legal sense.

Even as a matter of analogy, though there are some resemblances between the social or political unit and the biological or physiological organism, the differences are very pronounced.

As has been already pointed out the social unity is discrete rather than concrete; the governmental form of organization of any given State is an arbitrary one and is in a process of continual change; the living organism is an aggregate whose parts exist solely to support and continue the life of the whole and the individual units have no life of their own, no independent powers of volition or of action. Also, while, in the organism, the tendency is for the influence and control of the whole over the action of its parts to increase not only in exactness but in scope, this is not the necessary tendency in the State, whose control, though tending to become more and more perfect, at the same time may secure to the individual a continually increasing sphere of free undetermined action. Again, it is a universal rule that all natural organisms derive their life from pre-existing living beings, whereas the State does not, and cannot, obtain its vitality from other political powers.

Finally, and what is absolutely conclusive upon the subject, in the organism the laws of development, though acting from within, are blindly and intuitively followed; whereas the growth of the State, though also from within, is, to a considerable extent at least, consciously felt by its constituent units, and the form of its organization controlled by them. "A time arrives in the progress of social development," says Professor Cairnes, "when societies of men become conscious of a corporate existence, and when the improvement becomes for them an object of conscious and deliberate effort. We cannot, by taking thought, add a cubit to our stature. The species, in undergoing the process of improvement, is wholly unconscious of the influences that are determining its career. It is not so with human evolution. Civilized mankind are aware of the changes taking place in their social condition, and do consciously and deliberately take measures for its improvement." [10]

Thus, the living individual of the biologic world is given no choice of the laws that are to govern its growth, though it may influence, to some extent, the direction of such growth. For it, the physical laws of assimilation and organic increase are rigidly fixed. The State, upon the contrary, is created by, and subject to, the will of human beings as regards, not only its governmental structure, but as to the range and character of its functions, and the ends to be realized through its power.

The Force Theory. The present work is predicated upon the assumed proposition that there is such a thing as moral obligation, and the answer to purely antinomian views is left to metaphysicians or writers upon theoretical ethics. In other words, it is taken for granted that the State, as an institution exerting authority and control over men, requires ethical justification.

There are some writers who, like Hobbes, find in the commands of the State rules of morality for the individual; or who, like Spinoza, say that the individual is released from his obligation to obey the State when the State loses power to protect him; or who, like Treitschke, make power the essential element of the State, and its increase the chief duty of the State; or who deny, as does

---

[10] *Fortnightly Review*, Vol. XXIII (January 1875), quoted by Ward; *Psychic Factors of Civilization*, p. 299. Cf. on this topic, Gunton, *Principles of Social Economics*, Pt. VI, Chap. II, Sec. 2.

Machiavelli, that the ordinary canons of morality are applicable to the acts of those who govern States. However, as we shall later see, these writers by no means identify might and right, but insist upon the necessity of a moral justification for political authority, and emphasize the moral tasks which States are called upon to perform. They are by no means antinomians. However, there have been ethical or political speculators who have held, either that might makes right, or at least, that the exercise of force by those capable of exercising it, is not subject to moral reprobation.

Pushed to its logical limits, it is clear that a might theory of right is as available to justify resistance to political authority as it is to support it. All forms of control or coercion being of a *de facto* character merely, every individual and all groups of individuals, under this theory, are justified in evading or wholly escaping from that control when they are, or believe themselves to be, strong or cunning enough to do so.

The question whether Force or Power may create right was raised by the Sophists in Greece, in the fifth century B. C. and so important was the ethical issue thus raised, that, in his *Republic,* Plato discusses, as his central theme, the nature of Justice. In Book I, we find examined the various views which, it would appear, were more or less current in his time. Through the mouth of Cephalus the doctrine of tradition is advanced; by Glaucon the conventional or compact principle is stated; while by Thrasymachus of Chalcedon the force theory, that justice is "the interest of the strongest" is put forward. This, indeed, was the typical position of the radical Sophists of the fifth century which Plato was especially anxious to refute. For the sake of brevity, instead of quoting from *The Republic,* we give the following summary by Ernest Barker of Thrasymachus' position:

"In the view of Thrasymachus there is no such thing

at all as natural right. Right is simply whatever is enforced by the strongest power in the State in accordance with its own view of its own interests. It does not matter what it enforces, whether the right of the strong or the right of the weak, whether inequality or equality: whatever it enforces is right. Thrasymachus does not hold that might is fundamentally right by nature's ordinance; he holds that right is nothing more than the enactment of might, whenever might may reside in any given State, and whatever its enactment may be. If the weak make laws in their interest, or in accordance with their conception of their interest, those laws, and the right they establish, are just and right so long as the weak can enforce them, and they cease to be right so soon as they cannot be enforced. While Callicles is something of an idealist, believing in a natural right which is always right, Thrasymachus is thus an empiricist, who believes that there is no such thing as a single and permanent right. His affinities are with Hobbes rather than with Nietzsche; and, like Hobbes, he believes that the only right is the enactment of the sovereign power. This, it has been said, is ethical nihilism. It is the logical complement in the sphere of morality to the intellectual nihilism of Gorgias, though it is a complement that was absent in Gorgias' own teaching. As Gorgias holds that you could not know Being, so Thrasymachus holds that you cannot know right; as Gorgias, by implication, throws you back on the 'appearance of things,' so Thrasymachus explicitly throws you back on the appearances or enactments ($\tau\grave{\alpha}$ $\delta o\kappa o\tilde{v}\tau\alpha$) of the different laws enforced by different sovereigns." [11]

When stated in this bold form, the Force theory, it scarcely needs to be pointed out, is a denial that there is any such thing as moral obligation. Rousseau makes this

[11] Ernest Barker, *Greek Political Theory: Plato and His Predecessors*, p. 72.

sufficiently plain when he says: "Force is a physical power, and I fail to see what moral effect it can have. To yield to force is an act of necessity, not of will—at the most, an act of prudence. In what sense can it be a duty. Suppose for a moment that this so-called 'right" exists. I maintain that the sole result is a mass of inexplicable nonsense. For, if force creates right, the effect changes with the cause: every force that is greater than the first succeeds to its right. As soon as it is possible to disobey with impunity, disobedience is legitimate; and, the strongest being always is in the right, the only thing that matters is to act so as to become the strongest. But what kind of right is that which fails when force fails? If we must obey perforce, there is no need to obey because we ought; and if we are not forced to obey, we are under no obligation to do so. Clearly, the word 'right' adds nothing to force: in this connection it means absolutely nothing. Obey the powers that be! If this means yield to force, it is a good precept but superfluous: I can answer for its never being violated. . . . Let us admit then that force does not create right, and that we are obliged to obey only legitimate powers.[12]

Stirner. In 1844, under the name of Max Stirner, Caspar Schmidt, a Bavarian, published a volume entitled *Der Einzige und sein Eigentum* which, though evidently a work with a sincere moral or spiritual purpose, set forth a doctrine which, if it does not declare that might makes right, at least declares that the exercise of effective force or compulsion in whatever form by any individual so circumstanced as to be able to exercise it, cannot be stigmatized as ethically wrong.

Every man can say, he declares, "I am entitled to everything that I have in my power. I am entitled to overthrow Zeus, Jehovah, God, etc., if I can: if I cannot, then these gods will always remain in the right and in

[12] *Social Contract*, Book I, Chapter III.

power as against me." [13] And again: "*I decide whether it is the right thing in me, there is no right outside me. If it is right for me, it is right.* Possibly this may not suffice to make it right for the rest: that is their care, not mine: let them defend themselves. And if for the whole world something were not right, but it were right for me, i.e., I wanted it, then I would ask nothing about the whole world. So everyone does who knows how to value himself, everyone in the degree that he is an egoist; for might goes before right, and that with perfect right." [14]

The conception "right" has, indeed, in Stirner's thought no real meaning, for he goes on to say: "In fact, with the concept [of "right"] the word too loses its meaning. What I called 'my right' is no longer 'right' at all, because right can be bestowed only by a spirit, be it the spirit of nature or that of the species, of mankind, the Spirit of God of that of His Holiness, or His Highness, etc. What I have without an entitling spirit I have without right; I have it solely and alone through my *power*. I do not demand any right, therefore I need not recognize any either. What I can get by force I get by force, and what I do not get by force I have no right to, nor do I give myself any airs, or consolation, with my imprescriptible right." [15]

This last statement is an interesting one, for it serves to mark off Stirner's views from those of most of the other advocates of anarchy. They, as a rule, start with the premise that men have an inherent, inalienable, indefeasible *right* to seek what they conceive to be their own interests, and in the ways which to them seem most suitable or desirable. Therefore, they declare, all coercion exercised upon them by a power outside themselves—they are especially concerned with political power—is a violation

[13] *The Ego and His Own*, English translation by S. T. Byington; Modern Library edition, p. 197.
[14] *Idem*, p. 198.
[15] *Idem*, p. 218.

of their right to freedom of action, and, therefore, ethically unjustifiable. This means, though they are not always careful to see where this, in practice, would lead them, the limitation of the liberty of action of each individual by the qualification that no one, in the pursuit of his own interests may justly interfere with the freedom of other individuals to seek their respective interests according to their own ideas as to the means that will be most efficient for the purpose. Where interests or desires conflict (or are thought to conflict), the only legitimate solution is a composition of the differences upon a basis of voluntary agreement. Stirner's doctrine, however, is almost the antithesis of this. He invests the individual with what amounts to an inescapable, inherent or natural inclination to seek to satisfy the desires that are born within himself, to realize the potentialities with which he feels himself endowed. His world is an absolutely egocentric one. In the pursuit of his ends, as determined by himself, he need not be influenced by what other individuals may wish to do or have. All forms of coercion are thus justified, including, of course, the coercion which those who happen to possess what they call political authority may be able to exercise. But, as to this coercion in the name of a State or Government, Stirner has this to say: [16] There is nothing sacrosanct about political authority, nothing that serves to give to it a right of control beyond the desire of those who happen to occupy the seats of political power to seek their own several interests by any means available to them. Therefore, there is no obligation upon any one to heed the commands of those claiming political authority over him. If one has the power or desire to disobey these orders he is ethically justified in doing so, or, at least, it is not unethical that he should do so.

[16] This is not stated explicitly, but is certainly implicit in his general philosophy.

As a matter of fact, Stirner is prepared to admit that the existence of political authority has been indispensable to the progress of humanity, but he denies that to the individual the progress of humanity is an end for which he is under any obligation to strive. To the statement that "the State is the most necessary means for the complete development of mankind," he answers: "It assuredly has been so as long as we wanted to develop mankind, but, if we want to develop ourselves, it can be to us only a means of hindrance." To the question whether the State cannot be reformed, he replies: "As little as the nobility, the clergy, the church, etc.: they can be abrogated, annihilated, done away with, not reformed. Can I change a piece of nonsense into sense by reforming it, or must I drop it outright?" [17]

Nietzsche. There are superficial resemblances between the egoism of Stirner and the assertive individualism of Nietzsche, but the inner spirit and ideals of the two writers are different. Stirner has a high regard for every individual because he is a rational human being. Nietzsche is contemptuous of the individual as such. He looks with satisfaction upon the overriding, and even the extermination, of the weaker units of humanity, and hails with his highest approval the appearance of strong men who, conscious of their own strength, will use it ruthlessly, undeterred or unrestrained by any mawkish feelings of sympathy or justice or of religious scruples for the wishes of others. Thus, as distinguished from Stirner, Nietzsche holds that only a few men deserve to rule—to be free— and that all others are natural-born slaves. "At the risk of displeasing innocent ears," he says, "I submit that egoism belongs to the essence of a noble mind. Aggressive and defensive egoism are not questions of choice or of free will, but they are fatalities of life itself." [18] Furthermore,

[17] *The Ego and His Own*, p. 245.
[18] *Beyond Good and Evil*, Sec. 265.

to Nietzsche, what the individual should seek to obtain is not simply to escape from control of an extraneous character, leaving others similarly free, but himself to exercise power to the utmost possible extent. This "will to power" should dominate him. "Exploitation belongs to the nature of the living being as a primary organic function." [19] If he has a truly noble mind, the individual should dare to live dangerously. The gist of Nietzsche's indictment of the State, as he saw it, was that it protected the weak against the strong. Social and political regeneration will come, if it comes at all, he taught, through the work of men who will not scruple to use the power they are able to take unto themselves. Nietzsche's individualism is thus one that culminates in autocracy rather than in popular freedom.

Because it has been so often said that Nietzsche borrowed largely from Stirner, we may spare still further space to quote, in refutation of this view, the following from Mr. J. L. Walker's introduction to Mr. Byington's translation of Stirner's work:

"Stirner loved liberty for himself, and loved to see any and all men and women taking liberty, and he had no lust of power. Democracy to him was sham liberty, egoism the genuine liberty. Nietzsche, on the contrary, pours out his contempt upon democracy because it is not aristocratic. He is predatory to the point of demanding that those who must succumb to feline rapacity shall be taught to submit with resignation. When he speaks of 'Anarchistic dogs' scouring the streets of great civilized cities, it is true, the context shows that he means the Communists; but his worship of Napoleon, his bathos of anxiety for the rise of an aristocracy that shall rule Europe for thousands of years, his idea of treating women in the oriental fashion, show that Nietzsche has struck out in a very old

[19] *Idem*, Sec. 259.

path—doing the apotheosis of tyranny. . . . Stirner shows that men make their tyrants as they make their gods, and his purpose is to unmake tyrants. Nietzsche dearly loves a tyrant."

We shall later have occasion to deal with Nietzsche's influence upon Prussian political thought, especially as regards its justification of national egoism. As Muirhead has said in his *German Philosophy and the War*,[20] "Let Nietzsche's Ego be interpreted in terms of the *Nation*, let it come to be taught in high places with all the fervour of prophecy that it was from the loins of the German Nation that the Superman was destined to appear, while upon its chief enemies in the direction in which its hopes were set decay had already set her mark; finally, let it be announced with all the authority of expert knowledge that the hour was about to strike, and it is not difficult to see what the harvest of this long sowing was likely to be."

[20] *Op. cit.*, p. 80.

CHAPTER III

THEORIES OF ANARCHY

FROM those theories which have sought to evade rather than to answer the problem of political obligation, we turn to a consideration of the views of those who so strongly assert the ethical right of the individual to be free from external coercion that they deny that political coercion can ever be ethically justified.

These theories of anarchy, it will be found, differ not only as to their premises and as to the social or political régimes which they deem desirable, but as to the modes by which they think the abolition of political authority should be brought about. As to the character of the communal life which they desire, there is a divergence of opinion as to how economic goods should be held or distributed, and as to the kind of social organization that should exist; but, so long as the fundamental principle is accepted that these arrangements, whatever they are, are supported wholly by continuing voluntary action or agreement upon the part of those persons affected, (*volenti non fit injuria*) these are differences of economic or social theory and not of political philosophy, and need not, therefore, be here considered.

As regards differences of opinion of anarchists as to the mode in which a régime of no-government is to be brought about, it will be found that there are those who declare that existing political rule should be resisted, whenever possible, and destroyed by any forcible means that may be available. Others hold that anarchy is to be established by the peaceful processes of persuasion, the potency of which will be continually increased as men become more and more intellectually enlightened. Some of these so-called philosophical anarchists, as distinguished from the anarchists of deed or of action, have a confidence, as will presently be pointed out, that there is an irresistible momentum in the evolutionary process operating in human societies towards a régime in which coercive political power will become useless and will therefore disappear.

William Godwin. Although the writings of William Godwin cannot be said, as an historical proposition, to have furnished the reasoning upon which modern theories of anarchy have been founded, they do, in fact, antedate by two generations their attempt to furnish a philosophical justification of anarchy as an ideal social state for men. Godwin's ideas are to be found in his *An Inquiry Concerning Political Justice and Its Influence on General Virtue and Happiness,* first published in 1793. In later editions he somewhat modified some of his more extreme doctrines, but did not abandon his belief in anarchy as a goal for the attainment of which men should strive.[1]

In common with most social and political idealists, Godwin was a firm believer in the natural goodness and rationality of men, and, therefore, in the feasibility of securing any desired social or political end if intellectual enlightenment is diffused and arbitrary impediments to progress are removed. Political government with its oppressive hand, he asserts, has been, in the past, the chief of these impediments.

"All vice," he declares, "is nothing more than error and mistake reduced into practice and adopted as the principle of our conduct. . . . Vicious conduct is soon discovered to involve injurious consequences. Injustice, therefore, by its own nature is little fitted for a durable

---

[1] In the second edition of his work Godwin substituted in the title the word "Morals" for the words "General Virtue" as used in the first edition.

existence. But Government lays its hand upon the spring there is in society, and puts a stop to its motion. It gives substance and permanence to our errors." [2]

Again, he says: "Man is not originally vicious. He would not refuse to listen, or to be convinced by the expostulations that are addressed to him, had he not been accustomed to regard them as hypocritical, and to conceive that, while his neighbor, his parent, and his political governor pretended to be actuated by a pure regard to his own interest, they were in reality, at the expense of his, promoting their own. Such are the fatal effects of mysteriousness and complexity. Simplify the social system in the manner in which every motive but those of usurpation and ambition powerfully recommend; render the plain dictates of justice level to every capacity; remove the necessity for implicit faith; and the whole species will become reasonable and virtuous. It will be sufficient for juries to recommend a certain mode of adjusting controversies, without assuming the prerogative of dictating that adjustment. It will then be sufficient for them to invite offenders to forsake their errors. If their expostulations proved in a few instances ineffectual, the evils arising out of this circumstance would be of less importance, than those which proceed from the perpetual violation of the exercise of private judgment. But in reality no evils would arise, for, where the empire of reason was so universally acknowledged, the offender would either readily yield to the expostulations of authority: or, if he refused, though suffering no personal molestation, he would feel so uneasy under the unequivocal disapprobation and observant eye of public judgment, as willingly to remove to a society more congenial to his errors. The reader has probably anticipated me in the ultimate conclusion, from these remarks. If juries might at length cease to decide

---

[2] *Political Justice*, Book I, Chap. IV. This and the quotations to follow are from the first edition.

and be contented to invite, if force might gradually be withdrawn and reason trusted alone, shall we not one day find that juries themselves and every other species of public institution, may be laid aside as unnecessary? Will not the reasoning of one wise man be as effectual as those of twelve? Will not the competence of one individual to instruct his neighbors be a matter of sufficient notoriety, without the formality of an election? Will there be many vices to correct and much obstinacy to conquer? This is one of the most memorable stages of human improvement. With what delight must every well-informed friend of mankind look forward to the auspicious period, the dissolution of political government, of that brute engine, which has been the only perennial cause of the vices of mankind, and which, as has abundantly appeared in the progress of the present work, has mischiefs of various sorts incorporated with its substance, and not otherwise to be removed than by its utter annihilation!" [3]

Godwin, while viewing anarchy as an ideal to be striven for, does not deny that, until men are generally enlightened and therefore moralized, governments have a right to exist. But it would appear that, in no case, would he justify governmental control except as a police measure for preventing oppression of individuals by each other. "Government," he declares, "can have no more than two legislative powers, the suppression of injustice against individuals within the community, and the common defense against external invasion." [4]

Proudhon. Stirner, as has been pointed out, was not a political agitator, but wrote, it would appear, simply under the impulse of a deep conviction that the reverence which he saw paid by the individual to powers outside himself or to principles not the product of his own reason, was a pernicious and irrational check upon the realization

---
[3] *Political Justice*, Book V, Chap. XXIV.
[4] *Idem*, Book V, Chap. XXII.

of his own ego. Reverence for the Bible, for the Church, or for the Christian God thus fell into the same category as reverence for the political State, or, indeed, for the opinions of any person or group of persons, political, social or private. In his opinion, individuals enjoy the freedom to which their own natures entitle them only when they form their judgments as to what they shall do wholly uninfluenced by tradition, social opinion, or the demands of any external authority, temporal or spiritual, public or private. In short, it was especially against intellectual and spiritual servitude that Stirner inveighed. As contrasted with this purpose and motive we find practically all other modern advocates of anarchy controlled by a profound dissatisfaction with existing economic conditions. These conditions they view either as the product of, or maintained by, political authority. Therefore, though primarily critics of economic society (organized as they find it upon a capitalistic basis), and, holding certain views as to the manner in which economic values are created, and the principles of justice in accordance with which economic goods should be distributed and the burdens of production apportioned, they turn their attention to political theory because they are convinced that their social and economic ideals can be realized only by abolishing coercive political authority. The founder of this politico-economic school of thinkers is perhaps Mikhail Bakunin (1816-1876), but he did not develop, at least in printed form, any systematic philosophy of anarchism. For this we must turn to Proudhon and Kropotkin.[5]

Influential as Proudhon's writings have been upon later socialistic as well as anarchistic thought, they do not reveal a clear-cut political philosophy, for he does not begin with an examination of the fundamental question as to the rightfulness of coercion, but, having convinced him-

[5] Proudhon was the first to use the word "Anarchy."

self that economic society should be so organized that all individuals will labor equally, and receive equal amounts of the products (that is, products equal in value as measured by labor-time),[6] and also being persuaded that the legal ownership of property (including especially the right of inheritance) renders this impossible, without further argument he declares that the State, which he finds is founded upon the idea of property, should be abolished, and its place taken by coöperation among individuals based upon agreements freely and voluntarily entered into. Proudhon thus parts company with both the socialists and communists like St. Simon, Babœuf, and Cabet, for the double reason that they accept the idea of property and rely upon political authority for the maintenance of the economic and social régimes which they advocate.

Proudhon's best known work is *What Is Property?* (*Qu' est-ce que la propriété?*) published in 1840, but an adequate knowledge of his doctrines can be obtained only by studying also his later works, and especially his *System of Economic Contradictions, or the Philosophy of Misery,* which appeared in 1846.

In common with almost all other Utopians, Proudhon has a confident belief in the power of reason to control human action, and has, therefore, the assurance that, if individuals are given a fair opportunity to know the truth and are relieved from coercion and thus made subject to all the consequences of their own acts, they will spontaneously bring their conduct into consonance with principles of justice, and, by voluntary coöperation, secure such united action or adjustment of apparently conflicting interests as may be needed for harmonious and efficient social life. Summarizing the results reached in his *What Is Property?* he says: "I have accomplished my task: property is conquered, never again to rise. Whenever this work is read and discussed, there will be deposited the

[6] Cf. Ely, *French and German Socialism,* p. 138.

germ of death to property; then, sooner or later, privilege and servitude will disappear, and the despotism of will will give place to the reign of reason. What sophisms, indeed, what prejudices, however obstinate, can stand before the simplicity of the following propositions."

Proudhon then goes on to state what may be termed his Ten Commandments of the new social order. In these will be seen the extent to which his system is a mixture of economics and politics.

"I. Individual possession is the condition of social life; five thousand years of property demonstrate it. Property is the suicide of society. Possession is a right; property is against right. Suppress property while maintaining possession, and, by this simple modification of the principle, you will revolutionize law, government, economy, and institutions; you will drive evil from the face of the earth.

"II. All having an equal right of occupancy, possession varies with the number of possessors; property cannot establish itself.

"III. The effect of labor being the same for all, property is lost in the common prosperity.

"IV. All human labor being the result of collective force, all property becomes, in consequence, collective and unitary. To speak more exactly, labor destroys property.

"V. Every capacity for labor being, like every instrument of labor, an accumulated capital, and a collective property, inequality of wages and fortunes (on the ground of inequality of capacities) is, therefore, injustice and robbery.

"VI. The necessary conditions of commerce are the liberty of the contracting parties and the equivalence of the products exchanged. Now, value being expressed by the amount of time and outlay which each product costs, and liberty being inviolable, the wages of laborers (like their rights and duties) should be equal.

"VII. Products are bought only by products. Now, the condition of all exchange being equivalence of products, profit is impossible and unjust. Observe this elementary principle of economy, and pauperism, luxury, oppression, vice, crime, and hunger will disappear from our midst.

"VIII. Men are associated by the physical and mathematical law of production, before they are voluntarily associated by choice. Therefore, equality of conditions is demanded by justice; that is, by strict social law: esteem, friendship, gratitude, admiration, all fall within the domain of equitable or proportional law only.

"IX. Free association, liberty—whose sole function is to maintain equality in the means of production and equivalence in exchanges—is the only possible, the only just, the only true form of society.

"X. Politics is the science of liberty. The government of man by man (under whatever name it be disguised) is oppression. Society finds its highest perfection in the union of order with anarchy."

Kropotkin. The founder of modern communistic anarchism was Mikhail Bakunin. However, as he published no systematic and reasoned statement of his views, for the political and social philosophy of this school we shall turn at once to the writings of the best known of its members, Prince Peter Kropotkin. These writings, so far as they attempt the justification of anarchy are in the form of articles or short pamphlets, but are nevertheless philosophical in character and plainly present the premises upon which the argument is based.

Kropotkin's ideal is "anarchist communism, communism without government, free communism." [7]

"The Anarchists," says Kropotkin, "conceive a society in which all the mutual relations of its members are regulated, not by laws, not by authorities, whether self-imposed or elected, but by mutual agreements between

[7] "The Coming Anarchy," *The Nineteenth Century*, August, 1887.

the members of that society, and by a sum of social customs and habits—not petrified by law, routine, or superstition, but continually developing and continually readjusted, in accordance with the ever growing requirements of a free life, stimulated by the progress of science, invention, and the steady growth of higher ideals . . . no ruling authorities, then—no government of man by man; no crystallization and immobility, but a continual evolution—such as we see in Nature. Free play for the individual, for the full development of his individual gifts —for his individualization. In other words, no actions are imposed upon the individual by a fear of punishment; none is required of him by society, but those which receive his free acceptance. In a society of equals this would be quite sufficient for preventing those unsociable actions that might be harmful to other individuals and to society itself, and for favoring the steady moral growth of that society." [8]

Like most other anarchists, Kropotkin emphasized the idea that capitalism and political coercion are so united that the one cannot be abolished without the other being destroyed. "The State," he says, "is, for us, a society of mutual insurance between the landlord, the military commander, the judge, the priest, and, later on, the capitalist, in order to support each other's authority over the people, and for exploiting the poverty of the masses and getting rich themselves. Such was the origin of the State; such was its history; and such is its present essence. Consequently, to imagine that Capitalism may be abolished while the State is maintained, and with the aid of the State . . . is as unreasonable, in our opinion, as to expect the emancipation of Labor from the Church, or from Cæsarism or Imperialism. A new form of economic organization will require a new form of political structure." [9]

[8] *Modern Science and Anarchism*, p. 45.   [9] *Idem*, p. 81.

Kropotkin's ideal social State, and the one towards which he believes humanity to be tending, is one in which the private ownership of land, capital and other instruments of production will disappear; they will become the common property of society and be managed in common by the producers of wealth, and such public administration as is needed will be provided by voluntary coöperation of individuals, or of groups and federations of groups of individuals.

Kropotkin believed that the establishment of this régime will be the inevitable outcome of competition, of the struggle for existence, as operating among men. He saw, therefore, a definite, if not a providential, purpose in human history. The final result is inescapable, the process irresistible, and, therefore, it is not necessary that anarchists should resort to violence,—to propaganda of the deed. It would appear, however, that he held that men will be well advised if, recognizing the existence of an evolutionary force or tendency which it is hopeless fully to check, and the outcome of which will be eminently desirable, they do nothing to check its operation, but, upon the contrary, so far as possible, seek to promote its progress.

In his article "The Scientific Basis of Anarchy," [10] he said:

"The Anarchist thinker does not resort to metaphysical conceptions (like the 'natural rights,' the 'duties of the State' and so on) for establishing what are, in his opinion, the best conditions for realizing the greatest happiness of humanity. He follows on the contrary, the course traced by the modern philosophy of evolution, without entering, however, the slippery route of mere analogies so often resorted to by Herbert Spencer. He studies human society as it is now and was in the past; and, without either en-

[10] *Nineteenth Century*, February, 1887. Republished in Parson's *Anarchy*.

dowing men altogether, or separate individuals, with superior qualities which they do not possess, he merely considers society as an aggregation of organisms trying to find out the best ways of combining the wants of individuals with those of coöperation for the welfare of the species. He studies society and tries to discover its *tendencies*, past and present, its growing needs, intellectual and economical; and, in his ideal, he merely points out in which direction evolution goes. . . . He concludes that the two most prominent, although often unconscious, tendencies throughout our history are: a tendency towards integrating our labor for the production of all riches in common, so as finally to render it impossible to discriminate the part of the common production due to the separate individual, and a tendency towards the fullest freedom of the individual for the prosecution of all aims, beneficial both for himself and for society at large. The ideal of the anarchist is thus a mere summing-up of what he considers to be the next phase of evolution. It is no longer a matter of faith; it is a matter for scientific discussion. . . . Anarchists recognize the justice of . . . tendencies towards economic and political freedom, and see in them two different manifestations of the same need of equality which constitutes the very essence of all struggles mentioned by history. Therefore, in common with all Socialists, the Anarchist says to the political reformer: 'No substantial reform in the sense of political equality, and no limitation of the powers of government, can be made so long as society is divided into two hostile camps, and the laborer remains, economically speaking, a serf to his employer.' But to the Popular State Socialist we say also: 'You cannot modify the existing conditions of property without deeply modifying at the same time the political organization. You must limit the powers of government and renounce parliamentary rule. To each new economical *phasis* of life corresponds a new political *phasis.* Absolute monarchy—that is, court rule—corresponded to the system of serfdom. Representative government corresponds to Capital-rule. Both, however, are class-rule. But in a society where the distinction between capitalist and laborer has disappeared, there is no need of such a government; it would be an anacronism, a nuisance. Free workers would require a free organization, and this cannot have another basis than free agreement and free coöperation, without sacrificing the autonomy of the individual to the all-pervading interference of the State. The no-capitalist system implies the no-government system.'

"In arriving at these conclusions anarchy proves to be in accordance with the conclusions arrived at by the philosophy of evolution. By bringing to light the plasticity of organization, the philosophy of evolution has shown the admirable adaptivity of organisms to their conditions of life, and the ensuing development of such faculties as render more complete both the adaptations of the aggregates to their surroundings and those of each of the constituent parts of the aggregate to the needs of free coöperation. It familiarized us with the circumstance that throughout organic nature the capacities for life in common are growing in proportion as the integration of organisms into compound aggregates becomes more and more complete; and it enforced thus the opinion already expressed by social moralists as to the perfectibility of human nature. . . . By showing that the 'struggle for existence' must be conceived, not merely in its restricted sense of a struggle between individuals for the means of subsistence, but in its wider sense of adaptation of all individuals of the species to the best conditions for the survival of the species, as well as for the greatest possible sum of life and happiness for each and all, it permitted us to deduce the laws of moral science from the social needs and habits of mankind. It showed us the infinitesimal part played by positive law in moral evolution, and the immense part played by the natural growth of altruistic feelings, which develop as soon as the conditions of life favor their growth. It thus enforced the opinion of social reformers as to the necessity of modifying the conditions of life for improving men, instead of trying to improve human nature by moral teachings while life works in an opposite direction. Finally, by studying human society from the biological point of view, it came to the conclusions arrived at by anarchists from the study of history and present tendencies, as to further progress being in the line of socialization of wealth and integrated labor, combined with the fullest possible freedom of the individual."

This reliance by Kropotkin upon the evolutionary process, as indicating both the ideal of human progress and the means by which it is to be attained, opens up a field of speculation which it would be tempting to explore. To do so would, however, carry us beyond the boundaries set for the present volume. It may, however, be pointed out that this line of argument involves the false assumption that changes brought about by competition, that is, by what is called evolution, necessarily mean progress when measured by moral or other standards suggested by reason to men. The fittest individuals or species that survive in a competitive struggle are "fittest" only in the sense of being best adapted to the environment in which they happen to find themselves. As Huxley says in his famous Romanes lecture, "Evolution and Ethics": [11] "In cosmic nature what is fittest depends upon the conditions. . . . If our hemisphere were to cool again, the survival of the fittest might bring about in the vegetable kingdom a population of more and more stunted and humbler and humbler organisms, until the fittest that survived might be nothing but lichens, diatoms, and

[11] *Collected Essays*, Vol. IX.

such microscopic organisms as those which give red snow its color; while, if it became hotter, the pleasant valleys of the Thames and Isis might be uninhabitable by any animated beings save those that flourish in a tropical jungle. They, as fittest, the best adapted to changed conditions, would survive."

It is, therefore, futile to look to Evolution, as does Kropotkin, simply as a competitive process, as a force that will necessarily lead to the realization of human ideals. Confidence in this can be had only if one also believes that there is some sort of overruling Providence which determines the destiny of humanity and sees to it that men so act that, ultimately at least, this destiny will be realized.

The character of social or political existence towards which, in point of fact, humanity appears to be tending is a matter of personal judgment upon the part of each student of history, and Kropotkin is, of course, entitled to his opinion as to this fact. But, even if it should be granted, *arguendo,* that social, economic and political changes are tending in the direction of a régime of community of economic goods and total absence of coercive political authority, it would not follow that such a consummation would be one to be devoutly wished, or one that it is beyond the power of human effort to avoid.

Herbert Spencer. Herbert Spencer is properly classified as an extreme Individualist rather than as an Anarchist. However, he is in agreement with Kropotkin that political authority is, *per se,* an evil; that a study of the evolutionary process, as operating throughout the world of life, teaches that governmental interference with the competitive struggle between men is ill-advised; and that the time will come when government will wholly disappear. As regards man's audacity in attempting to interfere with the cosmic process, he says: "If the political meddler could be induced to contemplate the essential meaning of his plan, he would be paralyzed by the sense of his own temerity. He proposes to suspend in some way or degree that process by which all life has been evolved."

As to the possibility, indeed the probability, that anarchy will be the product of social evolution, he says: "It is a mistake to assume that government must necessarily last forever. The institution marks a certain stage of civilization—is natural to a peculiar phase of human development. It is not essential, but incidental. As amongst Bushmen we find a state antecedent to government, so there may be one in which it shall become extinct." [12] And, in another place in the same volume he says: "Does it [government] not exist because crime exists? . . . Is there not more liberty, that is, less government, as crime diminishes? And must not government cease when crime ceases, for the very lack of objects on which to perform its function? Not only does magisterial power exist because of evil, but it exists by evil." [13]

In a later chapter of this volume in which are discussed theories regarding the legitimate sphere of governmental control, we shall have occasion to consider the individualistic doctrines which Spencer deduces from evolutionary biological principles. It is sufficient here to say that, pending the time when, through the evolutionary process, the State becomes no longer necessary, Spencer holds that the exercise of its coercive authority should be limited to purely police measures.

In the next chapter it will be shown that present-day Communists—including the Bolshevists—look forward to the time when the State will "wither away" and finally disappear.

Denial that the Use of Physical Force, Whether through the State or Otherwise, Is Ever Legitimate. Allied in some respects to philosophical anarchists are

[12] *Social Statics*, ed. 1873, p. 24.
[13] *Ibid.*, p. 230.

THEORIES OF ANARCHY

those persons who deprecate the use of physical force under any circumstances. Among these may be included Tolstoi. It scarcely needs be pointed out that such a view not only denies the legitimacy of coercion by the State, but, at the same time, denies that the individual is justified in using force to repulse the authority which an existing government seeks to exercise over him. Tolstoi, it may be observed, founded his pacifism upon the teachings of the Holy Scriptures, as he interpreted them, and not upon a philosophically reasoned system of ethics.

Other persons, among whom may be included those known during the Great War as "Conscientious Objectors," have limited their objection to force to its use in the form of war. It would appear that those holding this view do not assert that the employment of force in any form is necessarily wrongful, but merely that war, because it involves the loss of human life, great human suffering, and the stimulation of evil passions among men, is so great an evil that the results possible to be attained by it can never furnish an adequate compensation. The religious element is also often stressed, the position being taken that war springs from the lower impulses of men and is contrary to the spirit of the Christian Gospels.

Gandhi's doctrine of non-violent resistance to British authority in India was also founded on a religious basis, although the element of expediency had without doubt a place in his thought.[14]

Criticism. A full criticism of the premises and reasoning of those who deny the ethical validity of all forms of political control, or of those who assert that, at any rate, a condition of no-government is an ideal to be approached as nearly as circumstances will permit, will not

---

[14] Gandhi says that the principle of passive resistance first came to him in 1893 after reading the Sermon on the Mount. *Young India*, February 25, 1920. Cf. Romain Rolland, *Mahatma Gandhi*, p. 40.

be attempted at this stage of our inquiry. This can be better done after we have examined the positive theories upon which the exercise of coercive public authority has been upheld. It may, however, here be pointed out that those who assert that political coercion is ethically unjustifiable, irrespective of its results, are logically obligated to demonstrate that human individuals are, by their very nature, endowed with an inalienable and indefeasible ethical right to live their own lives according to their own unrestrained several wills; and also (unless the position is taken that one individual should never determine his conduct towards other individuals according to his approval or disapproval of their characters or acts), to assert that there is a quality that inheres in the control exercised through political agencies that distinguishes it, *in genere,* from all other forms of social control, that is, from the pressure which individuals may bring to bear upon each other by refusing to have social or business relations with those persons whose acts are disapproved. It does not need to be pointed out that such a refusal, or a threat of it, can be, and, in many cases, is as deterrent in its influence upon the conduct of others as is the threat or infliction of the punishment provided for in the penal laws of a State.

CHAPTER IV

THE NATURE AND FUNCTIONS OF THE STATE AS ENVISAGED BY SOCIALISTS AND COMMUNISTS

THERE are few persons, in any State, who are fully satisfied with the general economic and political conditions which prevail, but, in the great majority of instances, this discontent is not so profound as to lead to the belief that the very basis of our present political society is so wrong that present unsatisfactory conditions can be corrected only by action, essentially revolutionary in character (whether accompanied by violence or not) which will lead to the establishment of an entirely new political régime—new, both as to its forms of governmental organization and operation, and as to its economic and social aims. There are some, however, who do take this view, and it is with the political theories of these revolutionists—as distinguished from reformers—and especially with those who found their doctrines upon the political and economic theories of Karl Marx, that the present chapter will deal.

It is, of course, possible to be discontented with present social and political conditions for other than economic reasons, but the historical fact is that, where this discontent has led to the demand for a new social and political order, it has been founded, primarily, upon a dissatisfaction with the manner in which, under existing conditions, economic burdens and benefits are distributed. Those who have advanced schemes for a new ordering of social and political life have, to be sure, claimed that, under such schemes, cultural and other than purely economic interests will be better advanced than they now are, but the emphasis has always been laid upon the economic advantages, whether of production or distribution and consumption, which will be secured.

Those who have demanded a new order of things may be grouped into various schools, as, for example, Anarchists, Socialists, Communists, Syndicalists, Guild Socialists, Political Pluralists, etc. Some of these schools are elsewhere discussed in the present volume. The present chapter will deal with Socialism and Communism.

State Socialism and Social Reform Distinguished. It is necessary to distinguish between State Socialism and Socialism, for, as will presently appear, the term Socialism, when used without the qualifying adjective "State," is used by present day Communists as synonymous with Communism.

As the term indicates, a Social Reformer is one who believes that the results which he deems desirable can best be reached by progressively extending the regulatory and operating activities of existing Governments within the economic field. Those reformers who look forward to the time when the State will own and operate all, or practically all, the instruments of production, and thus control also the distribution of their products or services, may fairly be denominated State Socialists, if we accept the ordinary definition of Socialism as a régime under which all the instruments of production are owned and operated and their products distributed by the State. Thus R. T. Ely, in his *French and German Socialism* [1] says: "A Socialist is one who looks to society organized in the State for aid in bringing about a more perfect distribution of economic goods and an elevation of humanity." [2]

According to this definition every one is socialistic in his

---
[1] P. 30.
[2] Dr. Ely goes on to say that there is a more popular meaning given to Socialism which renders it nearly equivalent to Communism.

beliefs to the extent that he favors State intervention in, or control of, economic operations; but it is scarcely fair to term one a State Socialist unless he desires, and looks forward to, complete governmental ownership and control of all the instruments of production.[3]

Socialism and Syndicalism Distinguished. Distinguishing Socialism and Syndicalism, Macdonald says:[4] "Whilst Socialism asks that economic power should be put in the hands of the community, Syndicalism asks that each industrial group of workers should control the instruments of production which it uses." But, observes Macdonald, "the Syndicalist really has in mind the control of the means of production by a working class State, because he is always careful to explain that industrial machinery, though owned by those who work it, would be used for the benefit of all. . . . The fact that the Syndicalist founds his community on common property in the means of production used for common convenience and benefit, gives him, without being a Socialist, a right to stand on a small bit of the same ground as the Socialist. The Syndicalist, however, is poles asunder from the Socialist in method, and method counts for everything in the process of social change. The Socialist believes in a combination of political and trade union action; the Syndicalist believes in trade union action alone; the Socialist appeals to the whole body of public opinion; the Syndicalist considers the working classes only; the Socialist brings about his changes by legislative moulding, he uses the organic State to transform itself by making such alterations in its own mind and circumstances as must precede all permanent change; the Syndicalist, cutting himself off from these organic formative influences, has to fall back upon force, either the passive force of paralysis

[3] It is in this light that Socialism is viewed, and, in the main, defended, by J. Ramsay Macdonald in his volume *The Socialist Movement* (Home University Library).
[4] In his little volume entitled *Syndicalism*, p. 3.

or the active force of riots, to effect his changes with revolutionary suddenness. . . . In fact, Syndicalism is largely a revolt against Socialism. Socialism must be parliamentary or nothing."

Hsio, in his volume on *Political Pluralism,* gives the following definition of Syndicalism: [5] "Syndicalism . . . agrees with Marx that economics is the ruling force of all organization. In common with Socialism, also, it takes the class war as its starting point. It differs from Marxism in this that for the Syndicalist the end of the capitalist régime is not to be marked by the final elimination of all class distinctions; and class war simply means the struggle of the proletariat to dominate society. It is not surprising, therefore, that the Syndicalists do not profess to work for the welfare of the whole society, but confine their attention to the good of the working class alone. Furthermore, being indifferent to society, syndicalism has no use for political power. Parliamentarianism and legislation are sneered at by good Syndicalists, and 'direct action' is to them the only sane and legitimate means to achieve their end." [6]

State Socialism and Communism Distinguished. Both Socialists and Communists agree that the instruments of production should be owned and operated, and their products distributed by the organized community, but they differ in that the State Socialist desires the community to be organized as a political body, that is, as a State. The State, therefore, according to State Socialists, is to be the owner and operator of instruments of production and the distributor of their products. The Communists, upon the other hand, look forward to the time when the State will disappear: their ideal is that the whole body of the people, organized for productive pur-

---
[5] Page 112.
[6] The direct action that is recommended is generally sabotage and the general strike.

SOCIALISTIC AND COMMUNISTIC VIEW OF STATE 63

poses, but not armed with legal coercive power, will own and operate the instruments of production. Furthermore, the extreme Communists would abolish private proprietary rights not only in land and other instruments of production, but in all other objects or things. Some of them go still further, and would have community with regard to family life, the breeding and raising and educating of children, and even the living in common quarters. This last feature, however, it is to be said, does not appear conspicuously in present-day theories of Communism.

Present-day Communists, as to this matter of repudiating what may be called "State Socialism," emphasize the point that such Socialism would be an essentially capitalist one—that it would be nothing more than the substitution of State capitalism for bourgeois capitalism. Thus, Engels, who, together with Marx, has supplied present-day Communists or Socialists, with their social and political philosophy, in his *Socialism, Utopian and Scientific,* says: "The transformation, either into joint-stock companies and trusts, or into State ownership does not do away with the capitalistic nature of the productive forces. In the joint-stock companies and trusts this is obvious. And the modern State, again, is only the organization that bourgeois society takes on in order to support the external conditions of the capitalist mode of production against the encroachments, as well of the workers as of individual capitalists. The modern State, no matter what its form, is essentially a capitalist machine, the State of the capitalists, the ideal personification of the total national capital. The more it proceeds to the taking over of productive forces, the more does it actually become the national capitalist, the more citizens does it exploit. The workers remain wage-workers—proletarians."

A further distinction between State Socialism and

Communism is that, generally speaking, State Socialists look to the gradual and peaceful introduction of the régime which they advocate; whereas, the Communists believe that their régime may, and, in most cases, must, be ushered in by revolutionary action, which, in the beginning at least, will take the form of a seizure by the working classes—the proletariat—of control of the State —of its political governmental organs.

Utopian Socialistic Schemes. The construction of ideal "Utopian" schemes of social life has been an activity of ardent minds from the time of Plato. As to this, one need only think of Plato's "Republic," More's "Utopia," Bacon's "New Atlantis," Campanella's "City of the Sun" and Harrington's "Oceana."

In the early years of the nineteenth century we again find put forward proposals for the social and economic regeneration of human society the immediate practicability of which was urged by their authors, but which later Socialists and Communists have criticized not only as Utopian, in the sense of not being practical, but as "unscientific" because based upon a lack of understanding of the true nature of modern industrial society. Thus stigmatized by Socialists and Communists since the time of Marx have been the schemes of such writers as Babeuf, Saint Simon, Fourier, Cabet, Blanc and Owen.[7] And yet it cannot be denied that, from the theories of these writ-

---

[7] Speaking of the earlier Utopian socialistic or communistic schemes of St. Simon, Fourier and Owen, Engels, in his *Socialism, Utopian and Scientific*, says: "One thing is common to all three. Not one of them appears as a representative of the interests of that proletariat, which historical development had, in the meantime, produced. Like the French philosophers, they do not claim to emancipate a particular class to begin with, but all humanity at once. Like them, they wish to bring in the kingdom of reason and eternal justice." And, a little later: "At this time, however, the capitalist mode of production, and with it the antagonism between the bourgeoisie and the proletariat was still very incompletely developed. Modern industry, which had just arisen in England, was still unknown in France."

St. Simon published his Geneva letters in 1802; Fourier published his first work in 1808; Owen began the direction of New Lanark in 1800.

ers, later Socialists and Communists have derived some of their own doctrines.[8]

Marxian Socialism and Communists. Present-day Communists, while repudiating State Socialism in the strongest terms, call themselves also Socialists, but declare that their Socialism has a scientific character which socialistic theories prior to the time of Karl Marx had lacked. This claim to a scientific character they found upon the analysis, made by Marx, of human society in its various stages of development and in its present industrial or capitalistic form.[9]

The central thesis of Marx was that, at all times, eco-

[8] Thus, Hertzler, in his *History of Utopian Thought* (p. 222), says: "Without exception they [these earlier so-called Utopian Socialists] believed in the abolition of that enemy of the 'very obvious and simple system of natural liberty'—private property—upon which their predecessors had set their hopes; therefore, they were all exponents of the socialization of property. Private property was personal; it narrowed the feelings and sympathies; it prevented the utilization of a common gift for the common welfare; therefore, it must be taken out of the minds of individuals. Production also had to be socialized and supervised by society in its own interests. Hence the Utopian Socialists were true forerunners of the Marxians."

Further characterizing these Utopian Socialists, Hertzler continues: "There was [among them] no uniformity on the question of equality. Babeuf and Cabet had the idea of absolute equality, sheer dead monotony; Fourier and Saint Simon recognized differences in capacity, and had schemes of reward according to capacity; Blanc was the most advanced, accepting inequality, but demanding reward, not according to capacity, but according to needs. He struck the most adequately social note of all. Nor did they agree on their views of the State. Fourier's idea of a central executive, if one had to be, was to domicile it nowhere nearer than Constantinople. Saint-Simon thoroughly believed in the State. Louis Blanc not only believed that the State was the main hope of good government, he took his ideals into the heart of political affairs and addressed a National Assembly in support of his views. Owen looked upon the State as an incapable institution that did not count very much one way or the other, that might be of small use temporarily for social purposes, but would gradually become obsolete."

See also Shadwell, *The Socialist Movement;* Laidler, *A History of Socialist Thought;* and Ely, *French and German Socialism in Modern Times.*

[9] It is often said that Marx's "labor theory" of value is the main premise of his socialistic conclusions,—that, in other words, upon this theory he founded an ethical claim upon the part of workers to the products of their labor which can be satisfied only under a socialistic régime of production and distribution. This would appear to be a mistake, as is pointed out by Simkovitch in his *Marxism Versus Socialism.*

nomic interests and motives had dominated men's actions, and that all human history is but a record of this fact. This history shows, he said, that economic conditions have determined the character of the political, social and cultural conditions that have prevailed at any given time. Also, that there has ever been a struggle for power between economic classes, and that that class which has secured economic power has organized and controlled the State for the protection and advancement of its own interests. Hence, he declared, men's history is but a record of these class struggles. This is what he meant by the "economic interpretation of history."

Speaking of the economic interpretation of history, as stated by Marx, Engels, in his *Socialism, Utopian and Scientific*, says: "Then [for the first time] it was seen that all past history, with the exception of its primitive stages, was the history of class struggles, that these warring classes of society are always the product of the modes of production and of exchange—in a word, of the economic conditions of their time; that the economic structure of society always furnishes the real basis, starting from which we can alone work out the ultimate explanation of the whole superstructure of juridical and political institutions as well as of the religious, philosophical, and other ideas of a given society. . . . From that time forward Socialism was no longer an accidental discovery of this or that ingenious brain, but the necessary outcome of the struggle between two historically developed classes—the proletariat and the bourgeoisie. Its task was no longer to manufacture a system of society as perfect as possible, but to examine the historico-economic succession of events from which these classes and their antagonism had of necessity sprung, and to discover in the economic conditions thus created, the means of ending the conflict. . . . The Socialism of earlier days criticized the existing capitalistic mode of production and its consequences. But it could not explain them, and, therefore, could not get the mastery of them. . . . For this it was necessary—(1) to present the capitalistic method of production in its historical connection and its inevitableness during a particular historical period, and, therefore, also, to present its inevitable downfall; and (2) to lay bare the essential character, which was still a secret. This was done by the discovery of *surplus value*. It was shown that the appropriation of unpaid labor is the basis of the capitalist mode of production and of the exploitation of the worker that occurs under it; that even if the capitalist buys the labor power of his laborer at its full value as a commodity on the market, he yet extracts more value from it than he paid for; and that, in the ultimate analysis, this surplus value forms those sums of value from which are heaped up the constantly increasing masses of capital in the hands of the possessing classes. . . . These two great discoveries, the materialistic conception of history and the revelation of the secret of capitalistic production through surplus-value, we owe to Marx."

It thus appears that Marx, more or less influenced by Hegelian dialectic, held that there operates in human history what amounts to a natural or inevitable law, according to which each phase of historical development, that is, each type of economic class domination, leads to the growth of antithetical forces, which, finally, lead to the destruction of the type; whereupon a new type of class struggle begins, which, in turn, will be superseded by another type. In the modern industrial world, Marx declared, the capitalists are in power and are using their power continually to advance their own interests at the expense of those who have only their labor to sell; but, he declared, the workers are becoming conscious of their situation and of their possible power, should they unite as a class; that modern capitalism is bringing into being the very forces and instrumentalities which will lead to its own destruction; and that the time is thus near at hand when political power will be wrested from the hands of the propertied bourgeoisie and assumed by the proletariat; whereupon, common ownership and operation of the instruments of production will be established, the former profits of the private capitalists done away with, and the entire products of labor—industrial and agricultural—distributed among the laborers. Thus will be ushered in the Communist régime.

It appears that, although he would seem to have held that there is an inevitableness to the processes of human history, Marx believed that it was proper, and, perhaps, necessary that an exploited class should exert itself to bring about the transition from one phase or stage of economic life to the one that is to succeed it. Thus, he taught that, as a rule, this transition is usually marked by more or less violent action upon the part of those who are oppressed under the existing régime. Hence, he declared, history is to be viewed as a series of revolutions. In other words, though each economic class, while in power, creates the forces, and thus prepares the way, for its own overthrow, the overthrow itself comes by revolutionary action upon the part of the new class which is to occupy the seats of political and economic power.

As has been said, Marx was convinced that the next stage in history would see Capitalism destroyed and replaced by Communism.[10] The first phase of this revolution would be brought about by the seizure of political control by the proletariat, which, for a time at least, would use the political power—the State—as a means for bringing the Communistic régime into full operation.

[10] It would seem that he thought that this Communist phase would be the final one for man, for, as will later appear, he expected it to be one in which there would be no more classes, and, therefore, no opportunity for the class struggles, which, according to him, have, in the past, constituted the essential element in human history.

SOCIALISTIC AND COMMUNISTIC VIEW OF STATE 69

However, he believed that, when this régime was brought into full operation, the need for the maintenance of the State would disappear, and, in its place, non-political organs for the direction and control of the production and distribution of economic goods would be created.

The Communist Manifesto. Marx's and Engel's views found their most concise statement in their famous Communist Manifesto of 1847, and from that document may be quoted the following paragraphs: [11]

"The history of all hitherto existing society is the history of class struggles. Freeman and slave, patrician and plebeian, lord and serf, guild master and journeyman, in a word, oppressor and oppressed, stood in constant opposition to one another. . . . The modern bourgeois society that has sprouted from the ruins of feudal society, has not done away with class antagonisms. It has but established new classes, new conditions of oppression, new forms of struggle in place of the old ones. Our epoch, the epoch of the bourgeoisie, possesses, however, this distinctive feature; it has simplified the class antagonisms. Society is more and more splitting up into two great hostile camps, into two great classes directly facing each other: Bourgeoisie and Proletariat."

After detailing the evils of bourgeois rule, the Manifesto declares that this rule needs to be supplanted by Communism, the distinguishing feature of which will be "not the abolition of property generally, but the abolition of bourgeois property." "Communism deprives no man of the power to appropriate the products of society: all that it does is to deprive him of the power to subjugate the labor of others by means of such appropriation." "The proletariat will use its political supremacy (when ob-

[11] Engels was co-author with Marx of this Manifesto. In a Preface, written in 1888, to an edition of this Manifesto, Engels says: "The Manifesto being our joint production, I consider myself bound to state that the fundamental proposition which forms its nucleus, belongs to Marx."

tained) to wrest, by degrees, all capital from the bourgeoisie, to centralize all instruments of production in the hands of the State, that is, of the proletariat organized as the ruling class; and to increase the total of productive forces as rapidly as possible. . . . When, in the course of development, class distinctions have disappeared (all persons being drawn into the working or proletariat body), and all production has been concentrated in the hands of a vast association of the whole nation, the public power will lose its political character. Political power, properly so-called, is merely the organized power of one class for oppressing another. If the proletariat, during its contest with the bourgeoisie, is compelled by the force of circumstances, to organize itself as a class, if, by means of a revolution, it makes itself the ruling class, and, as such, sweeps away by force the old conditions of production, then it will, along with these conditions, have swept away the conditions for the existence of class antagonisms, and of classes generally, and will thereby have abolished its own supremacy. In place of the old bourgeois society, with its classes and class antagonisms, we shall have an association in which the free development of each is the condition for the free development of all."

The Manifesto closes with the words: "Let the ruling classes tremble at a Communist revolution. The proletarians have nothing to lose but their chains. They have a world to win. Working men of all countries, unite!"

Bolshevist Theory. The arch-exponent of Bolshevism, until his death in 1924, was, of course, Lenin. The official edition of his writings is in process of publication, and, when completed, will extend to thirty or more volumes. The essentials of his economic and political philosophy may, however, be found in his small volume entitled *The State and Revolution,* a work which the Communists declare to be the most important contribu-

SOCIALISTIC AND COMMUNISTIC VIEW OF STATE

tion to thought since the publication of the first volume of Marx's *Das Kapital*.[12]

Lenin claims, and with substantial justice, that, in Bolshevism, is to be found a thoroughgoing application of the doctrines of Marx, especially as found in his and Engel's "Communist Manifesto" of 1847.

Before further examining, however, the essentials of Bolshevist theory, it will be well to state, as briefly as possible, the manner in which the Bolshevist party of Russia developed out of, and is at present connected with, the International Communist Party.

What is known as the "First International," was established in 1847, and had for its creed the Manifesto which Marx and Engels had prepared.[13] This organization, after holding various meetings, reached its peak of development in 1869. It began rapidly to decline after the Franco-Prussian War of 1870, which had led to the futile outbreak of the Paris Commune in 1871, to which the International had lent its approval and support. Though existing for some years after this, the First International was without considerable influence, and, by 1880 may be said to have ceased to exist.[14]

What is known as the Second (Communist) International was formed at Paris in 1889. The program which

[12] An inexpensive English translation of *The State and Revolution* is published by the Communist Party of Great Britain, 16 King Street, Covent Garden, London, W. C. 2.

[13] The Preamble and Rules of the International were also written by Marx.

[14] Lorwin, in his *Labor and Internationalism* (p. 56) says: "It is usually said that the International went under as a result of the struggle between Marx and Bakunin. The fact is that this struggle was merely one phase of the decline of the International. The first blow to the International was its desertion by the English trade unionists who became apprehensive of its socialistic tendencies. The strong nationalistic sentiments aroused by the Franco-Prussian War and the specter of revolution conjured up by the Paris Commune made its existence in Germany impossible and destroyed it in France. The suppression of the Paris Commune broke the courage of revolutionists and their faith in a speedy triumph of socialist ideas; while the prolonged industrial depression of 1873-79 weakened trade union organization in all western countries."

it then adopted served as a basis for most of the discontented economic radicals until the outbreak of the Great War, although there were constant differences of views among the different schools of Socialists and Communists. There was an expectation upon the part of many that the internationalist, as distinguished from the nationalist, views which had been spread among the working men, would cause them to refuse to support a war between the greater European powers, but this hope was disappointed in 1914.[15] This marked the end of the Second International, and the birth, soon after, of the Third International.

This Third International, as were its predecessors, is an international organization, but with national units in many of the countries of the world. In historical fact, however, it has been closely associated with the Bolshevists of Russia, and has had its headquarters at Moscow where, in 1919, it was formally established. Though the Third International thus has an existence and organization distinct from the Soviet Government of Russia and from the Bolshevist party which is in control of that government, the fact is that the same persons who control the policies and actions of the one direct also the policies and actions of the other.

In its "Manifesto to the Proletariat of all Countries," issued by the first conference or congress of the Third International, it was declared that the World War had been an "Imperialist War"; that it had been brought about by imperialistic rivalries, and had been fought for imperialistic ends; and that the time had come for the workmen—the proletariat—of all nations to unite to bring to an end the capitalistic régime which had been responsible not only for this great disaster but also for the long continued exploitation of those who had only their labor to sell. The Manifesto declared: "Only the

[15] As to this, see Chapter VI of Lorwin's *Labor and Internationalism.*

Proletarian Dictatorship, which recognizes neither inherited privileges nor rights of property but which arises from the needs of the hungering masses, can shorten the period of the present crisis; and for this purpose it will mobilize all materials and forces, introduce the universal duty to labor, establish the régime of industrial discipline, and, in this way, heal in the course of a few years the open wounds caused by the war, and also raise humanity to now undreamed-of heights. . . . It is the proletariat which must establish real order, the order of Communism. It must end the dominion of capital, make war impossible, wipe out State boundaries, transform the whole world into one coöperative commonwealth and bring about real human brotherhood and freedom."

To do this, the Manifesto declared, the political power would need to be seized by the proletariat, in order that, by it, the power of the capitalist class—the bourgeoisie—might be destroyed. "The organized power of the bourgeoisie is in the civil State, with its capitalist army under the control of bourgeois—junker officers, its police and gendarmes, jailors and judges, its priests, governmental officials, etc. . . . The dictatorship of the proletariat, which gives it a favored possession in the community, is only a provisional institution. As the opposition of the bourgeoisie is broken, as it is appropriated and gradually absorbed into the working groups, the proletarian dictatorship disappears, until finally the State dies and then there are no more class distinctions. . . . Democracy so-called—that is, bourgeois democracy—is nothing more nor less than veiled dictatorship by the bourgeoisie. . . . Bourgeois democracy, with its parliamentary system, uses words to induce belief in popular participation in government. Actually, the masses and their organizations are held far out of reach of the real power and the real State administration. In the Soviet system the mass organizations rule, and through them the mass itself, inasmuch as the Soviets draw constantly increasing numbers of workers into the State administration, and only by this process will the entire working population gradually become part of the government. . . . The Soviet system . . . unites the masses with the organs of government by right of recall, amalgamation of legislative and executive powers and by use of working boards. Above all, this union is fostered by the fact that in the Soviet system elections are based not on arbitrary territorial districts, but on units of production."

From time to time, in successive world congresses of the Third International, the aims and policies of the Communists have been further elaborated, but without introducing any essentially new doctrines.[16]

In Lenin's *The State and Revolution,* are found the same criticisms of bourgeois rule that were stated by Marx; the same declaration as to the necessity of a revolution; the same defense of a temporary dictatorship by the proletarian party; the same promise that, ultimately, this dictatorship will give way to communal nonpolitical rule.

"The State," Lenin declares, "is the product and manifestation of the irreconcilability of class antagonisms. . . . The State only exists where there are class antagonisms." He agrees with Marx that "the State is the organ of class domination, the organ of oppression of one class by another. Its aim is the creation of order which legalizes and perpetuates this oppression by moderating the collisions between the classes." This being so, "it is clear that the liberation of the oppressed classes is impossible without a violent revolution, and without the destruction of the machinery of State power."

Just how long the State, dictatorially operated by the

---

[16] For a recent and elaborate statement, see the program adopted, in September, 1928, by the Sixth Congress of the Third International. The translated text of this is given by Batsell in his *Soviet Rule in Russia.*

proletariat, will need to last, Lenin does not venture to predict, but, as to this it is worthy to note that, in a letter, published in *L'Humanité,* in July, 1919, he said: "A very long period of transition is necessary to pass from Capitalism to Socialism; the transformation of production is a difficult thing; we need time to transform all the conditions." "When the meaning of this is considered," says Ramsay Macdonald, "it is ominous." [17]

Just exactly what forms of regulatory or coercive control is expected by the Communists to exist when the Communist régime is in full operation, it is difficult to say. As regards some of the characteristics of this régime, they are, however, fairly clear. The régime will be a democratic one, but not in a political sense. Those regulatory or directing organs which will exist will owe their being to the direct will of the entire populace, and, by recall or other means, those in authority will be kept in close touch with, and responsible to, the public will.

The Communists have laid great emphasis upon the necessity of abolishing standing armies and gendarmeries, and of getting rid of the bodies of civil officials bureaucratically organized. Apparently, they believe that, if the people can rid themselves of these two distinct classes, who, under existing circumstances, are outside of the general body of private citizens, and whose function it is to uphold the power of the State rather than to advance the interests of the people, a very long step will be taken toward abolishing the State. Sometimes, indeed, it would seem as though the Communists believe that thus the political State can be said to be wholly done away with. With respect to this point we find Lenin saying: "The centralized power of the State, peculiar to capitalist society, grew up in the period of the fall of feudalism. Two institutions are especially characteristic of this machine: the bureaucracy and the standing army.

[17] *Parliament and Revolution,* p. 23.

More than once in the works of Marx and Engels we find mention of the thousand threads which connect these institutions with the capitalist class; and the experience of every worker illustrates this connection with extraordinary clearness and impressiveness." A little later on he says: "Once the majority of the nation itself suppresses its oppressors a special force for suppression is no longer necessary. In this sense the State begins to disappear. Instead of the special institutions of a privileged minority (privileged officials and chiefs of a standing army) the majority can itself directly fulfil all these functions; and the more the discharge of the functions of the State devolves upon the masses of the people, the less there is need for the existence of the State."

Included in this demotion of military and civil officials from their official status as agents of the State, is the reduction of the salaries of those persons who take over their duties to an equality with the salaries or wages of the other workers of the proletariat. "The control of all officials, without exception, by the unreserved application of the principle of election and, at any time, recall; and the approximation of their salaries to the ordinary pay of the workers—these are simple and self-evident democratic measures, which harmonize completely the interests of the workers and the majority of the peasants."

Again, he says: "In order to destroy the State, it is necessary to convert the functions of the public service into such simple operations of control and book-keeping as are within the reach of the vast majority of the population, and, ultimately, of every single individual." And, finally: "We set ourselves, as our final aim, the task of the destruction of the State, that is, of every organized and systematic violence, every form of violence against man in general. We do not expect the advent of an order of society in which the principle of the submission of the minority to the majority will not be observed. But, striving for Socialism, we are convinced that it will develop further into Communism, and, side by side with this, there will vanish all need for force, for the subjection of one man to another, of one section of society to another, since people will grow accustomed to observing the elementary conditions of social existence without force and without subjection." "We are not utopians, and we do not in the least deny the possibility of excesses by individual persons, and equally the need to suppress such excesses. But, in the first place, for this no special machine, no special instrument of repression is needed. This will be done by the armed nation itself, as simply and as readily as any crowd of civilized people, even in modern society, parts a pair of combatants or does not allow a woman to be outraged. And, secondly, we know that the fundamental social cause of excesses which violate the rules of social life is the exploitation of the masses, their want and their poverty. With the removal of this chief cause, excesses will inevitably begin to 'wither away.' We do not know how quickly and in what stages, but we know that they will be withering away. With their withering away, the State will also wither away."

The Communists have, of course, the problem of determining the rule in accordance with which the products of communized property are to be distributed among the workers.

Each worker is expected to be compelled by one form of pressure or another, to work according to his ability, for the welfare of his community, and, as a minimum, he, equally with every other worker, will be entitled to receive products in kind and to an amount necessary to him in order that he may maintain for himself a decent existence. When all have been thus provided for from the common fund of products, it appears that the surplus is to be divided according to the needs of each individual.

Thus will become operative the Communist canon of distributive justice—"From everyone according to his ability; to everyone according to his needs." [18]

Summary. We are now in a position to state, in summary form, the Marxist (Bolshevist) economic and political conceptions.

It is seen that, though the Marxians stress the idea that, under a capitalistic régime, the proletariat are prevented from receiving their full share of what is socially produced, they do not make any conspicuous efforts to lay down abstract, fundamental ethical principles, whether of economic justice or of political right, in accordance with which economic goods shall be distributed. Marxians claim that, in the modern world, economic goods are something more than the product of the labor of the individual workmen—they are a social product. Notwithstanding this, they assert, this entire social product, except such as is needed by the laborers in order to maintain a bare existence, is seized upon and absorbed by the capitalist classes. Apparently, they claim this to be unjust,—an injustice which will not be corrected until each man receives from the total of products according to his needs. At the same time, it is expected of him that each one will contribute to the production of goods and services according to, and to the extent of, his abilities. During the period of transition after the proletariat have obtained political control, they hold that it may be necessary to

---

[18] It may be observed that, according to Marx, in the first or "lower" phases of Communism, that is, before Communism has come into full operation, a somewhat less ideal rule of distribution would probably have to be applied. According to this rule, every member of the communist society, performing a socially necessary service or work, would receive a certificate that he had done a specified amount of work. By presenting this certificate, he would receive from the public stores a corresponding quantity of products. In the higher phase of Communist society, however, distribution would be according to needs. "There will then," says Lenin, "be no need for any exact calculation by society of the quantity of products to be distributed to each of its members; each will take freely 'according to his needs.'"

compel every one to work, to a certain extent at least, and to pay each one according to the amount of work actually and individually done by him. But, it is asserted, this is not a completely satisfactory or wholly just rule of distribution for it does not take into due account the fact that economic goods are, truly speaking, a social product. The truly rational, and, presumably, just result is reached only when every one works according to his abilities, and receives according to his needs. So much for the social or economic theory of the Marxists.

As for their political theory, it is evident that they hold that the present political state has no firm ethical basis. When society is placed upon its proper operating basis, there will, according to them, be no practical need for the continued existence of the State. Until now, they say, the State has had for its *raison d'être* and as its actual effect, nothing more than the maintenance in power of the capitalists, and the protection of their economic interests.

As regards the belief of the Communists that, when their régime obtains full operation, the State will disappear, it must be pointed out that, granting all that they say, this will be true only if we so limit the term "State" as to make it inapplicable to the form of social organization which the Communists expect will take its place.

The Communists, so far as the author is aware, have not attempted to give a clear picture of just what will be the structural organization of society after the State has disappeared, but it would appear that they expect that the Communist community (at least, if of any considerable size) will have an organization for the purpose of carrying on production in a scientific and rationalized manner, that is, in a way which will not only employ the most efficient means of production but also determine what commodities shall be produced and in what amounts. In these respects there will be required a much more elaborate machinery of direction and operation than that now exemplified by any modern government, and the only grounds upon which the Communists can claim that this will not be a governmental or State machinery are: (1) that the end subserved by this communist machinery will no longer be the maintenance of the interests of a dominant class, but, instead, will be the advancement of the interests of the entire community as a single class; (2) that, because of the readiness with which its directions will be obeyed by all, or nearly all, the people, there will be no need for it to issue commands, obedience to which will be enforced, or violations of which will be punished; (3) as flowing from the foregoing, that there will be no armed forces attached to the administrative machinery which will be distinct from, and, in a sense, outside of and above the body of the people; and (4) that those who operate the communistic machinery will not constitute a magistracy or bureaucracy, but, upon the contrary, will be a body of men, performing, to be sure, certain public functions, but not marked off in any way from the whole body of the workers of the community; that is, that these functionaries will have no public rights or special privileges and will be rewarded for their work in just the same manner, and to the same extent, that other workers are rewarded.

Even if one shares the optimism of the Communists as to the possibility of establishing a régime under which political compulsion will no longer need to be exercised toward the persons organized under it, there still remains the problem of protecting such a community against foreign foes—a problem which can cease to be a real one only when the adjoining or near-by communities have themselves adopted Communism, or, at any rate, have become so moralized as to abandon all forms of foreign aggression. Until such a situation has come into

SOCIALISTIC AND COMMUNISTIC VIEW OF STATE

being a Communistic community must make provision for possible aggression from outside itself. This will mean the maintenance of armed forces, military or naval, or both. It is, of course, possible to argue that such forces can be provided by voluntary enlistments, and maintained and made militarily effective without the necessity of placing powers of coercion in the hands either of the civil authorities or of those directing the field operations of these forces. To assent to this is certainly to levy a high tax upon the optimism of the most optimistic.

It does not lie within the province of the present work to consider the administrative difficulties that would necessarily be met by Communists in the operation of the social organization which they envisage for the future. It may be said, however, as regards their canon of distributive justice that every one will be expected to work according to, and to the extent of, his abilities, and that he will receive according to his needs, that there seems to be no way, and certainly Communists have suggested none, by which it will be possible to determine what are a person's abilities or what are his needs. Thus, whatever may be the abstract merits of the formula as a canon of distributive justice, the practicability of its application is not great.[19]

The doctrines of the Bolshevists with regard to the type of government required in order that their ideals may best and most rapidly be realized, is, to a certain extent dependent upon their economic doctrines and their conception of the nature and province of the State. It is not necessary, however, here to describe the Soviet form of government which has been established in Russia. It can, however, be pointed out that, under this form of government, the attempt has been made, as required

---

[19] The author, in a work entitled *Social Justice*, has sought to determine the nature of distributive justice, and to estimate the theoretical and practical value of the various views advanced by ethical writers and social reformers.

by the general doctrines of Communism, to exclude the bourgeoisie from influence or control, and, ultimately if not immediately, to vest political, or, rather, social, control in the people regarded as a single producing and consuming class. It may also be observed that, involved as an integral element in communist or Bolshevist social philosophy, is the substitution of the internationalistic for the nationalistic point of view; that is, the acceptance of the conception of the solidarity of interests of the working people of all nations as distinguished from the interests of the people of a single nation. This premise leads, in theory at least, to conclusions which, in important respects, are not in consonance with doctrines of international rights and obligations founded upon orthodox nationalistic conceptions of State sovereignty and independence. Interesting as it would be to trace these implications, the scope of the present work will not permit this to be done.

CHAPTER V

DIVINE RIGHT THEORIES

THE Divine Right theory, as applied to the State, declares that it is God's will that men shall live in a condition of political society. As applied to Government, it asserts that a *de facto* political authority, or a given form of political rule—the monarchical, for example—is sanctioned by the Supreme Being, and, therefore, that obedience to its commands is a moral obligation laid upon those over whom its claim to authority extends. The theory has also included the doctrine that those persons who exercise the powers of government, or, at any rate, those who are at the head of the administration (and in whom all rights of sovereignty are assumed ultimately to be vested), are either themselves super-human or divine beings, or vicegerents of God with a directly divine mission to exercise supreme political authority over their subjects.

In one or another of these forms the divine right theory, since the earliest times to the present day, has played an important part in the history of political thought. As is well known, among all primitive peoples practically every precept of social or political conduct was deemed to be supported by a divine sanction and their rulers considered to be, if not themselves gods, at least possessed of a divine right to rule. In the ancient empires of the East, religion and law were confused to such an extent that political science can scarcely be said to have existed as an independent branch of knowledge. The ultimate sanction of all law was supposed to be found in the sacred writings. In all of the vast Asiatic monarchies of early days the rulers claimed a divine right to control the affairs of the State, and this was submitted to by the people with but little question.

By the Hebrews the theocratic theory was carried to the extent not only of maintaining that the authority of their rulers rested upon divine delegation and sanction, but of alleging a direct oversight and participation by Jehovah in the control of public affairs.

The Greeks were too rationalistic to explain or justify political laws and institutions by referring them to a postulated divine will. Instead, as we have already seen, their chief thinkers, Plato and Aristotle, felt it necessary to show that political life is validated because in consonance with men's essential nature as moral, rational beings. Ultimately, thus, the State was deemed to be divine, but only in the sense that the entire cosmos was conceived to be governed by natural or divine law. Furthermore, there was in the Greek mind no doubt that the specific governmental structures which the States should possess, the persons who should exercise authority, and the public policies to be pursued, were matters that properly lay within the right of each political group of persons to determine for themselves. To the Greek his State was of such comprehensive significance that the performance of religious rites by the individual was but a part of his obligation to the State. With the interior religious beliefs, or opinions, of the citizen the State did not much, if at all, concern itself, and no priesthood, distinct from the State's magistracy, was created. In fact, in their thought there did not arise the idea, so well known to the medieval and modern world, of a distinction between Church and State.[1]

[1] "It is a famous saying of Plato that philosophy is the child of wonder. It was the gift of the Greeks that they were prone to wonder; and they naturally turned to inquire into the things which excited their wonder. They inquired rationally into the properties of speech, and so

With the Romans began, in practice, a clearer distinction between divine and civil authority. By them, law was considered as created by the State, and its final authority sought in the Roman people. They may thus be said to have been the first to attempt to give to the structure of the State a definite legal form, and thereby, while limiting its governmental power, to give to it greater stability and regularity in action. At the same time, as is well known, the Romans were practical lawyers and administrators rather than philosophers, and, so far as they did indulge in philosophical speculations, followed closely Grecian thought, and made slight, if any, advances upon it. In Republican Rome, political authority came to be placed upon a human or rationalistic basis; but, with the rise of the Empire, and the entrance of Asiatic influences, there was a return to theocratic doctrines, and divine attributes were ascribed to the Cæsars, some of whom, there is reason to suppose, actually believed themselves to be gods.[2]

With the rise to power of the Christian Church began a struggle between temporal and spiritual authorities which has lasted to the present day, and which has given rise to a wide variety of theories regarding the extent to which it is proper to ascribe a divine origin to, or justification for, political authority.

In its early history, the Church of Christ was distinctly and avowedly an organization claiming dominion over only the spiritual interests of mankind. In the patristic writings obedience to the State in all things not contrary to the law of God was distinctly taught. The supremacy

produced the science of logic; they inquired rationally into the spatial properties of matter, and so produced Euclidean geometry—perhaps the most typical expression of their genius. In the same spirit they inquired rationally into the composition and properties of the State. There is no speech of 'divine right' or supernatural sanctions in Greek political theory, except, perhaps, in some of the speculations of the later Pythagoreans." Ernest Barker, *Greek Political Theory: Plato and His Predecessors*, p. 1, note 1.

[2] Cf. Sweet, *Roman Emperor Worship*, passim.

of the civil power in all things temporal was freely admitted. The command to render unto Cæsar that which is Cæsar's was uniformly held during these earlier years as providing the principle according to which the relations between Church and State should be governed. "If the Emperor demand tribute," said Saint Ambrose, "we should not refuse. . . . If the Emperor desire our fields, he has the power to take them, no one of us can resist. . . . We will pay to Cæsar that which is Cæsar's."[3]

However, in proclaiming the kingdom of God, the Church gave to the individual a law in spiritual affairs outside of and superior to that of the State. And, as the See of Rome increased in power and importance, it began to claim powers embraced within this principle. It maintained its right to preserve the peace, to decide as to the justice of quarrels between temporal princes, to enforce with temporal might the purity of morals, to defend the oppressed, and to enforce its decisions by anathema and excommunication, and, when necessary, even by force of arms.

Thus, by degrees, the temporal power of the Church increased until it became itself a civic organization, promulgating laws and enforcing obedience to them by military coercion, and contesting with the temporal rulers of Europe the right of supreme control. Dante,[4] Occam,[5] and Marsilius of Padua[6] defended in their writings the claims of the temporal powers in this controversy. Hincmar, Hildebrand, Thomas Aquinas,[7] and Giles of Rome[8] supported the papal pretensions.

In this great medieval strife between papal and temporal power, both parties remained, however, united upon one point; namely, that this dualism of Church and State

[3] *Epist. de basilicis tradendis*, 38, t. II. (Ed. Bened., p. 872.)
[4] *De Monarchia.*
[5] *Octo questiones super potestate summi pontificis. Dialogus Magistri.*
[6] *Defensor pacis.*
[7] *De regimine principum.*
[8] *De Regimine principum. De ecclesiastica potestate.*

found an ultimate union in a divine order. They were not divided as to the ultimate nature of all political authority, but only as to the manner of its delegation by its supreme author to particular hands.

In this polemical literature, we would not expect, nor do we find, systematic treatises upon the nature of the State. The writings deal with utilitarian interests, quote the patristic writings and the Scriptures as the highest authorities, and depend upon conflicting interpretations as to the historical relations between the Church and the Empire. Thus, in all these writings we find political philosophy confused with religious dogma, and its results largely vitiated by the extent to which the minds of men were dominated by theological beliefs. Aquinas, for example, argued as follows: "The highest aim of mankind is eternal blessedness. To this chief aim all earthly aims must be subordinated. This chief aim cannot be realized through human direction alone, but must obtain divine assistance, which is only to be obtained through the Church. Therefore, the State, through which earthly aims are attained, must be subordinated to the Church. Church and State are as two swords which God has given to Christendom for its protection; both of these, however, are given by Him to the Pope and the temporal sword by him handed to the rulers of the States. Thus the Pope alone received his power directly from the Almighty, the Emperor his authority indirectly through the Pope's hand." [9]

Against this argument, the supporters of the supremacy of the temporal power replied: "Between spiritual and temporal affairs there is a distinction that cannot be destroyed. The control of temporal affairs belongs exclusively to the State, and the Roman Bishop possesses no power either to enact or to suspend laws regulating affairs other than those of the spirit. The kingdom is

[9] Cf. Janet, *Histoire de la Science Politique*, Vol. I, pp. 381-401.

necessarily and avowedly declared by the Scriptures to be not of this earth, but of the world to come; not over the bodies of men, but over their souls."

The Protestant Reformation, rather than lessening this confusion of divine and political power, tended to increase it. All of its leaders, Luther, Melanchthon, Zwingli, and Calvin, reiterated the divine origin of civil authority and the necessity of the citizens' obedience thereto. The opponents of the Reformation, especially the Dominicans and Jesuits, directed all their energies to proving the purely mundane character of the State. This they did in order to give to the Church the sole claim to spiritual origin and divine authority, and, therefore, to the placing of political power upon a lower basis as compared with it. It was at this time, and in the writings of these ecclesiastics, that the doctrine of *Naturrecht* was given a prominence in political speculations that it was thenceforth to maintain until the present century.[10]

When, however, the contest became no longer one between Pope and Emperor, between ecclesiastical and temporal power, but between ruler and ruled, and the scope and legitimacy of political rule in particular hands became questioned, the controversy assumed a new shape. The point in dispute then came to be, not so much the origin of political power itself, as the hands by which, and the manner in which, it could rightfully be exercised. By the end of the thirteenth century it had become an axiom accepted by all parties, that the will of God and the nature of man were to be considered only as *causae remotae*, and that all rulership lay in the free contractual gift of the community (*per viam voluntariae subjectionis et consensus*), the debated point being only as to the effect of such a popular contract; that is, whether resulting in a total alienation or merely a revocable dele-

[10] Upon this point see especially Gierke, *Johannes Althusius u. die Entwicklung der naturrechtlichen Staatstheorien*, pp. 64 *et seq.*

gation, of the supreme political power. And, in this connection, it is to be especially noted that, during the sixteenth and seventeenth centuries, it was the Roman Catholic writers, and particularly the Jesuits, who were foremost in advocating the original sovereignty of the peoples and the contractual basis of their governments.

We now find the temporal princes, who, in their contests with the Pope, had been willing enough to separate entirely their authority from the sanction of support of the Church, looking to the Church to uphold them in their rule by declaring tyrannicide and popular deposition impious; while the Clergy, especially in France and other countries whose rulers remained loyal to Rome, were found refusing to accept the full consequences of the theories of Contract and Natural Law which they were willing enough to support in the Church's struggles against the Empire.[11] But it was only in the absurd and extravagant patriarchal theory of Filmer,[12] according to which royal authority is based upon the dominion given by God to Adam at the time of his expulsion from Eden, and in the subservient writings of Bossuet,[13] that the divine theory was again openly argued.

At the same time, it cannot be denied that the idea of a "divinity that doth hedge a King" continued to be of great actual influence upon the ideas of the people—an influence which, though crushed in the French Revolution, revived during the counter-revolutionary period that followed 1815, and remained in the thought of the common people of Europe, especially of those under the more autocratic of rulers. But, for all purposes of

[11] During the counter-revolutionary period that followed the Congress of Vienna, the absolutist attitude of the Church was very pronounced. President Andrew D. White, in the *Papers of the Am. Hist. Assn.* (Vol. IV, Part I). gives an extreme instance of this in an article entitled "A Catechism of the Revolutionary Reaction."
[12] *Patriarcha, or the Natural Power of Kings*, published in 1680. For refutation of Filmer's views, see Sidney, *Discourses on Government*, and Locke, *Two Treatises of Government*, Book I.
[13] *Politique tirée de l'Écriture sainte*.

political philosophy, the divine theory disappeared before that of natural law and contract, and received its *coup de grâce* on the continent from the writings of Hugo Grotius, and in England from those of Hobbes and Locke.[14]

Japan. The purpose of the present work being one of criticism rather than of history, no further attempt will be made to trace, even in outline, the course of the divine right theory in political thought. Mention will be made, however, of certain modern or current manifestations of the doctrine.

There is, inherently, no reason why the Divine Right theory should not be alleged in support of any form of government. Indeed, to those who are convinced that "the voice of the People is the voice of God (*vox populi, vox dei*) the theory is advanced to sustain all forms of government under which the principle is accepted that the expressed will of the governed should determine the policies of the State. In general, however, the theory has been employed almost exclusively to justify the title to authority of autocratic monarchs.

Of present-day States belonging to what international law terms the "Family of Nations," Japan alone asserts, officially, the divine right theory of government. This doctrine it holds in the radical form of declaring the essentially divine character of the monarch,—not that he acts as an agent or vicegerent of God or the Gods, but that he is himself, in his own person, divine, and that he is a direct successor of the Sun Goddess the greatest figure in the Japanese pantheon.

[14] Mr. Spencer remarks how remarkable it is that a system of thought may often be seen going about in high spirits after having committed suicide. Thus it is that the divine theory, though killed and buried, is from time to time revived and seen going about in habiliments changed, to be sure, but so thin as but slightly to hide its true self. Instances of this are to be seen in Stahl, *Die Philosophie des Rechts*, Haller, *Restauration der Staats-wissenschaft*, and Mulford's apocalyptic rhapsody (as Professor Dunning terms it), *The Nation*.

The Preamble to the Japanese Constitution speaks of the reigning Emperor as occupying the throne by "a lineal succession unbroken for ages eternal," and the same allegation is made in Article I.

The Marquis (later Prince) Ito, commenting on the statement of Article III of the Constitution that "the Emperor is sacred and inviolable," says: [15] "The Sacred Throne was established at the time when the heavens and the earth became separated (*Kojiki*). The Emperor is Heaven-descended, divine and sacred: He is preëminent above all His subjects. He must be reverenced and is inviolable. He has indeed to pay due respect to the law, but the law has no power to hold Him accountable to it. Not only shall there be no irreverence for the Emperor's person, but also shall He neither be made a topic of derogatory comment nor one of discussion."

In most countries, the progress of political liberalism and of intellectual enlightenment has caused the divine right theory to lose, by degrees, whatever acceptance it may have had in the minds of the people. And no doubt this has been true among the better educated of the Japanese people. But there can be little doubt that it is still held, as a matter of faith, if not of reasoned thought, by the great mass of the Japanese people, and thus, emotionally, is of great influence in Japan. The most significant fact is, however, the deliberate manner in which those who have been in political authority in Japan since the so-called Restoration of 1867 have deliberately transmuted the old Shinto religion, originally one of nature and ancestor worship, into a religion of political patriotism and of emperor worship. This new Shintoism has been spread through the schools and by all the other instrumentalities of propaganda available to an auto-

---

[15] Marquis Ito, as is well known, was the chief draughtsman of the Constitution, which fact gives an especially authentic character to his Commentaries.

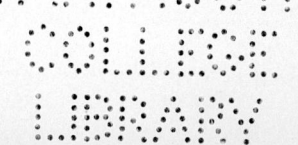

cratic and paternalistic government. This manufacture and successful inculcation in a people of what has amounted to a new religious faith, has been treated by B. H. Chamberlain, one of the best known authorities on things Japanese and for a considerable time professor at the Imperial University of Tokyo. In his pamphlet entitled *The Invention of a New Religion*,[16] Mr. Chamberlain says:

"Mikado-worship and Japan-worship—for that is the new Japanese religion—is, of course, no spontaneously generated phenomenon. Every manufacture presupposes a material out of which it is made, every present a past on which it rests. But the twentieth-century Japanese religion of loyalty and patriotism is quite new, for in it pre-existing ideas have been sifted, altered, freshly compounded, turned to new uses, and have found a new centre of gravity. . . . Shinto, a primitive nature cult, which had fallen into discredit, was taken out of its cupboard and dusted. The common people, it is true, continued to place their affections on Buddhism. . . . The governing class determined to change all this. They insisted on the Shinto doctrine that the Mikado descends in direct succession from the nature Goddess of the Sun, and that He himself is a living God on earth who justly claims the absolute fealty of his subjects. Such things as laws and constitutions are but free gifts on His part, not in any sense popular rights. . . . The new Japanese religion consists, in its present early stage, of worship of the sacrosanct Imperial Person and of His Divine Ancestors, of implicit obedience to Him as head of the army (a position, by the way, opposed to all former Japanese ideas according to which the court was essentially civilian); furthermore, of a corresponding belief that Japan is as far superior to the common ruck of nations as the Mikado is divinely superior to the common ruck

[16] Published in 1912; London; D. Watts and Co.

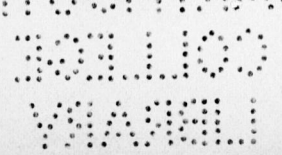

of kings and emperors. Do not the early history-books record the fact that Japan was created first, while all other countries resulted merely from the drops that fell from the Creator's spear when he had finished his main work?"

In another and earlier work, Professor Chamberlain had given the following account of Shintoism:

"Shinto, so often spoken of as a religion, is hardly entitled to that name. It has no set of dogmas, no sacred book, no moral code. The absence of a moral code is accounted for, in the writings of the modern native commentators, by the innate perfection of Japanese humanity, which obviates the necessity for such outward props. It is only outcasts, like the Chinese and Western nations, whose natural depravity renders the occasional appearance of sages and reformers necessary: and, even with this assistance, all foreign nations continue to wallow in a mire of ignorance, guilt, and disobedience towards the heaven-descended, *de jure* monarch of the universe—the Mikado of Japan." [17]

In a standard treatise on Japanese political life, by a Japanese, we find, in a chapter entitled "The Nation and its Political Mind," the following estimate of the influence in Japan of the divine right theory:

"The Divine Right of the Emperor, however absurd it may seem to the theorists of individualistic idealism, still holds a predominant place in the minds of the Japanese; and its political value seems to be as important to the Japanese nation as the religious value of miracles and mythological and allegorical stories is to certain religions. . . . The Divine Right of the Emperor is the fundamental principle on which the Japanese polity was first established and on which it still rests. . . . That the Mikado reigns and governs the country absolutely, by a right inherited from His Divine Ancestors, is the un-

[17] *Things Japanese*, verb, "Shinto."

conscious belief or the instinctive feeling of the Japanese people. Indeed, it may be said to be their religion. . . . The foreign religions, philosophies, ethical theories, and political principles which have come into Japan from the earliest ages of her civilization, however great their influence generally, have done very little, if anything at all, to modify the traditional attitude of the people towards their Emperor. . . . Since the middle of the nineteenth century almost all of the influential political dogmas, theories, and principles of the Western world, such as the law of Nature, the rights of man, individualism, utilitarianism, laissez faire, the theory of the *contract social*, socialism, democracy, republicanism, and constitutionalism, have penetrated Japan, and have exercised considerable influence upon her political thought, so that the system of government was in a short period of time revolutionized; but the dogma of the divine right of the Emperor and the loyalty of the people has never mingled with or been affected by these new ideas." [18]

China. In Chinese political philosophy, under the Empire, was found a peculiar combination of democratic and divine right theories. Confucianism was a system of conduct rather than a theology, and taught the obligations that children owe their parents, the obligations parents owe their ancestors, and the obligations due by the people in general to their rulers. By the Taoist doctrine, which was a system of metaphysics as well as of religion, the universe was regarded as an ordered one controlled by uniform, unchangeable natural laws imposed by an omnipotent, wholly rational, but impersonal, power, the name for which, when translated into Western phraseology, was termed Heaven. The Emperor was viewed as holding a "Mandate" from Heaven to rule

[18] Uyehara, *The Political Development of Japan, 1867-1909.* Published in 1910.

his people. This Mandate he was believed to retain only so long as he ruled wisely and justly. He was, in other words, obligated, in all his acts, to conform to *Tao*, the Road, the Way, or the Natural Order of the Universe. The proof that he was so ruling was the fact that his people were prospering under his rule. If, for any reason, they did not prosper, this was evidence that the Emperor had departed from Tao. Thus he was held responsible for whatever might happen,—even for those events, like floods, earthquakes, droughts, etc., leading to famine, over which, regarded as merely an ordinary human being, he could have had no control. It was old and settled doctrine that "Heaven sees as the people see; Heaven hears as the people hear"; that their welfare is the constant wish of Heaven. It sees that the people need to be ruled, and, therefore, provides rulers for them. Thus, in the proclamation announcing the foundation of the Shang dynasty in 1766 B. C., we find elaborated the following argument:

"Heaven gives birth to people with such desires and passions that they, without a ruler over them, would fall into disorder and confusion. It also gives birth to men of intelligence, whose business it is to regulate these desires and passions. The King of the overthrown dynasty had his virtue obscured, and the people, as it were, fell into quagmires and burning charcoal. Thereupon, it endowed the present King with valor and wisdom to serve as the mark and standard to the princes of the myriad states and to continue the work of Yu, the founder of the overthrown dynasty. Now our King is ruling after the example set by that great King to fulfil the appointment of Heaven. The defeated King was really an offender in the eye of the Supreme Being. He, possessing no virtue equal to the sacred task, pretended to the sanction of Heaven to issue commands. Thereupon the Supreme Being viewed him with disapprobation and caused our King to receive the appointment and to govern the multitude of the people." [19]

Also worthy of quotation is the following paragraph, an excerpt from the address to T'ai-Kiah, the second emperor of the Shang dynasty, by his eminent minister I-Yin:

"The throne, conferred by Heaven, is a seat of hardship. If you have virtue, nothing but good government will prevail; but if you have none, disorder and rebellion will be rife. Combine your rule with Tao, and in all respects you must prosper. If an emperor's virtues are constant, they protect his throne; if they are unstable, he loses his nine possessions [provinces]. When the sovereigns of the Hia dynasty were no longer able to practise virtue, they offended the gods and oppressed the people. Therefore, Imperial Heaven no longer protected them, and its eye wandered over the myriads of regions to see whether there existed any person to whom it might tender the appointment; with a look of affection it sought a man of virtue of the first order, to make him chief of the gods. None but myself and (your father) T'ang possessed such first-rate virtue, and could therefore obtain the enjoyment of Heaven's favor; so it was he who received the glorious appointment from Heaven, became the owner of the people in the nine possessions, and was able to change the calendar of the Hia dynasty. It was not that Heaven had any partiality for our Shang dynasty; it simply sided with the man who possessed virtue of the first order. Nor was it that Shang sought the allegiance of the lower people; the people simply turned to the man of highest virtue. So, if your virtue is of the first order, none of your actions will be unsuccessful; but if it is of the second or third order, all your acts will produce misfortune. Happiness and misfortune are not unreasonably forced upon

[19] Quoted by Hawkling L. Yen, *Constitutional Development of China*, p. 29.

men; but Heaven sends down misfortune or happiness according to the state of their virtue." [20]

In the works of Mencius we find still more particularly described the manner in which an Emperor obtained his right to rule, as witness the following dialogue:

"Wan Chang said, 'Was it the case that Yaou gave the empire to Shun?' Mencius said, 'No. The emperor cannot give the empire to another.'

" 'Yes:—but Shun had the empire. Who gave it to him?' 'Heaven gave it to him,' was the answer.

" 'Heaven gave it to him,—did Heaven confer its appointment on him with specific injunctions?' Mencius replied. 'No. Heaven does not speak. It simply showed its will by his personal conduct, and his conduct of affairs.' . . . The empire can present a man to Heaven, but he cannot make Heaven give that man the empire. A prince can present a man to the emperor, but he cannot cause the emperor to make that man a prince. . . . Therefore I say, Heaven does not speak. It simply indicated its will by his personal conduct and his conduct of affairs. . . . The sentiment is expressed in the words of the great Declaration—'Heaven sees according as my people see; Heaven hears according as my people hear.' . . .

"In the case of a private individual obtaining the empire there must be in him virtue equal to that of Shun or Yu, and moreover there must be the presenting of him to Heaven by the preceding emperor." [21]

This last requirement, that the new Emperor should be presented, that is, nominated, to Heaven by his predecessor, though ordinarily required, was not, in practice, deemed absolutely essential, and, of course, was not met when, as every now and then occurred, new dynasties were established by the forcible overthrow of the old.

---

[20] The book *T'ai-Kiah*, III, quoted by de Groot, *Religion in China*, p. 99.
[21] Legge, *The Chinese Classics. The Works of Mencius*, Book V, Chap. V.

It is worthy of note that, under the Republic, the presidents of China have, in various of their proclamations, continued to give at least verbal expression to the doctrine that when the people have suffered from either civil discord or foreign aggression or even from disasters due to disease or the failure of crops, the fundamental cause has been a lack of virtue and wisdom upon their ruler's part.

Germany.[22] We shall later have occasion to consider the manner in which, before the Great War, there was built up in Germany an apotheosis of the State as a mystical entity or person. In consonance with, if not correlative to, this view, was the doctrine strenuously and repeatedly asserted by William II that he derived his right to rule as King of Prussia directly from God, and not by delegation of authority from his subjects. Note, for example, the following from a considerable number of similar utterances by him:

In Bremen, on April 21, 1890, William said: "The fact that we have been able to achieve what has been achieved is primarily due to the fact that in our House the tradition prevails that we regard ourselves as appointed by God to reign over the peoples whom we have been called to rule, and to guide them in accordance with their welfare and the furtherance of their material and spiritual interests."

In Berlin, on February 20, 1891, he said: "You know that I regard my whole position and my mission as one entrusted to me by God, and that I am called upon to execute the mandate of a Higher Being to whom I shall hereafter have to render account."

In a speech delivered August 25, 1910, he said: "Here [Königsberg] my grandfather again, by his own right, set

---

[22] In the paragraphs which immediately follow the author has made liberal use of material appearing in his volume *Prussian Political Philosophy*. (D. Appleton & Co., 1918.)

the Prussian crown upon his head, once more distinctly emphasizing the fact that it was accorded to him by the will of God alone . . . and that he looked upon himself as the chosen instrument of heaven. . . . Looking upon myself as the instrument of the Lord, without regard to the opinions and intentions of the day, I go my way."

In his proclamation to the Army of the East, in 1914, the Kaiser said: "Remember that you are a chosen people. The spirit of the Lord has descended upon me because I am the Emperor of the Germans. I am the instrument of the Almighty, I am his sword, his agent. Woe and death to those who shall oppose my will. Woe and death to those who do not believe in my mission. . . . Let them perish, all the enemies of the German people! God demands their destruction, God who, by my mouth, bids you to do His will."

It would appear from these and other utterances of his majesty, that William II believed that the Hohenzollern family had been selected from among the other members of the human race as instruments of divine providence to rule the Prussians, just as he also believed, and frequently asserted, that the Germans had been selected out from among the other races of mankind to spread *Kultur* and extend political salvation to the remainder of the world. Thus he evidently believed that he gained his personal right to rule because he was a Hohenzollern, and the heir to the throne of his ancestors, as marked out by the rules of hereditary descent that prevailed in his family. And this, of course meant, logically, that this particular method of reckoning descent had direct divine approval. For the marks or criteria which apodictically indicated that the Hohenzollern family had this divine mission, no firmer foundation was advanced than the fact that the course of history had so indicated—*Die Weltgeschichte ist das Weltgericht.* By the same judgment the Teutons had been pointed out as the protagonists of culture for all mankind. In other words, there is no evidence that the Kaiser believed that, in any explicit and unmistakable manner, God had spoken directly to him, giving to him the political mission which he claimed to have. Nor has it been reported that he claimed to have had an apocalyptic vision in which this endowment of authority was made. Not in this direct and immediate sense, then, did the Kaiser claim to be the vicegerent of God. Rather, he was convinced that, as Hegel taught, there is a rationality to human history; that, in the unfolding events of this world, there can be discerned a divine or providential factor; and that, regarded in this light, his right to rule was but a part of the divine right of the Hohenzollern family to rule, of the divine right of Prussia to take the leadership of the Teutons, and of the divine right of the Teutons to exercise the dominant authority in the world.

To what extent the divine right theory found acceptance by the German people it is impossible to say. Certainly it did not seem to shock their reason or offend their religious views. And, judged from the purely emotional point of view, there can be little question that the conception of their ruler as an agent of God, or as an instrument of divine Providence, stimulated the loyalty and self-sacrificing patriotism of the people, and tended to induce them to accept as just and proper the policies pursued by those in political power.

It may be doubted, however, whether, as a matter of reasoned conviction, any considerable number of the Prussian people ascribed an essentially divine character to the authority of their rulers. Certainly, we find no explicit acceptance of the doctrine in the writings of German jurists and political philosophers. Bluntschli, in his *Allgemeine Staatslehre,* published in the middle of the nineteenth century, openly repudiated it. "Authority," he wrote, "is indeed in principle and in fact dependent on God, but not in the same sense that God has exalted particular privileged persons above the limitations of human nature, set them nearer to Himself and made them demigods, nor in the sense that God has named human rulers as His personal representatives, identical with Himself as far as their authority extends. Such theocratical ideas contradict the human nature of those to whom the Government of the State is entrusted. The proud words of Louis XIV, 'We princes are the living images of Him who is all holy and all powerful,' are a blasphemy towards God and an insult towards his subjects—men as much as he.''[23]

It is true that, at the time that Bluntschli wrote, the rulers of Prussia were not making such explicit claim to divinely given authority as was later to be made by William II, but it remains true that in the commentaries on German public law during the reign of William we do not find the divine right doctrine upheld. Upon the other hand, it is equally true that we seldom find publicists openly denouncing it.[24] By way of exception to this

[23] Book IV, Chap. VII. English translation, ed. 1892, p. 286. Bluntschli was here writing in refutation especially of the views of Stahl, who, in his *Staatslehre* had sought, in a somewhat mystically or metaphysically disguised form, to preach a doctrine of divine right. Thus, Bluntschli continued: "Many understand the authority, distinct from the persons who exercise it, as superhuman and politico-divine. Stahl says, (*Staatslehre*, II, Sec. 43) 'The authority of the State is of God, not only in the sense that all rights are of God, property, marriage, paternal authority, but in the quite specific sense, that it is the work of God which He regulates. The State rules, not merely in virtue of the rights which God has given it, as a father does over his children, but it rules in the name of God, therefore it is that the State is clothed with majesty.' But this is to come back to an objective theocracy, which would practically lead to the ruler being considered the personal representative of God—a view which Stahl himself rejects—and would introduce again all the assumptions and abuses bound up with it."

[24] There were undoubtedly prudential reasons for this silence. Dawson, the well-known authority on Germany, in his volume *What is Wrong with Germany*, instances the case of Dr. W. Schücking, Professor of Jurisprudence at Breslau, who was warned by the Minister of Education simply for remarking in his lecture dealing with royal succession that he would pass over the doctrine of monarchy by God's grace as being a non-juristic question.

Treitschke in his *Politics* (English translation, Vol. II, p. 58) said: "The claim to rule by the grace of God is no more than a devout aspiration which does not attempt to formulate a mystical and spiritual right

academic reticence, is the following discussion of the subject by Dr. Otto Hintze, Professor of History at the University of Berlin—a discussion contained in a volume of papers by eminent German scholars issued after the outbreak of the Great War and with the purpose of presenting to the world a true picture of German thought and ideals. "Our rulers," he says, "declare themselves to be such 'by the grace of God,' but not in the sense in which Englishmen understand the notorious *jure divino* of the Stuart kings. The meaning of this characterization from the viewpoint of political law is simply that the royal power was not granted by the people, but that it rests upon ancient, historical right that has grown and ripened coincident with our history, thus proceeding from a combination of factors which piety may be inclined to ascribe to a higher dispensation. Exalted, mystic conceptions such, for example, as those indulged in by Frederick William IV, are of a purely subjective, individual nature and without the faintest constitutional significance. The monarch is not, in our eyes, the representative of God upon earth, but merely, as Frederick the Great expressed it, the first servant of the State, and when William II takes pleasure in acknowledging himself to be the instrument of the Most High, this is intended in no other sense than might be employed in the religious con-

to power, but simply to assert that the inscrutable will of Providence has decreed the elevation of a particular family above its rivals. Piety is a fundamental requirement in a monarch, since the notion that he stands immeasurably above all other men may actually unsettle his reason, if it be not balanced by personal humility which compels him to acknowledge himself God's instrument. All this does not abrogate the axiom that it is the nature and aim of monarchy to be of this world. Genuine monarchy does not aspire to partnership with the Almighty. On the other hand, monarchy stands opposed to republicanism. In a republic, authority is founded upon the will of the governed, while in a monarchy it is derived from the historical claim of a particular family and concentrated in the will of one man who wears the crown and who, though surrounded by more or less responsible advisers, ultimately decides every question himself."

The recognition by Treitschke of the Providential element of course gives to monarchy and to the reigning family a supra-rational or transcendental basis of right.

ception of any other calling. It intensifies moral elevation and the sense of responsibility, but does not in any manner touch constitutional prerogatives." [25]

Implications of The Divine Right Theory. It has been pointed out that the divine right theory may conceivably be predicated of any form of Government, but that, as an historical fact, it has been used almost exclusively to support the right of kings. As a theory or royal right, Figgis, in his scholarly volume, *The Divine Right of Kings*, says:

"The theory of the Divine Right of Kings in its completest form involves the following propositions:

"(1) Monarchy is a divinely ordained institution.

"(2) Hereditary right is indefeasible. The succession to monarchy is regulated by the law of primogeniture. The right acquired by birth cannot be forfeited through any acts of usurpation, of however long continuance, by any incapacity in the heir, or by any act of deposition. So long as the heir lives, he is King by hereditary right, even though the usurping dynasty has reigned for a thousand years.

"(3) Kings are accountable to God alone. Monarchy is pure, the sovereignty being entirely vested in the King, whose power is incapable of legal limitation. All law is a mere concession of his will, and all constitutional forms and assemblies exist entirely at his pleasure. He cannot limit or divide or alienate the sovereignty, so as in any way to prejudice the right of his successor to its complete exercise. A mixed or limited monarchy is a contradiction in terms.

"(4) Non-resistance and passive obedience are enjoined by God. Under any circumstances resistance to a King is a sin, and ensures damnation. Whenever the King issues a command directly contrary to God's law, God is

---

[25] *Modern Germany in Relation to the Great War.* By various writers. Page 18.

to be obeyed rather than man, but the example of the primitive Christians is to be followed and all penalties attached to the breach of the law are to be patiently endured." [26]

To this analysis of the doctrine the following comments may be added. The second proposition seems to be too absolutely stated. It is true that, no matter for what time dispossessed, a monarch or his descendants may claim that, *jure divino,* he or they have a right to the throne. But it is equally true that, if the divine theory but not royal divine right be pushed to its logical limits, as by many it was, all reigning monarchs, as *de facto* rulers, may claim a divine right to authority.

The third proposition that a King, ruling *jure divino,* must be regarded as the exclusive ultimate source of all law, that is, as the depositary of sovereignty, is one of great constitutional importance, and cannot be avoided. Therefore it is only what we would expect, when we find this principle emphasized in the constitutional jurisprudence of Japan and of Prussia before the Great War.

The Japanese constitution in its preamble declares that it is the product of the sovereign will of the Emperor, and that any proposal to amend it must be initiated by the Emperor. He is declared to be the head of the Empire and to combine in himself the rights of sovereignty, and the law-making power remains in him. As Marquis Ito, the chief draughtsman of the Constitution in his *Commentaries on the Constitution* says: [27] He is "not only the centre of the executive, but is also the source and fountain-head of the legislative power." He has graciously declared that he will exercise his powers in accordance with the terms of the Constitution, but this declaration he has the legal right at any time to withdraw.

In Prussia, prior to the Great War, the same constitutional principle as that prevailing in Japan, was ac-

[26] *Op. cit.,* p. 5.   [27] P. 10.

cepted. The Constitution itself declared that it emanated from the will of the King, and German publicists were in unanimous agreement that, under it, the sovereign legislative as well as executive power remained vested exclusively in the monarch. Schulze, in his *Preussisches Staatsrecht*, declared of the King: "He possesses the whole and undivided power of the State in all its plenitude. It would therefore be contrary to the nature of the monarchial constitutional law of Germany to enumerate all individual power of the King or to speak of royal prerogative.... His sovereign right embraces all branches of the government.... He is the personified power of the State."

To the same effect declared von Rönne in his *Preussisches Staatsrecht*. "All the prerogatives of the State," he said of the King, "are united in his person, and his will is supreme, the officials being only organs through which he acts."

The foregoing principles of constitutional jurisprudence, logically resulting from the acceptance of the divine right political theory, have been emphasized since they show that, while that theory is compatible with constitutional government—that is, one under which the executive rules according to established laws, and not according to casual or arbitrary expressions of his personal will—it is not compatible with constitutional systems which recognize that the governed have an inherent right to determine their own form of government or to select their own rulers, or which even concede to them or to their elected representatives a portion of the legislative powers of the State.

The divine right theory logically carries with it a conclusion from which those who have held it have vainly sought to escape.

When applied simply to the State, that is, in justification of the existence of political society, the theory is of no practical importance—except possibly in refutation of the premises of the anarchists—since it throws no light upon the question as to the right to existence of any particular government, or as to the rightfulness of the claim of particular persons to operate the government. Upon the other hand, when applied to governments, it becomes impossible to avoid the recognition of the legitimacy of every *de facto* government whatever its historical origin. Thus, it becomes necessary to accept as divinely intended and sanctioned a government erected upon the ruins of a pre-existing government that has been forcibly overthrown. The theory thus, while asserting, upon the one hand, that resistance to the authority of an existing government is not simply a political or civil offense but a sin in the theological sense, is, upon the other hand, obliged to admit that if resistance is offered and the rebels or revolutionaries are successful in overthrowing the old government and establishing a new one in its place, then, by the very fact that it is in existence, the new government, or the new set of officials, may claim a divine right to the obedience of the people. Revolution is a sin, but, if successful, receives divine sanction. From this dilemma, the upholders of divine right can escape only by asserting that the divine being by some definite and unequivocal revelation has indicated that a particular government or particular ruler enjoys its special favor. This proof, in specific instances, they, of course, have not been able to supply.

A further disadvantage of the divine right theory is its absolute character. It necessarily includes the corollary that no matter how inefficient or oppressive a given rule may be, its authority may not, without sin, be resisted. The rulers, to be sure, are responsible to God as to how they exercise their divinely given powers, but the governed have no alternative but to obey, and, even when ordered to do things which their consciences and religious beliefs do not approve, they have, at the most, only the moral right of passive disobedience, that is, of refusing to do what they deem iniquitous, but of offering no open resistance to their political rulers, and accepting with pious resignation such punishments as may be inflicted upon them because of their refusal of active obedience.

Criticism of the Divine Right Theory. It will be seen that the application of this theory to political conditions has been of a twofold order: first, as justifying political authority in general; and, secondly, as legitimizing the exercise of such political authority in particular hands by viewing *de facto* rulers as either direct agents of the Almighty, or as wielding a power indirectly delegated. But, however understood, the theory is devoid of value, and open to much of the same logical criticism as that applied to the theory of the State as a purely "natural" institution. To those who are deists, the two theories are not, in fact, separable. The deist must hold that all power is from God, and, if this be so, the individual may maintain that his inclinations and powers are as truly of divine origin as are the powers of the State.

Were it, indeed, a fact that the actual presence and activity of divine action, as distinguished from human action, could be seen in the enactment and enforcement of the law of the State, it would be another thing; but what we actually see, whatever may be its ultimate basis, is the State acting through human agencies. The question thus is as to whence has come the prerogative of rule of these human agencies, whoever or whatever they may be. Even though the substance of the State, or, rather, the tendency to political life, be implanted by Nature or by God in human nature, the realization of this political tendency, its actual manifestation and operation, has been left to human agencies, and it is the justification of the authority exercised by these human agencies which men seek. Grant all that the divine theory necessarily maintains; namely, that ultimately all power is from God, that by Him is implanted in the nature of man the need and demand for the State, we get no nearer to knowing why, in any particular case, there should exist in a community a definite set of individuals arrogating to themselves the right of exercise of this divine prerogative of rule. All that necessarily follows from the divine theory is that political rule of some sort or other is divinely justified. No test, or suggestion of a test, is thereby afforded for determining whether any particular empiric manifestation of such order is exercised according to this divine purpose, or by the hands divinely appointed; unless, indeed, we say that the mere fact that the given State does exist, and that its government is in the hands that it is, is evidence that this is according to the will of Him who is omnipotent and directs all human things. But, of course, this is nothing more than saying that "whatever is, is right," which is also the motto of the Force Theory. Thus, instead of affording a basis for true political authority, it logically justifies every conceivable act, whether such act tends to uphold or to subvert the existing state of rule.

The divine right theory, even if it does not wholly exclude utilitarian considerations deduced from human experience, necessarily involves propositions that are to be accepted as matters of faith rather than of reason. If, then, at the present time, the theory finds little acceptance in the Western World it is because there is a general belief, either that reason should reign supreme, or that, if faith, as distinguished from reasoned conviction, be conceded to have a proper place in the intellectual life of men, its precepts should relate exclusively to matters spiritual and leave men free to regulate their temporal concerns according to their own judgment as to what, under given circumstances, is for their own best good. This general premise accepted, it follows that it lies with

DIVINE RIGHT THEORIES

each group of individuals to determine the character of political rule which they will create and support, or, indeed, to decide whether political rule of any sort shall exist. In other words, political institutions are placed upon a purely human or rationalistic or utilitarian basis above which they can be raised only by calling to aid mystical conceptions of the State which differ from the divine conceptions only as resting upon alleged metaphysical instead of theological principles. This metaphysical or mystical theory of the State we shall consider in Chapter VII.

CHAPTER VI

THE PATRIMONIAL THEORY [1]

CLOSELY allied to the Divine Right Theory, as applied to monarchies, is the Patrimonial Theory according to which the ruler is regarded as owning or possessing the right of rulership as though it were a piece of property. The right thus regarded and sustained has, in general, been deemed not only indefeasible but absolute and comprehensive, and, as carrying with it the moral as well as the legal right upon the part of the ruler to do as he may see fit with his subjects, their lands and other property.

This doctrine logically must rest upon the major premise that property rights are the creation of either natural or divine law, and that, by such law, these rights may be acquired by inheritance, according to definite rules of descent (usually of primogeniture), or that they may be obtained by conquest, occupation or other means.

The doctrine that the people of a State, together with their lands and other goods and chattels are, in a very real sense, in the last resort, the property of the ruling monarch was widely held in Europe during the sixteenth, seventeenth and eighteenth centuries. That this view should have prevailed, is historically explainable. The entire feudal system, out of which the modern monarchy had evolved, was founded upon the idea that the ownership of land carries with it, as one of its incidents, the right of political rulership. When, then, by a process of development, the idea of a contract between the feudal

[1] Considerable material for this and the next chapter has been drawn from the author's *Prussian Political Philosophy*, D. Appleton and Co.

lord and his followers had gradually disappeared, and the king had obtained a supremacy over his feudal lords; when his "peace" had become higher than theirs, and had extended over the whole country; and when these lords, and those who in turn held of them, were forced to concede that they held their lands by a conditional grant from the king, their liege lord, the idea that the monarch was the owner of the entire realm was complete. In him lay the final legal title to all land. All other persons had "tenures" rather than rights of ownership. And, as for the people themselves, the idea that one person might be another person's "man" was universal. The influence of these ideas on even comparatively recent political conceptions may be indicated by recalling that serfdom did not disappear from Germany until well into the nineteenth century.

This patrimonial conception of monarchy explains the accepted idea that the throne might be inherited, or willed away by testament, like a piece of property, and that it might be bought or sold or acquired by marriage. It explains also the recognized right of the king to requisition, upon occasion, the goods of his subjects, and even to sell those subjects themselves to foreign powers, as, for example, was done when the Hessian soldiers were sold by their ruler to England for use against the Americans in the Revolutionary War.

It might seem that a political practice such as this would have been based upon postulates which denied the possession by the governed of moral rights to consideration, or which placed the conduct of monarchs outside the realm of ordinary morality. It is quite clear, however, that the argument in behalf of royal absolutism and selfishness was not stated in terms as bold as these. The rulers in their dealings with their subjects did not feel themselves free from the moral restraints which humanity and sympathy impose, but it is clear that the moral obligations which they recognized were those of generosity and charity, rather than those of justice which imply the possession of rights by those to whom justice is due.

It would seem, in fact, that the rights claimed and exercised by the eighteenth century monarchs were not different in essential nature from those claimed at the present time by those holders of private property who regard the institution of private property as devoid of social or political implications, and who therefore regard themselves as vested with the rights of use and disposition the free exercise of which may not be interfered with except under very special circumstances. Thus, as we know, there are at the present time many owners of large fortunes, the possession of which has come to them by accident of descent, by the favoring operation of law, or by the working out of economic forces, who feel themselves free to use their wealth, if they see fit, for their own selfish welfare, and, as employers of labor, consider that those who work for them have no moral claim, and certainly no legal claim, beyond such as is founded upon their contracts of employment:—that anything beyond this which they do for the benefit of those subject to their economic rule is an act of charity or generosity rather than an obligation of distributive justice.

With reference generally to the patrimonial royal idea, it is to be pointed out that, even when accepted, no answer is given to the question as to the means or marks by which is indicated the particular person who is to be recognized as the owner or monarch. As to this, it may be said, that, in former years, the people were willing to accept as their rightful ruler the one who by accident of descent, or result of established conquest, became the *de facto* occupant of the throne.

Combination of Divine Right and Patrimonial Theories. Those holders of the Divine Right Theory who sought to avoid the conclusion that any *de facto* government is *ipso facto* divinely sanctioned, even though brought into existence by the forcible overthrow of a prior-existing government, had recourse to the patrimonial theory. Thus, they endeavored to prove that the right to rule of a reigning monarch was indefeasible and remained vested in him and his heirs even though he or they might, for a time, be deprived of the throne. This, for example, was the doctrine of James I of England. His right to rule he asserted was both hereditary and divine, or, rather, that the divine right included, as one of its special qualities, that it should become automatically vested in the eldest son or other heir of the ancestor.[2]

[2] See especially James I, "The True Law of Free Monarchies," p. 62, in McIlvain's edition of *The Political Works of James I*.

CHAPTER VII

MYSTICAL OR TRANSCENDENTAL THEORIES

SOMEWHAT similar to the Divine Right doctrine which seeks to vest in Kings and other rulers political authority that may not be questioned by their subjects, are certain theories which have attempted to vest this absolute and not-to-be-questioned authority in the State viewed as a mystical or transcendental being with ends of its own to realize, with corresponding inherent rights, with a personality of an order higher than that of its citizens or subjects, and, therefore, with its acts not amenable to the rules of morality which apply to individual human beings. As thus viewed, the State does not exist primarily for the advancement of the interests of individuals but for the advancement of its own interests. The State is not regarded as established and maintained by individuals, and is not a creation of their effort. It comes into being as a result of natural or metaphysical forces operating in and through human history. The governmental machinery through which it acts has, of course, to be created and operated by individual men who are necessarily guided by what their several judgments tell them is just and expedient. But, this theory teaches, the basis upon which the State itself rests—its right to existence—is a metaphysical and absolute one. What is declared in its name must be accepted by its citizens as right, and is to be obeyed even at the sacrifice, if need be, of their own particularistic interests or of life itself.

The formulation of such a doctrine as this could be the result only of a dialectical *tour de force,* but this was achieved by the German school of idealistic metaphysicians of the nineteenth century, and, what is still more remarkable, the German peoples were persuaded to give practical application to some of its most pernicious conclusions.

This mystical envisagement of the State as a superentity or person, so foreign to American and English ideas, can perhaps be best grasped by likening it to the conception of the Christian Church held by Roman Catholics and high Anglicans—a conception which Morley, in his *Life of Gladstone,* states in the following terms. After asking whether the Church is a purely human creation "changing with time and circumstance, like all the other creations of the heart and brain and will of man," Morley writes:

"To the Erastian lawyer the Church was an institution erected on the principles of political expediency by act of Parliament. . . . To the Evangelical, it was hardly more than a collection of congregations commended in the Bible for the diffusion of the knowledge and right interpretation of the Scriptures, the commemoration of gospel events and the linking of gospel truths to a well-ordered life. To the high Anglican, as to the Roman Catholic, the Church was very different from this; not a fabric reared by man, nor in truth any mechanical fabric at all, but a mystically appointed channel of salvation, an indispenable element in the relation between the soul of man and its Creator. To be a member of it was not to join in external association, but to become an inward partaker in ineffable and mysterious graces to which no other access lay open. Such was the Church, Catholic and Apostolic, as set up from the beginning, and of this immense mystery, of this saving agency, of this incommensurable spiritual force, the established Church of England was the local presence and the organ."

Transferring such a conception as this from the ecclesiastical to the political field, and employing abstract metaphysical rather than theological principles, the German political philosophers satisfied themselves and their followers not only that the State was the most exalted of all human institutions, but that it had the transcendent function of objectifying and realizing the metaphysically absolute principles of existence which pure reason discloses.

Hegel was the chief proponent of this doctrine, but we find the way prepared for it by Kant, who, in his *Rechtslehre*, published in 1796 as the first part of his *Metaphysik der Sitten*, used expressions which made it possible to charge him with a conception of the State which raised it above reason of the citizen and rendered inapplicable to it the utilitarian tests that apply in the lower walks of life. Thus he said: "the origin of the supreme [political] power, from the practical point of view, is inscrutable by the people who are under its authority." In other words, he continued, "the subject should not reason too curiously as to its origin, as if the right of obedience due it were to be doubted."

Of the will of the State he declared: "A law which is so holy and inviolable that it is practically a crime even to cast doubt upon it, or to suspend its operation even for a moment, is represented of itself as necessarily derived from some supreme, unblamable lawgiver. And this is the meaning of the maxim 'All authority is from God'; which proposition does not express the historical foundation of the civil constitution, but an ideal of the practical reason. It may be otherwise rendered thus: 'It is a duty to obey the law of the existing legislative power, be its origin what it may.' Hence it follows that the supreme power in the State has only rights and no (compulsory) duties towards the subject."[1]

---

[1] *Philosophy of Law*, translated by Hastie, p. 174. Cf. Mattern, *State Sovereignty and International Law*, pp. 30-35.

In another place in the same work Kant asserted: "From the very nature of government the executive function of the supreme ruler should be regarded as irresistible." He denied that resistance to royal oppression is ever justified. "If," he said, "the ruler or regent as the organ of the supreme power proceeds in violation of the laws . . . the subject can interpose complaints and objections to this injustice, but not active resistance." And a little later on he said: "There can not even be an article contained in the political constitution that would make it possible for a power in that State, in case of transgression of the constitutional laws by the supreme authority, to resist or even to restrict it in any way." Thus we find it stated not merely as an advisable principle of constitutional law that the King should be above the law, but as metaphysically involved in the very idea of political rule. Indeed, Kant in one place went so far as to state that there is in the State a unity resulting from a trinity of powers which is apparently patterned after the triune character of the Christian God.[2]

To do Kant justice, it should be said that, elsewhere in his writings his political thought was more utilitarian in character, and that he even accepted the theory which places the sovereignty originally in the people and founds the State upon a social compact, but it none the less remains true that, when speaking of the State as an abstract entity, he used language which implied that it has transcendental or mystical qualities.

Hegel. In the philosophy of Hegel the State appeared in full light as a transcendental being, and as having an essentially divine purpose to fulfill. "The State," he said, "is the march of God in the world; its ground or cause is the power of reason realizing itself as will. When thinking of the idea of the State, we must not have in our mind any particular State, or particular institution,

[2] Cf. Duguit, *The Law and the State*, translation, p. 46.

but must rather contemplate the idea, this actual God, by itself." [3]

As thus conceived, it is what we would expect when we find the State declared by Hegel to be morally supreme and able to transmute into duties to itself whatever rights may seem to belong to its subjects as individual human beings. "This substantive unity [of the State]," he said, "is its own motive and absolute end. This end has the highest right over the individual, whose highest duty in turn is to be a member of the State." In another place in the same work he said: "The State is indeed the reality of the moral idea"—*Der Staat ist die Wirklichkeit der sittlichen Idee.*[4]

This State conception of Hegel was founded upon his philosophy of history. It was his belief that whatever is, is rational; that the real is the rational, and that, if the history of men be studied with sufficient critical insight, a meaning or rationality can be discerned in the sequence of events which that history discloses. If this were not so, he pointed out, human history would have no meaning whatever; it would be a mere record of proximate rather than of final or ultimate causes, and, therefore, would constitute a series of happenings which, however long continued, could never be summed up. As opposed to such a view, he conceived that men, by their very nature, are destined to progress toward some definite end or goal. As thus regarded, human history was made to appear as a process by means of which certain "absolute ideas," as revealed by metaphysical inquiry, obtain objective realization. As a result of his dialectic, Hegel found that men, if not born free, are at least born for freedom; that is, they are potentially qualified for absolute freedom. This freedom, however, is not one to be realized in a régime of complete individualism in which each one seeks

---

[3] *Philosophy of Right*, trans. by Dyde, p. 247.
[4] *Idem*, p. 240.

his own selfish and particularistic ends. Rather, it is conceived of as a condition of rational liberty, in which each one, guided by his own reason, is led to identify his own interests with those of others and with those of the social whole of which he is a constituent unit. Logically, it would seem that the full realization of the ideal society thus pointed out would be secured only when, in turn, a complete harmony of efforts and interests among all the nations of the world was attained. It does not appear, however, that Hegel pushed thus far the application of his philosophy.

The liberty posited by Hegel as something ever to be striven for and at any given time to be enjoyed in as full a measure as possible, is, he declared, a rational, inward, or spiritual, rather than a political freedom. It is one, he asserted, which is possible of measurable enjoyment only in a community which is organized upon a basis higher than that of a mere "Civil Society," which is concerned primarily with the definition and protection of the particularistic interests of individuals. Above the individual, above the family, and above what he called the "Civic Community," there must be that highest political type, the State.

In the "Civic Community," individualism prevails; that is, the end or purpose of the authority which exists is the regulation of individual interests. A community, thus viewed, cannot, therefore, according to Hegel, provide the means for bringing these interests into essential unity and harmony. Thus, to quote the language of Hegel: "In this society every one is an end to himself; all others are for him nothing. And yet, without coming into relation with others, he cannot realize his ends. Hence, to each particular person others are a means to the attainment of his end. . . . Here the fountains of all the passions are let loose, being merely governed by the sum of reason. Particularity limited by universality is the only standard to which the particular person conforms in promoting his well-being." [5]

In the next section he expressed the idea more simply in the statement that "individuals in the civic community are private persons, who pursue their own interests."

As contrasted with the Civic Community, Hegel's State has a totally different relation to the individual. Here the dominant note is the State's unity and universality, and the individual has a significance only as a member of it. "The State is the realized ethical idea or ethical spirit"; "it is the objective spirit," and the individual has "his true, real existence and ethical status only in being a member of it"; "Union, as such, is itself the true content and end, since the individual is intended to pass a universal life. His particular satisfactions, activities, and way of life have in this authenticated substantive principle their origin and result; the State is the ethical whole and the actualization of freedom. It is the absolute purpose of reason that freedom should be actualized. The State is the spirit, which abides in the world and there realizes itself consciously."

The foregoing quotations are from Hegel's *Philosophy of Right*. In his *Philosophy of History*, he wrote as follows: The State is the "realization of freedom," "it exists for its own sake." "Truth is the unity of the universal and subjective [individual] will; and the Universal is to be found in the State in its laws, its universal and rational arrangements. The State is the Divine Idea as it exists on earth." [6]

---

[5] *Philosophy of Right*, trans. by Dyde, p. 186.

[6] Dewey, in his *German Philosophy and Politics*, p. 64, gives the following luminous statement of the difference between the American and English, and the German conception of the State: "In English and American writings the State is always used to denote society in its more organized aspects, or it may be identified with Government as a special agency operating for the collective interests of men in association. But in German literature *Society* is a technical term and means something empirical and, so to speak, external, while the *State*, if not avowedly something mystical and transcendental, is at least a moral entity, the

MYSTICAL OR TRANSCENDENTAL THEORIES

Translating these assertions into language less abstruse, it would appear that Hegel's order of argument was as follows: Man's highest aim and destiny is to be free; men are free when they are required to do only what their reason recommends; therefore, freedom is not secured by civic processes which aim to adjust or compromise, and, if necessary, to protect, by police power, the particularistic interests of individuals as suggested by their several subjective wills; therefore, transcending individual human beings, there is needed some entity or being whose will will be universal (in a philosophical sense) and acceptable to individuals as the voice of reason itself, so that, in yielding obedience to it, they will not feel themselves coerced to do other than what their own individual reason approves. Such a being is the State. The State thus becomes, in Hegel's view, a wholly abstract being. It is not the aggregate of the individuals subject to its authority, nor is it the social or civic unit into which they are compacted by mutual agreement or by the pressure of physical force. The State is that higher and more abstract entity which lives or operates through governmental organs and public magistrates, but, in its own self, it is a Spirit or Idea, which, abstract in character, finds realization and objectification, or concreteness, in laws and their enforcement. Thus, having a will of its very own, it may properly be viewed as a person.

The personality, thus ascribed to the State, as a mystical or spiritual attribute, finds its analogue in the legal personality which, as described by the author in his *Fundamental Concepts of Public Law,* the jurist gives to

creation of self-conscious reason operating in behalf of the spiritual and ideal interests of its members. Its function is cultural, educative. Even when it intervenes in material interests, as it does in regulating law-suits, poor laws, protective tariffs, etc., etc., its action has ultimately an ethical significance: its purpose is the furthering of an ideal community. . . . Hence the significance of the force or power of the State. Unlike other forms of force, it has a sort of sacred import, for it represents force consecrated to the assertion and expansion of final goods which are spiritual, moral, rational."

the State. But, where the jurist uses his conception merely as a convenience, that is, as a starting point or central idea in order that he may give system and logical coherence to public law thinking, Hegelian political philosophers attribute to the State a real personality. They make of it a genuine moral being that has a will and ends of its own divorced from, and superior to, those of the individual human beings subjected to its authority;[7] and, predicating this, they draw conclusions that are more than formalistic in character. The State is to them not solely, or even primarily, a means for securing the welfare of its citizens or subjects, but a being carrying out a cosmic process, or the dictates of universal reason, and, therefore, impelled by its own nature and destiny to seek its own perfection. If it appears as a means at all, it is to secure the objective realization, in human history, of certain providential or metaphysically absolute principles. It becomes, in this sense, a supreme being, the ultimate source of authority for the individuals who are of an inferior order of beings, and is able to determine for itself what action upon its part is ethically justifiable.

The idea of divine right is thus transferred from the ruler to the State that rules. But it is not necessarily in substitution of the theory of the divine right of the monarch. Indeed, it is especially congenial to such a doctrine, for it necessarily denies to the ruled an inherent right to

[7] Eduard Meyer, probably the most eminent of then living German historians, writing in 1915, said: "The State is of much higher importance than any one of these individualistic groups, and eventually is of infinitely more value than the sum of all the individuals within its jurisdiction. For it has a life apart; its mission is unending, and, in theory at least, unless it is unchecked by a force from without, endless, encompassing, as it does all the generations yet to come, and welding them into a great unit,—the mighty life of a nation acting its part in the history of the world. This conception of the State, which is as much a part of our life as is the blood in our veins, is nowhere found in the English Constitution, and is quite foreign to English thought, and to that of America as well. . . . The German word *Staat* is untranslatable into English. There is absolutely no English equivalent to express the idea which the word conveys to us." *England: Its Political Organization and Development and the War against Germany*, p. 32.

determine how and by whom they shall be governed. And thus it is that we find ante-World War German political philosophers denying, not merely that, as a practical proposition, it is expedient to permit the people to determine their own form of government and to participate actively and decisively in its operation, but that, from the very nature of political authority, it is improper that they should have this right. It is not maintained that in all cases monarchy is the only possibly legitimate form of government, but it is asserted by those of this school that the ultimate source of political right, ethically viewed, is to be found, not in the wills and judgments of the governed, but in the State, which, in practice, of course, means the will and judgment of those who happen to occupy the seats of political power.

Treitschke. In the *Politics* of Heinrich von Treitschke we find a more or less transcendental conception of the State as a super-person. This phase of his philosophy we earlier referred to. He has also been credited with worshipping mere Power when possessed by the State. This, however, is hardly a fair statement of his views. It is true that Treitschke sees in the State an entity or being of so exalted and special a character as to render inapplicable to its acts the criteria of right by which the conduct of private individuals is to be judged; and also that he deems the possession of power by the State, in the greatest possible amount, so eminently desirable that nothing should be allowed to stand in the way of this consummation; but, after all, he views the State as having a high moral end to realize—albeit, that end is an end of its own as distinguished from the welfare of its body of subjects.

Having declared the State to be "the most supremely real person, in the literal sense of the word, that exists," and as "thoroughly capable of bearing responsibility and blame," he goes on to declare that "power is the vital principle of the State, as faith is that of the Church, and love that of the family"; and that "if it neglects its strength in order to promote the idealistic aspirations of man, it repudiates its own nature and perishes. This is, in truth, for the State equivalent to the sin against the Holy Ghost." [8]

Elsewhere Treitschke speaks not so much as though Power were one of the attributes of the State as that the entire nature of the State is exhausted in its Power. The statement that "the State *is* Power" he repeatedly makes.[9]

In Chapter III, which is entitled "The State in Relation to the Moral Law," he says of Christian morality: "It comes at last to this, that he [the individual man] attains the highest perfection possible when he has recognized and developed the most essential part of himself. When we apply this standard of deeper and truly Christian ethics to the State, and remember that its very personality is Power, we see its highest moral duty is to uphold that power. The individual must sacrifice himself for the community of which he is a member, but the State is the highest community existing in exterior human life, and therefore the duty of self-effacement cannot apply to it. As nothing in the world's history is its superior, the Christian obligation of sacrifice for a higher object is not imposed. . . . The injunction to assert itself remains always absolute. Weakness must always be condemned as the most disastrous and despicable of crimes, the unforgivable sin of politics."

However, as has been said, the State, according to Treitschke, has a high moral purpose to perform in the world. In the last chapter of his treatise, in which he dis-

[8] *Politics*, Chap. I.
[9] *E.g.*, "Since the State is Power, it can obviously draw all human action within its scope, so long as that action arises from will which regulates the outer lives of men, and belongs to their visible common existence" (Chap. II). In Chap. III he praises Machiavelli for being "the first to declare distinctly that the State is Power."

cusses "International Law and International Intercourse," he says: "We must insist that the State is absolute physical power, but if it insists upon being that and nothing else, unrestrained by conscience or reason, it will no longer be able to maintain itself in a position of security. . . . The State does not identify itself with physical power for its own sake; it is Power, in order to protect and to further the highest welfare of the human race. Taken without qualification, the doctrine of Power, as such, is quite empty of meaning, and unmoral as well, because it can find no justification within itself."

Treitschke makes this assertion only by way of denial of the doctrine, ascribed to Machiavelli, that a State can bind itself by no law in its relations with other States. When, however, we come down to the foundation of Treitschke's statement that States may so bind themselves, we find, in the first place, that he holds that when a State deems it expedient to violate an agreement entered into by it with another State, it has a moral right to do so; and, furthermore, that the only reason why these provisionally binding agreements should be entered into is the purely utilitarian one that "a State which went upon the principle of despising faith and loyalty would be constantly threatened by enemies, and would consequently be unable to fulfill its purpose of being physical power."

A little later on he says: "Every State . . . will of its own accord pay a certain respect to the neighboring Powers. A more definite feeling of law will be evolved by time out of the dictates of reason and a mutual recognition of personal advantage. Every State will realize that it is an integral part of the community of other States in which it finds itself placed, and that it must live with them on some kind of terms, bad or good, as the case may be. These reflections will arise from very real considerations of reciprocity, and not from love to mankind."

Why the Transcendental Theory Found Acceptance in Germany. Despite the highly abstract and essentially sophistical character of the reasoning by which this apotheosis of the State is sustained, the doctrines undoubtedly found wide acceptance among the German people. Where it was not explicitly asserted it was implicitly accepted in German literature. This extraordinary result was due to a variety of causes.

In the first place, the doctrine, as we have seen, was especially sponsored by Hegel, and of the great influence of his general philosophy and dialectical philosophical method upon his own and immediately following generations the world knows. In the second place, it would seem that, either by accident of intellectual development, or by inherent racial prepossession, the Germans have taken kindly to abstract, idealistic, and universalistic interpretations of human history, that is, to the formulation of what they themselves have termed, *Weltanschauungen*. Professor Ernst Troeltsch, of the University of Berlin, in an essay entitled "The Spirit of German Kultur," written subsequently to the outbreak of the Great War, and in which he attempted to present in its true light, to English speaking peoples, the character of the German political thought, emphasizes the proneness of his people to abstract speculation. Commenting upon what he terms "the German metaphysical and religious spirit," he says: "Our sense of order is not founded on its usefulness for material and social ends, but emanates from the sense of duty, from an ideal conception of the spirit which is the rule and law of human life and of the universe. Nor is this feeling identical with a sentimentality that clothes, covers and seeks to compensate the asperities of life. It is rather the child of an elemental cosmic conception which realizes that this feeling is basic in the universe. The German is by nature a metaphysician who ponders and strives, from the spiritual inwardness of the universe,

MYSTICAL OR TRANSCENDENTAL THEORIES 127

to grasp the inner meaning of the world and of things, of man and destiny. It will always be idle to explain the origin and development of this predominant, though by no means universal, characteristic. It remains the final German life secret, much discussed among the Germans themselves, the cause of sacrifice and suffering, the motive power of wonderful achievements—the problem of an ever-new compromise with the practical life and its realistic demands." [10]

A third, and undoubtedly powerful reason why the transcendental conception of the State should have found such a fertile field in the German mind was that it was linked up with the conviction which the Germans had come to hold—a connection due to deliberate indoctrination through the schools, the universities, and the press—that, in the working out of the providential purposes of human history, the German people had been selected as the highest exponents of culture; that, in order that this healing *Kultur* be applied as widely as possible, the extension of German political control, by force if necessary, was an eminently proper end to be striven for; and that the all-powerful State was the instrument by which this destiny of the German people was to be fulfilled.[11]

[10] *Modern German* (by various writers), p. 78.
[11] Profesor Dewey, in his *German Philosophy and Politics*, p. 15, thus describes the means available in ante-World-War Prussia for the propagation of doctrines approved by the bureaucracy: "Germany is the modern State which provides the greatest facilities for general ideas to take effect through social inculcation. Its system of education is adapted to that end. High schools and universities in Germany are really, not just nominally, under the control of the State and part of the State itself. In spite of freedom of academic instruction, when once a teacher is installed in office, the political authorities have always taken a hand, at critical junctures, in determining the selection of teachers in subjects that have a direct bearing upon political policies. Moreover, one of the chief functions of the universities is the preparation of State officials. Legislative activity is distinctly subordinate to that of administration conducted by a trained civil service, or, if you please, bureaucracy. Membership in this bureaucracy is dependent upon university training. Philosophy, both directly and indirectly, plays an unusually large rôle in the training. The faculty of law does not chiefly aim at the preparation of practicing lawyers. Philosophies of jurisprudence are essential parts of the law teaching, and every one of the

Corollaries. Certain corollaries that result from this German conception of the State deserve to be noted.

It has already been pointed out that the theory necessarily denied the fundamental premise upon which all theories of popular government are based—that, to quote the words of the American Declaration of Independence, governments are instituted to secure to the governed certain rights of life, liberty and the pursuit of happiness, that they derive "their just powers from the consent of the governed," and that "whenever any form of government becomes destructive of these ends, it is the right of the people to alter or abolish it, and to institute new government, laying its foundation on such principles and organizing its powers in such form, as to them shall seem most likely to effect their safety and happiness."

A second corollary which followed from the German apotheosis of the State was the freedom of its acts, especially in its dealings with other States, from the control of the rules of morality applicable in other fields of human conduct.

A third corollary was the conception of the State as a *Kulturstaat,* as distinguished from a mere *Polizeistaat.* That is to say, its purpose was viewed as comprehending not only the negative one of preventing or punishing offenses against persons and property, but as embracing the affirmative task of advancing the spiritual as well as the material interests of its subjects. Thus the sphere of the State's authority was viewed as properly including matters of secular, as well as of religious, education, the promotion of the arts and the sciences, and the extension

classic philosophers took a hand in writing a philosophy of Law and of the State. Moreover, in the theological faculties, which are also organic parts of State-controlled institutions, the theology and higher criticism of Protestant Germany have been developed, and developed also in close connection with philosophical systems—like those of Kant, Schleiermacher, and Hegel. In short, the educational and administrative agencies of Germany provide ready-made channels through which philosophic ideas may flow on their way to practical affairs."

Cf. also the author's *Prussian Political Philosophy,* Chap. VIII.

of direct aid in matters of finance, commerce, and industry.

Fourthly, and finally, the doctrine led to a conception of human Liberty that was quite different from that which is necessarily connected with the doctrines of popular government which have found acceptance in most of the other politically developed countries of the world. It has already been pointed out that what Hegel and his followers understood by freedom, was moral or intellectual freedom,—the freedom of man's reason and spirit from the restraints of dogma, tradition and external authority. It did not mean political liberty. But, more than this, the German conception of the State led, within the field of private legal rights of person and property, to the laying of emphasis upon the idea of order, to the approval by the individual of multitudinous restraints, governmentally imposed, upon his own freedom of action, because, these restraints, being applied to all other individuals, he is thereby secured against exactions or damaging conduct upon their part. To this relation between law and liberty, and to the possibility of emphasizing this phase of the problem at the expense of the other, we shall later on have occasion to return.

Mulford. An interesting reflection of Hegelian thought in American political literature is seen in Elisha Mulford's *The Nation,* published in 1870.

Here we find the Nation substituted for the State as a mystical, transcendental person or entity to which what amounts to divine worship is to be accorded. The concrete purpose which Mulford had in view was to strengthen the allegiance of the American people to the United States as single body-politic, and to stigmatize as impious any efforts to destroy or weaken this unity. A Nation he declared to be a moral person with a real will and consciousness, as of divine foundation, and as the instrument through which freedom is to be realized. That the people of the United States, taken as a whole, constituted such an entity, he appears to have thought, needed no demonstration. He assumed the fact, and devoted himself to a statement of the conclusions that are deducible from that fact. A single quotation will sufficiently indicate the character as well as the purpose of his work:

"The confederacy is the necessary antagonist to the Nation in history. This antithesis becomes apparent in every respect in which they may be regarded. The Nation, as the organism of human society, presumes an organic unity; and its being, as organic, is that which no man can impart. The confederacy assumes the existence of society as artificial, as formed through an association of men in a certain copartnership of interests, and as only the aggregate of those who, before living separately, voluntarily entered it. The Nation is formed in the development of the historical life of the people in its unity; the confederacy as a temporary arrangement which is formed in the pursuance of certain separate and secular ends. The Nation in its necessary being can have its origin only in the divine will, and its realization only in that. The confederacy assumes the origin of society in the voluntary act of those who separately or collectively enter it, and its institution has only this formal precedent. The Nation is constituted in a vocation in history, and therefore has its own purpose and work; and of this it cannot divest itself, as if it was an external thing, nor alienate, nor transfer it to another. . . . The Nation exists in an organic and moral relation to its members, and between the Nation and the individual no power on earth can intervene. . . . The Nation exists in its unity in the divine guidance of the people." [12]

In the next chapter will be shown the mystical or transcedental character of the State as viewed by Fascists.

[12] *The Nation* (ed. 1899), p. 324.

CHAPTER VIII

FASCISM

FASCIST political theory closely approximates, if it does not fully accept, the transcendental conception of the State. It also is strongly influenced by organismic doctrines, and, at the hands of some of its proponents, seems committed to divine right premises. The analysis of Fascism which follows is taken from expositions which may be said to have received official or quasi-official authentication.[1]

In order to point out the distinctive, and, as he conceives it to be, the novel character of Fascist political

[1] These are: J. S. Barnes, *The Universal Aspects of Fascism.* Signor Mussolini furnishes a preface to this volume in which he says that Mr. Barnes has correctly stated the fundamental concepts or premises of Fascist theory. Alfredo Rocco, *The Political Doctrine of Fascism.* Dr. Rocco was minister of Justice in the Government of Italy, and of his address, which is published as number 223 of the International Conciliation pamplets, Signor Mussolini says: "I have just read your magnificent address which I endorse throughout." Corrando Gini, *The Scientific Basis of Fascism.* This appeared as an article in *The Political Science Quarterly*, Vol. XLII, pp. 99-115. Professor Gini is Professor of Economic Policy and Statistics in the Royal University at Rome, and Director of the Royal Institute of Statistics and Economic Policy.

Another work to which Signor Mussolini has given his approval is *The Fascist Movement in Italian Life* by Dott. Pietro Gorgolini, an English translation of which was published in 1923. It has not been found necessary to quote from this work, but, in general, it may be said that the conception of the State ascribed to the Fascists is not inconsistent with that ascribed to them by the other writers who have been quoted.

Especial mention should also be made of Schneider's *Making the Fascist State*, published in 1928. This work, though it has not received what may be called official approval by Mussolini or by the Fascist party is a scholarly and well documented examination of Fascist theories in their various phases and in their relation to the political views of such other Italian writers as Croce, Gentile. Mazzini and Machiavelli. The relations of Fascism to Syndicalism and to the Catholic Church are also traced. In an appendix are given illustrative excerpts from Fascist literature and official documents.

theory, Signor Rocco begins his exposition with an illuminating, and essentially correct, analysis of modern Liberalism and of the socialistic and democratic implications from that body of doctrine. He shows that, from the beginning, so-called "liberalists" have viewed society as a sum total of individual persons, and have regarded the ends of societies as nothing more than the ends of the individuals of which the societies are composed.

As a corollary from this, he says, until comparatively recent times the doctrine of *laissez-faire* was declared as an absolute *principle,* namely, that societies as politically organized, that is, as States, are not justified in exercising more than the minimum of control needed in order to prevent individuals from unduly interfering with each other's rights and interests. This corollary has been abandoned by the Socialists, and even by the Communists and Sovietists, and the ground taken that Governments are justified in exercising any authority they may see fit in order to bring about that distribution among their peoples of social and economic goods which will satisfy the canons of distributive justice as determined by ethical philosophy. But, in taking this new position, as Signor Rocco points out, the Liberalists have not abandoned their fundamental conception of societies or States as nothing more than sums total of the individuals composing them, and that social or political control has for its sole end the promotion of the welfares of these individual persons.

This conception, Signor Rocco declares, Fascist political theory absolutely rejects. He says: "The social concept has a biological aspect, because social groups are fractions of the human species, each one possessing a peculiar organization, a particular rank in the development of civilization with certain needs and appropriate ends, in short, a life which is really its own." Again, he says: "As the human species is not the total of living beings of the world, so the various groups which comprise it are not the sum of the several individuals which at a given moment belong to it, but rather the infinite series of the past, present, and future generations constituting it. And, as the ends of the human species are not those of the several individuals living at a certain moment, being occasionally in direct opposition to them, so the ends of the various social groups are not necessarily those of the individuals that belong to the groups but may even possibly be in conflict with such ends, as one sees clearly whenever the preservation and the development of the species demand the sacrifice of the individual, to wit, in times of war."

Based upon the foregoing assertions, Signor Rocco draws the conclusion that each of the social and political groups of individuals has an organic existence of its own and with ends of its own which it is ethically entitled to pursue.

The author of the present work is by no means disposed to deny that the true ends or interests of individuals include considerations arising out of the welfare of not only other living individuals, but of individuals of future generations. This will appear more fully when consideration is given to the grounds upon which all forms of social and political control or coercion are to be justified. But this is a different thing from admitting that there exist social or political entities or beings whose ends and interests are superior to those of the individual human units, or cells, of which they are composed.

Signor Rocco continues: "Fascism replaces . . . the old atomistic and mechanical state theory which was at the basis of the Liberal and democratic doctrines with an organic and historic concept." He goes on to say that, by this, he does not accept the so-called, "organic theory" of the State; but this denial, it appears, applies only to the repudiation of the idea that States are veritable living beings in the same sense in which are the species of the biological world. That societies or States have existences and interests independent of those of the individuals composing them he asserts. He says: "It is irrelevant in this connection to determine whether social groups, considered as fractions of the species, constitute organisms. The important thing is to ascertain that this [Fascist] organic concept of the State gives to society a continuous life over and beyond the existence of the several individuals." He immediately continues: "The relations between the State and citizens are completely reversed by the Fascist doctrine; instead of the Liberal democratic formula, 'society for the individual' we have, 'individuals for society.' [2] For Fascism, society has historical and immanent ends of preservation, expansion, improvement, quite distinct from those of the individuals which at the moment compose it; so distinct in fact that they may even be in opposition. Hence the necessity, for which the older doctrines make no allowance, of sacrifice, even up to the total immolation of individuals, in behalf of society; hence the true explanation of war, eternal law of mankind."

In the next paragraph, Signor Rocco is still more outspoken. He says: "For Liberalism, the individual is the end and society the means. For Fascism, society is the end, individuals the means, and its whole life consists in using individuals as instruments for its social ends. The State, therefore, guards and protects the welfare and development of individuals not for their exclusive interest, but because of the identity of the needs of individuals with those of society as a whole—individual rights are only recognized in so far as they are implied in the rights of the State. In this preëminence of duty we find the highest ethical value of Fascism." [3]

[2] This, says Signor Rocco, does not eliminate the individual, but it subordinates him to the group.
[3] Other statements of Signor Rocco to the same effect are: "Our concept of liberty is that the individual must be allowed to develop his

Professor Gini, in the article to which footnote reference has been made, is in full agreement with Signor Rocco as to the organismic character of States, and as to the possession by them of ends which take precedence of the ends or interests of their citizens. With reference to the essential distinction between the orthodox "liberal" doctrine of the State, and that of Fascists, he says: "The Liberal theory assumes that society consists of an aggregate of individuals who must look after their own interests, and it regards the State as an emanation of the individual wills intended to eliminate the conflicts between the interests of individuals. The Nationalist [or Fascist] theory, on the contrary, views society as a true and distinct organism of a rank superior to that of individuals who compose it, an organism endowed with a life of its own and with interests of its own. The interests result from the coördination of the desires for the time being of the current generation together with the interests of all the future generations which are to constitute the future life of the nations. Often enough these are in harmony one with the other, but occasionally the interests of future generations are opposed to those of the present generation, and in any case they may differ notably, if not in direction, at least in intensity. The agency destined to give effect to these higher interests of society is the State, sacrificing, whenever necessary, the interests of the individual and operating in opposition to the will of the present generation. Hence the concept of the gov-

personality *in behalf of the State*" (italics not in the original) ; "Fascists make of the individual an economic instrument for the advancement of society, an instrument which they use so long as it functions and which they subordinate when no longer serviceable."

Elliott in his recent volume, *The Pragmatic Revolt in Politics* (p. 221), says:

"Fascism is a more real danger than pluralism. It interprets syndicalism as merely a means to an end of social solidarity, organizes its State functionally to promote efficiency, not to protect group rights, and subordinates every moral value to the maximum production of which the disciplined nation is capable, under the integrating will of a 'super-man.'"

ernment as an agency to which is entrusted a mission of historical character, a mission which summarizes its very reason for existence. It is an agency, not for the changeable wishes of numerical majorities or of major interests, but rather for the effectuation of a program corresponding to the interests of the national organism. The justification of measures of restraint upon individual liberties follows from this point of view, although these measures may be opposed to the desire of the majority or, theoretically, of even the entire body of citizens, when such measures of restraint are thought to be necessary in order to give effect to a program identified with the interests of a nation."

"Fascism," says Barnes, in his book previously referred to, "regards it as the duty of the individual so to continue his life that the pursuit of his interests coincides with those of the community. The State is and can be the only impartial judge as to whether the individual is doing this or not. If he is not, the State has the right and duty to interfere."

It seems clear to the author of the present work that the Fascist conception of the State, if not purely a transcendental one, is at least a composite of transcendental, organismic and even, it would appear, of divine right theories.[5]

Barnes, in his exposition of Fascism, attempts to divorce Fascist theories from Hegelian assumptions, but not, in the author's opinion, with success. Barnes denies in an unqualified manner that Fascism views the State as an end in itself. He says: "The notion of the State as an end in itself forms no part whatever of orthodox Fascism."[6] But it seems clear to the writer that he is not warranted in making this statement. This sufficiently

[4] *Op. cit.*, p. 176.
[5] As to the divine right element in Fascism, see especially the statement of Barnes quoted in the next paragraph.
[6] *The Universal Aspects of Fascism*, p. 95.

appears from the quoted statements of the official expounders of Fascism. Indeed, Barnes' statement is scarcely consistent with that made by himself only two pages later on. He there says: "Man is by nature a social animal. . . . Authority is implicit in every society. Authority therefore belongs to the natural order of things as much as society itself, and, having thus its source in nature, it has God for its author. So the principle of authority is a divine principle. Whenever a supreme authority exists, acknowledging no higher authority save the sovereignty of God alone, we call that authority the State, which is society juridically organized for the purpose of promoting the general welfare. The State is thus a political unity, and every political unity is an organism, with a life which transcends that of the individuals which compose it, and outlasts that of any particular generation of men."

According to Fascism, then, it is the *duty* of the individual to subordinate his own interests to those of the State, and it is the *right* of the State, if necessary, to make him do so.

All Fascists agree that the State should have regard for the welfare of its individual citizens, but this obligation exists, they would appear to hold, because the welfare of the State, to a considerable extent at least, is bound up with the welfare of its citizens, and, therefore, can be stated only in terms of such individual welfares. But, to whatever degree the doctrine may, in practice, lead to public policies which coincide with those that result from individualistic premises, the two theories are fundamentally wide apart. The one attaches primary value to the interests of the State and, essentially speaking, makes the welfare of individuals subordinate to it as means to an end; the other views the welfare of the individual members of a State as the real end to be sought, but is willing to concede that, in many respects, individuals can secure their true or ethically highest ends only by having regard for, and seeking, the welfare of others, and that this, in many cases, can best be obtained by supporting the State under whose authority they live, and by promoting policies on its part which look to the general good of the whole community. Thus, according to this view, each citizen is entitled to seek his own welfare, but, if he be intellectually and morally enlightened, he sees that, as a means to his end, he needs to support his State and approve of its policies so far as they tend, or are believed to tend, to promote the general welfare.

Although the Nation or State is thus conceived of as an independent being or entity with ends of its own to be subserved, the Fascists are emphatic in the assertion that these ends cannot be determined by an appeal to any general or collective will of its constituent individual citizens. As to the fallacy of appealing to popular opinion, or to a so-called "general will" of the people, we find Mussolini himself saying: "The masses by themselves alone are incapable of forming spontaneously a collective will of their own, and even less capable of proceeding spontaneously to a selection of men to represent them. The problem of government, therefore, is never solved by relying on an illusory will of the masses; it is solved by a wise choice of the directing minds." But, as he goes on to declare, this choice cannot be effectively made by the instrumentalities or methods found operating in the so-called popular or parliamentary governments of the world. "Experience teaches," he says, "that it is the schemers, the agitators, the demagogues who guide the masses when they are left uncontrolled. To place the choice of candidates and deputies completely in the hands of the electoral body, composed of an inchoate mass of heterogeneous individuals, means in reality placing this choice in the hands of a few intriguers who appoint themselves to be the spiritual guides and teachers of the masses."[7]

"There is a natural instinctive force possessed by every living organism and directed to maintain that organism's existence. With respect to that organism which is the State, this instinctive force finds expression in the 'general will,' which is consequently a useful touchstone for every Government to sound, however this may be possible. . . . But there is no sure means of ascertaining the 'general will,' and in any case, unless Reason [8] supports the direction apparently pointed out by the 'general will,' no cause is shown why that direction should be followed." [9]

As to the Fascist rejection both of the dogma of popular sovereignty as a basis for the State and of the popular voice as a means of fixing the form of government which is to exist and of controlling its policies, Signor Rocco says: "Fascism therefore not only rejects one dogma of popular sovereignty and substitutes for it that of State sovereignty, but it also proclaims that the great mass of citizens is not a suitable advocate of social interests for the reason that the capacity to ignore individual private interests in favor of the higher demands of society and of history is a very rare gift and the privilege of the chosen few."

As regards the determination of the form of government which a State is to possess, Barnes says that the Fascist doctrine is that "authority is not derived from the community, because the community is incapable of either creating it or abolishing it, since it is inseparable from the very notion of community. The precise form

---

[7] These quotations are from the report by Mussolini laid before the Italian Chamber of Deputies on March 2, 1928, explaining to that body the fundamental features of Italy's new electoral law. For partial text of this report, see *Current History* for May, 1928, pp. 180-188.
[8] Whose reason?
[9] Barnes, *The Universal Aspects of Fascism*, p. 105.

which authority takes, however, is a question . . . of organic growth, authority being a vital principle of all society. To the question, who is to decide the form of government, the answer is, whoever is, in fact, the efficient authority at any given phase of social development." [10]

If, then, according to the Fascist theory, the will of the State, viewed as an entity or being, with distinct ends of its own to be realized, cannot be obtained by an appeal to the will of the governed, regarded as a heterogeneous mass of individuals, in accordance with any of the electoral or other constitutional devices which have hitherto been employed by States, but two other alternatives for determining such State will would seem to be open. These are: either that the State may be able itself,— *in propria persona,* as it were—to declare its own will; or that its citizens may be so grouped or organized that they will be qualified to declare the will of the State.

It is possible to assert that Fascism adopts the second of these alternatives, but it will be found that, in actual fact, the popular will, as expressed in the modes, and through the instrumentalities, sanctioned by the laws which the Fascists have promulgated, leave but little scope for the exercise of the people's will as distinguished from that of the person or persons who happen to be in control of the governmental machinery of the State. Let us see how this is.

As regards the manner in which the people are to be grouped for the purpose of ascertaining their opinions, it is to be observed, first of all, that, according to Fascist theory, this grouping is to be determined by considerations of State welfare rather than of the welfare of the citizens. There is the express repudiation of the idea that these citizens are given a voice in the determination of public policies because of an inherent or ethical right

[10] *Op. cit.,* p. 101.

possessed by them to exercise this function. It is flatly asserted that such parliamentary or other bodies as may be allowed to operate, represent and speak for the State rather than for the people themselves. "Fascist doctrine," declares Mussolini in the report from which we have already quoted, "denies the dogma of popular sovereignty, which is contradicted every day by reality, and in its stead proclaims the dogma of the sovereignty of the State, the State being the juridical organization of the Nation and the instrument of its historical necessities." [11]

In a report which Professor Gini submitted in 1925 to the Italian Government with reference to constitutional reforms, he said: "When the State is regarded as an entity, that is, as an organism standing apart with its own objects and its own requirements, and when individuals are regarded as means to satisfy such objects and such requirements, it is natural that individuals should be called upon to participate in the political life of the nation in no other proportion than that of the importance which they assume in the life of the State."

It is necessary, then, according to the Fascist theory, that the people of the State shall be so organized that they shall give voice to the interests of the State rather than to their own interests, and this requirement the Fascists have sought to secure, and believe that they have secured, by grouping the people into functional rather than territorial groups. This has meant the establishment of juridically organized professional associations, which include trade unions, employers' associations, coöperative bodies, guilds, etc., in which is exclusively vested the right to speak in behalf of the people or to act in their behalf. This organization, then, is one imposed upon them by the State and because it is be-

---

[11] It is clear that Mussolini is not here speaking of the sovereignty of the State in its juristic aspect, *i.e.*, as dealt with, for instance, in the author's *Fundamental Concepts of Public Law*.

lieved that thus national interests, that is, interests of the State, will be best advanced. And the same criterion applies with regard to the national parliamentary body which is created. Its function is to coöperate with, rather than to control or dictate to, the Executive. Thus, to quote again from Mussolini: "The Deputies . . . are organs of the State. Their selection cannot, therefore, proceed as a logical consequence from an abstract principle; it must be concretely regulated and controlled in the best way possible, in order that the ultimate objectives of the institution may be attained. And, since the first duty of the Chamber of Deputies is to collaborate with the Government in shaping the laws, making itself an interpreter of the needs and sentiments of the various social groups, which constitute such a great and important part of the national life, and harmonizing them with the historical and inherent necessities of that national life, it is clear that a good electoral system must be based above all upon the concurrent action of the totality of the organized forces of the country, and must further guarantee that the men chosen to constitute the Chamber shall be fully aware of the national interests, shall be, that is, statesmen in the loftiest sense of the word."

The deputies to be elected, it is to be noted, are only those presented for election by the organizations recognized by national law for the purpose, and who have been approved by the National Grand Council of the Fascist Government. As Mussolini has frankly said: "With the designation of the Grand Council the Deputy's election may be said to be completed, except for the ratification of the electoral body. That is why the projected law calls the persons included in the list of the Grand Council 'designated Deputies.' [The electoral body] is not, according to the usual fiction of the old electoral systems, called upon to choose the Deputies, but rather to approve the choice made by the organ which sums up in itself all the forces of the Nation. This approval does not, and cannot, apply to the individual names; it concerns the list as a whole, in which names are only the expression of a political trend. It is then essentially this trend which the electors are called upon to approve."

One other feature of the Fascist doctrine of the State needs to be mentioned, and this is as to the relation which, according to this doctrine, the various States of the world should stand toward one another. As to this it would appear that the exaltation of States into independent and self-seeking entities tends to diminish, if it does not wholly destroy, their obligation to have regard for the welfare of the Family of States or to the whole of Humanity. Upon this point we find the official exponents of Fascism expressing open disapproval of the doctrines of Internationalists who attach a higher value to the welfare of all humanity than they do to the welfare of individual States. Thus we find Professor Gini saying: "The essential difference between Fascism and the Socialistic current of thought, which has drifted off from the original programs of Communism and Collectivism, consists to-day in the concept of organic unity to which the interest of the individual must be subordinated. The Fascists perceive this unity in the nation, while the Socialists recognize it, at least theoretically—even at the cost of sacrificing their native lands—in the larger human society." In another place Professor Gini says: "It is an attitude of natural aversion from organisms tending to place limits upon the free action of the national organism, and, consequently, in a certain sense actually to weaken that organism. On this basis is to be explained the effort not to extend one iota beyond what is necessary the function of such international organisms or the participation of the national government in their proceedings."

As regards the Fascist conception of the State in its world or international aspects, Barnes says: [12] "The highest form of State is the national State, because the most perfect harmony is brought about where national unity, based on a community of traditions,[13] coincides with political unity." The Fascist says, indeed, and, in this respect Barnes does not seem to be in full agreement with Professor Gini, that "the political ideal or goal of mankind is, indeed, one universal national State, owning one supreme authority and integrated by one common national consciousness, however varied and intense might be the local differences and loyalties." But, he adds: "Fascism insists that progress toward this goal can only be made by upholding the principle of authority in existing States, and not, as would humanitarian Internationalists, by weakening authority and national sentiment, which sustains authority. It seems to stand to reason that man cannot hope to construct a higher authority by a process of destruction that brings the very principle of authority into contempt."

Again, Barnes says: "If the world at large, if the big Empires that to-day control the raw materials and the empty spaces fit for colonization, hem in a vital and prolific nation, not naturally enjoying the possession of abundant raw materials and empty spaces for her sons to settle in, and prevent, thereby, that Nation from maintaining a proper standard of life for her sons, by closing their doors to colonization or exacting a monopoly toll for the raw materials on which her industry may thrive, it is they who will be responsible for any wars which may break out in consequence of such a Nation's right to live and to enjoy a better life." [14]

The reference here to the conceived needs of Italy, and

---
[12] *Op. cit.*, p. 98.
[13] Not necessarily based on ethnic unity, Barnes elsewhere says.
[14] *Op. cit.*, p. 157.

to ambitions very generally ascribed to her, is obvious. It is, perhaps, of interest to note that we find almost identical arguments advanced by certain Japanese writers and statesmen in support of Japan's right to obtain for herself, from outside her own present political boundaries, such *materiel* as may be necessary in order that she may realize what she conceives to be her legitimate national development.[15]

It is clear that the Fascists are not affirmatively committed to the support of any specific type of governmental machinery. They can sanction any way of operating a State so long as, and to the extent that, it effectively seeks to promote the welfare of the State; but they believe that, in fact, they have developed in Italy a State machinery which is far more efficient, as thus tested, than any which has preceded it. They also believe, there appears to be grounds for holding, that, in this respect, Italy is ahead of most, if not all, of the other States of the world. Still, it does not appear that they would assert that it would be advisable for these other States to establish governments of precisely the type of that now existing in Italy, for they would agree that, after all, the test of a good government is a purely pragmatic one: Does it seek the right ends, and seek them by the most effective possible means? It is only upon the purely negative side, as denying the validity of the doctrine of popular sovereignty, namely, that the governed have an inherent and inalienable right to determine for themselves the form of political rule to which they are to be subjected, to participate in its operation and to dictate its specific policies, that the Fascists are dogmatic. This denial, the Fascists supplement by the opinion that the policies of the State may be more wisely determined by a few leaders than by the general body of the citizens

---

[15] Cf. the author's article, "Japan and the Natural Resources of Eastern Asia," *North American Review*, August, 1923.

themselves. This, however, is not a matter of dogmatic theory: it is but an opinion regarding a matter of fact, an opinion, therefore, which may be justified with regard to certain citizen bodies, but which may not be justified with regard to a people more intelligent, or more highly educated, or more highly moralized with regard to matters social and political.

What criticism, it may be asked, may be made of the Fascist doctrine as thus summarized? As for the assertion that, by the electoral and other governmental means which it employs, it provides a more efficient administrative machinery than is otherwise attainable, or that it secures the adoption of wiser public policies, it can only be said that this is an assertion of a matter of fact regarding which each person is entitled to his own opinion, and, therefore, it cannot be met by a flat denial. It may or may not be true, but, at any rate, no question of teleological political theory is involved. Furthermore, to anticipate conclusions which will be later reached in the present treatise, the denial that there are inherent in the individual citizens of a State spheres of liberty which it is essentially unethical that the State's controlling power should invade, is a proper one. Its denial of popular sovereignty, if by that be meant the inherent ethical right of every citizen to participate actively in the administration of the government of their State or in the determination of its policies, is also valid. The one essential vice in the Fascist theory, then, is the doctrine that the nation or State has an existence and ends of its own to subserve which are independent of the existence and the ends of its citizens. It is, in short, the transcendental character which it ascribes to the State which is the erroneous and vicious element in the theory. The demonstration or full exposition of this vital error cannot be made until the argument of the present volume has advanced beyond the critical to the constructive stage, but the following fact regarding the mystical or transcendental conception of the State may here be referred to. Even those who hold that the State is, essentially speaking, a being or entity which has a life and ends of its own, are not able to point out how these ends may be certainly and truly determined except through the judgments of individual human beings. Whatever independent existence the State may be declared to have, it is not such a being as is able to declare for itself what its ends or wishes are. Therefore, in the final result, these must be determined by those who happen to be in control of its policy-forming governmental organs, and thus, at one step, we descend from the mystical to the practical plane of action, from the superpersonal to the individual personal sphere of thought and judgment. This is admitted by Professor Gini when he says: "The uncertain point in connection with the system of Fascism, . . . is the lack of an objective standard whereby to interpret the interests of the nation. We must not conceal from ourselves the danger that a minority, which has come into power through the exercise of force or in consequence of unexpected developments, will go on maintaining itself by force and yet retain the intention of serving in good faith the true interests of the nation and purporting to carry on the program inspired by those interests, but not in reality corresponding to them." [16]

It is not surprising that we find among Fascists a great and revived admiration for Machiavelli. This is not merely because he was an Italian, or because he sought to promote Italian unity: the additional and

[16] Professor Gini, however, hazards the opinion that the danger that the true interests of the nation will not be perceived and followed is less when the power of determining these interests is possessed by a limited number of persons rather than by a larger number. This is but an individual opinion, and its soundness will, of course, depend upon the character of the citizen body. If they are not, generally speaking, an intelligent and politically educated body of people, the opinion may have a presumptive validity; but, if they have this character, the presumption may be the other way.

weighty reason is that he exalted to such a high place what may be called *la raison de l'état*.[17]

[17] Cf. Lion, for example, in the *Pedigree of Fascism, passim*. Signor Rocco says of Machiavelli: "His writings, an inexhaustible mine of practical remarks and precious observations, reveal dominant in him the State idea, no longer abstract but in the full historical concreteness of the national life. Machiavelli therefore is not only the greatest of modern political writers, he is also the greatest of our countrymen in full possession of a national Italian consciousness."

CHAPTER IX

THE CONTRACT THEORY

HISTORICALLY the Contract Theory has been the most important of all the philosophical attempts to find a rational basis upon which to rest the exercise of political authority. While not a correct theory in its pure form it will be found to contain elements of truth of such fundamental value that it will be necessary to consider with some degree of particularity the manner in which it has been argued by its chief proponents.

In analyzing this method of approaching the problem it is necessary to advert to the distinction between State and Government and to bear in mind the distinction, earlier pointed out, between the abstract question as to the right of the State to be, that is, of political society itself to exist, and the ethical *quo warranto* of the form of government under which a given political society is organized; and, secondly, the source whence the persons who operate that government derive their ethical right to rule.

When one speaks of an agreement between the individual persons concerned as the basis of the political society in which they live, the term Social Contract is employed. It might, perhaps, be more accurately descriptive to speak of it as the Political Contract since its assumed effect is to create a political out of a non-political group of individuals, but usage has so firmly fixed the phrase that an attempt to displace it is not feasible. The term Compact is often used instead of Contract, and attempts have also been made to distinguish between the meaning of the two words, but in this treatise they are used interchangeably.

The agreement which is brought forward to justify the existence of a given form of government, and, incidentally, to support the right to rule of those who operate it, is, or should be, known as the Governmental Contract. This contract is almost uniformly conceived of as one between the body of the governed and those who govern them. So conceived, it should, as a logical proposition, be preceded by the Social or State Contract, since it is necessary to view the individuals concerned as having been, in some way, combined into a single corporate body in order that they may constitute one of the parties to the Governmental Compact. Historically, however, the logical necessity for the two operations was not recognized until comparatively modern times. This failure was due either to a failure to distinguish between the origin of political society and the creation of a particular government over it, or to the acceptance of political society as a direct product of Nature, that is, of the instinctive, undeliberated action of men, or as divinely dictated. The existence of political society being posited upon any one of these three grounds, no other explanation, by way of common agreement or otherwise, was deemed to be required, and, therefore, only the matter of finding an ethical basis for the existence of a particular form of Government was thought to be at issue. Furthermore, a distinction was not drawn between groups of men viewed as social units, and the same groups regarded as bodies-politic. The terms society and social were used as comprehending both ideas.

It is in Greek thought that we find the earliest coherent political thinking,—the first attempts squarely to meet, upon rational grounds, the ethical problem raised by the subjection of individuals to the coercive processes of government. From the time of Protagoras this fundamental question was never absent from Greek philosophical thought. Indeed, it remained one of its central themes of discussion.

Aristotle in his *Politics* speaks of the Sophist Lycophron as having placed civil law, and therefore political authority, upon a basis of agreement, but it is in the doctrines of Glaucon in the fourth century, as reported in Plato's *Republic* that we find the compact theory stated and argued, though without distinguishing between a social and a governmental contract. Men, finding a non-political state to be intolerable, and moved by fear of each other, it was argued, make a contract to do justice to each other, and agree upon laws, which they mutually accept as binding upon themselves, and as defining what actions shall be regarded as right or wrong. It was to refute such an arbitrary or conventional basis of social and political obligation as this, as well as the other individualistic doctrines of the Sophists, as, for example, the force theory of Thrasymachus, earlier referred to, that Plato wrote his *Republic;* and the same purpose, though perhaps not so predominant, is found in Aristotle's *Politics* and *Ethics.*

In Roman political theory, during the time of the Empire, as well as under the Republic, we find the Governmental Compact theory explicitly asserted; that is, the theory that those who rule obtain their authority from the consent of those whom they govern, or, at any rate, from the consent of those who enjoy the full rights of citizenship, and that there is thus an implied compact between the rulers and the ruled. This idea was almost universal throughout the Middle Ages. The fact is that the whole feudal system was saturated with ideas of contract. Thus, as says Sir Henry Maine: "The earliest feudal communities were neither bound together by mere sentiment nor recruited by a fiction. The tie which united them was a Contract, and they obtained new associates by contracting with them. The relation of the lord to the vassals had originally been settled by express engagement, and a person wishing to engraft himself in the brotherhood by commendation or infeudation came to a distinct understanding as to the conditions on which he was to be admitted. It is therefore the sphere occupied in them by Contract which principally distinguishes the feudal institutions from the unadulterated usages of primitive races. The lord had many of the characteristics of a patriarchal chieftain, but his prerogative was limited by a variety of settled customs traceable to the express conditions which had been agreed upon when the infeudation took place." [1]

The thesis of an original sovereign capacity of the people, and the transfer of this power to their rulers by a compact was held during the middle and early modern ages by many of those who asserted that rulers possessed absolute political powers as well as by those who strove to establish the idea that their powers were or might be constitutionally limited. The point at issue was as to the character and scope of this compact.

Upon the one side it was held that the surrender of this supreme power by the people was necessarily entire, and resulted in total and irrevocable alienation of their political rights. This was the view held by Suarez and other Jesuitical writers, and later, by Grotius and Pufendorf. Upon the other side, it was maintained that this governmental pact effected nothing more than a delegation of power to the rulers, such power to be used by them only for the purpose for which granted, and liable to be recalled upon being misused.

Suarez, whose development of the idea of sovereignty was especially profound for his time, likened the birth of the State to that of a child, and, from that analogy, derived its necessarily absolute character. Just as man, he

[1] *Ancient Law*, p. 353.

said, is free and has full power over all his members, as soon as he exists, so is the political body. Just as the father of the child only gives to it existence, while God gives it freedom, reason, and power, so the sovereignty of the community is created by the free will of men uniting; and, just as the father can procreate the child or not, as he sees fit, but, if created, cannot deny it full power and freedom; so, likewise, the community may or may not create the body politic at its option, but, when created, cannot refuse it freedom from all control. As regards the power to alienate sovereignty, Suarez likened the temporal powers of the people to the spiritual power of the Pope. The sovereign pontiff, he said, although holding his power from God, is able to abdicate it, and, in the same way, the republic, though receiving the legislative (*i.e.* sovereign) power from God, is able to abandon this, if it should see fit, and to transfer it to another person.[2]

Grotius endeavored to maintain the possibility of a people surrendering its sovereignty without reservation or power of revocation, upon the ground that the conquered may purchase their lives at the hands of their conquerors by an acceptance of political slavery,—a doctrine that excited the especial indignation of Rousseau who clearly showed the impossibility of founding a "right" of control upon such a basis, not to speak of the false principle of international law that it contained.[3]

By those whose views differed from the above, it was held, either that it was inherently impossible for a people to alienate its sovereignty; or, that, if it could be done, the presumption would be, in absence of any exact knowledge of such a compact, that the surrender of power would be coupled with the condition that its exercise

[2] *Tractatus de legibus et legislatore*, Bk. III, Chap. III. Cf. Gierke, *Althusius u. die Entwicklung der Naturrechtlichen Staatstheorien*, pp. 67 et seq.
[3] *The Social Contract*, Bk. I, Chap. IV.

should be directed to the general welfare of the community.

In accordance with these views we find many of the political discussions of these centuries turning upon such points as the power of the people to offer resistance to tyrants *absque titulo* and to tyrants *ab exercitio,* that is, to tyrants without legitimate title to power, and to those who, though possessed of proper title, exercised their control in an oppressive manner. The general view held was, that, towards tyrants of the first class, both natural right and civil right permitted resistance, as there was really no compact on the part of the people with them. But as regarded those of the second class, views differed, some holding that citizens were individually bound, but that collectively they had the right of resistance. Others held that implicit obedience was in all cases demanded.

With the development in England, especially during the seventeenth century, and, later, in America and Europe, of doctrines of popular government, the theory of a governmental compact between governors and governed came to the front as the chief argument against monarchical absolutism.

The Social or Political Compact. In accepting the contractual origin of governments, even the absolutists had to concede an original sovereign power of the people; for the people must, of course, have first had that which they were regarded as having granted away. But this surrender of power could only be imagined as performed by a community acting as a single body in a corporate capacity. That is to say, it was necessary that it should first assume the character of a corporate or legal subject. Hence, it came to be agreed that a given aggregate of men must first constitute a single social or political body, as distinguished from a mere horde or arithmetical sum of persons, before they can contract with the particular rulers to whom the political power is to be given.

It thus became necessary to account for the manner in which this transition from a sum of individuals to a united community was effected.

In the earlier and more theological times, society was held by some to be as much a direct creation of God as is man himself. In general, however, God was considered simply as the *causa remota,* and Nature, or the "instinctive sociability" of man viewed as the proximate cause. That is to say, the Aristotelian doctrine was maintained. This was the general view until the end of the sixteenth century. We thus find no mention of an original Social Compact in the writings of Bodin, the body politic being considered by him as an aggregation of families. Nor did the Monarchomachi advance beyond this point.

It is not until the appearance of Richard Hooker's *Ecclesiastical Polity,* in 1594, that we find in political literature an application of the compact theory to the establishment of political society itself, and, even by Hooker, the point was only incidentally raised, and not pursued to its logical conclusions.

In this work, Hooker attempted the defense of an established church, such as existed in England, by denying that the church was necessarily subject to direct divine regulation in all matters; and by asserting that, for its government, laws may be made by men, so long as they are not contrary to the Scriptures. In sustaining this thesis, he was led to an inquiry regarding the origin of all authority, and found it in the consent of the governed. A pre-civic condition of man was distinctly premised, and, to escape from this state, which was one of lawlessness and war, the Social Compact was entered into.[4] Having

[4] By some writers, and especially by Gierke in his *Johannes Althusius und die Entwicklung der naturrechtlichen Staatstheorien,* great credit is ascribed to Althusius for developing the Social Compact idea. It is, indeed, alleged by Gierke that from Althusius' *Politica methodicé digesta,* first published in 1603, Rousseau derived the most important of his doctrines. For a destructive criticism of this claim, see C. E. Vaughan's *Political Writings of Rousseau,* Vol. II, pp. 4-8. As Vaughan points out,

asked that those who complained of present evils should compare them with those times "wherein there were no civil societies, with those times wherein there was as yet no manner of public régime established," Hooker went on to say: "To take away all such mutual grievances, injuries, and wrongs, there was no way but only by growing into composition and agreement among themselves, by ordaining some kind of government public, and by yielding themselves subject thereunto; that unto whom they granted authority to rule and govern, by them the peace, tranquillity, and happy estate of the rest might be procured. . . . Strifes and troubles would be endless, except they gave their common consent all to be ordered by some whom they should agree upon: without which consent there was no reason that one man should take upon him to be lord or judge of another. . . . In a word all public regiment of what kind soever seemeth evidently to have arisen from deliberate advice, consultation, and composition between men, judging it convenient and behoveful." [5]

Grotius in his famous *De Jure Belli ac Pacis,* published in 1625, accepted the Social Compact theory though he laid no special stress upon it. It is important to note, however, that he appears to have had in mind a distinction between Society and the State, for, while he referred to social life as a natural condition of man, he found the origin of the State in a deliberate agreement between men.[6] This assertion he made incidentally while discussing the right of resistance to constituted authority. Whether or not the obligation to obey should hold good in all cases, he said, depends "upon intention of those

---

Althusius, so far as he used the compact idea, applied it in the establishment of the smaller social units, the clan, tribe, village and city, which he conceived to be the constituent elements of the State. The individual as such, was thus given no part in the establishment of the State.

[5] *Ecclesiastical Polity,* Book I, X.
[6] As to this see Dunning, *History of Political Theories,* Vol. II, p. 180.

who first entered into civil society, from whom the power of sovereigns is originally derived. . . . We must observe that men did not at first unite themselves in civil society by any special command from God, but their own free will, out of a sense of the inability of separate families to repel violence, whence the civil power is derived." [7]

From the time of Grotius the Compact Theory played a part in almost all speculative political writings for the next two hundred years. For the purpose of the present treatise, however, it will not be necessary to trace its course in any detail. It will be sufficient if an account is given of its employment in the writings of its chief exponents, Hobbes, Locke and Rousseau, with a word as to its use by Spinoza. Before examining the reasoning of these writers, however, it will conduce to clearness of thought if we first speak briefly of the notions of Natural Laws and Natural Rights which have constituted the starting point of all the compact theories.

Natural Law.[8] The term Natural Law or Laws of Nature has been (and is) widely used in the so-called Natural Sciences to designate the sequences uniformly observed in the phenomenal world. Here, though "laws" are spoken of, there is no idea of commands addressed to rational beings except in so far as Great Nature (*natura naturans*) is regarded as a creative and volitional entity, or as God is viewed as fixing, by His will, the operations of the cosmos. And, even when thus regarded, there is involved no idea that men may, if they would, successfully resist the operation of these commands. Man may disobey

[7] *De Jure Belli ac Pacis*, Bk. I, Chap. IV, Sec. 7. Pufendorp in his *De Jure Naturae et Gentium*, published in 1672, adopted the social compact as the logical basis upon which to found political society, and, furthermore, developed the contract idea by predicating a separate agreement as to the form of government to be established and also a third agreement between the governed and those particular persons who were to govern them.

[8] See Professor A. R. Lord's *The Principles of Politics*, pp. 28-42, for an excellent brief discussion of the various meanings which have been attached to the term "natural law."

them only in the sense that, by unwisely regulating their own conduct, they will have visited upon themselves the results of certain of these so-called natural or phenomenal laws which otherwise would not, as to them, be called into operation.

As applied only to living beings (to animals or lower orders of life as well as to men), the term Natural Law has also been used to indicate instinctive, as distinguished from deliberated action. Thus the instinct to preserve, one's own existence and to satisfy such desires as hunger, thirst, and, in general, to avoid those things which cause bodily pain, and to do or obtain those things which give physical satisfaction or pleasure appears to be universal. In this sense also the so-called laws are not laws at all in the sense of being commands addressed by a superior rational being to inferior rational beings. They are, as Huxley has pointed out in one of his essays, "nothing but a statement of that which a given being tends to do under the circumstances of its existence, and which, in the case of a living being, it is necessitated to do if it is to escape certain kinds of disability, pain and ultimate dissolution." [9] There is, however, this much to be said of these laws of life: they are used to support the claim of ethical right upon the part of rational beings, that is, of men, to do what is required in order that their lives may be preserved and their other needs satisfied. This emergence of an ethical claim has furnished the basis for the third sense in which the term Laws of Nature has been employed, and introduces as well the correllative idea of "Natural Rights."

In this third sense the Laws of Nature have been conceived of as rules of conduct for men dictated by Nature, or by God, and made known to men by right reason or by divine revelation. Hence, these laws, as independent of human enactment, or of political society, have been

[9] "Natural and Political Rights," *Essays*, Vol. I, p. 349.

regarded as of absolute and universal validity, morally binding at all times, in all places, and over all peoples.

By some, as we shall see, these Natural Laws were conceived of as the rules of human conduct that would be binding in a non-political society,—a condition which was spoken of as a "State of Nature." That men once existed, as an historical fact, in such a non-political society was assumed by some; by others it was merely asserted that, if such a society were conceived to exist, these Natural Laws would apply.

Necessarily there were conflicts of opinion as to what it is proper for individuals to do when there is conceived to be an inconsistency between these Natural Laws and the civil commands of political authority, and also disputes as to whether the human reason, unaided by divine direction, is competent to determine with certainty the substantive provisions of these laws; but, in general, there was agreement that these laws should furnish at least the norms for human law, and that their principles should guide rulers in the exercise of their discretionary political power. By some, Natural Law in the sense in which we are now considering it, was declared to be identical with Divine Law; by others, that, though distinct, it was necessarily in harmony with Divine Law; by others (Grotius for example) that these Natural Laws, as given by Reason, would exist and be binding even were there no God.

History of the Theory of the Law of Nature.[10] As already shown, Divine Law, pure and simple, swallowed up, in the beginning, all ideas of law. Though necessarily

---

[10] In beginning this division of our subject, it is proper that special mention should be made of the extremely able and lucid treatment of this subject by Mr. John W. Salmond (*Law Quarterly Review*, April, 1895, article "Law of Nature") as well as of the volume of Professor Ritchie, entitled *Natural Rights*. From these two sources has been derived much of the historical matter contained in the next following paragraphs. Other valuable sources are Gierke, *Johannes Althusius u. die Entwicklung der naturrechtlichen Staatstheorien;* Lasson, *Rechtsphilosophie;* and of course Maine, *Ancient Law*, Chap. III.

uttered and enforced by human agents, a supramundane sanction was conceived to attach to all rules to which the obedience of the people was demanded. This was the condition that existed in all the Oriental countries, and during the Heroic period of Grecian history.

It is first in the time of the Sophists, representing, as Janet says, the period of enlightenment (Aufklärung) of Greece, that we find the question raised whether there are fixed canons of right and wrong that are settled for all time by divine dictation or by Nature, or only provisions changeable at the caprice of men. It is clear that certain of the Sophists, because they saw those norms of conduct differing among different peoples and at different times, rejected the very idea of right and the good, and asserted that each individual had to determine for himself, whether from motives of self interest or merely by caprice, what it would be proper for him to do.

At the hand of the Cynics, the appeal to the State of Nature took the form of a protest against human conventionalities and so-called artificialities of life, as opposed to simple primitive conditions. This principle they applied not only in their philosophic thought, but in their practice of life. In the conduct of Diogenes, who disowned the State, became a "citizen of the world," lived in a tub, and discarded all superfluous clothing, we see the practical results obtained.[11]

By Plato, we find the pre-existence of eternal ideas again upheld. In fact, the chief object of his *Republic* was the demonstration of a natural justice apart from human origination, and of which human justice is but an imperfect reflection. The idea, however, of a natural *law* declaring and rendering practically valid this natural justice, was not made prominent. In the writings of

---

[11] An entertaining revival of this doctrine is to be found in Mr. Edward Carpenter's essay, *Civilization: Its Cause and Cure*. It plays a part, also, in all "back to nature" movements.

Aristotle we find a correction of the Cynic view that had characterized the civilized, conventional life of man, as unnatural, and as morally inferior to simpler and cruder forms. A natural law as well as a natural justice was spoken of, but so far as this law was made to apply to human conduct, it was practically identified with the unwritten divine law, or that of reason.

In the systems of the Stoics we at last find a well-defined philosophical meaning given to the term "Nature," according to which it appears as the "manifestation of the single and homogeneous spirit of the world, whose several phenomena are connected together through the common law of right reason. The Law of Nature is therefore that common, universal, divine, and good rule of reason which governs creatures combined in a natural association, regarding it as a reflection of the process of nature, in instinct as well as in the human understanding: it is the harmony of human justice with the law of the world, which results from the identity of moral and of material nature, independently of any positive institution." [12]

By this postulation of human reason as the revealer of the laws of nature, and as thus the judge of right conduct, the Stoics avoided the absurdities of the Cynic maxims and made their application to ordinary life conformable to the practical and reasonable conditions by which men are surrounded. Thus "Nature to the Stoics is not the mere chaos of sensible things *minus* whatever results from man's rational efforts. It is objective reason; it is, as with Aristotle, the divine element in the Universe; the reason of the individual man is only a partial manifestation of it; his reason is a divine element in him, and it is in virtue of this divine element in him that man can understand the reason that is in the Universe and can live the life according to nature. Thus,

[12] Pulszky, *Theory of Law and Civil Society*, p. 79.

reason is not something that separates the judgment of one man from that of another. The appeal to reason is an appeal to the common reason of mankind. Human laws and institutions, therefore, are no longer despised as merely conventional. They are a realization, however imperfect, of the Law of Nature which is behind and above them." [13]

It was in the Stoic form that the idea of "Law of Nature" was introduced into Roman Law. It will not be necessary to trace the manner in which Rome was obliged to recognize laws not emanating primarily from her own will in the administration of justice between members of her Latin provinces who were not entitled to the benefit of her own peculiar *jus civile;* how, from those laws, found to be common to all the Latin tribes, a body of *jus gentium* was formed; how, subsequently, under the Stoic influence, the Roman jurists began gradually to see in these laws, so uniformly accepted by independent tribes, the lost "code of nature"; nor, finally, how, this conception once accepted, the Roman Law avoided the danger of arrest of development by her code, and became furnished with an ideal, in the effort for the attainment of which, unlimited possibilities of growth were contained.[14]

The Romans did not distinctly affirm the historical reality of a "State of Nature" in which Natural Law had held full sway. Furthermore, the Natural Law was not held by them as at any time legally valid unless adopted and accepted by Rome as her own, whereby in fact, it thus became a part of her own *jus civile.* In other words, this hypothetical Natural Law was regarded as an ideal towards which the civil law should tend; not as a code

[13] Ritchie, *Natural Rights,* p. 34.
[14] See the account of Maine in his *Ancient Law,* Chaps. III and IV. Maine also calls especial attention to the service of the *jus naturale* in France as supplying general principles through which the diverse elements of her law were partially harmonized and unified.

which had actual, present validity. Its actual applicability depended upon the peculiar conditions of a civil society, and, until these were favorable, the civil law prevailed. There was a strong tendency to view the *jus gentium* as a partial manifestation of this ideal law.

In the Christian conception of the world, the State of Nature was frequently conceived of as the original state of sinlessness and grace, from which men had fallen by Adam's sin. It was thus only the corruptness of this world that made the political power and the civil law a necessity. This was especially the conception developed by St. Augustine in his *Civitas Dei*. Natural Law thus became divine law (*lex aeterna*) and was held by the Church to be actually applicable, so that disobedience to it on the part of the temporal powers might be punished by deposition or might even justify regicide.

As might be expected, the doctrine of Natural Law did not escape further analysis in the keen dialectics of the Schoolmen. In their hands, the Natural Law in general or *lex aeterna*, became distinguished from that particular part of it which applies to man alone (*lex naturalis*). According to this, the *lex aeterna* has its source in divine reason, and the *lex naturalis* immediately in man's reason. Thus the *lex naturalis* governs man's actions only. Though *revealed* by his reason, it is not, however, *commanded* by such reason, but by the divine reason, of which man's reason is only a partial manifestation. Thus the *lex aeterna* says to beasts and all non-reasoning beings, you *must;* while to man, because of his reasoning faculties and his moral nature, you *ought*. It is of course apparent that this distinction is very nearly identical with that between the second and third conceptions which we have stated at the beginning of this chapter. The reign of Scholasticism may be roughly said to have lasted from the eleventh to the sixteenth century, its greatest influence being in the thirteenth century. During these years the distinctions that we have given dominated European thought.

With Grotius and Hobbes began a new period, characterized by the severance of natural and divine laws, that is, a return to the principle of nature as *natura naturans,* as itself legislative, and as providing rules for human conduct binding upon man by his very own nature. As such, the obligatory character of these rules was viewed as independent of a belief or disbelief in a deity to which this nature might be ultimately referable. The reasonableness of these laws, as founded upon considerations of utility, rather than their ascription to a divine source, was regarded as giving validity to them.

The influence of the doctrine of Natural Law upon the development of International Law, through the work of Grotius and his school, was immediate and all-important. The *jus gentium* of the Romans was made to mean the law *between* nations. By thus ascribing to it a source in Nature itself, a validity was given to it which went far towards securing its recognition at the hands of sovereign rulers. States were viewed as independent individuals, as without a common superior for the enunciation of mutually binding rules of intercourse, and, hence, as in a "State of Nature" towards each other—a State of Nature, however, which was governed by Natural Law. This view long persisted among writers upon international law. Thus Vattell writing in the middle of the eighteenth century, distinguished between "the *necessary* law of nations, which consists in the application of the law of nature to nations" (being *necessary* "because nations are absolutely bound to observe it"); and the *positive* or *arbitrary* law of nations, which he again divided into *Voluntary, Conventional,* and *Customary.*[15] What

[15] The title of Vattell's work is *The Law of Nations, or Principles of the Law of Nature Applied to the Conduct and Affairs of Nations and Subjects.* The quotations are taken from the Preface, p. lvii, of the 4th Am. ed., 1835.

Vattell called the "necessary" law of nations, Grotius termed the "internal law of nations" because obligatory in point of conscience. He also termed it the "natural law of nations."

Having made this preliminary survey of doctrines of Natural Law, we are prepared to consider in some detail the chief philosophers who, starting with a postulation of Natural Law have, by means of a social or political compact, sought to explain and justify the existence of political authority over men. And first among these is Thomas Hobbes.

CHAPTER X

HOBBES

GROTIUS, more emphatically than his predecessors, had divorced Natural Laws and Natural Rights from Divine Law and Divine Rights, and had thus placed their discussion more nearly upon a rationalistic basis, and opened the way to purely utilitarian arguments. This process was completed by Thomas Hobbes. His political and ethical views were stated in a number of works, but most completely in his *Leviathan,* published in 1651, and, for our present purposes, it will not be necessary to go outside the pages of that book.

In order to understand Hobbes' ethical and political theories it is necessary first to speak of the psychological premises upon which he grounded them.

According to Hobbes, men, in their actions, are moved either by appetite or desire toward an object, or by aversion away from it. That which they desire, men love and term good; that which they are averse to, they hate and term evil. Therefore, since different men (or the same men at different times) love or hate different things, the terms good and evil are relative in character. "These words of good, evil, and contemptible, are ever used with relation to the person that useth them; there being nothing simply and absolutely so; nor any common rule of good and evil, to be taken from the nature of the objects themselves; but from the person of the man, where there is no commonwealth; or, in a commonwealth, from the person that representeth it; or from an arbitrator or judge, whom men disagreeing shall by consent set up, and make his sentence the rule thereof." [1]

It follows from this that men in all their voluntary actions are purely egoistic, and that, since men always aim at that which at the time will secure for them that which they desire, or which will render them immune from that which they hate or have an aversion to, a rigid determinism results.

Now, the aim of every man being, as Hobbes asserts, to obtain the means of gratifying his desires, and of avoiding what he has an aversion to, his supreme aim is to obtain Power,—a power that will enable him not only to satisfy his present needs, but give to him an assurance that he will continue to have the means of satisfying his needs. "I put," he says, "for a general inclination of all mankind a perpetual and restless desire of power after power that ceaseth only in death. And the cause of this is not always that a man hopes for a more intensive delight than he has already attained to, or that he cannot be content with a moderate power; but because he cannot assure the power and means to live well, which he hath present, without the acquisition of more." [2]

Men being egoistic in their acts, and ever seeking more power for themselves, it results that, where there is no restraining authority over them all which compels them to act according to certain fixed rules or laws, a universal competition between them arises, a competition that means the war of every man against every man which is regulated by no considerations of morality or of justice. Indeed, he says, in such a non-political state, the ideas of right and wrong, of justice and injustice, have no application. "To this war of every man against every man, this also is consequent; that nothing can be unjust. The notions of right and wrong, justice and injustice, have no place. Where there is no common power, there is no

[1] *Leviathan*, Chap. VI.   [2] *Ibid.*, Chap. XI.

law; where no law, no justice. Force and fraud, are, in war, the two cardinal virtues. Justice and injustice are none of the faculties neither of the body nor mind. . . . They are qualities that relate to men in society, not in solitude. It is consequent also to the same condition, that there can be no propriety, no dominion, no 'mine' and 'thine' distinct; but only that to be every man's, that he can get; and for so long, as he can keep it. And thus much for the ill condition, which man by mere nature is actually placed in; though with the possibility to come out of it, consisting partly in the passions, partly in his reason." [3]

It is clear, then, that, according to Hobbes, the non-political state is for man a very undesirable one—undesirable for every one, for no one is by nature so superior in power to his fellow men that he need not be fearful either of their strength or of their cunning. "Nature hath made men so equal in the faculties of the body and mind: as that though there be found one man sometimes manifestly stronger in body or of quicker mind than another, yet, when all is reckoned together, the difference between man and man, is not so considerable, as that one man can thereupon claim to himself any benefit, to which another may not pretend, as well as he. For as to the strength of body, the weakest has strength enough to kill the strongest, either by secret machination, or by confederacy with others that are in the same danger with himself." [4]

"Hereby," Hobbes continues, "it is manifest, that during the time men live without a common power to keep them in awe, they are in that condition which is called war; and such a war, as is of every man, against every man. . . . In such a condition there is no place for industry, because the fruit thereof is uncertain, and consequently no culture of the earth; no navigation, nor use

[3] *Leviathan*, Chap. XIII.   [4] *Ibid.*, Chap. XIII.

of the commodities that may be imported by sea; no commodious buildings; no instruments of moving and removing such things as require much force, no knowledge of the face of the earth; no account of time; no arts; no letters; no society; and, which is worst of all, continued fear and danger of violent death; and the life of man solitary, poor, nasty, brutish, and short." [5]

Man is, however, says Hobbes, a rational being, able to conceive of conditions better than those by which he happens to be surrounded, and able to devise means for realizing those better conditions. The fundamental prerequisite to this betterment is the abolishment of this condition of universal war of men against men, which, even when not actually raging, is ever impending. The first and fundamental precept of nature is therefore to establish peace.

This fundamental utilitarian purpose of securing peace, Hobbes declares, could conceivably be realized by men mutually agreeing to forego aggression upon each other. But, such an agreement or agreements would be of no operative value because no one would have assurance that, if he abided by his agreement, all the others would do likewise. This assurance, he says, can only be provided if all agree to vest in some definite individual, or set of individuals, the right to determine what it shall be proper for men to do, and clothe him or them with power to compel obedience to the corresponding laws or commands which he or they may issue. In other words, it becomes necessary to establish a society political,—to create a State or Commonwealth. "Covenants without the

[5] Apparently he views such an evil condition of life as having been, in many cases at least, a matter of historical fact. He says: "It may peradventure be thought that there was never such a time nor condition of men as thus; and I believe it was never generally so, over all the world but there are many places where they live so now. For the savage people in many places of America, except the Government of small families, the concord whereof dependeth on natural lust, have no government at all, and live at this day in that brutish manner, as I said before."

sword, are but words, and of no strength to secure a man at all." [6]

Thus Hobbes is led to the conclusion that the State must be viewed as founded upon a compact between the individuals subjected to its authority. His statement as to the nature and scope of this social or political compact deserves to be quoted at length. He says:

"The only way to erect such a common power, as may be able to defend them from the invasion of foreigners, and the injuries of one another, and thereby to secure them in such sort, as that by their own industry, and by the fruits of the earth, they may nourish themselves and live contentedly, is to confer all their power and strength upon one man, or upon one assembly of men, that may reduce their wills, by plurality of voices, into one will; which is as much as to say, to appoint one man, or assembly of men, to bear their person, and every man to own, and acknowledge himself to be author of whatsoever he that so beareth their person, shall act, or cause to be acted, in those things which concern the common peace and safety; and therein submit their wills, every one to his will, and their judgments, to his judgment. This is more than consent, or concord; it is a real unity of them all, in one and the same person, made by covenant of every man with every man, in such manner, as if every man should say to every man 'I authorize and give up my right of governing myself, to this man, or to this assembly of men, on this condition, that thou give up thy right to him, and authorize all his actions in like manner.' This done, the multitude so united in one person is called a 'commonwealth,' in Latin *civitas*. This is the generation of that great 'Leviathan,' or rather, to speak more reverently, of that 'mortal God,' to which we owe, under the 'immortal God,' our peace and defence. For by this authority, given him by every particular man in the

[6] *Leviathan*, Chap. XVII.

commonwealth, he hath the use of so much power and strength conferred on him, that by terror thereof, he is enabled to perform the wills of them all, to peace at home, and mutual aid against their enemies abroad. And in him consisteth the essence of the commonwealth, which, to define it, is one person, of whose acts a great multitude, by mutual covenants one with another, have made themselves every one the author, to the end he may use the strength and means of them all, as he shall think expedient, for their peace and common defence.

"And he that carrieth this person is called 'sovereign,' and said to have 'sovereign power'; and every one besides, his subject." [7]

From this contract the rights of absolute government are deduced. The contract once made, not only does the power of the ruler or rulers become absolute, but all right, that is, rational right, based on reason, of revolution on the part of the people is, according to Hobbes, forever lost. "They," he continues, "that have already instituted a commonwealth, being thereby bound by covenant to own the actions and judgments of one, cannot lawfully make a new covenant amongst themselves to be obedient to any other, in anything whatsoever, without his permission. And, therefore, they that are subjects to a monarch, cannot without his leave cast off monarchy, and return to the confusion of a disunited multitude; nor transfer their person from him that beareth it, to another man, or other assembly of men; for they are bound every man to every man, to own, and be reputed author of all, that he that already is their sovereign, shall do, and judge fair to be done; so that any one man dissenting, all the rest should break their covenant made to that man, which is injustice: and they have also every man given the sovereignty to him that beareth their person; and therefore if they depose him they take from him that which is his

[7] *Leviathan*, Chap. XVII.

own, and so again it is injustice. Besides, if he that attempteth to depose his sovereign be killed, or punished by him for such attempt, he is author of his own punishment, as being by the institution, author of all his sovereign shall do: and because it is injustice for a man to do anything for which he may be punished by his own authority, he is also upon that title unjust. And whereas some men have pretended for their disobedience to their sovereign, a new covenant, made not with men, but with God; this also is unjust: for there is no covenant with God but by mediation of somebody that representeth God's person; which none doth but God's lieutenant, who hath the sovereignty under God. But this pretence of covenant with God is so evident a lie, even in the pretenders' own consciences, that it is not only an act of an unjust, but also of a vile and unmanly disposition.

"Secondly, because the right of bearing the person of them all is given to him they make sovereign, by covenant only of one to another, and not of him to any of them, there can happen no breach of covenant on the part of the sovereign and consequently none of his subjects, by any pretence of forfeiture, can be freed from his subjection. That he which is made sovereign maketh no covenant with his subjects beforehand, is evident; because either he must make it with the whole multitude as one party to the covenant; or he must make a several covenant with every man. With the whole, as one party it is impossible; because as yet they are not one person; and if he makes so many several covenants as there be men, those covenants after he hath the sovereignty are void; because what act soever can be pretended by any one of them for breach thereof is the act both of himself, and of all the rest, because done in the person, and by the right of every one of them in particular. Beside, if any one, or more of them, pretend a breach of the covenant made by the sovereign at his institution; and others, or one other of his subjects, or himself alone, pretend there was no such breach, there is in this case no judge to decide the controversy; it returns therefore to the sword again; and every man recovereth the right of protecting himself by his own strength, contrary to the design they had in the institution. It is, therefore, vain to grant sovereignty by way of precedent covenant. The opinion that any monarch receiveth his power by covenant, that is to say, on condition, proceedeth from want of understanding this easy truth, that covenants being words and breath, have no force to oblige, contain, or protect any man, but what it has from the public sword: that is, from the united hands of that man, or assembly of men that hath the sovereignty, and whose actions are avouched by them all, and performed by the strength of them all, in him united. . . . Because every subject is by this institution author of all the actions, and judgments of the sovereign instituted, it follows, that whatsoever he doth, it can be no injury to any of his subjects; nor ought he to be by any of them accused of injustice. For he that doth anything by authority from another, doth therein no injury to him by whose authority he acted." [8]

From this form of dominion, termed "sovereignty by institution," Hobbes next turns to dominion acquired by conquest or victory in war. "This power of rule is acquired," he says, "when the vanquished, to avoid the present stroke of death, covenanteth either in express words, or by other sufficient signs of the will, that so long as his life and the liberty of his body is allowed him, the victor shall have the use thereof at his pleasure. . . . It is not, therefore, the victory that giveth the right of dominion over the vanquished but his own covenant. . . . In sum, the rights and consequences of both paternal and despotical dominion" [*i.e.* dominion by conquest] "are

[8] *Leviathan,* Chap. XVIII.

the very same with those of a sovereign by institution." [9]

The crucial point in Hobbes' theory is undoubtedly his ascription of an original as well as a continuing moral obligation upon the part of individuals to yield obedience to the social or political covenant into which they are conceived to have entered for the creation of the commonwealth.[10] An important, though perhaps a less fundamental question is as to whether it was logically necessary to predicate a covenant in which the parties place themselves, practically without reservation, under the control of their constituted rulers.[11]

Both of these questions we shall examine.

Hobbes is emphatic in his assertion that, in a State of Nature there is no distinction between what it is morally right and what it is morally wrong that one should do to another. "The desires and passions of man," he says, "are in themselves no sin. No more are the actions that proceed from those passions, till they know a law that forbids them; which till laws be made they cannot know,

[9] *Leviathan*, Chap. XX. It will be observed that here Hobbes is compelled to depart from his fundamental conception of a compact between the governed, and is obliged to found authority upon an agreement between the rulers and those whom they rule. In both cases the moving force is fear—fear, in the one case, of each other; in the other case, of the ruler.

[10] Only those living at the time of the making of the compact could have been the original parties to it. It must have been assumed by Hobbes that all persons thereafter living in a given political society are to be deemed to have given an implied assent to the agreement upon which it is conceived to rest.

[11] *Leviathan*, Chap. XXI. The only qualifications upon the individual's obligation of absolute obedience to the commands of the civil power recognized by Hobbes are that the subject is not called upon to commit violence against himself, and that, when the government that asks his obedience is not able, in fact, to defend him against violence from others, his duty to obey its commands ceases. "The obligation of subjects to the sovereign," Hobbes says, "is understood to last as long, and no longer, than the power lasteth, by which he is able to protect them. For the right men have by nature to protect themselves, when none else can protect them, can by no covenant be relinquished." Hobbes, however, in no case admits that the individual has the moral or legal right to weaken, by his own act, the power of the State to give protection to himself or to others.

nor can any law be made till they have agreed upon the person that shall make it." [12]

Only when such laws exist can there be a distinction between justice and injustice, he says in another place. "Before the names of just and unjust can have place, there must be some coercive power, to compel men equally to the performance of their covenants, by the terror of some punishment, greater than the benefit they expect by the breach of their covenant; and to make good that propriety, which by mutual contract men acquire, in recompense of the universal right they abandon: and such power there is none before the erection of a commonwealth."

In effect, then, Hobbes asserts that, in a State of Nature, there are no such things as Natural Laws, at least as those laws had been previously understood. Hobbes uses the term but is careful to say that a so-called law of nature (*lex naturalis*) is nothing more than a "precept or general rule, found out by reason" which leads a man to do what will preserve his life and to avoid doing what will tend to destroy it. It is only in this sense of the word that he says "the first and fundamental law of Nature" is "to seek peace, and follow it." And, because a general covenant, such as he describes is, in his opinion, the only means by which peace may be obtained, therefore, this law of Nature provides that the covenant should be entered into and obeyed. Ancillary to this first law of Nature, Hobbes states a number of other laws or precepts of Nature the observance of which, he declares, necessarily tends to the preservation of the peace, all of which may however be summed up in the general rule "Do not that to another, which thou wouldst not have done to thyself." [13]

In essence, then, these "precepts" of Nature "are immutable and eternal; for injustice and ingratitude, arro-

[12] *Leviathan*, Chap. XV. [13] *Ibid.*, Chap. XV.

gance, pride, iniquity, acception of persons, and the rest, can never be made lawful. For it can never be that war shall preserve life, and peace destroy it." "The science of them is the true and only moral philosophy," but they are not laws in any true sense of the word. "These dictates of reason, men used to call by the name of laws, but improperly: for they are but conclusions, or theories concerning what conduceth to the preservation and defence of themselves, whereas law, properly, is the word of him that by right hath command over others." Only as we consider them as delivered in the word of God, "that commandeth all things," can they, says Hobbes, be properly called laws.[14]

This concession, however, does not detract from the absolutism of the State, for Hobbes denies that an individual has any certain means of determining what is the will of God in any particular instance, that is, what specific application shall be made of these precepts of Nature which result from the will or command of God. These precepts are morally binding upon the ruler, but for obedience or disobedience to them he is responsible only to his God and never to his subjects. Thus, a civil law may be a *morally* bad one, because it does not conduce to the preservation of the peace and the advancement of the welfare of the people; but it can never be deemed an *unjust* one, "for no law can be unjust. The law is made by the sovereign power, and all that is done by such power is warranted and owned by every one of the people; and that which every man will have so, no man can say is unjust."

In effect, then, Hobbes does not identify the two ideas of legality (or justice) and morality. The morality of an act depends upon whether or not it tends to preserve the lives and advance the fortunes of the people. It is, therefore, an intrinsic quality. Nevertheless, the individual,

[14] *Idem.*

in a civil society, is warranted in accepting as morally right every command issued to him by his sovereign, whatever action or forbearance it may order. To him, no command of the sovereign can be unjust, that is, illegal, because, in the original covenant, the individual is conceived to have agreed to accept as willed by himself whatever may be willed by the person or persons whom he and his fellows have vested with supreme political power. Furthermore, it cannot be immoral, because the maintenance of the authority of the State unimpaired is indispensable if peace and security are to be obtained and these ends are the prime objects of morality. "The first and fundamental" precept of Nature directs that he should enter into and continue to fulfill the original covenant as the sole means whereby peace may be effectively maintained. Thus, to repeat, even for the private individual the ideas of legality and morality, of justness and intrinsic rightfulness, are not identified, but, in actual conduct, what the State orders him to do is both morally and legally right, and sums up for him the entire code of moral conduct.[15]

What are the defects, if there be any, in this course of reasoning?

In the first place it may be denied that, as a matter of fact, individual men are, by their very nature, actuated only by self-regarding motives. In other words, it may be asserted, as did Grotius, and, as we shall presently see, did Locke also, that men have natural instincts or desires which lead to sociability rather than to dominion, and that, therefore, if given free play, these altruistic sentiments will tend to create friendly coöperation rather than a war of all against all.

[15] It will be observed that, according to Hobbes, the sphere of moral conduct is a limited one. It does not include the performance of other than self-regarding acts, that is, morality never rises above enlightened prudence. Hence, he is satisfied to sum up moral obligation in the negative form as calling upon individuals not to do to others what they would not have others do to themselves.

Those who agree with Hobbes, as well as those who side with Grotius and Locke, rest their case upon mere assertion. As regards the question whether men are, or are not, by inherent nature, sociable, and actuated, to an extent at least, by altruistic motives, the truth can be known only when genetic psychologists have cleared up the problem of the origin of such ideas as sympathy, benevolence, justice, and the like. This much is certainly true: that, in creatures of the sub-human orders, which, we may possibly assume, act without intellectual deliberation, we do find parents sacrificing themselves for the protection or sustenance of their young, and even individuals sacrificing themselves for the welfare of the groups to which they belong.[16]

Admitting, however, Hobbes' premise that men are naturally unsociable and self-regarding, but withal reasoning beings, is a contract of each with all the others, according to which all become subjected to a single sovereign authority, the only means by which peace may be secured and political society established? Would it not be conceivable that men, seeing that, by failure to exercise forbearance towards each other, they were defeating their own purposes, should come to a common determination to coöperate and mutually refrain from aggression and violence towards their fellow-beings? If to this it should be responded that it would be absurd to think that there would not always be some individuals who would not come to, or abide by, such a determination, and that those peaceably inclined would have to protect themselves against such, the rejoinder would be that the peaceable and more rational ones could combine for this purpose and coerce, by their superior power, the refractory ones. This, of course, would mean the establishment, to

[16] See the interesting work of Prince Kropotkin, *Mutual Aid among Animals*. It may be argued that these self-sacrificing acts are purely instinctive, and therefore without any conscious motive upon the part of those committing them.

this extent, of political government, but it would not be a government over the individuals creating it, nor can it be said that it would be formed upon, and its sphere of control determined by, an original social or political covenant.

And this leads to what is, after all, the chief question raised by Hobbes' political philosophy. Can it be said that, from a strictly logical point of view, he is able to endow political authority and civil laws with an additional moral force by founding them upon an original social compact? He himself says that, in a State of Nature, such as exists before the covenant is entered into, men are under no moral obligation as to their outward or actual conduct, that is, *in foro externo*. But, if this is so, there is no possible basis upon which they can be morally bound to abide by any agreement that they may enter into. Hobbes concedes that this is the case as long as there exists no power strong enough to compel obedience to agreements. Is it not illogical, however, for him to say that, by an agreement, individuals can bring into being a status in which there is a moral obligation to obey the agreement upon which that status is itself based? Is this not reasoning in a circle? Can a stream rise higher than its source? In other words, would not Hobbes' argument have been more logical, and have reached the same practical conclusion, if he had disregarded entirely the contract idea, either as the original or continuing basis of political society, and frankly said that the only moral justification for the existence of a supreme coercive political authority is derived from its utility to wholly self-regarding individuals; that, therefore, after its establishment, the individual has as much right as he had before, to act as he sees fit and in the manner that his own powers of mind and body make possible; but that, as a matter of fact, he will be wise to give implicit obedience to a common political authority, that is, that, in the long run, it will be to his own individual advantage to do so?

It is the opinion of the present writer that this, from the logical point of view, should have been the course of Hobbes' argument. By introducing the idea of an original covenant he appears to gain something more than a purely utilitarian support for his doctrine of supreme and absolute political power, but it is an adventitious and logically illegitimate one.

Leaving aside, however, this vital defect, and accepting Hobbes' covenant at its face value, certain of its characteristics are to be noted.

By arguing that the necessities of peace (which it is the first and fundamental law of nature that individuals should seek), are such as can be met only by entering into a compact which closes the door to the future right of the individual to withdraw, and by making the agreement one by which each individual covenants with each other individual, and, finally, by making this original social compact include the vesting in the hands of a definite person or number of persons, of the sovereignty of the body politic which sovereignty is indivisible and inalienable, and without legal limit, Hobbes sought to forestall a future claim of right by individuals, or, indeed, by the whole citizen body, to change the location of the sovereignty, or to withdraw from or dissolve the body politic itself. For, the agreement being one between each individual and every other individual, severally regarded, he was able to argue that a withdrawal of any one individual from the compact would be a breach of faith unless the consent of every other person with whom he severally covenanted was obtained. And, the government being instituted, and those in the possession of its powers being vested with authority, not as a result of an agreement between them and the ruled, but as an immediate and necessary product of the social compact itself, Hobbes was able to argue that a State, once established, or created by whatsoever means and having received the implied allegiance of its subjects, resistance to its authority would be a violation of the original social compact—a violation which could not be excused by a claim that those in authority had first violated their agreement, for the rulers were conceived to have secured their authority independently of any agreement to which they were a party.

The fallacies of this highly ingenious reasoning are, in the first place, that, accepting the purely utilitarian basis upon which the existence of political authority is rested by Hobbes, it becomes logically impossible to deny to individuals or to the citizen body the right, when they conceive it to be useful or utilitarian to do so, to alter their form of government, to change their rulers, or to dissolve the State itself. To Hobbes himself, peace undoubtedly appeared of such transcendent importance that anything that would endanger its continuance could be deemed an evil; and, therefore, he thought that, from a purely selfish or utilitarian viewpoint, it was rational that individuals should run the danger of oppression by a government to which they had promised practically unlimited obedience, rather than that they should, by leaving the way open to resistance to those in political authority, render less certain the peace to which is attached such supreme value. But this could be nothing more than his personal opinion regarding what was, or would be, a condition of fact.

If others should disagree with him as to this, and therefore deny that the original compact must rationally contain the terms he gave to it; or if, having agreed to such a compact, individuals, or the whole citizen body, should later come to believe that it would be to their advantage no longer to abide by the agreement, there are no possible logical grounds upon which, granting the utilitarian premises, such a modification of, or withdrawal from, the compact could be morally condemned.

In the second place, as a mere logical proposition, it can be argued that it is not possible for a moral being, by his own act, so to bind his future conduct that, under no circumstances, will it be right, that is, as a utilitarian proposition, for him to refuse to do what he has promised to do. Whenever an act is proposed to be done, at that time the agent must decide, the circumstances being what they then are, what it is right for him to do. The fact that he has promised to do a certain thing, and that the rights of other persons are thus involved, are considerations that must be given their due weight. But these considerations can never be absolutely controlling. The agreement may have been improvidently entered into, fraud, ignorance, or coercion may have been present, or the present circumstances may or could not have been foreseen. Indeed, whatever may be the moral standard adopted, hedonistic or idealistic, utilitarian or transcendental, egoistic or altruistic—a contract absolutely binding for the future is morally an unwarranted one.

In fine, then, even adopting Hobbes' utilitarian premises, such an original contract as he describes would not be the only conceivable one which individuals could enter into as a means of escaping from the evils of a "state of nature," or, if entered into, would not necessarily be of continuing force.

Apparently Hobbes does not distinguish between a group of men as constituting a social unit, and the same group as a body-politic. The purpose and effect of his covenant is, by a single stroke, to create the latter out of a previously existing non-social, non-political, disparate number of individuals. Furthermore, his covenant operates to establish also a definite form of government and to place particular individuals in charge of it. Hobbes clearly recognizes that the question as to what form of government shall be provided is one distinct from the question whether or not a political society shall be created, and this he declares to be a matter of choice upon the part of the individuals who are to be governed.[17] But, apparently, he does not conceive it to be possible to separate the two acts of creating a State and establishing a government for it. And, correspondingly, he is not able to view the overturning of an existing government as anything else than a return to a non-political State of Nature. And, although he admits that there may be a choice between vesting supreme power in the hands of a single individual and the giving of it to a number of persons, he does not admit that the sovereign power itself can be divided or limited. If monarchy be decided upon, it must therefore be an absolute monarchy. A limited monarchy in which supreme power is conceived of as divided between the King and a parliament or other organs of government, he declares, would create an impossible situation. So, also, if the sovereignty be vested in an assembly of men, it must be vested in them in its totality.

In result, then, Hobbes saw no practical distinction between the State as a political entity, to which sovereignty belongs, and the government which is the instrumentality through which the State operates and exercises its sovereignty. Had he accepted this distinction he probably would not have found it necessary to assert that a government must be absolute in character. He would, in other words, have seen that a constitutionally limited monarchy, or other form of constitutional government, is not a contradiction in terms; that the sovereignty of the State is not destroyed by the establishment of constitutional laws which divide the exercise of sovereignty among its several governmental organs and

[17] Hobbes is, however, strongly of opinion that Monarchy is to be preferred. See Chapter XIX of his *Leviathan*.

which deny to any or all of them the exercise of any but specifically delegated powers.

By insisting upon the essential and necessary unity of Sovereignty, as well as by distinguishing, as sharply as he did, civil laws from so-called natural laws, Hobbes prepared the way for the English School of Analytical Jurisprudence which was later to be created by Bentham and Austin.[18] But, it is to be observed, Hobbes does not insist upon the indivisibility and supremeness of sovereignty as a conclusion of formal juristic logic, but rather as a conclusion of practical politics. The State is established to create and maintain peace. It is Hobbes' opinion that

[18] The following quotations from Chapter XXVI of the *Leviathan* entitled "Of Civil Laws" will show how fully Hobbes prepared the way for, and even provided the terminology of, Austin. "Natural are those [laws] which have been laws from all eternity; and are called not only 'natural,' but also 'moral' laws; consisting in the moral virtues, as justice, equity, and habits of the mind that conduce to peace and charity, of which I have spoken in the fourteenth and fifteenth chapters. 'Positive' are those which have not been from eternity; but have been made laws by the will of those that have had the sovereign power over others; and are either written or made known to men by some other argument of the will of their legislator. Again of positive laws some are 'human,' some 'divine' and of human positive laws some are 'distributive,' some 'penal.' . . . 'Divine positive laws' (for natural laws being eternal and universal are all divine) are those which being the commandments of God, not from all eternity, nor universally addressed to all men, but only to a certain people, or to certain persons, are declared for such by those whom God has authorized to declare them." [Hobbes, however, goes on to deny that any persons can infallibly know by natural reason that another has had supernatural revelation of God's will.] "Positive human or Civil Law, is to every subject those rules, which the commonwealth hath commanded him, by word, writing, or other sufficient sign of the will, to make use of, for the distinction of right from wrong; that is to say, of what is contrary and what is not contrary to the rule. The legislator in all commonwealths, is only the sovereign, be he one man as in a monarchy, or one assembly of men, as in a democracy, or aristocracy. For the legislator is he that maketh the laws. . . . The sovereign of a commonwealth, be it an assembly or one man, is not subject to the civil law. For having power to make and repeal laws, he may when he pleaseth free himself from that subjection. . . . When long use obtaineth the authority of a law, it is not the length of time that maketh the authority, but the will of the sovereign signified, by his silence, for silence is sometimes an argument of consent; and it is no longer law, than the sovereign shall be silent thereon."

Austin followed Hobbes in respect to denying a positive legal character to so-called constitutional laws purporting to regulate the exercise of their powers by governmental organs.

the State cannot effectively do this if its power is weakened by division or limited by a reservation of individual rights. This, it will be seen, is an argument different from that which is used to support the unity of sovereignty as a juristic proposition. Most publicists of the present day accept this proposition as a matter of legal logic, but, as a matter of practical expediency, that is, as a question of political policy, they do not believe that it is wise to authorize a single man, or even an assembly of men, to determine by his or their arbitrary and conclusive will what it is desirable that the Government should do. This conviction is based upon certain other beliefs that serve as its premises. These are: (1) that, in a community in which intellectual and moral enlightenment has advanced to any considerable extent, the governed are able to form a wiser judgment as to what is for their own interest than can a monarch or assembly of men; and, (2), that rulers possessing autocratic powers cannot be trusted to put aside selfish interests and always seek the welfare of those whom they govern. Therefore, as a matter of policy, it has seemed best, either to leave to the governed the decision of the more important public policies, or, where rights of initiating and determining these policies are placed in the hands of governmental officials, to provide that they shall act under full legal responsibility, civil and criminal, for acts in excess of their delegated powers, and under political responsibility to the governed, —a responsibility that can be enforced by impeachment, by failure to re-elect, or by other practically effective modes of removing from office those officials whose policies or acts are not approved of by the governed.

CHAPTER XI

SPINOZA AND LOCKE

Spinoza. The criticisms which we have made of Hobbes' theories furnish us with an introduction to those of Spinoza and Locke. Spinoza's doctrines nearly resemble those of Hobbes, but, where they differ, they improve upon them.[1] He makes even more plain than had Hobbes the proposition that if one premises the existence of a non-political, non-social régime there cannot be said to exist any individual rights and duties nor any natural rules that may properly be termed laws. A single quotation will sufficiently show this.

"By the right and ordinance of Nature," he says, "I merely mean those natural laws wherewith we conceive every individual to be conditioned, so as to live and act in a given way. For instance, fishes are naturally conditioned for swimming, and the greater for devouring the less; therefore fishes enjoy the water, and the greater devour the less by sovereign natural rights. For it is certain that nature, taken in the abstract, has sovereign right to do anything she can; in other words, her right is co-extensive with her power. . . . Now it is the sovereign law and right of nature that each individual should endeavor to preserve itself as it is, without regard to anything but itself; therefore this sovereign law and right belongs to every individual, namely, to exist and act according to its natural conditions. We do not here acknowledge any difference between mankind and other in-

---

[1] Spinoza's political theories are to be found in his *Theologico-Political Tractate*, published in 1670, and his unfinished *Political Tractate*, published in 1677.

dividual natural entities, nor between men endowed with reason and those to whom reason is unknown. . . . The natural right of the individual is thus determined, not by sound reason, but by desire and power." [2]

In agreement with Hobbes, Spinoza says that men in a State of Nature are in a condition of war and consequent misery, and are led by their reason to enter into a covenant of each with all whereby a political society is created. Spinoza does not, however, lay the emphasis upon this covenant that Hobbes does. He does not enter into any detailed discussion of its terms, and, what is still more important, he does not, in the political society that is thus established, lessen the natural and moral right of the individual to refuse obedience to such of the commands of the State as it may appear to him inexpedient to obey, and which as a matter of power, he is able to disobey. In other words, in the civil, as well as the natural, state, the question remains one of power, and, in fact, Spinoza describes the original compact rather as a union of powers than as a union of wills. "The sovereigns only possess this right of imposing their will," he says, "so long as they have the full power to enforce it: if such power be lost their right to command it is lost also, or lapses to those who have assumed it and can keep it." This he said in his *Theologico-Political Tractate*.[3] In his *Political Tractate* he says: "If we weigh the matter aright, the natural right of every man does not cease in the civil state. For man, alike in the natural and in the civil state, acts according to the laws of his own nature, and consults his own interest. Man, I say, in each state is led by fear or hope to do or leave undone this or that; but the main difference between the two states is this, that in the civil state, all fear the same things, and all have the same ground of security, and manner of life; and this certainty

[2] *Theologico-Political Tractate*, Chap. XVI.
[3] *Idem.*

does not do away with the individual's faculty of judgment. For he that is minded to obey all the commonwealth's orders, whether through fear of its power or through love of quiet, certainly consults after his own heart his own safety and interest." And, of course, the same is true where the individual is minded to disobey the law, because he believes that thereby he will benefit himself.[4]

In result Spinoza comes to the conclusion that men will find it to their advantage in most cases to yield obedience to the commands of their rulers.[5] This, however, is to be observed as to Spinoza's view regarding the sphere of political authority, that his chief concern seems to be to show that, by its very nature, the political power is not able to control the inner thoughts of men, and that it is inexpedient that it should attempt to prevent their free outward expression "unless they be seditious and overthrow the foundations of the commonwealth." Thus we find in his two Tractates eloquent and convincing arguments in favor of freedom of thought and of speech and press. In the religious field, however, he holds that the State may expediently regulate external rights and the operations of ecclesiastical establishments. In this respect Spinoza is in complete agreement with Hobbes.

Locke.[6] Locke founds his system of political philosophy upon the conception of a State of Nature from

[4] Chapter III. In answer to a correspondent who had asked him to state the difference between himself and Hobbes he wrote (Epistle 50): "I ever save natural right harmless and hold that the sovereign magistrate has no more right over his subjects than is measured by the excess of his power over theirs."
[5] Spinoza, however, differing from Hobbes, finds greater practical advantages in a democratic than in a monarchical form of government. But democracy he defines so as to make of it an aristocracy rather than a democracy as that term is understood at the present time.
[6] Locke's political system is to be found in his *Two Treatises of Government*, published in 1689. The first Treatise is devoted almost exclusively to a refutation of the doctrines of Sir Robert Filmer's *Patriarcha*. In the pages which follow the references are all to the second Treatise.

which man emerges into a political society by means of an agreement to which they are all regarded as parties. Locke, however, comes to conclusions regarding the extent of legitimate governmental control over the individual very different from those of Hobbes. This he is able to do by ascribing to the men living in a state of nature qualities which Hobbes denied. He does not disagree with Hobbes as to the miserable conditions of human life when there is no overruling political authority, but he does assert that in such a pre-political state of society men have an appreciation of their obligation to act socially, and, therefore, that, in such a state, there are moral obligations, even though, for reasons which he states, it is often impracticable for them to be exercised. Thus, while Hobbes had given to the so-called Natural Laws a meaning different from that which they had previously received, Locke revived their meaning as rules or commands intrinsically binding upon men.

Hobbes, as we have seen, starts from the proposition that men are by nature moved wholly by self-regarding desires, and that, therefore, they are essentially nonsocial beings, all seeking dominion over their fellow men rather than friendly coöperation with them. Hobbes' State of Nature is, therefore, a condition of neither social nor political organization. Locke, upon the contrary, views men as by Nature sociable beings who should be moved, whether, in fact, they are or are not so moved, by altruistic feelings, and by mutual recognition of, and respect for, the rights of other persons—rights which owe their origin to ascertainable Natural Laws. Thus, according to his conception, men in a State of Nature should recognize each other as equals, and as entitled to be treated as such, and in accordance with the laws of justice—not merely of expediency or prudence—which Nature or Nature's God supplies. Thus he says: "The State of Nature has a law to govern it, which obliges every one, and reason, which is that law, teaches all mankind who will but consult it, that, being all equal and independent, no one ought to harm another in his life, health, liberty or possessions; for being all the workmanship of one omnipotent and infinitely wise Maker; all servants of one sovereign Master, sent into the world by His order and about His business; they are His property whose workmanship they are made to last during His pleasure, not one another's pleasure. And, being furnished with like faculties, sharing all in one community of Nature, there cannot be supposed any such subordination among us that may authorize us to destroy one another, as if we were made for one another's uses, as the inferior ranks of creatures are for ours." [7] Thus, as he goes on to say, even one who has transgressed against the natural law is not to be treated by those injured thereby as having no rights: retribution is to be exacted not according to "passionate heats of boundless extravagancy," but "as calm reason and conscience dictate, what is proportionate to his transgression, which is so much as may serve for reparation and restraint."

Though thus living in a state of society in which laws and individual rights prevail,[8] there are "inconveniences"

[7] *Two Treatises of Government*, Bk. II, Chap. II. The doctrine here stated, upon theological grounds is essentially the same as that later declared by Kant and his followers, that no human being should be treated by other human beings simply as means for reaching their several ends, but that always these other beings should be regarded as having ends of their own to realize: each one to be a "person" and to treat others as "persons" and not as "things." These Laws of Nature, Locke was confident, could be definitely and fully determined by the human reason if properly applied.

[8] Locke lays great emphasis upon the point that property rights exist in a State of Nature. Indeed, in some places, his language is so unqualified as to suggest that the main purpose of creating governments and civil law is to protect property rights. He declares that the individual's rights to life and health and liberty are in the nature of property rights. As for other kinds of property, he accepts the labor theory that material wealth is the creation of men's labor and belongs to him by whose labor it is created. "Every man has a 'property in his own person.' This nobody has a right to but himself. The 'labor' of his body and the 'work' of his hands, we may say are properly his. Whatsoever, then, he removes out of the state that Nature hath provided and

in a State of Nature which make it appropriate that a political régime be substituted for it. These inconveniences are: (1) that there is no "established, settled, known law received and allowed by common consent to be the standard of right and wrong, and the common measure to decide all controveries between them," (2) that there is no one known and "indifferent" [impartial] judge with authority to determine all differences according to the established law; and (3) that there is often needed a "power to back and support the sentence when right, and to give it due execution."

Even the control exercised by the parent over the child, asserts Locke, is not an arbitrary one, and is permitted by nature only because the child has not a reasoning power that qualifies it to exercise its freedom in a rational manner. Thus, children are not born *into* a full state of equality with adults, but they are born *for* it and become automatically entitled to it as soon as they reach years of discretion. "Thus we are born free as we are born rational; not that we have actually the exercise of either: age that brings one, brings with it the other too." [9]

The problem, then, is, how to establish a political authority that will supply these needs and, at the same time, not violate that natural right which each individual has "to be free from any superior power on earth, and not to be under the will or legislative authority of man, but to have only the law of nature for his rule." The only solution, says Locke, is to establish, and continue to

left it in, he hath mixed his labor with it, and joined it to something that is his own and thereby makes it his property." The whole of Chapter V, from which this quotation is taken, is an interesting discussion of the ethical basis of property rights, and especially interesting is Locke's theory as to the part that has been played by money (the use of which is founded by him upon common consent), in making possible and justifying the building up of large individual fortunes.

[9] The concession here made by Locke, that, until years of discretion are reached, the child is rightfully subject to the control of its parents, is a very important one, and, logically, destructive of much of Locke's reasoning regarding man's natural right to liberty. This will be later shown.

maintain a political authority or government upon the freely given consent of those who are to be controlled by it.

Though not stated as clearly as one could wish, it is evident that Locke distinguishes between a covenant by which individuals are conceived to unite themselves into a single body-politic or corporate, and the two later acts by which a particular form of government is established, and its operation entrusted to specific individuals.

As regards the original or social compact, Locke says: "When any number of men have, by the consent of every individual, made a community, they have thereby made that community one body, with power to act as one body." [10]

Applying strictly this doctrine that a man's natural liberty may not justly be limited except with his consent, Locke maintains that an individual by living, or having possessions in, and enjoying the advantages of, a given commonwealth gives his tacit assent to its laws. He does not, by that fact alone, however, become a member of its body-politic, for he retains the right to remove himself from beneath its control whenever he sees fit. The original signers of the covenant which created the body-

[10] And he adds: "which is only by the will and determination of the majority. For that which acts any community, being only the consent of the individuals of it, and it being one body, must move one way, it is necessary the body should move that way whither the greater force carries it, which is the consent of the majority, or else it is impossible it should act or continue one body, one community, which the consent of every individual that united into it agreed that it should; and so every one is bound by that consent to be concluded by the majority. And therefore we see that in assemblies empowered to act by positive laws where no number is set by that positive law which empowers them, the act of the majority passes for the act of the whole, and of course determines as having, by the law of nature and reason, the power of the whole."

This argument of Locke in behalf of the controlling right of a majority is by no means an adequate one. Especially unsatisfactory is his ascription of argumentative value to the analogy between a body-politic and a material body which, as a matter of physics, must move in the direction in which the greater force is applied. For a further discussion of the relative rights of majorities and minorities, see *post* Chapter XIII.

politic have no such right of removal or secession from the body-politic. Upon this point Locke says:

"Every man that hath any possession or enjoyment of any part of the dominions of any government doth hereby give his tacit consent, and is so far forth obliged to obedience to the laws of that government, during such enjoyment, as any one under it, whether this his possessions be of land to him and his heirs for ever, or a lodging only for a week; and whether it be barely travelling freely on the highway; and, in effect, it reaches as far as the very being of any one within the territories of that government. . . . He is at liberty to go and incorporate himself into any other commonwealth, or agree with others to begin a new one *in vacuis locis,* in any part of the world he can find free and unpossessed, whereas he that has once, by actual agreement and any express declaration, given his consent to be of any commonwealth, is perpetually and indispensably obliged to be, and remain unalterably a subject to it, and can never be again in the liberty of the State of Nature, unless by any calamity the government he was under comes to be dissolved." [11]

The absolutely and eternally binding force of the original compact upon the individual parties to it seems a severe doctrine, especially in a political philosophy designed to support political liberalism, but, in fact, its severity is greatly mitigated by the terms declared by Locke to be necessarily embodied in that compact. This compact, he says, does not, and, reasonably, cannot justify the establishment of absolutism, that is, of a form of government under which those in executive authority are authorized to rule according to their own personal and

[11] As to the historical character of the original compact, which Locke seems to accept, see Chapter VIII of his Second Treatise. Hume, in his essay on the Social Contract, points out that the liberty to leave a society and its territory is, for the ordinary individual, a barren one. It is, he says, as though the captain of a ship, in mid-ocean, were to say to one of his men or passengers: "If you don't like the way I am sailing this ship you are free to leave it."

arbitrary wills. There must be constitutional limitations restraining autocratic power, and the commands of the State must be in the form of general established laws. Locke's doctrine in this respect is thus the antithesis of that of Hobbes. To Hobbes, a limited monarchy is a contradiction of terms, a logical impossibility; to Locke, a monarch is necessarily a constitutionally limited ruler,—a result following from the purposes for which political society is created. He says: "It is evident that absolute monarchy, which by some men is counted for the only government in the world, is indeed inconsistent with civil society, and so can be no form of civil government at all. For the end of civil society is to avoid and remedy those inconveniences of the State of Nature which necessarily follow from every man's being judge in his own case by setting up a known authority to which every one of that society may appeal upon injury received, or controversy that may arise, and which every one of the society ought to obey. Whenever any persons are, who have not such an authority to appeal to, and decide any difference between them there, those persons are still in a State of Nature. And so is every absolute prince in respect to those who are under his dominion. For he being supposed to have all, both legislative and executive power, in himself alone, there is no judge to be found, no appeal lies open to any one, who may fairly and indifferently, and with authority decide, and from whence relief and redress may be expected of any injury or inconveniency that may be suffered from him, or by his order. So that such a man, however entitled Czar, or Grand Seigneur, or how you please, is as much in the State of Nature, with all under his dominion, as he is with the rest of mankind."

In effect, then, Locke stands out conspicuously as the defender, upon abstract or philosophical grounds, of Constitutional Government, which, in his eyes, means three things: (1) that the executive and ultimate legislative powers are placed in different hands; (2) that all the organs of government are to operate through fixed laws known to the people; and (3) that the legitimate powers of all governments, whatever their form, are limited by the natural rights of life, liberty, and property possessed by their citizens or subjects, and that, in fact, the province of political power is confined to the protection of these rights.

Upon this interpretation of the purpose for the attainment of which civil government is established, and upon these conclusions as to the inherent limitations upon political authority, Locke bases his famous justification of the continuing and indefeasible right of a people to determine the form of the government under which, and the rulers by which, they are to be governed.

Here we find drawn the distinction between the original compact by which a people establishes civil society and becomes a body-politic, and the agreement as to the form of government to be erected. Locke writes: "the majority having, as has been shown, upon men's first uniting into society, the whole power of the community naturally in them, may employ that power in making laws for the community from time to time, and executing those laws by officers of their own appointing, and then the form of the government is a perfect democracy; or else may put the power of making laws into the hands of a few select men, and their heirs or successors, and then it is an oligarchy; or else into the hands of one man, and then it is a monarchy; if to him and his heirs, it is a hereditary monarchy; if to him only for life, but upon his death the power only of nominating a successor, to return to them, an elective monarchy. And so accordingly, these make compounded and mixed forms of government, as they think good."

It will be observed that Locke here makes of the establishment of government an operation distinct from the creation of political society. Government is established by an act of the people, as a body-politic, and by a majority of the voices of its constituent individuals, this right of the majority being derived from the original compact. The government, therefore, derives its existence from the constitutive right of the citizen body in which the ultimate sovereignty is vested. Its powers, in other words, are wholly delegated ones, and the authority of those who operate it none other than a fiduciary one. This is to say: the citizen body is the principal, and the government its agent, which latter, consequently, may legitimately act only in accordance with the terms upon which its agency is granted. This means, in the first place, that rulers must respect the provision that has been made for the allocation of specific powers among the several organs of government, and that all public action must be directed to securing the purposes for which political authority has been established.

Governmental authority being of this character, it necessarily results that, when it disregards the purposes for which it exists, or disregards the constitutional modes provided for the exercise of its powers, the sovereign people may refuse obedience to its orders, or, in extreme cases, may withdraw their mandate from the whole government in order that a new form of government may be established, or a new set of rulers placed in power. Locke says:

"For all power given with trust for the attaining of an end being limited by that end, whenever that end is manifestly neglected or opposed, the trust must necessarily be forfeited, and the power dissolve into the hands of those that gave it, who may place it anew where they shall think it best for their safety and security. And thus the community perpetually retains a supreme power of saving themselves from the attempts and designs of any body, even of their legislators, whenever they shall be so foolish or so wicked as to lay and carry on designs against the liberties and properties of the subject."

Locke, however, makes it plain, that this ultimate sovereignty of the people is, essentially, though not illegal, in the sense of being a violation of the original governmental compact, nevertheless, a revolutionary one, and is, to be exercised only in cases of extreme need. Thus, as long as a Government lasts, the exercise of political powers is exclusively in its hands. "The community may be said in this respect to be always the supreme power, but not as considered under any form of government, because this power of the people can never take place till the government be dissolved." And, he adds: "In all cases whilst the government subsists, the legislature is the supreme power."

The last chapter of Locke's *Two Treatises* deals with "The Dissolution of Governments." He begins with the statement that "he that will, with any clearness, speak of the dissolution of Government, ought in the first place to distinguish between the dissolution of society and the dissolution of the Government." After again stating the fundamental purposes for which political society is established, he states his doctrine of the right of revolution in the following terms:

"Whensoever, therefore, the legislative shall transgress this fundamental rule of society, and, either by ambition, fear, folly, or corruption, endeavor to grasp themselves, or put into the hands of any other, an absolute power over the lives, liberties and estates of the people; by this breach of trust they forfeit the power the people had put into their hands for quite contrary ends, and it devolves to the people, who have a right to resume their original liberty, and by the establishment of a new legislative (such as they shall think fit), provide for their own safety and security, which is the end for which they are in society. What I have said here concerning the legislative in general holds true also concerning the supreme executor, who, having a double trust put in him, both to have a part in the legislative and the supreme execution of the law, acts against both, when he goes about to set up his own arbitrary will as the law of society."

If, against this doctrine, it be charged that it "lays a ferment for frequent revolutions," Locke says, "I answer, such revolutions happen not upon every little mismanagement in public affairs. Great mistakes in the ruling part, many wrong and inconvenient laws, and all the steps of human frailty will be borne by the people without mutiny or murmur. But if a long train of abuses, prevarications, and artifices, all tending the same way, make the design visible to the people, and they cannot but feel what they lie under, and see whither they are going, it is not to be wondered that they should then rouse themselves, and endeavor to put the rule into such hands which may secure to them the ends for which Government was at first erected."

There is little question that the conclusions which Locke reaches are in substantial agreement with those of modern political thought, and are those upon which are founded the constitutional systems of nearly all present-day civilized peoples.[12] To what extent he has employed the proper reasoning in support of them will be considered after the doctrines of Rousseau have been stated and thus the way prepared for a general estimate of the merits of the compact theory.

[12] Japan, at the present time, stands as the only Power, claiming to be civilized, which repudiates these conclusions.

CHAPTER XII

ROUSSEAU

UNTIL recently writers have found it difficult to give a satisfactory statement of Rousseau's political theories because of what has appeared to be glaring inconsistencies between his views as stated in his discourses, *Has the Restoration of the Arts and Sciences Had a Purifying Effect upon Morals?* and *What is the Origin of Inequality among Men, and Is It Authorized by Natural Law?* and his *Social Contract.* For the *"Discourses"* have seemed to defend an individualistic system of moral and social or political philosophy, whereas his *Social Contract,* except in its first few pages, has seemed to emphasize the rightful authority of the State over the individual. However, Professor A. O. Lovejoy in a notable essay entitled *The Supposed Primitivism of Rousseau's Discourse on Inequality* [1] has shown that difficulties in harmonizing Rousseau's various statements, especially with reference to conditions that may be supposed to have prevailed before men became politically organized, disappear when it is seen that Rousseau used the term "State of Nature" in four distinct senses, which represented in his mind four clearly marked stages in the evolution of human society, and that, while one of these stages—the third—presented to his mind conditions of life that were ideal, and preferable to those which were later secured when men had become politically organized, the other pre-political or "natural" stages presented to men conditions of life which were emphatically less desirable. In the pages

[1] Published in the November, 1923, issue of *Modern Philology* (Vol. XXI, No. 2, pp. 165-186).

which immediately follow, this analysis by Professor Lovejoy of Rousseau's conceptions of non-political conditions of life will be closely followed and thus the way paved for a satisfactory statement of the doctrines of the *Social Contract* as to the ethically legitimate grounds upon which, and upon which alone in Rousseau's belief, political coercion may be defended.

According to Rousseau, in the first stage of human development, when men were just as they had been created by nature, they differed but little, except potentially, from the other animals. No social life existed, the family had not been created, and the relations between the sexes were impermanent and only casual. "Let us conclude, then," he says in his *Discourse on the Origin of Inequality*, "that man, in a State of Nature, wandering up and down the forests, without industry, without speech, and without home, an equal stranger to war and to all ties, neither standing in need of his fellow-creatures nor having any desire to hurt them, and perhaps not even distinguishing them from one another; let us conclude that, being self-sufficient and subject to so few passions, he could have no feelings or knowledge but such as befitted his situation; that he felt only his actual necessities, and disregarded everything he did not think himself immediately concerned to notice, and that his understanding made no greater progress than his vanity. If by accident he made any discovery, he was the less able to communicate it to others, as he did not know even his own children. Every art would necessarily perish with its inventor, where there was no kind of education among men, and generations succeeded generations without the least advance; when, all setting out from the same point, centuries must have elapsed in the barbarism of the first ages; when the race was already old, and man remained a child."

Only if man be viewed as a purely physical being, and

the matter of his health alone be considered, could this type of existence, said Rousseau, be considered a desirable one for man. "If," declared he, in an often quoted sentence, "she [Nature] intended us to be healthy, I venture to affirm that the state of reflection is a state contrary to nature and that the man who thinks is a man depraved." But it scarcely needs be said that Rousseau did not view man as nothing more than an animal or purely physical being.

In this first, or animal, state of existence, men were not conceived by Rousseau to have been, except potentially, moral beings, although he conceived that they probably had innate feelings of sympathy for, or at least repugnance to, the sufferings of others,—feelings that ultimately were to lead to the establishment of social relations among themselves. In the Preface to his *Discourse on Inequality* he said: "Contemplating the first and most simple operations of the human soul, I think that I can perceive two principles prior to reason, one of them deeply interesting us in our own welfare and preservation, and the other exciting a natural repugnance at seeing our species suffer pain and death. It is from the agreement and combination which the understanding is in a position to establish between these two principles, without its being necessary to introduce that of sociability, that all the rules of natural right appear to me to be derived—rules which our reason is afterwards obliged to establish on other foundations when by its successive developments it has been led to suppress nature itself."

The second stage of human development, one that existed many centuries, was one during which, according to Rousseau, men learned to use simple tools and weapons, to unite into groups for mutual protection, to establish permanent family relations, and to recognize private ownership of personal belongings such as the instruments of production and of warfare.

The third stage of pre-political development was reached when this process of social evolution had been completed, village life established, and patriarchal authority recognized. This is the stage which Rousseau lauds as the ideal one for man and from which he regrets that man should have separated. He writes: "This period of expansion of the human faculties, keeping a just mean between the indolence of the primitive state and the petulant activity of our egoism, must have been the happiest and most stable of epochs. The more we reflect on it, the more we shall find that this state was the least subject to revolutions, and altogether the very best man could experience; so that he can have departed from it only through some fatal accident, which, for the public good, should never have happened. . . . So long as men remained content with their rustic huts, so long as they were satisfied with clothes made of the skins of animals and sewn together with thorns and fishbones, adorned themselves only with feathers and shells, and continued to paint their bodies different colors, to improve and beautify their bows and arrows and to make with sharp-edged stones fishing boats or clumsy musical instruments: in a word, so long as they undertook only what a single person could accomplish, and confined themselves to such arts as did not require the joint labor of several hands, they lived free, healthy, honest and happy lives, so long as their nature allowed, and as they continued to enjoy the pleasure of mutual and independent intercourse."

It is, then, to this State of Nature, when social life was simple and unaffected, and when substantial equality in economic conditions among all the members of each group prevailed, that Rousseau devotes his praise and commendation. The "unfortunate accident," of which he speaks, that took men out of this idyllic existence, was when men entered upon forms of economic activity which made them dependent upon one another, and, especially, when private property in land was established. "From the moment," he says, "when one man began to stand in need of the help of another, from the moment it appeared advantageous to any man to have enough provisions for two, equality disappeared, property was introduced, work became indispensable, and vast forests became smiling fields, which man had to water with the sweat of his brow, and where starving and misery were seen to germinate and grow up with the crops." "The first man," he says in another place, "who, having enclosed a piece of ground, bethought himself of saying 'This is mine,' and found people simple enough to believe him, was the real founder of civil society. From how many crimes, wars and murders, from how many horrors and misfortunes, might not any one have saved mankind, by pulling up the stakes, or filling up the ditch, and crying to his fellows, 'Beware of listening to this impostor; you are undone if you once forget that the fruits of the earth belong to us all, and the earth itself to nobody.' "

Thus, according to Rousseau, man ushered in that fourth non-political state of human existence which became evil in the extreme and which corresponded to that State of Nature which Hobbes had described. From this condition of life it became indispensable to escape, and the means of escape which the people sought was the establishment of political authority, the creation of the State. But, unfortunately, believes Rousseau, because the peoples of the world had not founded their several States upon proper grounds,—had not based them upon a common and continuing popular consent—the remedy had led to a slavery greater than that from which they had sought to release themselves. Though born free, they found themselves everywhere in chains.[2]

[2] *Social Contract*, Bk. I, Chap. I. Rousseau was convinced that there was an inherent tendency in governments to become autocratic and oppressive. "As the particular will acts incessantly against the general will, so the government makes a continual effort against the sover-

In his *Discourse*, written in 1749 and published in 1751,[3] Rousseau had examined the question whether the restoration of the Sciences and the Arts had contributed to the purification of morals, and had come to a negative conclusion. Indeed, he went further than this and maintained the thesis that the development of social relations, and of what is ordinarily termed Civilization, had operated to corrupt the natural innocency of man, and bring to an end the pleasures of simplicity and freedom which, in his primitive, natural state, man had enjoyed. The essay was, however, rather an attack or satire upon the evils and vices of the society of his day than a constructive attempt to establish a system of morals upon a purely naturalistic basis. It was in his second *Discourse upon the Origin of Inequality among Men,* published in 1755 that he entered more definitely the political field, and stated his conceptions of the conditions that had prevailed prior to, and which had led to, the establishment of political authority.

In his *Social Contract,* published in 1762, which bears the sub-title *Principles of Political Right,* he undertook the affirmative task of establishing the grounds upon which political authority should rest in order that the benefits of supreme coercive rule and generally binding laws might be secured without the evils which, as history showed and existing conditions manifested, had resulted from the substitution of political for non-political or "natural" modes of human existence. In his very first sentence he said: "I wish to inquire whether, taking men as they are and laws as they can be made, it is possible

eignty [of the people]. . . . Therein is the inherent and inevitable vice which, from the birth of the body-politic, tends without intermission to destroy it, just as old age and death at length destroy the human body." *Social Contract,* Bk. III, Chap. X. The title of this chapter is "The Abuse of Government and Its Tendency to Degenerate."

[3] *Discours sur les Sciences et les Arts.*

to establish a just and certain rule of civil administration.[4]

In his *Social Contract*, Rousseau devotes but a few paragraphs to the ideas of nature and natural law. He is, however, emphatic upon the point that a political mode of existence is far preferable to that stage of "natural" development into which, prior to the establishment of political society, and as described in the *Discourse on Inequality*, mankind had been brought. He says:

"The passage from the state of nature to the civil state produces in man a very remarkable change, by substituting in his conduct justice for instinct, and by giving his actions the moral quality they had previously lacked. It is only when the voice of duty succeeds physical impulse, and law succeeds appetite, that man, who till then had regarded only himself, sees that he is obliged to act on other principles, and to consult his reason before listening to his inclinations. Although, in this state, he is deprived of many advantages that he derives from nature, he acquires equally great ones in return; his faculties are exercised and developed; his ideas are expanded; his feelings are ennobled; his whole soul is exalted to such a degree that, if the abuses of this new condition did not often degrade him below that from which he has emerged, he ought to bless without ceasing the happy moment

[4] Book I, Introductory Note. In a Prefatory note Rousseau informs the reader that the present "little treatise" is extracted from a larger work earlier undertaken, but long since abandoned. Vaughan, in his Introduction to his edition of Rousseau's political writings, emphasizes the combination, in the *Social Contract*, of the practical and speculative purposes. That Rousseau was well aware that no one form of government or system of laws is the best for all peoples is shown in the following statements from his *Social Contract*. "The same laws cannot be suitable to so many different provinces, which have different climates, and cannot tolerate the same government," Book II, Chap. IX. "The wise lawgiver does not begin by drawing up laws that are good in themselves, but considers first whether the people for whom he designs them are fit to endure them," Book II, Chap. VIII. "We must assign to each nation a particular system of institutions which shall be the best, not perhaps in itself, but for the State for which it is designed," Book II, Chap. XI. Chapter VIII of Book III is entitled "That Every Form of Government Is Not Fit for Every Country."

that released him from it for ever, and transformed him from a stupid and ignorant animal into an intelligent being and a man. Besides the preceding, we might add to the acquisitions of the civil state, moral freedom, which alone renders man truly master of himself; for the impulse of mere appetite is slavery, while obedience to self-prescribed law is liberty." [5]

In his short chapter entitled "Primitive Societies" [6] Rousseau, aside from short animadversions upon the views of Grotius, Hobbes, and Aristotle, has no more to say of men's pre-social condition than that they are all born free and equal; that common liberty is a consequence of man's nature; that his first law is to attend to his own preservation, and that his first cares are those which he owes to himself.[7]

That Rousseau continued to hold the doctrine of his *Discourse on Equality,* that the State of Nature is one in which there are no moral laws, and that the liberty which men enjoy in such a state is determined wholly by their several powers, is shown in the paragraph already quoted in which he describes the Civil State. To that description he adds: "What man loses by the social contract is his natural liberty and an unlimited right to anything which tempts him and which he is able to attain; what he gains is civil liberty and property in all that he possesses. In order that we may not be mistaken about these compensations, we must clearly distinguish natural liberty, which is limited only by the powers of the individual, from civil liberty, which is limited by the general will; and possession, which is nothing but the result of force or the right

---

[5] Book I, Chap. VIII.
[6] Book I, Chap. II.
[7] The family Rousseau concedes to be the earliest and only natural form of society, but says that the natural bond of the child to its parents is dissolved as the need for protection disappears. "The children being freed from the obedience which they owed to their father, and the father from the cares which he owed to his children, become equally independent."

of first occupancy, from property, which can be based only on a positive title."

Rousseau, then, is scarcely behind Hobbes in asserting that morality, as well as legality, is the product of political society.[8] But, as will presently be seen, he is poles apart from Hobbes in his conception of the nature of ethically legitimate political authority, and what may be deemed to be an authentic expression of its supreme will.

Having posited the natural freedom and equality of all men, and admitted the need for, and advantages of, civil society, Rousseau sees clearly, and faces fairly, the problem that is presented, namely: "To find a form of association which may defend and protect with the whole force of the community the person and property of every associate, and by means of which each, uniting with all, may nevertheless obey only himself, and remain as free as before." [9] The only solution, he finds, is to base political authority upon the consent, freely given, of every individual subjected to it, but, at the same time, to maintain a régime under which every command of that power represents and reflects the true will of those whose acts are to be controlled by it. It is not enough, therefore, according to Rousseau, that an original social compact should be conceived as entered into. It is necessary that the terms of this compact shall be such as will leave still subsisting the liberty of the individual to guide his conduct by what he himself deems to be morally right and to his own true interest.

Rousseau states more explicitly than any of his predecessors had done the necessity of explaining how a group of individuals becomes a single corporate unit, and, as such, qualified to enter into an agreement for the institu-

---

[8] There appears here some inconsistency in Rousseau's thought, for, in his *Discourse on Inequality* there is an indication that, prior to the establishment of political society, human acts did not wholly lack a moral quality.
[9] Book I, Chap. VI.

tion of a particular form of government. "Before examining the act by which a nation elects a king," he says, "it would be proper to examine the act by which a nation becomes a nation, for this act, being necessarily anterior to the other, is the real foundation of society."

This original society-creating act is the Social Compact, the provisions of which are determined by its very nature, and are therefore unalterable and inviolable. Describing the nature and scope of this contract, Rousseau says:

"These clauses, rightly understood, are reducible to one only, namely, the total alienation to the whole community of each associate with all his rights." Thereby, he says, perfect equality is maintained, and, furthermore, liberty is not surrendered, for, "each giving himself to all, gives himself to nobody; and, as there is not one associate over whom all do not acquire the same rights which we concede to him over ourselves, we gain the equivalent of all that we lose, and more power to preserve what we have. . . . Each of us puts in common his person and his whole power under the direction of the General Will; and, in return, we receive, every member, as an indivisible part of the whole. Forthwith, in place of the individual personalities of all the contracting parties, this act of association produces a moral and collective body, which is composed of as many members as the assembly has voices, and which receives from this same act its unity, its common self (*moi commun*), its life and its will. This public person, which is thus formed by the union of all the individual members, "he continues," formerly took the name of city (*cité*) and now takes that of republic or body-politic, which is called by its members State when it is passive, Sovereign when it is active, Power when it is compared with similar bodies. With regard to the associates, they take collectively the name of People, and are called individually Citizens, as participating in the sovereign power, and Subjects, as subjected to the laws of the State."

The significant feature of this envisagement of the Social Compact is the ascription of personality to the unity that is created, and the investment of this *moi commun* with a will of its own—a General Will which is politically supreme. Sovereignty is thus stated in terms of will rather than of power, and is viewed as the essential attribute of the State and not of its Government—the ideas of State and Government being clearly differentiated.[10]

This conception of a real General Will (*volonté générale*) is Rousseau's most important contribution to political theory as well as to social psychology, and deserves to be carefully considered. The General Will is regarded, not as an arithmetical sum of the particular wills of the individual citizens, but as voicing the true will of each and every one of them. It, therefore, ever voices a unanimous will upon their part. Not that individuals may not, upon occasion, desire something else than is declared by this General Will, but that, when so desiring, they are to be deemed to be moved by accidental and casual motives, and thus, in effect, to wish for something other than what is consonant with their own true interests, and, therefore, something which, *ex hypothesi,* they do not truly desire. In such cases, says Rousseau, the conflict between the individual and the General Will is in appearance only. In reality there can be no opposition,

[10] In his article on *Political Economy,* antedating by several years his *Social Contract,* Rousseau had already developed his idea of the State as a corporate, or, as the French say, a "moral" person. He there wrote: "The body-politic, therefore, is also a moral being possessed of a will; and this General Will, which tends to the preservation and welfare of the whole and of every part, and is the source of the laws, constitutes for all the members of the State, in their relations to one another and to it, the rule of what is just or unjust." And, later on, he distinguishes between this General Will and the particular wills of individuals, and asserts that "the first and most important rule of legitimate or popular government, that is to say, of government whose object is the good of the people, is therefore, as I have observed, to follow in everything the General Will."

and, even should it be impossible to convince the dissident citizen of this, and coercion be applied to compel him to conform to the declarations of the General Will, he is, in essential fact, required only to do what his true and better judgment, if he would allow it to operate, would call upon him to do. "Indeed," he says, "every individual may, as a man, have a particular will contrary to, or divergent from, the General Will which he has as a citizen; his private interest may prompt him quite differently from the common interest; his absolute and naturally independent existence may make him regard what he owes to the common cause as a gratuitous contribution, the loss of which will be less harmful to others than the payment of it will be burdensome to him; and, regarding the moral person that constitutes the State as an imaginary being because it is not a man, he would be willing to enjoy the rights of a citizen without being willing to fulfil the duties of a subject. The progress of such injustice would bring about the ruin of the body-politic. In order, then, that the social pact may not be a vain formulary, it tacitly includes this engagement, which can alone give force to the others, that whoever refuses to obey the General Will shall be constrained to do so by the whole body; which means nothing else than that he shall be forced to be free."

As a practical proposition, says Rousseau, the majority are given, by the original compact, the right to coerce the minority. But, are not the ones thus coerced deprived of their liberty? This question, Rousseau avers is wrongly put. "The citizen consents to all the laws, even to those which are passed in spite of him, and even to those which punish him when he dares to violate any of them. The unvarying will of all the members of the State is the General Will; it is through that will they are citizens and free. When a law is proposed in the assembly of the people, what is asked of them is not exactly whether they approve the proposition or reject it, but whether it is conformable or not to the General Will, which is their own; each, in giving his vote, expresses his opinion thereupon; and from the counting of the votes is obtained the declaration of the General Will. When, therefore, the opinion opposed to my own prevails, that simply shows that I was mistaken, and that what I considered to be the General Will was not so. Had my private opinion prevailed, I should have done something other than I wished; and in that case I should not have been free." [11]

Returning to this subject, Rousseau, in a later chapter, says: "There is but one law which by its nature requires unanimous consent, that is, the social compact; for civil association is the most voluntary act in the world; every one being born free and master of himself, no one can, under any pretext whatever, enslave him without his assent. . . . If, then, at the time of the social compact, there are opponents of it, their opposition does not invalidate the contract, but only prevents them from being included in it; they are foreigners among citizens. . . . When the State is established, consent lies in residence; to dwell in the territory is to submit to the sovereign."

It is after the foregoing argument that Rousseau goes on to state the advantages of the civil over the natural state, in the paragraph which has been earlier quoted. The result, then, is that, in the civil state, the individual for the first time finds it possible to live a rational, moral life, not merely because, as Hobbes viewed it, peace and protection are provided, or because, as Locke declared, impartial judges and known rules of conduct and an executive power are supplied, but also because the individual is, as it were, protected against himself. He is compelled to be guided by the volitions of his truer and better self.

[11] Book IV, Chap. II.

Now, it does not need to be pointed out that the integrity of Rousseau's reasoning is dependent upon the securing in veritable fact of a General Will which will always seek the true welfare of each and every one of the persons controlled by it; otherwise, to the extent to which it does not do this, individuals will be compelled to do what their own true wills would not sanction, and, therefore, the freedom, which is inherently theirs, will be violated. Rousseau sees this very plainly, and, therefore, takes care to point out the circumstances under which the formulation and enunciation of a General Will is, in his opinion, possible, and to describe the qualities that must be exhibited by a law or command in order that it may properly claim to be an expression of this General Will.

In the first place, as regards its formulation, Rousseau says that care must be taken to exclude from it the particularistic elements that are ever present in individual wills. This, he says, can be done only when these particularistic elements are made to cancel one another; and this result can be obtained only when there are a considerable number of participants or voters so that there is opportunity for the application of what statisticians have since termed the law of compensating errors. "The General Will," says Rousseau, "is always right and always tends to the public advantage, but it does not follow that the resolutions of the people have always the same rectitude. Men always desire their own good, but do not always discern it; the people are never corrupted, though often deceived, and it is only then that they seem to will what is evil. There is often a great deal of difference between the will of all (*volonté de tous*) and the General Will (*volonté générale*); the latter regards only the common interest, while the former has regard to the private interests, and is merely a sum of particular wills; but take away from these same wills the pluses and minuses which cancel one another, and the General Will remains as the sum of the differences."

"If," he continues, "the people come to a resolution when adequately informed and without any communication among the citizens, the General Will would always result from the great number of slight differences, and the resolution would always be good. But when factions, partial associations, are formed to the detriment of the whole society, the will of each of these associations becomes general with reference to its members, and particular with reference to the State; it may then be said that there are no longer as many voters as there are men, but only as many voters as there are associations. The differences become less numerous and yield a less general result. Lastly, when one of these associations becomes so great that it predominates over all the rest, you no longer have a sum of differences, but a single difference; there is then no longer a General Will, and the opinion which prevails is only a particular opinion. It is important, then, in order to have a clear declaration of the General Will, that there should be no partial association in the State, and that every citizen should express only his own opinion."

Elsewhere Rousseau says: "Long discussions, dissensions, and uproar proclaim the ascendency of private interests and the decline of the State."

It is clear, then, that Rousseau would have legislation performed in the simplest form, and without preliminary discussions or "campaigns of education," and, of course, without the interference of political parties. Not much legislation, he thinks, should be attempted.[12]

[12] "A State thus governed needs very few laws; and insofar as it becomes necessary to promulgate new ones, this necessity is universally recognized. The first man to propose them only gives expression to what all have previously felt, and neither factions nor eloquence will be needed to pass into law what every one has already resolved to do, so soon as he is sure the rest will act as he does." Book IV, Chap. I. But see the interesting chapter (Book II, Chap. VII) in which Rousseau argues

So much for the manner in which, according to Rousseau, the General Will is to be determined. But equally, if not more, important to him is the question of the necessary content of the laws which are the expressions of this will, for it is an essential part of his theory not only that each individual shall consent to the laws which bind him, but that these laws, when so consented to, shall equally bind every other citizen. Only in this way, he says, does the individual, while obeying the State, remain as free as before the State was established; only when this is so is there a sure guarantee that the selfish motives of each voter will lead to the establishment of laws that are for the good of all. Thus, Rousseau's General Will is as much characterized by the generality of its application as by the generality of the mode of its creation. "The undertakings which bind us to the social body," he says, "are obligatory only because they are mutual: and their nature is such that in fulfilling them we cannot work for others without working for ourselves. Why is it that the General Will is always right, and that all continually will the happiness of each one, unless it is because there is not a man who does not think of 'each' as meaning him, and consider himself in voting for all? . . . It proves that the General Will, to be really such, must be general in its object as well as its essence; that it must both come from all and apply to all; and it loses its natural rectitude when it is directed to some particular and determinate object." [13]

that a person of superior intelligence, like a Lycurgus or Solon, is needed to give to a people their first code of law. Such a legislator would, however, not have the right to enact his laws, but merely propose them to the people for adoption who, says Rousseau, while unable themselves to determine what laws are needed, are able, collectively, to perceive the goodness of good law when presented to them. "Individuals see the good which they reject; the public desire the good which they do not see. All alike have need of guides. The former must be compelled to conform their wills to their reason; the people must be taught to know what they require."

[13] *Social Contract*, Bk. II, Chap. IV.

All true laws, therefore, according to Rousseau, must be of general application and must relate to "subjects collectively, and actions as abstract, never a man as an individual nor a particular action. Thus the law may indeed decree that there shall be privileges, but cannot confer them on any person by name; the law can create several classes of citizens, and even assign the qualifications which shall entitle them to rank in these classes, but it cannot nominate such and such persons to be admitted to them; it can establish a royal government and a hereditary succession, but cannot elect a king or appoint a royal family; in a word, no function which has reference to an individual object appertains to the legislative power." [14]

In result, then, the element of compact is employed by Rousseau as a means for bringing a State into ethically legitimate being; his conception of the nature of valid law as an expression of the *volonté générale* is employed to determine what a State may rightfully do after it has been created.

The *volonté générale* of the *moi commun,* brought into existence by the social compact, necessarily remains in the people. It is indivisible, indefeasible and inalienable, for, as Rousseau says, while power may be transmitted, will may not. And here we come to his distinction between legislative and executive authority,—between the State and its Government.

To the State, the body-politic, ever belongs the right of making laws, that is, laws general in character and directed to the general interest. To the Government, which is the minister or agent of the State, belongs the executive authority. Government is "an intermediate body established between the subjects and the sovereign for their mutual correspondence, charged with the execution of the laws and with the maintenance of liberty both civil

[14] Book II, Chap. VI.

and political." It is not founded upon a contract between the governed, or between them and their rulers. It is nothing more than a commission, or employment, and, apparently, never vested with true legislative authority. All that it may do is to interpret and apply the expressions of the sovereign legislative will, and, presumably, supplement them with the necessary orders or ordinances for carrying them into effect. If new laws are needed, or old laws require to be amended or repealed, resort must be had to the sovereign people.[15]

The people, Rousseau maintains, can act only directly; they cannot act through representatives. "Sovereignty cannot be represented for the same reason that it cannot be alienated; it consists essentially in the General Will and will cannot be represented. . . . The deputies of the people, then, are not and cannot be, its representatives; they are only its commissioners and can conclude nothing definitely. Every law which the people in person have not ratified is invalid; it is not a law."

But how, as a practical proposition, does Rousseau think it possible that the people can so act?

In the first place, Rousseau believes, as has been already pointed out, that few general laws are needed. In the second place, he holds that such an ethically legitimate State as he has in mind is possible only if it be one of very small size. "After careful consideration," he says, "I do not see that it is possible henceforward for the sovereign [the people] to preserve among us the exercise of its rights unless the State is very small." [16]

In order that the people may exercise their sovereign

[15] The establishment of a government, says Rousseau, is a complex act composed of two others. By the first, the form of government is determined upon. This is a law—an act of the sovereign people. By the second, the people nominate the persons who are to administer the government when established. This being a particular measure, is not a law, but a special order, resulting from the first act fixing the form of government.

[16] Rousseau relies upon confederations of small States to maintain themselves against foreign aggression.

will, it is necessary that they all meet together periodically, or in specially convened assemblies.[17] When so gathered together as a sovereign body "the whole jurisdiction of the government ceases, the executive power is suspended, and the person of the meanest citizen is as sacred and inviolable as that of the first magistrate." [18]

When assembled, says Rousseau, two propositions should immediately be laid before the people and separately voted upon: "Whether it pleases the sovereign [i.e. the people] to maintain the present form of government"; and "whether it pleases the people to leave the administration to those at present entrusted with it."

Inasmuch as, in the present treatise, we are dealing only with the ethical foundations of the State, it will not be necessary to give an account of Rousseau's views regarding the comparative merits of different forms of Government. It is, however, of interest to note that, in the abstract, democracy is declared to be the best form, but, as a practical proposition, suited only to few States. As to democratic government, he says: "How many things, difficult to combine, does not this form of government presuppose. First, a very small State, in which the people may be readily assembled, and in which every citizen can easily know all the rest; secondly, great simplicity of manners, which prevents a multiplicity of

[17] These assemblies, he says, must meet in accordance with existing law.

[18] There is to be noted the similarity of this theory to the doctrine which has received considerable acceptance in American constitutional jurisprudence, that, when a constitutional convention has met, the entire citizen body is deemed to be constructively present in its original sovereign capacity, and that, therefore, without regard to what may have been the terms upon which the convention was summoned, it may do anything it will. It can draft and promulgate an entirely new constitution, amend the old, or perform ordinary governmental acts, as, for example, the appropriation of public moneys or the issuance of executive orders. The American theory differs from that of Rousseau in that this sovereign power is conceived of as possible of exercise by a representative body, and that, though the Convention is superior to the existing government, the powers of that Government are not, *ipso facto*, in abeyance. See Jameson, *The Constitutional Convention*, and Hoar, *Constitutional Conventions: Their Nature, Powers and Limitations*.

affairs and thorny discussions; next, considerable equality in rank and fortunes, without which equality in rights and authority could not long subsist; lastly, little or no luxury, for luxury is either the effect of wealth or renders it necessary; it corrupts both the rich and the poor, the former by possession, the latter by covetousness; it betrays the country to effeminacy and vanity; it deprives the State of all its citizens in order to subject them one to another, and all to opinion. . . . If there were a nation of Gods, it would be governed democratically. So perfect a government is unsuited to men."

CHAPTER XIII

VIEWS OF HOBBES, LOCKE AND ROUSSEAU COMPARED AND THE CONTRACT THEORY CRITICIZED

IF now, by way of summary, we compare Rousseau's doctrines with those of Hobbes and Locke, we find, as the most important, the following resemblances and differences.

Rousseau agrees with Hobbes that men in a State of Nature are not sociable; but denies that they are natural enemies of each other. To the instinct of self-preservation with which alone Hobbes endows the natural man, Rousseau adds that of pity or sympathy. In agreement with Hobbes, Rousseau denies that, in a State of Nature, laws, or rights, or moral feelings, or even reason, to any degree of development, can exist. These are products of civil or political life.

There are, however, these differences between the two as regards the nature, location, and mode of exercise of supreme political right. Hobbes distinguishes between State and Government, but regards it as an ineluctable necessity that, at the time the social contract is entered into, and as, indeed, a part of that contract, absolutely unlimited discretionary authority to voice the State's will shall be vested in some definite monarch or assembly of men. Rousseau, upon the contrary, holds that this sovereign legislative power must ever remain in the people as united, that is, in the State. He agrees with Hobbes that there is no contract between the governed and their governors, but vests in the latter only the subordinate function of carrying into execution the State's General

Will. And, even this authority is subject to revocation at any time when the State, that is, the People, in their corporate capacity, so wills. Thus, while Hobbes and Rousseau both emphasize the supremeness and omnicompetence of the State's sovereignty, with Hobbes it is essentially a juristic conception (though its commands are also morally obligatory upon the citizen or subject). With Rousseau this sovereignty is rather the ultimate political and moral force in the community—a force exercised outside of and above the existing Government as he defines that term. Both Hobbes and Rousseau agree that the individual, in a political community, remains possessed of no rights which are exempt from the control of his State. "It is admitted," says Rousseau, "that whatever part of his power, property and liberty each one alienates by the social compact is only that part of the whole of which the use is important to the community." He adds, however, the qualification, "but we must admit that the sovereign alone is judge of what is important." [1] Thus both Rousseau and Hobbes agree that the original compact operates wholly to deprive the individual of any right henceforth to use his powers as he will for the satisfaction of his own desires. Both, in short, and to repeat, emphasize the sovereignty or omnipotence of the State.

Turning, now, to a comparison of the views of Rousseau and Locke we find, as regards the State of Nature, that, whereas Locke invests the natural man with nearly all the social virtues, Rousseau endows him only with pity or compassion. Also, and largely dependent upon this difference of view, whereas Locke asserts the existence in a State of Nature of a body of definite personal and property rights, Rousseau denies that there can validly be any such. To Locke, the original social compact is one whose terms are not definitely fixed by its very nature,

[1] *Social Contract*, Book II, Chap. IV.

but may be varied as the compacting individuals may see fit. They may not part with their rights to life, liberty and property, but, short of this, they can come to any agreement they desire. To Rousseau, upon the contrary, as with Hobbes, the nature of the agreement fixes its terms, and these necessarily provide for the total subjection of the covenanting individuals to the will of the political personality that is brought into being. In Locke, there is, apparently, little conception of the State as a moral or juristic personality whose will is sovereign. Nor do we find the fruitful conception of Rousseau that this will is ethically entitled to control because it represents the fundamentally true wills of the individuals to whom its commands are directed. Rousseau and Locke are, however, in agreement in stressing the fact that the essential sovereign function of the State is legislative rather than executive.

The Truth and Error in the Contract Theory

The inadequacy of the Contract Theory to furnish an ethical basis for the exercise of political coercion is now generally recognized. The review which has been given of the doctrines as stated by its leading proponents has, however, been amply justified not only by reason of the fact that the various phases of the problem have thus been set forth, but also because, as will be found, the theory itself, though not integrally valid, contains elements that are essential to a sound system of final political philosophy. In the criticism which follows the procedure will therefore be adopted of first pointing out the deficiencies of the theory, and then of showing, constructively, the extent to which the idea of individual consent must be accepted in ethical validation of the control which the State exercises over its citizens or subjects. First, however, as to certain illegitimate criticisms which have, at times, been directed against the theory.

The Contention That a Social Compact Would Have No Legally Binding Force. The validity of a Social Compact as a basis for political authority has often been denied upon the ground that to it could be ascribed no legal force for the reason that, *ex hypothesi,* there would be no antecedent political or civil law to support it. In other words, the assumed purpose and effect of the contract being the establishment of a civil society among individuals who previously had lived without political government or civil law, it has been argued that there clearly could have been, at the time of the entering into the contract, no legal obligation resting upon the parties to it to abide by their consent to it.

This statement, though logically correct, is irrelevant, since it represents an *ignoratio elenchi.* The Compact Theory has not been put forward as an explanation of the manner in which the State, and therefore legal obligation, is conceived to have been created: its primary purpose has been to show how it becomes morally obligatory upon individuals to obey the commands of the State. Therefore, it has been only the morally obligatory force of the original compact that has been asserted. Hence, to deny its legal character, does not meet the essential element of the theory.

The Contention as to the Non-Historical Character of the Compact Theory. Equally ineffectual as a criticism of the Compact Theory is the allegation that there is no affirmative historical evidence that, as an actual fact, political societies have been brought into being by covenants between their constituent individuals, and that, upon the contrary, there are good reasons for holding that, in truly primitive times, there would have been neither opportunity to enter into an original compact, nor mental capacity to conceive of its necessity or its terms. It does, indeed, appear that certain of the proponents of the theory believed that, in some instances, civil societies, as an historical fact, have originated in agreements between the individuals severally constituting them, but none of them has, to any considerable extent, rested their argument upon that alleged fact. The essence of his argument has been—whether or not they themselves have in all cases clearly seen it—that, if coercion by the State is to be ethically justified, it must be regarded as though it were founded upon an original social covenant.[2]

To this mode of approaching the problem of political obligation there is no logical objection. The conception or predication of an original compact may or may not be found logically adequate to support all the arguments founded upon it, but it furnishes the real key to the solution of the problem of political coercion. In other words, if a valid argument is to be found which will justify the coercion exercised by States over their subjects, it must take the form of a statement of the manner in which the individual is to be conceived to be related to his fellow-men and to the group to which he belongs, and without regard to whether or not, in actual fact, political authority originated, or has since been exercised, in accordance with the corollaries deducible from such a conception. Thus Kant was formally correct when he spoke of the Social Contract as "properly only an outward mode of representing the idea by which the rightfulness of the mode of organizing the Constitution may be conceivable," as also when he said that the contract "is but a mere idea of the reason, possessing nevertheless an indubitable [practical] reality in this respect that it obligates every legislator to enact his laws in such a manner as they might have originated in the united will of the people."

With regard generally to the matter of the historical

---

[2] The famous Mayflower compact of 1520 was between individuals already under the sovereignty of England, whose ultimate supreme political power they had no intention of disavowing.

origin of political authority among men it needs only to be added that, even were it possible to determine with certainty the manner in which this was brought about, no light would be thrown upon the question of its ethical legitimacy—unless, indeed, one accepts the doctrine that, at the time political authority originated, there was at work some mysterious or transcendental force that directed the actions of men into ethically correct channels. And, of course, the same is true as to any particular State now existing. It may have originated with the full approval of the governed, or by military conquest, or in some other way, but, having ascertained this, no final answer is thrown upon the question as to its ethical right to continue in existence. There still needs to be determined the subsisting obligations, if any. Thus the fundamental question is again raised.

Inherent Defects in the Compact Theory. Leaving aside, then, the irrelevant juristic and historical objections which have been raised to the Compact Theory, it becomes necessary to examine its inherent merits or defects. Viewing the theory as one explaining, conceptually, the origin of political society in general, or of any particular State, we are at once met by three difficulties which have already been referred to in our examination of the theories of Hobbes, Locke and Rousseau, but which have not been satisfactorily discussed. These three are: (1) granting, *arguendo*, that rightful political authority is founded upon an original covenant of each individual with all the rest, how can later generations of men be held bound by the agreement to which they did not personally give their assent; (2) whence comes the right of a majority or other dominant class in a political community to determine what the State shall do, and to compel obedience to such determinations upon the part of individuals who do not approve of them; and (3) what are the rights and obligations of those individuals who, by reason of infancy or defective mental equipment, cannot be said to have a reasoning power sufficient to enable them to appreciate the need for, or the nature and consequences of, a mutual agreement to establish and maintain a political society?

Continuing Force of the Original Compact. As regards the first difficulty it has been seen that the advocates of the Compact Theory have been obliged to assert that those who live in a given community give an implied assent to the original covenant upon which it is conceived to have been founded. To be valid, this implication must in turn imply that the assent is freely given, and thus, in fact, we find Locke asserting that if one does not wish to remain a member of a political community in which he finds himself, he should be free to depart from it. But, as every one knows, in many instances, it is practically impossible for men to avail themselves of this liberty. They have not the necessary financial means, and, if they have, it would, in many cases, be impossible for them to find a country to which they might go which would present political conditions more satisfactory than those of the country in which they already are. As Hume says in his essay on "The Social Contract," to tell the average individual that he has the right to leave the country where he is, if dissatisfied with the manner in which it is governed, is like telling a sailor or passenger upon a ship in mid-ocean that, if he does not approve of the manner in which the vessel is being sailed, he may step over its side, and leave it. In both cases the freedom of choice is a wholly empty one. If, then, we are to accept the doctrine that the rightfulness of all political authority must be based upon the consent of those subjected to it, it is not sufficient to predicate an original compact as the origin of political society, and imply a consent to it by later generations. We must find, or posit, a consent currently and continually given to the existence of political society, to the form of government that is maintained, and to each and every one of adopted policies of that government.[3]

If it be asked: Cannot people validly agree in advance to be bound by the decisions of a fixed proportion of their number, and, if they have so agreed, can they justly claim that their freedom of action has been illegitimately restrained, if, when the time comes, they find themselves dissenting from the decisions of that proportion, and are compelled to obey? the answer is: Certainly they can enter into and be morally bound by such an agreement, but, to be valid, the agreement has to be an express one, and not implied from the very nature of political society. Such an agreement would not differ in any way from the countless other agreements that individuals in a civil society enter into, and, therefore, cannot be relied upon as one of the supports of political authority itself. And, even as thus viewed, the individuals would not be absolutely bound in the sense that, under no conceivable circumstances, would they be morally justified in breaking their agreement.

Rights of Majorities and Minorities. Hobbes did not need to trouble himself with the respective rights and obligations of majorities and minorities after civil society is established, for his reasoning led him to deny to the governed, individually or collectively, any rights of opposition to those to whom, by the original compact, the exercise of the sovereign political power is given. As regards the original covenant itself he seemed to think that men, being led by their own reason to see that their natural desires can only be satisfied by the creation of some sort of civil society, each necessarily agrees to this,

[3] The argument that political rule originating in conquest may be justified by imputing to the conquered an agreement to obey in return for having their lives spared or being exempted from slavery, will be considered in connection with the examination which will later be made of the so-called "Governmental Contract."

and, furthermore, agrees that the form of political rule to be established shall be determined by a majority voice. Thus he says: "A commonwealth is said to be instituted when a multitude of men do agree and covenant, every one, with every one, that to whatever man, or assembly of men, shall be given by the major part, the right to present the person of them all, that is to say, to be their representative; every one, as well he that voted for it, as he that voted against it, shall authorize all the actions and judgments, of that man, or assembly of men, in the same manner, as if they were his own, to the end, to live peaceably among themselves, and be protected against other men." Because he held that this government, when instituted, was necessarily to have absolute power, it was not necessary for him to consider the rights of a minority or even of a majority of subjects as opposed to the will of the man, or assembly of men, to whom was given the sovereign authority.[4]

Locke and Rousseau, because of the character and result which they ascribed to the original agreement, were obliged to consider not only the case of individuals not approving this original agreement, but also the case of those who, after the creation of the State, might object to the form of its government, to the persons exercising its powers, or to its policies and commands. Both of them met this problem by asserting that those who remain in the community, as well as those who later become members of it, give thereby an implied assent to the covenant. As for the form of government to be maintained and its policies, both asserted that the minority are obligated to accept as ethically and legally just the decisions of the majority, either because that undertaking is conceived to be contained in the original compact or, as Locke ap-

---

[4] Just how differences of opinion between members of the assembly of men exercising the sovereign power were to be adjusted, whether by majority voice or otherwise, does not plainly appear.

pears to hold, because, from the very nature of things, a majority has this right of determination.

The paragraphs in which this right of the majority is asserted by Locke and Rousseau have already been quoted. From them it will be noted that Locke pushes his doctrine of consent to its logical limits by declaring that no one should be compelled to join in the original agreement, and that those not joining should not be held bound by its provisions. He says: "Men being, as has been said, by nature all free, equal and independent, no one can be put out of this estate and subjected to the political power of another without his own consent which is done by agreeing with other men to join and unite into a community. . . . This any number of men may do, because it injures not the freedom of the rest; they are left, as they were, in the liberty of the State of Nature." Locke nowhere discussed what would be the fate of those individuals who might be unwilling to unite with their neighbors in the establishment of a political society. He does, however, later say that residence within a political community carries with it an implied assent to its political organization and laws. It would therefore seem that those persons who were unwilling to enter into the original compact would have no other alternative but to abandon their then homes, and such of their property as would not be portable, and seek some other place, if such could be found, where political rule had not been instituted. Thus viewed, it is clear that the rights of the individual to liberty and property conceived by Locke to exist in a State of Nature, and upon which he laid such stress, would be substantially impaired by the original covenant as to those persons not wishing to become parties to it. Furthermore, Locke held that, having once agreed to the Social Contract, the individual, as an individual, has no right to withdraw from it. No right of secession upon the part of the individual is, or can be, reserved. This right belongs only to the whole people or citizen body.

Rousseau asserts that the Social Contract requires the unanimous consent of the individuals who are to constitute the body-politic created by it. But he does not discuss the situation or rights of those persons who, at the time of its being entered into, may be unwilling to agree to it. This, however, is not such a serious omission as it would have been in the case of Locke, for Rousseau does not recognize the existence, in the pre-political state, of those definite natural rights belonging to the individual which Locke had asserted. Indeed there then were, according to Rousseau, no moral rights and duties, but only instinctive impulses or desires. Rousseau, moreover, as we have seen, emphasized more strongly than did Locke the necessity that the consent of the individual to the maintenance of political authority should be a continuing one,— one that needed to be constantly renewed, and, therefore, that continuing opportunity should be given the citizens to say whether or not they wish to continue to live in political bonds, and that, even thus, the individual can rightfully be bound only by laws which truly represent the General Will, that is, the true will of each individual.

It does not certainly appear how far Rousseau went in admitting that an individual has a right to terminate at will his allegiance to his State. He says: "There is in the State no fundamental law which cannot be revoked, not even the social compact; for if all the citizens assembled in order to break this compact by a solemn agreement, no one can doubt that it would be quite legitimately broken. Grotius even thinks that each man can renounce the State of which he is a member, and regain his natural freedom and his property by quitting the country. Now it would be absurd if all the citizens combined should be unable to do what each of them can do separately."

Here Rousseau appears to accept without criticism

Grotius' statement that the individual may, when he sees fit, cancel his adherence to the Social Compact. He elsewhere says that the people, when gathered in sovereign assembly, must act by a unanimous vote, and it would therefore seem fair to assume that he held that the continuance of the contract might be brought to an end, as to any particular individual, by his refusal to continue his support of it. However, in a footnote to the paragraph that has been quoted he says: "It must be clearly understood that no one should leave [the country] in order to evade his duty and relieve himself from serving his country at a moment when it needs him. Flight in that case would be criminal and punishable; it would no longer be retirement, but desertion." This assertion seems to imply that the individual cannot escape from the contract after he has once agreed to it. If this is true, all that remains to him is the right to deny the binding force of political commands which, in their content and application, do not satisfy the requirements which Rousseau has laid down with reference to expressions of the General Will.

In truth, it was not logically necessary for Rousseau to save to the individual the right to separate himself from the body-politic to which he belongs, because, according to his doctrine of the General Will, the individual is construed to give his real assent to every act of the State, and, therefore, can never have a reason for secession from his State. Apart from this, however, as regards the statement in his footnote, he could have argued that the individual, having lived in a State and obtained the benefits of its law and order, has contracted obligations,—obligations that, legally speaking, are spoken of as accrued—which he may justly be compelled to satisfy before separating himself from the State.

Leaving now the matter of entering into and maintaining the original compact, and considering the position of those individuals who may not approve of the form of government that is maintained, or certain of its laws and policies, we find Rousseau and Locke in agreement that the will of the majority should control. Locke, as we have earlier seen, made only a feeble attempt to defend, upon logical grounds, this right of the majority to control. But Rousseau devoted all his dialectical skill to showing how it would be possible to ascribe absolutely controlling force to the will of the State and yet not impair the freedom of the individual who might not approve its acts. To the question of the success with which Rousseau developed his conception of an impeccable General Will we shall presently return. But, whether successful or not, it is certainly greatly to Rousseau's credit that he made no attempt to evade the issue raised when individuals do not approve the laws or policies of their governments but yet are compelled to obey or abide by them.

The question of the respective rights of majorities and minorities is, really, a simple and easily answered one. There is no right of a majority, as such, to have its will obeyed by a minority. And this is true, however large the majority may be, or however small the minority may be. That is, if one starts with the premise that men are entitled to determine their own acts in accordance with their own will, it becomes logically impossible to say that, if a majority or other dominant number of voices order that a certain thing be done or line of conduct followed, therefore, dissentient individuals may rightfully be compelled to act accordingly. Only by asserting that it is the will of God that the will of the majority shall be obeyed, or by making the assumption that, for some inherent, though unexplainable, reason, the judgment of the majority is necessarily a wise and just one, can the right of the majority to compel obedience to its will be successfully asserted. Certainly no reasonable man now maintains that a majority is always right. Indeed, all admit that, conceivably, a single individual opposing his judgment to the united judgment of every one of his fellow-men, may be in the right and they in the wrong,— *Athanasius contra mundum.* But, if this possibility be admitted, it is seen that the principle that the judgment of the majority or of any other pre-determined proportion of the populace should be uniformly accepted as just and expedient, and the will resulting therefrom be obeyed, is nothing more than a convenient and peaceable way of coming to a conclusion as to what shall be done and of establishing rules that shall be accepted as binding upon all. Thus, for many purposes, people have adopted the rule that they all will follow the decisions laid down by a mere plurality of voices. In other cases, they have deemed it wise that the rule or action should be supported by an absolute majority of persons entitled to vote upon it. In still other cases, a still larger proportion of the whole number of those voting, or of those qualified to vote, is demanded. Finally, in some cases, it has been considered wise to require a unanimous vote before sanctioning a specified act. The old Articles of Confederation adopted by the American States at the conclusion of the Revolutionary War provided that the Articles should not be amended except with the unanimous vote of all the States. As to many matters considered in International Conferences the rule is that only unanimously approved measures are to be considered as adopted. And by Article V of the Covenant of the League of Nations it is declared that "except where otherwise expressly provided in this Covenant or by the terms of the present Treaty [with Germany] decisions at any meeting of the Assembly or of the Council [of the League] shall require the agreement of all the members of the League represented at the meeting." The Constitution of the United States in a number of cases makes a majority of two-thirds or of even a larger proportion, necessary for a decision. Thus, amendments to the Constitution may be proposed only when two-thirds of both Houses of Congress concur or when the legislatures of two-thirds of the States deem amendment necessary; and the proposals thus recommended do not become effective until ratified by the legislatures, or specially convened conventions, of three-fourths of the several States.

Provisions such as these do not need to be further multiplied. They may be found, in practically every written constitution of the world, and furnish abundant proof that it is the general opinion that no inherent wisdom, or right of binding decision, is deemed to be possessed in all cases by a majority or any other fixed proportion of a populace or of a representative assembly of men.

Decisive of the existence of this opinion is also the fact that, under Anglo-American systems of law, a unanimous verdict of juries is, in almost all cases, required.

It may furthermore be pointed out to those in whose minds there still lingers the idea of some inherent right of a majority to coerce a minority, that the world presents no instances in which the voice of a majority of all persons living in a community, irrespective of their age, sex or other status, is regarded as decisive of political right. In all cases where the right of a majority is recognized it has always been a majority of a minority of the whole people, namely of adults, and, in most cases, of only adult males.

This much, then, at least we are justified in asserting: that there is no inherent merit in the right of majorities to coerce minorities, and, therefore, that Social Compact theorists are not justified in assuming that the principle is necessarily incorporated in the compact which serves as the basis of political authority.

It may further be pointed out, that the acceptance of the right of a majority to coerce a minority, even when accepted merely as a working principle, is dependent upon the assumption that there is an agreement of the entire community upon fundamental principles of right and policy, from which it results that such differences of opinion as may appear relate to matters of relatively less importance. When there are, within a political group, smaller bodies of "irreconcilables," that is, of persons who do not approve of the dominant political policy or prevailing form of government, or whose religious or other cultural views are radically different from those of the remainder of the group, then, as to these minority groups, the coercion exercised over them, in pursuance of the principle that the opinion of the majority should prevail, is obviously one of superior force and nothing else.

Finally, it is to be observed that, aside from its other defects, the majority principle rests upon the assumption that, to the opinion of all individuals, or, at any rate, of all individuals permitted to vote upon a proposition, equal weight should be given; that is, that differences in degrees of intelligence of moral character and of disinterested regard for the general welfare should count for nothing. We shall later have occasion to discuss the true meaning of Public Opinion and of the so-called "General Will" with a view to determining the validity of the grounds upon which Popular Government is ordinarily defended. We shall then see how improper it is to identify the proposition that governments and governmental policies should be subject to the control of the governed with the doctrine that numerical majorities, however large, have an inherent and absolute right to impose their will upon minorities.[5]

[5] One of the most satisfactory discussions of the topic we have been considering is that of Jellinek, in his short pamphlet *The Rights of Minorities*, translated by Baty (London: King & Son, 1912). Reference should also be made to A. L. Lowell's *Public Opinion and Popular Government* and *Public Opinion in War and Peace*, and A. V. Dicey's *Law and Public Opinion in England during the Nineteenth Century*.

The point that a man's freedom is just as much impaired when, against his will, he is compelled to obey the determinations of a majority as he is when he is coerced by a smaller number or even by a single individual will be further discussed later on and the conclusion reached, from which there would seem to be no logical escape, that, if we start from the premise that man has an inherent or moral right to determine for himself, and by his own judgment and desire, what he shall do, he is subjected to illegitimate coercion if compelled to act in a way in which, at the time, he does not wish to act.[6]

The Right of Persons Not Mentally Competent to Enter into Agreements. It is clear that, when, by reason of injury, or lack of mental power due to any other cause, one is unable to appreciate the significance of the terms of a contract, or even the nature of a contractural undertaking in itself, he can scarcely be held to have given his consent to any agreements into which he may have, in form, entered. Much less can he be held obligated by compacts to which only an implied consent upon his part may be alleged. Persons who fall within this *non compos mentis* class constitute a considerable portion of every community, and yet, to them, the Social Compact theory pays almost no attention, and, in fact, furnishes no basis for determining the consideration to be given to them by the intellectually qualified individuals of a community.

[6] When it is said "compelled to act," it is not meant that it is not within one's physical power to act otherwise, but that, by some power outside himself, he is threatened with such severe penalties, if he does not act according to the prescribed rule or order, that, balancing them with the possible benefits to be obtained by following his own desire, he finds it expedient to obey the prescribed rule or order. In a very true sense, in so obeying, he wills to obey, but only because a power foreign and of superior strength to himself has attached artificial disadvantages to the commission of the acts which, except for these artificially created disadvantages, he would have preferred to commit.

CHAPTER XIV

THE TRUE BASIS OF THE RIGHT OF POLITICAL COERCION

THE inquiry as to the true basis of the right of political coercion will perhaps, be simplified if we divide it into the following questions and consider them in the order stated.

(1) In what sense, if any, can an individual, viewed as an independent entity, that is, wholly apart from his status as a member of a social group, be said to have moral rights or to rest under moral obligations?

(2) Are there differences between the non-legal or purely social forms of coercion and those employed by the State which make it necessary to found the ethical right of political authority upon grounds essentially different from those which support other forms of social control?

(3) What absolute principles, if any, determine the manner in which, or the purposes for which, political coercion may be legitimately exercised?

(4) To what extent do the grounds upon which political authority is ethically justified determine the character of the government through which the State is to exercise its functions?

Natural Rights. The question as to what moral rights can be said to be possessed by, or moral obligations be held to rest upon, an individual considered apart from his status as a member of a human society is of first importance, because, if it be found that, as a logical proposition, no moral rights and obligations can exist except in a state of society, then, whatever limitations upon the individual's liberty of action are imposed upon him by those with whom he lives in social relations, or which necessarily grow out of his social life, do not need, in order to be ethically justified, to meet the objection that they derogate from rights possessed by him which spring from his very nature as a moral and rational being. In other words, if morality itself has no application except when men live in social relations with each other, then one can start with Society and need not consider how may be resolved the apparent antithesis between the complete individualism of a State of Nature and that subordination of the individual to the authority of others which is the outcome of social life. And if it be found that, as regards the right of coercion, there is no essential distinction between social and political coercion —that they differ only as to the means employed—, then the position that moral rights and duties exist only in a social régime, carries one well on towards the solution of political control. For a solution of the problem as thus stated, there is required a more critical examination of the idea of Natural Rights, and, incidentally, of the conception of moral obligation itself, than has thus far been attempted.

In its essence, the idea at the basis of the doctrine of Natural Rights has been that man is able, by his reason, to elaborate a code of human conduct, intrinsically ethical, covering all possible acts, and morally binding *urbe et orbi, semper et ubique*. As late as the seventeenth century we find Locke declaring that, starting with "the idea of a Supreme Being infinite in power, goodness, and wisdom, whose workmanship we are, and on whom we depend; and the idea of ourselves as understanding, rational beings," it is possible from these "self-evident propositions by necessary consequences as incontestable as those in mathematics," if one will apply himself with the same indifference [impartiality] and attention to the one as he does to the other of these sciences, to determine measures of right and wrong. Spinoza, writing at about the same time, went so far as to cast his ethics in the mathematical form of propositions, demonstrations, and corollaries.

Views such as these imply a naïve confidence in the human reason as a human faculty which, if allowed to operate free from corrupting influences, will lead all men to exactly the same conclusions; that is, in the moral field, to the discovery of what acts are, in themselves, that is, abstractly considered, absolutely right, and those that are absolutely wrong.

It was as much these absurd pretensions as it was the skeptical results of Hume's reasoning, that awoke the philosopher of Königsberg from his "dogmatic slumber." Negatively the result of Kant's work was to show the utter lack in the ethical systems of his time of a metaphysic or epistemology adequate for the support of the premises upon which they were founded. Positively, the result was to transfer to the individual human reason the legislative source of moral law. The significance of Kant's doctrine in this respect has been brilliantly stated by Salmond.[1] "In the system of Kant," says Mr. Salmond, "the law of nature, or, as he prefers to call it, the moral law, appears as the categorical imperative of the practical reason. . . . Law, for Kant, as for every one else, is a command; but he expresses this in his own way by saying that it is a 'proposition which contains a categorical imperative.' That the law of nature is a command or dictate of reason was already familiar doctrine in the time of Cicero; Aquinas and the schoolmen taught it, and from their day to that of Kant himself, it has not been rejected or forgotten. . . . The element of originality in Kant's system is his unreserved acceptance of what is

[1] In an article entitled "The Law of Nature," contributed to the *Law Quarterly Review* for April, 1895.

called the metaphysical doctrine of natural law. When Aquinas says that this law is the dictate of practical reason, he means primarily the reason of God, not of man—*ratio videlicet gubernativa totius universi in mente divina existens.* Human reason is not *per se* possessed of legislative authority, but is merely the secondary source of the law of nature, as being the means by which law is revealed to man. Kant, however, proclaims a new doctrine of the autonomy of the reason or rational will of man. The human practical reason is a lawgiving faculty, and its commands constitute the moral law. 'This law,' he says, '. . . is a single isolated fact of the practical reason announcing itself as originally legislative.' *Sic volo sic jubeo.* Reason is spontaneously practical and gives that universal law which is called the moral law. From this moral or natural law proceeds moral or natural obligation, as most of his predecessors taught. 'Obligation is the necessity of free action when viewed in a relation to a categorical imperative of reason.' "

Of course, Kant did not declare that it lies within the province of each individual to fix, arbitrarily, the distinctions between right and wrong. His theory was that what our reason tells us is right, becomes, *ipso facto*, categorically imperative upon us. But, in reaching its judgments, our reason is, by its very nature, governed by the principle that only that can be right which accords with a principle which we can wish to be a universal one. "Act on a maxim," he declared, "which thou canst will to be a universal law;" or, as he said in another place "Act externally in such a manner that the free exercise of thy will may be able to coexist with the freedom of others according to a universal law." And this maxim in turn implies the mandate of reason: "Be a person and respect others as persons."

Kant's writings inaugurated a new epoch in ethical speculation. Starting with his doctrines, present day transcendentalists, influenced to no inconsiderable extent by the arguments of the English utilitarians, declare that each individual should, and, in fact, must, determine for himself, in the last resort, what it is ethically right that he should do. And, furthermore, that, in reaching this determination, he must be guided by his own reason and without the assistance of any theological creed or mystical ecclesiastical or church authority, and also without the guidance of any independent and infallible faculty termed Conscience. Even when as in the case of the believer in Christianity the words of the Scriptures, or, in the case of a Roman Catholic, the *ex cathedra* utterances of the head of his Church, are taken as stating absolute truth, he still has to exercise his reason in order to arrive at the conclusion that the Scriptures or the dogmas or the ecclesiastical body to which he belongs are entitled to this implicit acceptance.

It is now generally accepted that, to the individual, the ethical character of his acts is dependent upon the motive or "good will" with which they are done, and that this is determined by the results that follow, or reasonably may be expected to follow, from the commission of specific acts. The desirability or undesirability of these acts must be fixed by the individual's conception of "the Good," that is, of what, ethically speaking, is by him deemed to be in the highest degree desirable. The acceptance of the "good will" of the agent, as here defined stands midway between the doctrine of Bentham who attached no moral value to the motive, and that of Kant who denied the determining force of the results of the act. Bentham says: "A motive is substantially nothing more than pleasure or pain operating in a certain manner. Now pleasure is in itself a good, nay, even setting aside immunity from pain, the only good. . . . It follows, therefore, immediately and incontestably that there is no such thing as any sort of motive that is in itself a bad one. If motives are good or bad, it is only on account of their effects." [2] So much for the utilitarian position.

Kant says: "Pure reason is practical of itself alone and gives to man a universal law which we call the Moral Law. . . . If this law determines the will directly the action conformed to it is good in itself; a will whose principle always conforms to this law is good absolutely in every respect and is the supreme condition of all good."

Professor John Dewey, after quoting these contradictory propositions, points out that the motive of the agent cannot be determined to be good or bad except in the light of the results which may reasonably be expected from the act that is willed; that, in other words, the individual must place his estimate upon the goodness or badness of these results. Thus the two ideas of good will or motive and results cannot be wholly separated. Intention, that is, deliberate willing to bring about a certain result thus becomes wedded to the motive that lies back of the intention and determines why the result is desired: Dewey says: "The insistence of utilitarianism that we must become aware of the moral quality of our impulses and states of mind on the basis of the results they effect, and must, control them—no matter how 'good' they feel —by their results, is a fundamental truth of morals. But the converse is equally true. Behind every concrete purpose or aim, as idea or thought of results, lies something, some passion, instinct, habit, interest, which gives it a hold on the person, which gives it motor and impelling force; and which confers upon it the capacity to operate as motive, as spring to action. Otherwise, foreseen consequences would remain mere intellectual entities which thought might speculatively contemplate from afar, but which would never possess weight, influence, power to stir effort. But we must go further. Not only is some active tendency in the constitution of the man responsible for

[2] *Principles of Morals and Legislation*, Chap. X.

the motive power, whether attractive or otherwise, which foreseen consequences possess, but it is responsible for the fact that this rather than that consequence is suggested." [3]

The author is in substantial agreement with the view of Dewey, but deems it advisable to add the observation that, in judging the moral character of an act, it is necessary to distinguish between the point of view of the one who commits the act and the point of view of the outsider who is called upon to pass ethical judgment upon the act and upon the actor. These points of view may not lead to the same judgments. What Dewey says, in the words which have been quoted, applies particularly to the individual when judging his own conduct, and to the outsider who is judging him in the light of his acts. When, however, the character of the act itself is judged by the outsider, he may deem it to be an ill-advised one, although, if he grant the conscientiousness of the actor, he may deem that the actor is not subject to moral disapprobation. In other words, the outsider may believe that the actor acted with or from a good will or motive and with a belief that, under the circumstances, his act was an ethically defensible or even meritorious one; at the same time, the outsider may, using his own judgment and estimate of what the situation ethically demanded, be of opinion that the act was not morally justified.

The central concept of modern ethics is the moral personality of man. This implies that each individual is able, and, in fact, is irresistibly impelled, to formulate for himself an ideal of perfection toward the attainment of which he is conscious of a moral obligation to strive. This consciousness of obligation, which takes the form of a categorical imperative posited by his own reason, carries with it the logical assumptions: first, of a freedom of the will, for without this there cannot be even the capacity

[3] Dewey and Tufts, *Ethics*, p. 252 (edition, 1908).

to obey the obligation which is felt; and, secondly, of an inherent right to be allowed by others to realize in fact, so far as is compatible with their reciprocal rights, those conditions of life which are implied in the ideal of personal development which each frames for himself.

In declaring the chief good to be the realization of one's best self, transcendental ethics necessarily distinguishes between those simple or material wants which the bodily passions and appetites create, and those desires which are the outcome of a craving to secure that moral perfection which the reason presents. The first express a demand for the satisfaction of an immediate want, without reference to, or recognition of, any ulterior end to be realized. The second are the outcome of the developed reason of an individual who is conscious that he is a moral being, who is able to see his life as a whole, who can conceive of a possible perfection, and who can adapt means to its attainment. This is the point which Green makes when he says: "The reason and will of man have their common ground in that characteristic of being an object to himself which, as we have said, belongs to him so far as the eternal mind, through the medium of an animal organism and under limitations arising from the employment of such a medium, reproduces itself in him. It is in virtue of this self-objectifying principle that he is determined, not simply by natural wants according to natural laws, but by the thought of himself as existing under certain conditions, and as having ends that may be attained and capabilities that may be realized under those conditions. It is thus that he not merely desires, but seeks to satisfy himself in gaining the objects of his desire; presents to himself a certain possible state of himself, which in the gratification of his desire he seeks to reach: in short, wills. It is thus, again, that he has the impulse to make himself what he has the possibility of becoming but actually is not, and hence not merely, like the plant or animal, undergoes a process of development, but seeks to, and does, develop himself." [4]

We are now prepared to say in what, if any, correct sense one may speak of "Natural Rights" belonging to the individual as such.

First of all it may be pointed out that the conception of so-called civilized life of men as being in any sense non-natural or unnatural, is essentially false. Man is himself a part of Nature, and his actions, whatever they may be, are necessarily "natural." In fact, to state that a thing *is*, is equivalent to stating that it is *natural*, for everything that exists is a part of *natura naturata*, and everything that happens is a part of the decree of nature as *natura naturans*.

Secondly, the idea of deriving from Natural Law definite, absolute rules of conduct is a vain one. Its rules are necessarily dependent upon the particular interpretation of Nature's will obtained through man's reason. What this interpretation will be obviously depends upon the given *data* from which men reason; and these, in turn, are only supplied by objective conditions of social, economic, and political life. All ethical obligation being posited upon that feeling of oughtness which is given to the individual as an original datum of consciousness that, when the rightness of a given line of conduct is recognized it should be followed, and all rules of moral obligation being thus considered as having their source in the legislative power of the human mind to set to itself principles of conduct, the idea of natural right becomes synonymous with those affirmative acts or forbearances which the individual, as a rational moral being, may claim from others as rational moral beings. As thus conceived, the only rights which may be claimed as natural, in the sense of being innate or essential, are those which are necessary for the realization of one's highest ethical

[4] *Prolegomena to Ethics*, paragraph 175.

self. Thus, as Green says, "they [rights] are 'innate' or 'natural' in the same sense in which according to Aristotle the state is natural; not in the sense that they actually exist when a man is born, and that they have actually existed as long as the human race, but that they arise out of, and are necessary for the fulfilment of, a moral capacity without which a man would not be a man." [5]

Justice to the individual, then, according to these principles, consists in the rendering to him, so far as possible, all those services, and surrounding him by all those conditions, which he requires for his highest self, that is, for the satisfaction of those desires which his truest judgment tells him are good. Conversely, opportunity for the fulfillment of highest aims is all that he may justly claim as his right.

The realization of one's highest ethical self is then the general categorical imperative addressed to every one. Therefore, the putting forward by an individual of a claim to a freedom of action implies at the same time the recognition of a duty by the individual making the claim; namely, that it is incumbent upon him to employ this liberty, when obtained, for the attainment of the end for which alone it is granted. Further still, the setting up by an individual of a claim for a given privilege or immunity logically implies the assertion by such individual that he has both the disposition and the ability properly to use it when obtained. For instance, the right of freely expressing one's opinions can be tolerated only when men have reached a certain level of reasonableness in the formation of their views.

But what does this mean? It means that the "rights" which different individuals may claim are not necessarily the same. It means, in the second place, that there are no absolute rights, no definite natural rights. The rights which different individuals may properly claim must

[5] *Philosophical Works*, Vol. II, p. 353.

vary according to their several ethical dispositions and capacities. Thus, the man who, by his striving, has built up for himself an upright character, has the right to demand from his fellow-men a respect to which his less honest neighbor can make no proper claim. Thus, also, a man who, by his wisdom and probity, is best qualified to direct a certain social force, has ethically the best right to be intrusted with its control. In this sense, and this sense alone, there is a "right" to rulership.

At this point it is to be noted that there is often a confusion between the proposition that all persons, by the very fact that they are persons, are entitled to the same rights, and the proposition that all persons are entitled to the same sort of respect for and protection of such rights as they are recognized to have. The distinction between these two propositions is so well brought out by Professor Dickenson in his work *The Equality of States in International Law* that a somewhat lengthy quotation is justified. He is speaking of nations, but his exposition is applicable, *mutatis mutandis,* to individual human beings. He says:

"The principle of equality has an important legal significance in the modern law of nations. It is the expression of two important legal principles. The first of these may be called the equal protection of the law or equality before the law. States are equal before the law when they are equally protected in the enjoyment of their rights and equally compelled to fulfill their obligations. Equality before the law is not inconsistent with the grouping of states into classes and the attributing to the members of each class of a status which is the measure of capacity for rights. Neither is it inconsistent with inequalities of representation, voting power, and contribution in international organizations. The second principle is usually described as equality of rights and obligations or more often as equality of rights. The description is a heritage from theories of natural law and natural right. What is really meant is an equality of capacity for rights. Equality in this sense is the negation of status. If applied without qualification in international organizations it requires equal representation, voting power, and contribution. Equality before the law is absolutely essential to a stable society of nations. If it is denied the alternatives are universal empire or universal anarchy. Equality of capacity for rights, on the other hand, is not essential to the reign of law. Strictly speaking, it has never been anything more than an ideal in any system of law. Among states, where there is such an utter want of homogeneity in the physical bases for separate existence, there are important limitations upon its utility even as an ideal.

"Notwithstanding these limitations, equality of legal capacity has its place as an ideal in the system of international law. It must be recognized that the international legal capacity of the state may be and frequently is restricted by its organic constitution. It must also be recognized that many important limitations upon the legal capacity of certain states are imposed by the positive law of nations. Thorough investigation of these problems from a more rational and more scientific point of view is urgently required. On the other hand, it is vital that the fundamental distinction between equality of legal capacity and equality in international organization be more widely understood and appreciated. At the risk of repetition, this distinction may be explained once more by reference to general legal principles which are more or less familiar to every one. It is generally assumed that equality of legal capacity among persons subject to law is the ideal toward which a system of private law ought to develop; but it has never been regarded as a necessary corollary that the same principle should be taken for an ideal in perfecting national organization, much less that it should be given practical application in the form of equal participation in government. No civilized state has ever tried to combine universal suffrage, the folk-moot, and the liberum veto. It may be suggested parenthetically that the organization of human beings on such a basis would be less unreal and would give greater promise of success than the organization of nations on the same principle. The problem of international organization should not be confused and complicated by attempting to insist upon the application of the principle of state equality. Conceding that equality of capacity for rights is sound as a legal principle, its proper application is limited to rules of conduct and to the acquiring of rights and the assuming of obligations under those rules. It is inapplicable from its very nature to rules of organization. Insistence upon complete political equality in the constitution and functioning of an international union, tribunal, or concert is simply another way of denying the possibility of effective international organization." [6]

There can be no absolute rights, furthermore, for the reason that whether or not a given right should be granted must depend upon all the concomitant circumstances which determine whether or not the special aim sought to be realized by the employment of the right claimed is the most desirable end which, under the given conditions, should be sought. Finally, even were the foregoing not true, it would be logically impossible to maintain the existence of more than a single absolute right. To say that any right is absolute means that it is one which, under all conceivable circumstances, should be granted to all individuals, *qua* persons, whatever their capacity for ethical development. To select any one right as absolute, means, then, that every other right must always be subordinated to it. Thus, for example, if the right to life be selected as absolute, no justification for its violation

[6] *Op. cit.*, p. 334.

can be offered, whether for the sake of the protection of one's own self from grievous bodily injury, or for the warding off of similar injury to one's own family. No injury to one's honor, or the honor of one's own family, will justify its violation. According to such a premise, life could never justly be taken or exposed to serious danger in war, however righteous the cause for which waged. In fact, no threatened evil to thousands or millions of other men, short possibly of what would entail death, would justify the taking of a single life. To state such logical consequences as these is a sufficient answer to those who would maintain the possibility of an absolute right, even did not the reasoning which has gone before show its impossibility.

So important is this point of the relativity of all rights that, though it be a repetition, a quotation from Green's *Prolegomena to Ethics* is justified. "We need not shrink," says Green, "from asserting, as the basis of morality, an unconditional duty, which yet is not a duty to do anything unconditionally except to fulfill that unconditional duty. . . . This is the unconditional ground of those particular duties to do or to forbear doing, which, in the effort of the social man to realize his ideal, have so far come to be recognized as binding, but which are in some way or other conditional, because relative to particular circumstances, however wide the range of circumstances may be, to which they are relative. . . . Every one . . . of the duties which the law of the State or the law of opinion recognizes must in some way be relative to circumstances. . . . Yet there is a true sense in which the whole system of such duties is unconditionally binding. It is so as an absolute imperative to seek the absolutely desirable, the ideal of humanity, the fulfillment of man's vocation. . . . It enjoins the observance of the whole complex of established duties, as a means to that perfection of which it unconditionally enjoins the pursuit. And it enjoins this observance as unconditionally as it enjoins the pursuit of the end to which this observance is a means, so long as it is such a means. It will only allow such a departure from it in the interest of a fuller attainment of the unconditional end, not in the interest of any one's pleasure." [7]

It results from what has been said that the attempt to find an absolute test of justice,—the giving to each one what he is rightly entitled to—, is a futile one. Justice, as an abstract term, has, of course, the definite meaning which has just been given to it, but it is impossible to say, for example, that any specific formula for the rendering to every one distributive or punitive justice is rightly applicable in all cases. What is social justice, or, to speak more concisely, justice—since all justice is social in character—, in any particular case depends upon the circumstances of the case. And the same is true of any general canon of justice, such as, with reference to economic goods, "to every one according to the labor done by him," or "according to the effort expended," or "according to the results of labor or effort expended," or "according to needs," or the simple egalitarian doctrine "an equal amount to every one." The degree to which any one of these, or other, rules of distribution, or a combination of two or more of them, can be said to lead to just results, necessarily depends upon the social conditions of the community to which they are applied; that is, depends upon the actual results to which their application will lead. Thus, it is conceivable that there be a community in which an absolute equality in the distribution of economic goods will lead to the most desirable social results. In another community, differently circumstanced, some other rule of distribution might lead to the best results. In each of these cases, the rule adopted can be said to realize "justice."

[7] §§ 197, 198.

Perhaps, the most general statement that can be made of an ideally just régime is that under which each person is required to contribute to the social good to the extent of his ability, and, from the general fund of economic goods (including services) is entitled to receive according to his needs,—"From every one according to his ability, to every one according to his needs."

The only difficulty, so far as this formula is concerned, is that it is impossible of actual application, since it is impossible, in any individual case, to determine, even approximately, what a man's abilities, or what his needs, really are. As for abilities, they are of many different kinds, and, of course, of varying degrees, and the determination of whether they are possessed by an individual, and of the degree to which they are possessed, can, in most cases, be determined only by experimentation,—an experimentation which may need to be carried on for years. And, as for a man's needs, these are still more variable, and still more difficult of determination. What a man is conceived really to need will, furthermore, depend upon social opinion as to what it is desirable that he should have, for, obviously, it could not be made to depend wholly upon what the man may want, or think that he needs, in order to satisfy such desires as he may happen to have. These, socially tested, may be bad rather than good.[8]

The result of our criticism thus shows us that an appeal to Natural Laws, or to the Natural Rights supposed to be founded upon them, has no other real meaning than an appeal to the ethical or ideal law which moral philosophy establishes, and that the so-called Natural Rights are no other than those rights which it is conceived that men, as rational moral beings in their dealings with one

---

[8] The author, in a volume entitled *Social Justice* (The Macmillan Co.), has discussed in considerable detail the various formulæ of distributive and punitive justice.

another should spontaneously and freely recognize and respect.

It now remains to be shown, however, that this conception while clear enough in itself is one which is logically inconsistent with the existence of a condition of complete individualism such as is predicated of a State of Nature:—that, in short, in such a non-social and non-political condition of life, the existence, and, indeed, the very idea of moral rights and moral obligations, would be an impossibility, and that, therefore, if it be conceived that individuals, so circumstanced, should enter into a compact for the establishment of social and political relations, their agreement would, under the conditions assumed, have not even a morally binding force.

Analyzing the idea of moral 'right' it has been seen that the claim of rights upon the part of one individual implies a reciprocal obligation upon the part of others to respect them, and this means that there is some sort of bond of common interest uniting those who have the rights with those who are obligated to respect them,—in other words, a social condition is implied, something more than a purely individualistic régime. Thus, one must agree with Green when he says: "There can be no right without a consciousness of common interest on the part of members of a society. Without this there might be certain powers on the part of individuals, but no recognition of these powers by others as powers of which they allow the exercise, nor any claim to such recognition, and without this recognition or claim to recognition there can be no right." [9] In a true "State of Nature," then, that is one which is conceived of as wholly individualistic—non-social and non-political—in character, only powers can exist, and what forbearance there may be upon the part of individuals to the exercise of their individual powers

[9] *Principles of Political Obligation: Philosophical Works*, Vol. II, p. 354.

of mind and body will be due wholly to considerations of prudence and not to conceptions of moral obligation. Indeed, there is some reason for holding that even the idea of moral obligation could never come into the mind of man, until social life has been instituted.[10] It is thus correct to say that society not only provides the *milieu* in which alone moral rules can find opportunity for application, but that it makes possible the very conception of the idea of morality itself. To what extent it would be possible for the isolated man to develop, in general, a power of reasoning beyond that possessed by the lower animals is also a question. Rousseau held that so long as men remained in a non-social state they did not guide their conduct by reason, but depended upon instinct and impulse. Certainly, morality cannot be predicated of unreasoning beings, but, in order to hold that morality has no application except in societies of men, it is not necessary to hold that men living in a state of complete isolation from each other would be wholly without reflective or even introspective mental powers. It is not even essential to show that the conception of moral obligation as

[10] The doctrine that the idea of a self as the possessor of rights can only come after the idea of a non-self has been developed and as set over against it, has been advanced, among others, by James Mark Baldwin and Josiah Royce. William McDougall in his *Introduction to Social Psychology*, accepting, in the main, the views of these two writers, has, upon this point, the following to say (p. 183): "It is helpful to try to imagine how far the idea of the self could develop in a human being of normal native endowment, if it were possible for him to grow up from birth onward in a purely physical environment, deprived, that is to say, of both human and animal companionship. It would seem that under these circumstances he could achieve at best but a rudimentary and crude idea of the self. It would be little more than a bodily self, which would be distinguished from other physical objects chiefly by its constant presence and by reason of the special interest that would attach to it as the seat of various pains. There would be a thread of continuity or sameness supplied by the mass of organic sensations arising from the internal organs and constituting what is called the coenæsthesia; and still more intimate and fundamental constituents of the empirical self would be the primary emotions, the conations, pleasures, and pains. The solitary individual's idea of self could hardly surpass this degree of complexity; for the further development of self-consciousness is wholly a social process."

an abstract idea could not frame itself in the isolated individual's mind. It is sufficient to show that, if he were to form such an idea, he would have to relate it to a situation in which men are united to each other by mutually recognized common interests, that is, to a condition of society; in short, that the ideas of moral rights and duties are meaningless apart from the idea of societies of men.

Moral philosophy must, then, start with the idea of Society and not with the individual man. And, if it be asked: How, as an historical proposition, did human society come to be created? we must turn to the results of anthropology and genetic psychology. If, as Hobbes maintained, men are by nature wholly self-regarding, we must ascribe the creation of social relationships, carrying with them mutual forbearances with regard to the exercise of individual powers, to the operation of the human reason which tells men that thus they can better satisfy their own several selfish interests. If, however, according to Rousseau, we regard men as having by their very nature sentiments of pity or sympathy as well as wholly self-regarding desires, then the creation by them of social life becomes all the more easy to understand. If it is as inherently natural to men to be sympathetic of the feelings of others, to feel pain or pleasure at the pain or pleasure of others, as it is for them to seek the satisfaction of what they regard as their own welfare, then, of course, we have ready at hand the explanation why men seek the society of others and are willing to recognize that, to a certain extent at least, they should exercise forbearance toward one another or even to extend affirmative aid to those of their fellow-creatures who seem to need their assistance.

From what has been said it is not to be understood that the writer claims that, granting that men are instinctively sympathetic, the origin of altruistic motives is

TRUE BASIS OF THE RIGHT OF POLITICAL COERCION 255

explained.[11] All that is meant to be asserted is that the feeling of sympathy leads to the establishment of social life, or at any rate renders more obvious to individuals the advantages to be obtained from a communal life in which the members of the group are recognized to have certain common interests. It tends, in other words, to create, if, indeed, it is not identical with, that "conscious-

[11] The action upon the part of an individual induced by sympathy may be wholly self-regarding in that he seeks to avoid the pain which the pain of others would give him, or to secure for himself the pleasure that the sight or knowledge of pleasure of others would give him. Upon this point the following observations of McDougall in his *Introduction to Social Psychology* are illuminating. "The fundamental and primitive form of sympathy is exactly what the word implies, a suffering with, the experiencing of any feeling or emotion when and because we observe in other persons or creatures the expression of that feeling or emotion." After describing the sympathetic induction of emotions displayed by many and probably by all gregarious animals, McDougall continues: "Sympathy of this crude kind is the cement that binds animal societies together, renders the actions of all members of a group harmonious, and allows them to reap some of the prime advantages of social life in spite of lack of intelligence" (pp. 92-93). "This primitive sympathy implies none of the higher moral qualities. There are persons who are exquisitely sympathetic in this sense of feeling with another, experiencing distress at the sight of pain and grief, pleasure at the sight of joy, who are utterly selfish and are not moved in the least degree to relieve the distress they observe in others or to promote the pleasure that is reflected in themselves. Their sympathetic sensibility merely leads them to avoid all contact with distressful persons, books, or scenes, and to seek the company of the careless and gay." Or, McDougall might have added, where they are led to action to relieve distress or to promote pleasure, they do so merely because of the effect that they themselves get upon their own feelings. As distinguished from mere passive sympathy, McDougall speaks of sympathy being active when it stimulates one to desire that others should feel the same emotions that he himself does. The root of this active sympathy he also finds in a gregarious instinct which man shares with animals. Here, also, the emotion may be a wholly egoistic one—a desire for one's own satisfaction.

As regards what is meant by terming a feeling "instinctive" we may also, with profit, quote the clear statement of McDougall. He says: "Among professed psychologists there is now fair agreement as to the usage of the terms 'instinct' and 'instinctive.' By the great majority they are used only to denote certain innate specific tendencies of the mind that are common to all members of any one species, racial characters that have been slowly evolved in the process of adaptation of species to their environment and that can be neither eradicated from the mental constitution of which they are the innate elements nor acquired by individuals in the course of their lifetime. A few writers, of whom Professor Wundt is the most prominent, apply the terms to the very strongly fixed acquired habits of action that are more commonly and properly described as secondarily automatic actions, as well as to the innate specific tendencies. The former usage seems in every way preferable."

ness of kind" which sociologists such as F. H. Giddings accept as the psychological basis of society.[12]

Distinction between Political and Other Forms of Coercion. Having shown that the term morality has no meaning apart from the idea of human society, and that, therefore, when solving the problem of justifying, upon moral grounds, the existence of political authority, we may start with social life as a given fact, we are ready to consider the second question earlier pointed out, namely, as to what differences, if any, distinguish political forms of coercion from those that are non-political, or purely social, in character.

If we take men as they have been known to be the world over and since the time when history furnishes any record of their acts, and not as they conceivably might be as perfectly moralized, intellectually enlightened beings, we find them conceiving themselves to have interests—whether real or mistaken is not here material—that are in conflict. This being so, coercion of some sort is inescapable. Some individuals will have to forego the satisfaction of their desires in order that the others may have free play to their will, or each will have to yield in part in return for the abandonment by the others of a part of their desires,—*do ut des*. In either case, limitations upon freedom of individual action make their appearance. The complete freedom of every one to do exactly what he wants to do is not possible, and the only questions are as to which desires shall be satisfied and which shall

---

[12] It is usual to deny to sub-human living beings any reflective or self-conscious life. If this be true then a human society, even of the most primitive type, is differentiated from the communal life of bees, wasps, ants, birds, or of mammals, by the fact that there is in the minds of the human beings a consciousness of common interests. "Human society," says Giddings, "truly begins when social consciousness and tradition are so far developed that all social relations exist not only objectively as physical facts of association, but subjectively also, in the thought, feeling, and purpose of the associated individuals. It is this subjective fact that differentiates human from animal communities." *The Theory of Sociology.* Supplement to the Annals of the American Acad. of Political and Social Science, July, 1894, p. 60.

remain unsatisfied and as to how this decision shall be brought about and enforced.

It may be imagined that in all societies, to a certain extent, all the individuals will willingly and peaceably agree to certain mutual forbearances. To what extent they will do so will depend upon the degree to which there is, in fact, a mutuality of interests, and an intellectual enlightenment enabling all to perceive that this common forbearance will redound to the advantage of each and every one. To the extent, however, to which individuals are not willing to subordinate their interests to, or compromise them with, the interests of others, it becomes necessary to exercise coercion. And thus the questions arise: Who are to exercise this coercion, and what form is it to take?

As to who shall exercise it, the decision will necessarily be one of power,—of the physical and mental power of individuals, acting individually or in concert. As to the kind of coercion, this may take a multitude of forms. It may be in the form of physical force directly applied, involving the taking of life, the infliction of bodily pain, imprisonment, or the forcible seizure of lands or goods. Or, it may act under the guise of social disapprobation, of refusal to have friendly or business relations with the persons proceeded against. In whatever manner this outside force is applied to the individual he is subjected to coercion, and this is true whenever he acts otherwise than he would have acted had he been free from the threat of evil to be inflicted upon him by his fellow men.

If, then, there must be coercion in some form to the extent that men's interests conflict, or are conceived to conflict, and if, as all will admit, subjection to coercion is, in itself, that is, detached from its purposes, an evil in the sense that it causes mental or physical irritation and pain, the two-fold problem is presented: (1) of eradicating as far as possible conflicts of individual interests, and (2) of applying in the best form possible the coercion that is demanded for solving the conflicts that are not avoided. The problem in its first aspect involves the whole matter of social organization and the application of correct canons of distributive justice with reference to all the desirable and undesirable things of life. The problem in its second aspect involves the establishment of agencies for applying coercion, when needed, in the most effective, and, as regards the amount of pain caused by it, the most economical form. It is with the problem in its second aspect that we are here concerned.

A Locke was not needed to show the inconveniences— to use his very mild term—of a state of society in which the individuals have no known general rules of conduct to which they are expected to conform, no impartial judges to which their disputes as to the meaning and application of these rules may be referred, and no set of persons possessing power for the enforcement of these rules and adjudications of such a paramount character that its exercise will not, except upon rare occasions, be resisted. These inconveniences of a non-political State, the political State, to the extent that it efficiently exercises its functions, overcomes. By its creation coercion is not for the first time employed: there is merely a substitution of a general, definite, paramount force in place of the uncertain, indefinite, unregulated force which public opinion or the physical powers and arbitrary wills of individuals would otherwise employ.

If, then, it be granted that by giving to a society a political organization and by vesting in a certain man or set of men the legal right of determining, in certain cases at least, when coercion shall be applied to individuals, the result, upon the whole, is to produce less evil or more good than would otherwise be secured, then political authority is justified.

However, because, as tested by the rule that has been

stated, it is deemed desirable that a political authority should be created in and over a given society, it does not follow that it should necessarily be given a monopoly of the right to exercise coercion. Nor has any commital been made as to the kind of governmental structure to be given to the State. It may be, that, with reference to many matters, it will still be preferable to have individuals controlled by "social" as distinguished from "political" forces, or even left free to secure what they are able to obtain in unrestricted competitive struggle with their fellow individuals. This is a topic to which we shall return in our chapter entitled "The Legitimate Sphere of the State." The ethical criteria to be applied in determining the merits of different forms of political control, that is, of government, will be considered in our chapter entitled "Government."

When political coercion of the individual is viewed in the light which we have thrown upon it, it is seen that, from the standpoint of ethics as well as of expediency, it is justified just to the extent that it provides a more efficient and less oppressive form of control than would exist without it. And this feature of operation deserves especial notice; namely, that, in very many cases, the effect of civil law is to decrease rather than to increase coercion because its effect is to protect individuals against coercion by other individuals, or groups of individuals.

That, taking it as a whole, coercion by political authority is preferable to unrestrained coercion few will deny. It is of course possible to take such an optimistic view as to the manner in which men would act if they were released from all political control, that a state of anarchy can be regarded as preferable to one of political society. This opinion, though unsupported by human experience, persons are entitled to hold as a matter of fact or of probability. But, for reasons that have already been given, they are not entitled to assert, as some anarchists do, that men, as individuals, have an absolute ethical right to complete exemption from coercion by their fellow-men. In so far, also, as they start with men as entitled to specific rights, as, for example, the right to the products of their own labor, or to participate upon equal terms in the use of land, they are, as our reasoning has shown, investing men with rights as individuals which they cannot, logically, be conceived to have. It is also to be observed that, in so far as anarchists view as ideal a state of society in which men are moved to act by mere public opinion and social censure or commendation, stopping short of physical coercion or the infliction of physical penalties, they in fact validate coercion, for when men are led to act otherwise than they would have liked to act because of their unwillingness to come under the disapprobation of their associates they are, to that extent, coerced. And this is true even when this disapprobation is not followed by a refusal of their associates to have social or economic or other relations with them.

The philosophical anarchist is thus offered only the following alternatives:

(1) He may mean by Anarchy, not a condition of complete individualism, but one in which individuals are coerced only by social opinion or by pressure taking the form of a refusal of others to have social or economic or other dealings with the reprobated one. In this case the difference of opinion between the anarchist and the upholder of political authority is merely one as to the relative merits of non-political as compared with political coercion. Or,

(2) The anarchist may assert that, under present conditions, political coercion is needed, but that, non-political coercion being a form of control preferable to that by the State, the former should be substituted for the latter whenever possible, and that every effort should be made to educate the people to this view, and prepare them as

rapidly as possible for the time when political authority may be wholly dispensed with. Or,

(3) The anarchist may hold that man is by nature ethically entitled to a freedom of action which makes illegitimate every form of coercion over him. This position, we have seen, is logically an impossible one, for it attempts to invest men with moral rights independently of their membership in a society. So far as the writer knows, no anarchist has advocated a condition of human life in which there would be no social relationships between men, and, even should they assert this, they would, as our reasoning has shown, have in mind a situation in which there would be no morality whatever, and, therefore, no basis for a claim, upon ethical grounds, to complete freedom of the individual.

In the position which has been taken in the preceding pages with regard to the ethical justification of political authority, one conclusion is involved which it is important to emphasize. This is that there is no inherent merit in political coercion which justifies it apart from the results reached, or expected to be reached, by it. In other words, to ask as an abstract proposition, and without reference to any particular political society, whether the State has a right to be, is as little sensible as to ask whether a given implement is of value without reference to the use to which it is to be put, or to inquire whether a picture is beautiful without designating some particular picture to which the judgment is to be applied. In short, the demand for an abstract or *a priori* justification of political authority, or, indeed, of any form of coercion, is an illegitimate, because meaningless, one. As near as one can come to making a general assertion that political coercion is justified is to say that the world has seldom, and perhaps never, seen a political rule that was not preferable to what would probably have resulted from a complete absence of political authority; but it cannot be denied that a political rule could conceivably be so unintelligent and so oppressive and self-seeking on the part of the rulers that, viewed from the standpoint of the ruled, a wholly non-political régime would be preferable.

Hobbes, Spinoza and Rousseau conceded that, in the State of Nature, there is no morality and yet thought that, because of the agreement that men enter into to establish a political society they come, in some way, under a moral obligation henceforth to abide by the terms of that agreement. Locke conceived of the pre-civil society as one in which nearly all the rules of morality exist and thus found a support for the morally binding force of the original covenant. By this assumption, however, he did not escape from false reasoning, for he did not explain how, starting with men as individually free and equal, they come to form a genuine society in which reciprocal moral rights and duties are recognized. In truth Locke took as granted the existence of nearly all the social features which the Social Compact was supposed to create.

Although Hobbes and Rousseau recognized that in a true State of Nature no such thing as morality can exist, and, therefore, no such thing as specific individual rights and duties, they yet viewed men as, in some way, entitled to a freedom from coercion of which they might not justly be deprived except with their own consent. They thus seemed to think that there is something artificial in the control exercised by political authority, something, as it were, against nature, and which distinguishes it in kind from the coercion exercised by individuals over one another when living without social or political bonds, which made it necessary to provide a special justification for it, which justification, they thought, could be found in an assumed consent of the people. If, however, they had more carefully examined the nature of moral obligation and of political authority they would have seen that they had created their own logical difficulties, and made insoluble the problem they had set themselves. This they did by assuming that there is an *a priori* objection to political coercion, and that, therefore, it is necessary to find a basis for political control that will not be in violation of the freedom of action that the individual has when viewed as a person living in absolute social detachment from his fellow-men. By recognizing that, in a State of Nature, there is no such thing as morality, Hobbes, Spinoza and Rousseau had the key to the question in their own hands, but they did not use it. They still held that they had to start with the individual as absolutely free, and therefore, that upon them lay the burden of proving that political control, as contrasted with this "natural" freedom of the individual, needs to be affirmatively and specially justified by obtaining in some way the consent of the individuals subjected to it.

Kant, as has been shown, was greatly influenced by Rousseau, and especially by his doctrine of a General Will growing out of a Social Compact and by the operations of which the individual remains free in an ethical or spiritual sense although subjected to the absolute control of his State. Kant was, therefore, led to accept, as a conceptual device, the Social Contract, but, in place of the instinctive or emotional elements that played so large a part in Rousseau's idea of man's will, Kant emphasized man's practical reason. "Obligation," he declared, "is the necessity of free reason when viewed in relation to a categorical imperative of reason." He still clung, however, to the idea that conflicting individual wills and interests needed to be harmonized by some such artificial means as a real or conceived compact between individuals. He had, apparently, no conception of a social or political society in which a true harmony might be affected between the wills of individuals *inter se,* and the interests of all made identical with the interests of each.

Hence, Natural Law, so far as it was viewed as *lex naturalis* rather than *lex aeterna* generally (which is the only sense in which it is pertinent to the present inquiry), became practically identical with the categorical imperative of practical reason. However, as Salmond points out,[13] there was this essential difference between the view of Kant and the position of Aquinas and the Schoolmen generally. When Aquinas spoke of the dictates of practical reason, he meant principally the reason of God, not of man; i.e., he held that man's reason is not in itself possessed of legislative, commanding authority. Kant, however, proclaimed the autonomy of human reason as itself possessing a law-giving faculty, and declared its commands to constitute the Moral Law. We thus see the *a priori* element in law carried to its extreme extent. The ascription to reason of the capacity for something more than mere generalization, comparison, and judging of the *data* furnished it from outside, and the giving to it of the capacity to evolve not only form but subject-matter, necessarily rendered the law to that extent independent of actual experience and historic relativity.[14]

It is thus to be observed that, though Natural Laws are conceived as commands either of the Deity or of Nature herself (*natura naturans*), there exists no means of actual coercion in the case of disobedience. Hence their actual binding force can only be upon the conscience. That is, Natural Laws, from their inherent nature, must necessarily be moral laws, and moral laws only. They may serve to represent what *should be,* but not what *is.* When they obtain actual acceptance and enforcement at the hands of a political power, they become *ipso facto* civil or positive laws.

---

[13] In his article "The Law of Nature," in the *Law Quarterly Review,* April, 1895.
[14] Cf. Pulszky, *Theory of Law and Civil Society,* pp. 75 *et seq.*

It is, then, their character as *ideal* rights, rather than as *actual* provisions of coercive law that has caused Natural Rights to be appealed to by those desiring a change from what is, and has thus made appeal to them ever the instrument of reform. It is its character as revealed only in the reason, and not in the explicit command of a human authority, that has given to Natural Law its influence against all customs and institutions that have lost their sacredness or outlived their usefulness. Thus the appeal to Natural Law is an appeal from established authority and judgment to the individual conscience as such,—the demand for a justification that is based upon grounds, utilitarian and moral, that will satisfy the practical reason of the individual making the demand.[15]

The Ethical Rights of Persons Deemed Mentally Incompetent. Reference has been earlier made to the difficulty with which the supporters of the Social Compact theory have had to contend with reference to the rights of persons who, by reason of infancy or other causes, are not able to exercise an intelligent judgment or will. The discussion of this difficulty was, however, passed over for the time being but now needs to be undertaken.

By the premise that all human beings are, by their very nature, free, and equally entitled to moral consideration, the Compact Theory was forced to give attention to the rights of intellectually incompetent as well as of intellectually competent persons.

Locke said: "Children, I confess, are not born in this full state of equality, though they are born to it. Their parents have a sort of rule and jurisdiction over them when they come into the world, and for some time after, but it is but a temporary one. The bands of this subjection are like the swaddling clothes they are wrapt up in and supported by in the weakness of their infancy.

[15] Cf. Ritchie, *Natural Rights*, pp. 6 *et seq.*

Age and reason as they grow up loosen them till at length they drop off, and leave a man at his own free disposal." [16]

Rousseau said: "The common liberty is a consequence of man's nature. . . . And as soon as he comes to years of discretion, being the sole judge of the means adapted for his own preservation, he becomes his own master." [17] It thus appears that both these philosophers—and the same is true of their followers—were obliged to recognize, dispite their premises regarding the natural, inherent, and inviolable rights of men, that, in fact, the enjoyment of these rights may be denied to them until they have reached "years of discretion." This concession they were obliged to make since they necessarily conceived of the Social Compact as something more than a mere formal mechanical act. It represented a meeting of minds and implied that the parties to it had the ability to form a conscious, deliberate judgment as to the undertaking contained in it.

John Stuart Mill, as we shall later on have occasion to point out, although asserting an absolute right of the individual to be exempt from political or social control so far as his self-regarding acts are concerned, found himself obliged to limit the application of this doctrine to those persons and to those races of men who have reached a stage of intellectual development equivalent to that of Locke's "age of discretion," and which he described as one in which the individual or race is able to profit by discussion, that is, is mentally qualified to appreciate the benefits and evils to himself to be expected from alternative lines of conduct. After declaring in his essay *On Liberty* that its object is "to assert one very simple principle as entitled to govern *absolutely* the dealings of society with the individual in the way of

---
[16] *Two Treatises of Government*, Book II, Chap. VI.
[17] *Social Contract*, Book I, Chap. III.

compulsion and control," Mill was forced in the very next paragraph to say: "It is, perhaps, hardly necessary to say that this doctrine is meant to apply only to human beings in the maturity of their faculties. We are not speaking of children, or of young persons below the age which the law may fix as that of manhood or womanhood. . . . Those who are still in a state to require being taken care of by others, must be protected against their own actions as well as against external injury. For the same reason we may leave out of consideration those backward states of society in which the race itself may be considered as in its nonage. Despotism is a legitimate mode of government in dealing with barbarians, provided the end be their improvement, and the means justified by actually effecting that end. Liberty, as a principle, has no application to any state of things anterior to the time when mankind have become capable of being improved by free and equal discussion."

Neither Locke, Rousseau, nor Mill and their followers seem to have seen that, in limiting the application of their consent doctrine to persons who have reached years of discretion they, in fact, abandoned the very citadel of their position. For they admitted that it lies within the power of those who exercise political or other forms of control to determine what persons have sufficient discernment to judge wisely as to their own interests, and that, as to those who have not this discernment, those in possession of actual power over them, may dictate to them what they shall or shall not do. The right to liberty was thus no longer asserted to be an absolute one, but dependent upon an ability to use it wisely, and, what is still more important, the governors and not the governed were given the authority to decide which persons or peoples are qualified to determine what it is wise or just for them to do. In truth, this is no more than is asserted by the autocratic monarch who asserts and believes that he knows better what is for the welfare of his people than they themselves know. It is no more than many Germans claimed before the Great War when they asserted that Germans were superior in culture to other races, and, therefore, that they would benefit those other races by bringing them, by force if necessary, under their own imperial control.[18]

It is clear, then, that the Contract Theory definitely breaks down at this point, for, in order not to assume the absurd position that a mere infant, with no appreciation of the nature or substance of a contract, can become a party to it and be bound by it,[19] consent is abandoned

[18] The criticism by Sir James Fitzjames Stephen of Mill's limitation of liberty to persons or races qualified to profit by discussion is vigorous enough to deserve quotation. In his *Liberty, Equality, and Fraternity* (Chapter I) he says: "Where, in the very most advanced and civilized communities, will you find any class of persons whose views or whose conduct on subjects on which they are interested are regulated even in the main by the results of free discussion? What proportion of human misconduct in any department of life is due to ignorance and what to wickedness or weakness? . . . If we look at the conduct of bodies of men as expressed in their laws and institutions, we shall find that, though compulsion and persuasion go hand in hand, from the most immature to the roughest ages and societies up to the most civilized, the lion's share of the results obtained is due to compulsion, and that discussion is at most an appeal to the motives by which the strong man is likely to be actuated in using his strength. Look at our own time and country, and mention any single great change which has been effected by mere discussion. Can a single case be mentioned in which the passions of men interested where the change was not carried by force —that is, to say, ultimately by the fear of revolution? . . . Parliamentary government is simply a mild and disguised form of compulsion. We agree to try strength by counting heads instead of breaking heads, but the principle is exactly the same. It is not the wisest side which wins, but the one which for the time being shows its superior strength (of which no doubt wisdom is one element) by enlisting the largest amount of active sympathy in its support. The minority gives way not because it is convinced that it is wrong, but because it is convinced that it is a minority." And a little later on, he says: "Estimate the proportion of men and women who are selfish, sensual, frivolous, idle, absolutely commonplace and wrapped up in the smallest of petty routines, and consider how far the freest discussion is likely to improve them. The only way by which it is practically possible to act upon them at all is by compulsion or restraint."

[19] A contract, *ex vi termini*, is a meeting of minds—a deliberate acceptance by the parties of the terms of the agreement, but this meeting of minds or acceptance of terms cannot take place except in so far as the parties are competent to understand not only the verbal meaning but the probable significance of the undertakings entered into.

as the only basis upon which control by one person over another may be justified, and in its place is accepted the doctrine that the individual has a right to coerce those whom he deems less enlightened than himself.

CHAPTER XV

THE LEGITIMATE ENDS OF POLITICAL COERCION

HAVING shown that men can be regarded as having moral rights and duties only in so far as they are viewed as members of a society, and that only a question of expediency distinguishes the coercion that is exercised in non-political or social form from that applied by the State through its Government, we are ready to consider the third group of questions propounded some pages back: What absolute principles, if any, determine the manner in which, or the circumstances under which, or the purpose for which, political coercion may be legitimately exercised.[1]

It is conceivable that those in political authority should seek any one of the following general ends: (1) the welfare of the State itself as an independent or transcendental being; (2) the welfare of those in control of the government; (3) the welfare of some particular class or classes of the citizen body; (4) the welfare of the whole body of citizens alike; (5) the welfare of all peoples, that is, of humanity, future as well as present.

The propriety of the first end can be maintained only by asserting the real existence of the State as a person or entity of a higher moral order than the individual human being, and, as such, subserving a purpose in human history so important that the interests of individuals, distributively or collectively considered, may, if necessary, be disregarded in order that the State's welfare may be advanced. The falsity of such a transcendental concep-

[1] See *ante*, p. 236.

tion of the State has already been indicated in what has earlier been said regarding that metaphysical doctrine.

The proposition that the welfare of the rulers as distinguished from the welfare of the ruled is an ethically legitimate end of a government can be sustained only if a patrimonial conception of political authority is accepted, or, possibly, if a divine right of rulership is upheld. However, so far as the writer knows, the divine right of rulership has never been argued except in company with the assumption that the ruler, as the agent of the Almighty, or as himself divine, is obligated to seek the welfare of those over whom he rules.

The proposition that government may rightly be operated for the benefit of some particular class or classes in the community can only be defended if to the members of these classes be ascribed certain inherent rights similar in character to those which are claimed by those rulers who assert a divine or proprietary right of rulership. To what extent, and in what manner the idea of the right of all men to an equality of consideration finds a place as an inherent element in the consideration of justice, that is, of ethical desert, has been discussed in another work,[2] but it may be said here that it is not possible to defend upon logical grounds the position that any one or more special classes of individuals have an inherent right, that is, apart from the personal merits and needs of their members, to have their particular interests raised above those of the other members of a community. This follows from the conception that all men, as moral persons, are essentially alike.

Discarding, then, the other conceivable possibilities, we are remitted to the proposition that all governments exist in order to advance the interests of the governed. Whether or not these interests are best determined by obtaining an expression of the judgment of the governed

[2] See the author's volume, *Social Justice*.

as to what they want the government to do, or whether this can best be determined for them by a monarch and his advisers, or by a select portion of the whole citizen body, is a distinct question with which we are not, at this place concerned, but which we shall later discuss. We are here concerned, however, to ascertain the fundamental principles or criteria which determine what are the true interests of the governed, and especially to know what relation exists between the welfare of a given individual and the welfare of other individuals or of the community as a whole. And, furthermore, it is of importance to determine in how far the welfare of one political group may be harmonized with the welfare of other political groups and with that of Humanity as a whole, including future as well as present generations of men.

Who Shall Determine What the Public Welfare Demands? If, then, viewing political government in all cases and under all circumstances as nothing more than a means to an end, and accepting as correct the doctrine that this end should be the welfare of the governed, one is met by the question: To what extent is it ethically justifiable that those who happen to be in political authority shall determine when, and the forms under which, coercion by the State shall be applied; and to what extent shall it be left to the individual to determine for himself what it is right that he should do? Or, stated in another way, the question is: When the political law has commanded that a certain thing be done or not done, with whom lies the final judgment as to the ethical propriety of the command?

The problem thus stated, in order to be satisfactorily solved, needs to be approached from three points of view: (1) that of the individual whose conduct is controlled; (2) that of the Government, or, what is the same thing, that of those who determine its policies; and (3) that of a disinterested third party viewing objectively the situation. These points of view will be considered in the order stated.

Applying the principles which were established in the preceding chapter, it is clear that the possession of rights by the individual is dependent upon the possession by him of a capacity and a disposition to employ them for the attainment of some desirable end. Applying them to the subject of political control, one is led to the declaration that the existence of a State is justified, as to each individual, in so far, and only in so far, as it tends by its activities to assist in developing the best self of that individual.

In thus bringing a particular State to the bar of moral criticism, it is rather its activities than its own right to existence which is brought to trial. The right to existence of the political authority itself is not in issue, for, as abstractly considered, that is, apart from any particular form of organization or manner of operation, there is no basis upon which a judgment may be founded. It is not until the State manifests its power and authority that material is afforded to which moral estimates may be applied. Furthermore, it is to be remarked, though it can hardly be necessary to do so, that, in considering the morality of a command of the State, there is no pretense that the fact that it is the command of the State enters as an absolutely determining factor. There is only to be asked by the individual in each particular case whether he, as a morally responsible person, shall obey or disobey. The act has a moral or immoral character only as to the individual, and what moral responsibility there is exists only for him.

When, however, the State has commanded a certain line of conduct, that fact, though not determinative of the morality of the command, abstractly considered, is yet one which the individual is morally bound to consider in determining what his own actions shall be. While it must be held that the individual has at times the moral right—nay, that he may be morally bound—to refuse obedience to those laws which, for any reason, he deems to be unjust or immoral, he is obligated to take into consideration, in estimating all the consequences of his act, that disobedience to a command of the State will tend to weaken to some extent the reverence for law in general, and will thus have an influence in dissolving those social and political bonds which in the aggregate promote the realization of morality as a whole. The moral right of resistance, as well as of revolution, cannot be denied, but it is a right only to be justified by a consideration of all the consequences, proximate and ultimate, individual and social, which attend its exercise.

The inescapable obligation which rests upon the individual as a rational being to judge for himself, by his reason rather than by any independent and infallible faculty termed conscience, or by the judgment of any other person, as to what it is right that he should do, is excellently given by Professor L. T. Hobhouse in his volume, *The Metaphysical Theory of the State*.[3] So luminously is this stated that a rather extended quotation is justified even though it covers ground already gone over. He says:

"In a simpler time, and in our own time to the more simple-minded men, conscience can be taken as the voice of God within and its deliverances may be fortified by an appeal to the written word of God without. So conceived, conscience is as much above State law in authority as it is below it in power; but in a sceptical age men realize more fully that there is a subjective element in conscience. Consciences differ, and the word of God, even if we take it to be an inspired document, is manifestly liable to the greatest diversities of interpretation. What I call my conscience is my final judgment, when

[3] *Op. cit.*, page 91.

all things bearing on the situation have been summed up, of my right and my duty. This judgment, common experience and psychological analysis will alike show, is in part dependent on idiosyncrasies of my own, on special experiences that have impressed me, on emotional tendencies that make me attach more weight to one thing and less to another, on partial application of principles, on obscurity of ideas. Conscience, then, would seem to have but little final authority. It falls short of the objectivity attached to law and the social tradition. How can it be set up as a standard of nonconformity in some vital matter? The answer of the individual in the first place is that conscience may be a poor thing, but it is his own; and the answer of the moral law must be that, though there may be many errors incident to the principle that men should do ultimately what is right in their own eyes, yet, if they do anything else than what is right in their own eyes, there is no moral law at all. Moral action is action in conformity with an inward principle, an action that the agent considers to be right and performs because he believes it to be right. If people are required to give up what they consider to be right, morality is annulled. May a man act, then, without regard to law or the judgment of others? On the contrary, what experience in practical matters will often teach him is that others are wiser than he, what morality will teach him is that the law which is right for him must in principle be a law of universal application, holding for all men similarly situated. What duty and practical sense will combine to show him is that he is a man among many, a member of an organized society, and if morality teaches him that he must do what he thinks good, it inculcates at the same time that what is good for him must be a common good. Nevertheless, he is in the end to stand by his judgment of the nature of the common good, and the means by which it is to be realized. Once given, as in the case of the churchman, that he has well and truly weighed all that law and society have to say, that he has taken into account the limitations of his own experience and the fallibility of his own judgment as one weak individual opposed perhaps to the millions of all organized society; when he has then asked himself frankly if it is not his final duty to waive his first judgment, to stifle the inward prompting from respect for an outward order built up by the organized efforts of men, valuable in itself and endangered if any one rebels against it; when, having duly tested the case in a spirit of humility, he has nevertheless come finally to the conclusion that, all said and done, the obligation is upon him to disobey, then, as a free agent, nonconformity is his only course.

"It should be observed that when we say he is right in following this course our proposition has two meanings, which must not be confused. To disentangle them, let us for a moment put ourselves on the side of the State. Let us suppose the State is justified in its behest, that if we were gods knowing good and evil, we should give our verdict on the side of the State, then, in that sense and from that point of view, the noncomformist is clearly wrong just as, if the verdict were given the other way, he would be clearly right. But, even in the case where he is wrong in one sense he is also right in another. It is right that he should do what he thinks right although, as it happens, he thinks wrong; the ultimate reason of this is that, though by so acting he is wrong on occasion, if he acted otherwise as a matter of principle he would never do right at all, and if every one so acted, right and wrong as moral terms would disappear. And by the same reasoning, the State, in so far as it holds itself trustee for the final good of society, will recognize that it is better for its members to be free men who will from time to time give trouble by mistakes of judgment, than conforming persons with whom everything is smooth because they never think at all. For this reason the State will avoid coercion of conscience up to the last resort, but, once again, as in the case of the Church, we have to admit as correlative to the ultimate right of conscience, an ultimate right of coercion. The State, a fallible organization of fallible men, has nevertheless to act according to its lights for the safety of the whole. Where it can see no escape from a universal rule, where this rule would be frustrated by individual acts of disobedience, where by disobeying A would in its judgment do a wrong to B, there in the end it has to exercise constraint, and there seems to be no appeal. The judgment of mankind may ultimately say that the State was wrong, but even so it will have to extend to the State the same charity which is due to the nonconforming individual. If the State acted *bona fida* by its best lights, it could do no better."

The State's Point of View. The individual's point of view with regard to the coercion that is exercised over him by his Government having been examined, the discussion of the point of view of those who, being in possession of the political power, determine what coercion shall be applied, will not be very difficult, for it will be found that the controlling principles are practically the same.

First of all there is to be repeated what has been earlier said, that the State, viewed as a person or as an abstract entity cannot be held responsible for its own acts. It is not a moral being. There is no way, therefore, in which moral responsibility can be imputed to it. It has no real will of its own. It cannot feel, have emotions, form motives, or exercise reason. It cannot, therefore, be said to have a conscience. And the same may be said of a People, when considered as a political unity as distinguished from the arithmetical sum of its constituent individuals.

In other words, morality applies only to human individuals. These have moral duties that arise from the fact that they are members of a society, and, when this society is so organized as to constitute a State, they may be said to have political as well as social obligations.[4] It is, indeed true, that individuals may, and, perhaps, necessarily must, form judgments as to what moral ends the State should seek to realize, and, in this sense, the State may be said to have a moral purpose and to be under a moral obligation. However, this is only nominally true, for this moral purpose, and the consequent moral obligation of the State, is one that is determined not by itself, but by the individuals who constitute the body-politic of the State, and it is upon them that, in final analysis, rests the obligation to see to it that what we described as the moral ends of the State are attained, or sought to be attained.

As to this obligation upon the part of the individuals constituting the body-politic of a State, it is to be observed that not all are able to contribute alike or equally to what may loosely be termed the will of the State. However, just to the extent to which one does, or can, contribute by his influence to the formation of an effective political opinion, he is under moral obligation to make that political opinion moral in character and directed to the securing of the highest possible ethical ideals as he sees them.

The moral responsibility for all political action may not, therefore, be shifted, either in whole or in part, upon an abstract political being, but rests wholly upon the individuals, whether they be public officials or private citizens; and this in exact proportion not only to the extent to which they actually do have an influence in directing the course of public affairs, but to the extent to which it lies within their individual powers, should

[4] It is sometimes said that individual human beings have moral duties which they owe to themselves, considered as distinct and independent persons. This is not correct for the reasons which have been earlier given.

they use their real opportunities, to direct the power of the State to the attainment of its proper ends.

Considering, then, the exercise of political control from the point of view of those that exercise it, it is clear that, in each specific instance, they must exercise their judgment in exactly the same way, and be moved by the same moral motives that apply when the individuals who are controlled pass their judgments upon the ethical rightfulness of the acts or policies demanded of them. In other words, those in authority are, of necessity, led to estimate the morality of their political acts in accordance with the ethical standards they set for themselves, and the conclusions which they reach as to how what they deem to be desirable may best be attained. Except, then, that the proposition is stated in terms possibly too hedonistic in character, we may accept the conclusion of Fitzjames Stephen when he says: "The character of laws or of morals is determined by the ideal of human life which it assumes, and this is the ideal of its author, not the ideal of those to whose conduct it applies. In a word, the happiness which the lawgiver regards as the test of his laws is that which he, after attaching to their wishes whatever weight he thinks proper, wishes his subjects to have. . . . If he has sufficient confidence in his own views, or if he is indifferent to their adoption by others, he can erect his system upon a conception of happiness as different from the common one of his own time and country as he pleases."[5]

It does not need to be repeated that those who determine the policies of a State are under a moral obligation to seek, not their own individual welfare, but the true welfare of the governed, and that, knowing that the interests of many persons are concerned in their decisions, they are under an especial moral obligation to be sure not only that they are seeking only the interests of the

[5] *Liberty, Equality, and Fraternity*, Chap. VI.

governed, but that they have, so far as has been possible to them, sought to make themselves acquainted with all the facts needed for an intelligent judgment and have fully considered the ultimate, as well as the proximate, results to be expected from the commands which they issue. Especially, should they appreciate that, where there is a difference of opinion between themselves and some or all of those whom they govern, it is imperative that they should reach their decision with an absolutely open and disinterested mind. But, the final judgment must be theirs in exactly the same manner that a parent determines for his children, or the director of a business corporation determines for his stockholders, or those in authority in a church or in any social organization, determine what, for the best interests of all concerned, shall be done.

The Objective Viewpoint. The same principles that have been stated as governing the rightfulness of an exercise of political authority when judged by either the governed or those governing applies when a disinterested third party passes ethical judgment upon political acts. He applies his own standards of conduct and his own conceptions of what are the true interests of the governed and what are the means by which they may best be attained. He thus forms his own opinion as to whether or not those in political authority are justified in applying coercion, and whether or not, all things considered, those to whom the coercion is attempted to be applied, should obey or seek to evade or openly to refuse to obey the commands of their political superiors.

CHAPTER XVI

THE LEGITIMATE SPHERE OF POLITICAL AUTHORITY

THE fundamental purpose of a system of final political philosophy has been fulfilled when it has determined the essential nature of political authority and the relation in which the individual stands to the State, and of the relation in which States stand to one another. This task, except as to the relations of States *inter se*, which will be later considered, has been performed, it is hoped, in the pages which have gone before. There remains, then, only to draw from the conclusions which have been reached certain corollaries with regard to the legitimate sphere of political authority, and the character of governmental organization through which it should operate. In this chapter we shall deal with the general principles, if any, which determine the extent to which a State may exercise the paramount powers which have been placed within its hands.

Inherent Limitations. Our examination of this question will be simplified if we first point out the respects in which the sphere of the State's control is limited by reason of the kind of coercion it is able to apply.

As regards these inherent limits, it is clear that, do what it will, the State cannot control the operation of man's judgment, that is, the determination by him of what he conceives to be right or wrong. Because of the sanctions which it attaches to its orders, the State may supply him with reasons which, added to those which exist independently of these sanctions, may persuade him to do or not to do specific acts. But, over the interior motives which move him to act, and which determine for him the essential morality of his conduct, it can exercise no control. In other words, the State can control only the external act. The determination by the individual whether or not a given act, all things considered, should or should not be performed, and his final decision as to whether in fact he will or will not perform it, must always lie with himself. In this sense the individual may be said to be, of necessity and always, free. As Green says: "Moral duties do not admit of being enforced. The question sometimes put whether moral duties should be enforced by law, is really an unmeaning one; for they simply cannot be enforced. They are duties to act, it is true, and an act can be enforced; but they are duties to act from certain motives, and these cannot be enforced." [1]

This is not to say that the State cannot enforce rules of conduct solely upon the ground that those who enact the laws deem that the rules are moral in character and content, but, it does mean that whether, in fact, they are such, the coerced individual must judge for himself, and his motive when obeying them may be either because he believes, as an ethical proposition, that he should so act, or simply because he deems it expedient not to subject himself to the consequences that would follow from a refusal to obey. And, even when he judges that it is ethically obligatory upon him to obey, this may be, not because he thinks that the rule is, in itself, an ethically sound one, but because he thinks that it will be better for him to obey it than, by resisting or evading it, to break down, to that extent, the authority of law in general and the law-abiding sentiment of his community.

It is also to be observed that, though the State is not able by its laws to limit the moral autonomy of the indi-

[1] *The Principles of Political Obligations*, § 10.

vidual, it may, none the less, exercise an influence for good or evil upon the moral standards of its citizens. By rendering legally compulsory acts that should be freely done because of their rightness, in many cases individuals will, not of necessity but in actual fact, be led to act in a purely formal or conventional manner. In other words, the essential rightness of the acts will be rendered obscure to them or, at least, not kept continually present in their minds. Upon the other hand, where acts are commanded by law which do not satisfy the ethical judgments of those ordered to commit them, but who, nevertheless, feel compelled to do them, the fact that these acts cannot be ethically justified becomes, by long continued commission of them, more or less or completely forgotten. Then, too, there is the well known fact that only a comparatively small part of even the most enlightened community gives earnest or philosophical thought to the rightness or wrongness of the customs or laws by which their social conduct is governed, with the result that all the remainder tend in very considerable measure to accept as right or wrong the rules of action and the standards of conduct which the law, in all its conceived majesty, establishes for them.

No Absolute Limitations. Having determined the possible scope of political control we turn now to consider whether there are any absolute ethical principles which operate to render illegitimate the exercise of the State's possible control with reference to certain matters, or for certain purposes. To this question the answer may be at once given that there are no such absolutely limiting principles. The doctrine which has already been established that the State has for its general purpose the promotion of the welfare of its citizens carries with it the corollary that whatever state action will tend to secure this end is ethically justified. And this doctrine is reinforced by the conclusion which we have earlier reached that the individual has no inherent, absolute rights which belong to him as a person and which, therefore, may not, as to their exercise, be infringed by any person or power external to himself. Those writers who, like Herbert Spencer, declare that "every man shall be free to do that which he will, provided he does not infringe the equal freedom of any other man"; [2] or who, like John Stuart Mill, assert that the State's authority may never be legitimately used to restrain the individual except to prevent harm to others,[3] were, as we have earlier seen, not only obliged to make exceptions to their doctrine which in fact utterly destroyed it as an absolute principle, but were utterly unable to state or to give any certain guidance as to when an act of an individual has consequences only to himself and is therefore one against which other individuals do not need to be protected. In truth, it is scarcely necessary to point out that under the conditions of our modern complex social life the life and prosperity of one individual is so intimately connected with the life and prosperity of others, that it is possible to find very few, if any, acts which are without social significance. And thus, even if one were to take Spencer's and Mill's doctrine at its face value, a range of State control could be justified that would extend far beyond that which any present State attempts to exert.

Fitzjames Stephen, in his *Liberty, Equality, and Fraternity* asserts that coercion of the individual, in whatever form applied, is justified when the following conditions are met: (1) that the object aimed at is desirable; (2) that the means employed are calculated to attain that purpose; (3) and at not too great an expense. This seems, upon first inspection, to be a drastic doctrine, but it is, we believe, a correct one. For example, let us apply it to what would be thought an extreme case, namely, to

---

[2] *Social Statics* (abridged and revised), p. 55; *Justice*, p. 46.
[3] *On Liberty*, Chap. I.

coercion in the matter of religious belief. There is no one who would maintain that we should recognize toleration as an absolute duty; that is, one to be exercised as to all persons and as to all acts. There are always some acts that we will not tolerate, even if performed in the name of religion. What, then, is the logical ground upon which we justify intolerance in such cases, and tolerance in all others? If we are convinced that a certain line of conduct will be for the best interest of another, and if we can by some means make that other adopt that policy without at the same time doing him a greater evil than benefit, is it not really a kindness to him to do so? If we are firmly convinced, for example, that the failure to accept a certain doctrine will doom the recusant to an eternity of awful torment, and if we are equally sure that coercion will be able to secure the saving acceptance, and without causing an amount of suffering anywhere near as great as that from which the coerced one is to be rescued, can we hesitate to declare that such coercion should be applied? Have we not, in fact, abandoned intolerance, where we have abandoned it, either because we have changed our minds as to the desirability of the end sought, or our faith in the efficiency of compulsion to reach it, or to reach it at a not disproportionate expense?

In taking this ground we again emphasize the fact that coercion being in itself painful, the one exercising it is morally bound first to convince himself that the conditions that have been mentioned are certainly present. No one is justified in intolerance, however slight, until he has informed himself by all means within his power as to the correctness of his opinion, and until he has taken into careful consideration all the effects, immediate and remote, of an exercise of coercion on his part. When such conditions are strictly observed it will be found, we think, that the doctrine will bring about a greater tolerance, individual, social, and political, than now actually obtains in any modern society.[4]

Alleged Limitations upon State Control as Fixed by Evolutionary or Competitive Processes. This chapter might close with what has already been determined regarding the province of the State, for it has been shown that, from the ethical point of view, there are no definite limits to the extent to which it may legitimately exercise the powers of control over human conduct which it possesses. However, inasmuch as the view has been widely held that the lessons to be learned from the so-called evolutionary process, which operates throughout all nature, warn us that evil results are certain to follow when the State extends its control beyond certain defined limits, and that, therefore, there are, in fact, certain, always applicable, prudential if not ethically inherent, limitations upon the sphere of political authority, it becomes desirable to consider this allegation. For, whether we speak of a limitation as inherent in political authority, when considered from the ethical point of view, or say that it is absolutely fixed by the very nature of the forces which control man's development upon this globe and which therefore cannot be escaped from, or, at any rate,

[4] In an article entitled "Force and Coercion" in the *International Journal of Ethics* for April, 1916, by Professor John Dewey are found the following statements which are pertinent to the point under discussion. "No ends are accomplished without the use of force. It is consequently no presumption against a measure, political, international, jural, economic, that it involves a use of force. Squeamishness about force is the mark not of idealistic but of moonstruck morals. But antecedent and abstract principles cannot be assigned to justify the use of force. The criterion of value lies in the relative efficiency and economy of the expenditure of force as a means to an end. . . . It follows from what has been said that the so-called problem of 'moralizing' force is in reality a problem of intellectualizing its use. . . . Only upon such a principle of expediency can the doctrine of non-resistance be urged, without committing ourselves to the notion that all exercise of energy is inherently wrong—a sort of Oriental absolutism which makes the world intrinsically evil. I can but think that if pacifists in war and in penal matters would change their tune from the intrinsic immorality of the use of coercive force to the comparative inefficiency and stupidity of existing methods of using force, their good intentions would be more fruitful."

that the disastrous effects following from an attempt to disregard them, cannot be avoided, the result is practically the same. In the one case, it is ethically illegitimate for the State to exercise powers actually possessed by it; in the other case, it is always inexpedient for it to do so. In either case, the State is called upon to recognize definite limits to the control which, except for these considerations, it might exercise.

Spencer. Herbert Spencer is the chief exponent of the proposition that an extension of the State's powers of control beyond the maintenance of security against foreign aggression, and the disregard of the principle that "every man shall be free to do that which he will, provided he does not infringe the equal freedom of any other man", is a dangerous and presumptuous attempt upon the part of politicians to interfere with the working of the great cosmic evolutionary processes through which progress in the past has, as he views it, been secured, and through which alone, in his opinion, it can continue to be obtained in the future. This evolutionary process, shortly stated, is one according to which individuals are forced to bear the consequences of their own acts and to profit or suffer from the qualities with which Nature has endowed them. In other words, that, throughout the biological sub-human world, development has been secured because practically unrestricted competition has prevailed. Identifying 'progress' with 'development,' Spencer argues that the welfare of men can be secured to an increasing extent only if they permit the same competitive process to apply to themselves.

Logically, it would result from such a conviction that all forms of social as well as political control among men should be abolished, and a régime of complete individualism or anarchy established, and, so far as the disappearance of political authority is concerned, this is, indeed, Spencer's ideal which he thinks may some day be realized. But, for the present, he sees the necessity of political life and urges merely that the State's control be confined to the performance of strictly police functions, leaving individuals otherwise free to compete with one another.[5]

In another work [6] the author has examined at some length the errors in Mr. Spencer's reasoning upon this matter of the proper extent of state control, and it is deemed sufficient here merely to summarize the points there made.

Spencer, without warrant, identifies change or development with improvement or progress, whereas the truth is that unrestrained competition leads to the survival only of those best fitted to meet what happens to be the conditions of their environment. Thus as Huxley pointed out in his famous Romanes Lecture, "Evolution and Ethics," "If our hemisphere were to cool again, the survival of the fittest might bring about in the vegetable kingdom a population of more and more stunted and humbler and humbler organisms, until the fittest that survived might be nothing but lichens, diatoms, and such microscopic organisms as those which give red snow its color; while,

[5] In addition to the support claimed to be derived from the empiric facts of biological evolution, Mr. Spencer, positivist though he is, relies also upon a bald doctrine of abstract natural rights. In that chapter of his *Justice*, which is devoted to the establishment of the authority of the individual formula which he has obtained, he avowedly rests it upon *a priori* grounds, and calls to his support the dicta of such men as Blackstone and Mackintosh, wherein they have declared the supreme, invariable, and all-controlling power of natural law. Spencer closes with the truly remarkable argument that "paying some respect to these dicta (to which I may add that of the German jurists with their *Naturrecht*) does not imply unreasoning credulity. We may reasonably suspect that, however much they may be in form open to criticism, they are true in essence." This is truly an argument that is remarkable, not only because of the method of demonstration involved, but because of the total misconception involved as to the connotation of the term *"Naturrecht"* in German jurisprudence. Mr. Spencer goes on, however, to assign a special and limited character to *a priori* beliefs in general, but in this we need not follow him, as we shall presently cover this point when we examine Mr. Spencer's system from a different standpoint.

[6] *Social Justice*, Chap. IX, "The Ethics of the Competitive Process."

if it became hotter, the pleasant valleys of the Thames and Isis might be uninhabitable by any animated beings save those that flourish in a tropical jungle. They, as the fittest, the best adapted to changed conditions, would survive."

Huxley might have gone even further than this, and pointed to the fact that the very conditions of an unrestricted competitive struggle often make impossible the survival of the exceptionally developed or endowed individuals, for this very difference often places them out of *rapport* with their environment. Thus it is, that the observed effect of competition in the sub-human world is the maintenance of a general level of uniformity rather than the preservation of exceptionally variant types. The process is much like the advance of a line of men in battle,—those who rush ahead are the most likely to be killed.

The competitive process in the sub-human world is not only a ruthless but an extraordinarily extravagant one. Thousands or even millions of progeny are produced in order that a single individual may be preserved and enabled to continue its kind.

Beings of the sub-human orders submit to this process simply because they have not the intelligence to check it, and the same is true with men themselves to the extent that they do not become conscious of their ability to substitute coöperation for strife. However, as soon as men reach a certain degree of intelligence, and have a consciousness of themselves as rational moral beings, they conceive of ends which they think desirable to be attained, and, in the light of these ends, give approval to ideal codes of conduct and consciously and deliberately adopt means for advancing towards the goals they have set up for themselves. Thus, as Huxley says in the address from which we have earlier quoted, "social progress means a checking of the cosmic process at every step, and the substitution for it of another which may be called the ethical process; the end of which is not the survival of those who may happen to be the fittest, in respect of the whole of the conditions which obtain, but of those who are ethically the best. . . . In place of ruthless self-assertion it demands self-restraint; in place of thrusting aside or treading down all competitors, it requires that the individual shall not merely respect but shall help his fellows; its influence is directed not so much to the survival of the fittest as to the fitting of as many as possible to survive."

Though thus spoken of as a checking of the cosmic competitive process, the efforts of civilized men, when correctly analyzed, are seen to seek not to put an end to competition, but, upon the one hand, to determine the *criteria* of fitness for survival in accordance with something more than the mere necessity of preserving existence—to enable, as Aristotle has said, that men may not only live, but live well—; and, upon the other hand, to make as efficient as possible the competitive struggle, that is, in the sense of securing the result desired for as many persons as possible and reducing to the lowest amount possible the sufferings of those who are not able to meet the requirements of the contest. And, it may be added, whereas, in the sub-human biological world, the aim is (if a teleological term may be used) to develop the species, the aim of human life, when interpreted in ethical terms, is to secure the increasing welfare of the individuals of the species.

In final criticism of Spencer may be pointed out how absurd is his statement that when men, by their conscious effort, check the operation of the competitive processes that prevail among the lower orders of life, they run counter to what Great Nature has herself prescribed. Even granting, which we cannot properly do, that there is some deliberate end aimed at by Nature, viewed as a creative or volitional entity, man is himself a part of that Nature and his intellectual faculties and his emotions, his ideals and his deliberated acts, are as "natural" to him as are the more instinctive or automatic actions of the lower orders of life. It is, then, nothing less than absurd when, to support his doctrine of extreme political *laissez faire,* Spencer says: "If the political meddler could be induced to contemplate the essential meaning of his plan, he would be paralyzed by the sense of his own temerity. He proposes to suspend in some way or degree the process by which all life has been evolved." It is reported that upon being shown by Rousseau a copy of his discourse on "The Origin of Inequality among Men," Voltaire said, "On reading your book one longs to walk on all fours." Spencer's advice to men is, in all seriousness, to much the same effect. Because an unrestricted and ruthless struggle for existence obtains among members of the brute creation, he says, it is clear that that is what Nature intends should prevail, and, therefore, that men would do well to allow that intention to prevail.

Spencer attempts to show that, as a matter of historical fact, the exercise in the past by the State of other than police functions has been attended by disastrous results. This, he has a rational right to do, and, if he could prove this to have been a fact, it would be a strong argument in support of his position. But, it would not be a conclusive proof, for it might well be that, in the past, political control has been exercised in an unintelligent manner, or that the conditions under which it was exercised were more unfavorable to successful political control than they now are. Even as it is, Spencer's presentation of the results reached in the past by political control shows no more than that certain results were unfortunate. He does not show, or even attempt to show, that the total results of State action were worse than they would have been had no political control whatever existed.

In final criticism of Spencer's views with regard to the proper province of the State it may be pointed out that his doctrine that the State may advisedly intervene to the extent of preventing individuals from interfering with the freedom which each of them individually and of right has to do what he likes, can, under modern complex conditions of social life, be made to justify, in fact, nearly all those acts of political power which he so severely condemns. Thus, even as a working proposition, he does not make the individual secure from State intrusion, any more than Mill was able to do by the formula which he sought to establish in his *Essay on Liberty*.

It is true that, under all systems of constitutional government, it is deemed desirable that the individual should be protected by law in the secure possession and use of certain kinds of private property, and that he should be permitted to exercise certain rights of action, as, for example, with regard to religious beliefs, the open expression and publication of personal opinions, the forming of associations, petitioning those in political authority, and the like. But with regard to these private or civil rights two facts are to be noted. Everywhere, and under the most liberal or democratic forms of government, these rights not only owe their existence to the laws of the State which creates and defines them, but they are never absolute in character. The rights of property are limited by the State's rights of eminent domain and taxation, and by what, in American jurisprudence, is known as the "police power." As to the extent of this power we can do no better than to quote the following description of it by Chief Justice Shaw in the often cited case of *Commonwealth v. Alger*.[7]

"We think it is a settled principle, growing out of the

[7] Cushing's Reports, p. 53.

nature of well-ordered civil society, that every owner of property, however absolute and unqualified may be his title, holds it under the implied liability that his use of it shall not be injurious to the general enjoyment of others having an equal right to the enjoyment of their property, nor injurious to the rights of the community. All property in this Commonwealth is . . . held subject to those general regulations which are necessary to the common good and general welfare. Rights and property, like all other social and conventional rights, are subject to such reasonable limitations in their enjoyment as shall prevent them from being injurious, and to such reasonable restraints and regulations established by law as the legislature, under the governing and controlling power vested in them by the Constitution, may think necessary and expedient. This is very different from the right of eminent domain,—the right of a government to take and appropriate private property whenever the public exigency requires it, which can [under conditions of American constitutional law] be done only on condition of providing a reasonable compensation therefor. The power we allude to is rather the Police Power; the power vested in the legislature by the Constitution to make, ordain, and establish all manner of wholesome and reasonable laws, statutes, and ordinances, either with penalties or without, not repugnant to the Constitution, as they shall judge to be for the good welfare of the Commonwealth, and of the subjects of the same. It is much easier to perceive and realize the existence and sources of this power than to mark its boundaries, and prescribe the limits to its exercise."

As regards the so-called personal rights to freedom of speech and press, of religious worship, etc., it can easily be shown that, under all systems of constitutional jurisprudence, they are limited to the extent that public order and the general welfare may seem to require. The individual may be required to offer even his life in the service of the State, as happens when he is compelled to perform military service in time of war, or as may happen when he is required to serve in a sheriff's *posse comitatus* in times of domestic disorder.

Alleged Limitations upon State Control Based upon Practical and Psychological Grounds. Without resorting to the lessons deemed to be taught by cosmic processes of evolution, there are many who hold that, as a practical proposition, because of the natural or instinctive motives which universally move men, and the opportunities which exist for determining what actions are most likely to benefit the governed, it is unwise that public control or operation should be substituted for private initiative and energy. Here we come to propositions that have a considerable measure of truth in them, and to which objection can be made only when they are stated in a too absolute form.

Analyzing the essential postulates upon which this individualistic doctrine rests, we find them to be, in effect, the following:

First, that each individual, in the long run, knows his own interests best, and, in the absence of arbitrary restrictions, is reasonably sure to seek them.

Secondly, that, in the absence of political restraint, free competition can and does exist; and

Thirdly, that such free competition always develops the highest human possibilities, by eliminating unfit elements and enabling each individual to do that for which he is best fitted.

As regards the truth of the postulate that the individual will best know his own interests, and that he will seek these interests as thus known, a denial may be made. Nothing is more obvious, for example, than that, in such matters as compulsory education, sanitation and the like, it is the very persons upon whom coercion is most needed who are least qualified to judge concerning the value of the conduct which such compulsion demands.

The second postulate, as to the necessary existence of free competition in the absence of external restraint by the State, is also not necessarily true. Genuine competition is possible only where the contesting parties possess comparative equality of strength or intelligence. Where there is not this equality, a contest does not mean effective competition, with the resulting benefits that the third postulate predicates, but simply a destruction of the weaker party. It is thus possible that, in many instances, interference by the State, by rendering conditions more equal, actually promotes competition rather than destroys it. Furthermore, legal regulation often serves not so much to check competition as to raise its moral plane. Proof of this is to be seen in the results following from factory legislation and the regulation of the employment of women and children.

Finally, as to the third assumption that the effect of free competition is ultimately beneficial, if not to all individuals, at least to the social group or the species, it is sufficient to refer to what has already been said with regard to the theories and arguments of Spencer and his school.[8]

Conclusion. It results from what has been said that we are brought to the conclusion that not only is there nothing in the nature of political rule to make ethically illegitimate the extension of its control beyond certain defined limits, but that, as a matter of expediency, no generally applicable limits, based upon evolutionary or psychological principles, can be laid down. In other

---

[8] See also L. F. Ward, *The Psychic Factors of Civilization;* and Ritchie, *Principles of State Interference.* A comparatively recent attempt to uphold the wisdom of keeping State control within a very narrow field is that of Sir Roland K. Wilson in his volume, *The Province of the State,* published in 1911. One point emphasized in this work is that when the State attempts to exercise other than police powers it is almost necessarily forced to neglect its more essential functions.

words, the attempt to confine the State to a performance of the merely negative police function, to make of it what the Germans call a *Polizeistaat,* must be abandoned. In its place we must definitely accept the conception of a *Kulturstaat,*—of a State that may legitimately exercise its controlling power for the rendering of whatever affirmative aid it can for the advancement of the welfare of its citizens. If this can best be done by establishing a socialistic or even a communistic régime, this will be ethically justified. In other words, the claims of the socialists and the communists cannot be properly met by asserting that they ask for an extension of State authority beyond limits which are absolutely fixed by ethical right. Instead, they must be answered, if answered at all, by showing that the canons of distributive justice which they would enforce through State action are false canons of justice; or by demonstrating that the evils practically certain to result from an application of their plans would more than balance the benefits probably obtained; or, finally, that it would not be possible, as a practical proposition, to establish and efficiently operate a governmental organization such as would be required for the performance of the tasks that would be laid upon it by a socialistic or communistic régime.[9]

Practical Considerations. Although we have rejected the view that there are any hard and fast limits to State action, it is, however, proper to refer to the fact that because of the mechanical and relatively crude manner in

[9] It perhaps does not need to be said that it would not be fair to the socialists and communists or to others who would radically change our present political or economic organization that they should state absolutely perfect canons of distributive justice, or that they should show that their schemes of governmental organization would work with perfect smoothness and efficiency. They would prove their case if they could show that their plans would, in all probability, produce better results than those obtained from present forms of political rule and economic life, and also better results than could be obtained from reforming or otherwise modifying present institutions without changing their essential character or the principles of distributive justice which they apply.

THE LEGITIMATE SPHERE OF POLITICAL AUTHORITY

which coercion by the State has to be applied it is often preferable to leave to regulation by social pressure or by the sense of justice and public spirit of the individual many matters which, except for these reasons, it would be desirable to regulate by law. Laws have to be stated in general terms, and therefore, justice in individual cases often has to be sacrificed; rules of evidence and of proof have to be formal in character; and, above all, the appeal has to be placed, in practically all cases, upon the low level of fear of pain or other personally disagreeable consequences. Thus Fitzjames Stephen, who perhaps as strongly as any one has emphasized and justified the use of physical force in the settlement of conflicting interests, is yet careful to say with reference to the province of criminal law: "In considering this question it must be borne in mind that criminal law is at once by far the most powerful and by far the roughest engine which society can use for any purpose .... It strikes so hard that it can be enforced only on the gravest occasions, and with every sort of precaution against abuse or mistake. Before an act can be treated as a crime, it ought to be capable of distinct definition and of specific proof, and it ought also to be of such a nature that it is worth while to prevent it at the risk of inflicting great damage, direct and indirect, upon those who commit it. . . . The excessive harshness of criminal law is also a circumstance which very greatly narrows the range of its application. It is the *ratio ultima* of the majority against persons whom its application assumes to have renounced the common bonds which connect men together. When a man is subjected to legal punishment, society appeals directly and exclusively to his fears. It renounces the attempt to work upon his affections or feelings."[10]

In another place in the same chapter, contrasting the operation of public opinion with that of law, Stephen

[10] *Liberty, Equality, and Fraternity*, Chap. IV.

says: "As for the influence of public opinion upon virtue and vice, it is incalculably great, but it is difficult to say much as to its extent, because its influence is indefinite, and is shown in an indefinite variety of ways. It must also be observed that, though far more powerful and minute than the influence of law, it is infinitely less well instructed. It is also exceedingly liable to abuse, for public opinion is multiform, and may mean the gossip of a village or the spite of a coterie, as well as the deliberate judgment of a section of the rational part of mankind. On the other hand, its power depends on its nature and on the nature of the person on whom it acts. A calm, strong, and rational man will know when to despise and when to respect it, though no rules can be laid down on the subject. It is, however, clear that this much may be said of it in general. If people neither formed nor expressed any opinions on their neighbors' conduct except in so far as that conduct affected them personally, one of the principal motives to do well and one of the principal restraints from doing ill would be withdrawn from the world."

With regard generally to the regulation of individual action by law, it may be observed that it has a two-fold aspect. Upon the one side it means that the individual is coerced by threat of penalties to be imposed by the State in case of disobedience to act or not to act in a certain way; upon the other side, it means that the individual, by reason of this legal regulation, is made reasonably secure against interference by others with regard to the prohibited acts. The one is necessarily felt by the individual, in many cases at least, as an irksome restraint upon his freedom of action; the other as a desirable fact. There is thus always a balancing of interests, and, depending upon whether the one of the results is deemed to more than compensate for the other, the legal regulation is justified or not. In some communities, whether, due to training, custom, or personal idiosyncrasies of the people, a greater value is attached to the security against the possible acts of others than is attached to the liberty to do as one will in the premises.

Thus, speaking generally, the peoples of Europe, and especially the Germans, as compared with the English, and still more as compared with the Americans, have preferred order, unity and system, legally imposed, to what appears to them to be the disorder and lack of individual security which results from the freer play which English and American law leaves to the conduct of individuals. But, whether one likes it or not, it would seem that, with the increasing complexity of modern social life, the individual will have to submit to a continually increasing regulation of his actions by the State.

State Functions Classified. With regard to their general aim, the activities of the State may be placed in three classes: those concerned with the Power of the State; those concerned with the maintenance of the Legal Liberties of the citizen; and those for the advancement of the General Welfare of the people, that is, with their economic, intellectual, moral, and æsthetic interests. The first relate to the military strength of the Government for domestic or international purposes; the second relate to the provision of as wide a field as possible to the citizen within which he is protected against both arbitrary governmental interference and molestation by private individuals; the third relate to the advancement of the interests of individuals in any way in which public action will be more efficient than private action.

Essential and Optional Functions. In order that a State may exist at all as a politically sovereign organization it is necessary that it should exercise certain powers. These include the raising of a public revenue, the maintenance of armed forces—an army, a navy, a constabulary or gendarmerie—, the establishment and operation of civil organs of government—executive, legislative, and judicial—, and the enactment and enforcement of such laws as are required by the foregoing. These may be termed the Essential functions of the State. All other functions which the State finds it expedient to exercise are Optional.[11]

Socialistic and Non-Socialistic Functions. The optional functions of the State may be divided into two classes according to whether they are socialistic or non-socialistic in character.

This implies an important distinction. The assumption by the State of an optional function is often loosely spoken of as a step towards socialism, but not always is this the case. Socialistic activities include only those which could or would be exercised by the people if left to their private initiative. Therefore, their assumption by the State, is, to that extent, a curtailment of the industrial freedom of the people. Examples of socialistic duties are

[11] Woodrow Wilson in the last edition (1918) of his *The State* (revised by Edward Elliott), groups the functions of the State under the two headings Constituent and Ministrant functions and, places under the first of these groups: the keeping of order and protection of persons from violence and robbery; the fixing of legal relations between man and wife and between parents and children; the regulation of the holding, transmission and interchange of property, and the determination of its liabilities for debt or for crime; the determination of contract rights between individuals; the definition and punishment of crime; the administration of justice in civil causes; the determination of the political duties, privileges, and relations of citizens; and the dealings of the State with foreign powers. "These will all be recognized," it is said, "as functions which persist under every form of government."

As to this it may be said that while it is true that all modern civilized peoples have found it necessary that their States should exercise these enumerated functions, this has not been true in the past, and is not now true in some countries which have not become highly industrialized. Only by degrees, for example, have States drawn within their control the compulsory adjustment of disputes regarding property rights and contract obligations of its subjects. And the same is true even with regard to the definition and enforcement of what are now known as criminal laws. As to this see Jenks, *Law and Politics in the Middle Ages*, and his shorter and more popular work, *A Short History of Politics*, which he has expanded into a volume entitled *The State and the Nation*.

the ownership and operation by the State of railroads, of canals or of telegraph lines; the ownership by the city of gas, water and electric light works, and the provisions of model tenement houses for the poor by the public authorities. These, it is clear, admit of private management, and, in fact, are, in the United States at least, very generally attended to by private enterprise.

Among the non-socialistic duties of the government are included those which, if not assumed by the State, would not be exercised at all. They are duties not essential to the State's existence, and yet, from their very nature, not likely or even possible of performance by private parties. Such duties as these are therefore not socialistic, because their public assumption does not limit the field of private enterprise, or in any way interfere with private management of any sort of industry. As a rule, they are powers educational in character rather than coercive; directive rather than controlling. Under this head come all those administrative duties that are of an investigating, statistical character, and consist not in the interference with industry, but in the study of conditions and the diffusion of the information thus obtained. Work of this kind is that performed by the United States Departments of Labor, and of Agriculture, by the Bureau of Education, the Fish Commission, the Coast and Geodetic Survey, the Decennial Censuses, etc. Public libraries and reading-rooms, boards of health, the provision of public parks, and certain branches of education also come under this head.

Likewise, of this character is that large class of governmental duties, which we have before mentioned, the exercise of which results in the raising of the plane of competition, rather than the destroying of it. Thus, when we consider closely, we see to what an extent the increase of governmental activity during the present century has been in this non-socialistic field, and all indications point to a continued expansion of the State's regulatory action within this field.

With reference to the relation of social or political control of the competitive process one feature of comparatively recent legal development deserves especial mention.

The general policy of modern law is to sustain the institution of private property, and to protect the individual in the possession of those economic goods which, as a result of the economic competitive process, as thus regulated, he becomes the owner of. Within comparatively recent years, however, the conviction has become stronger and stronger that, in many cases, this leads to unjust and socially inexpedient results, and, therefore, the law has been modified at many points with the deliberate purpose of bringing about a more satisfactory distribution of wealth than the competitive process is seen to produce. In other words, the State has itself intervened to enforce, in a measure at least, a system of distributive justice. It has not yet attempted to take property from the one individual to hand it directly to another individual deemed to be better entitled, ethically, to it, but it has, by means of its taxing and "police powers," brought this indirectly about. By levying taxes which fall for the most part upon the wealthier classes, as by inheritance and income taxes, the rates of which progressively increase as larger fortunes or incomes are concerned, and by spending the proceeds of these taxes not merely for the performance of the indispensable functions of government but for the performance of services or the provision of institutions like libraries, schools, hospitals, playgrounds and parks, and the like, which are open without charge to the entire public, the inequalities in wealth, produced by industrial and commercial competition, are *pro tanto* corrected. The same result is also secured by employers' liability laws and the insurance, at public expense, or at the expense of the employers, of workmen against the pecuniary losses due to unemployment, old age, sickness or accident.[12]

[12] It scarcely needs to be pointed out that the same result is secured by voluntary individual action, when wealthy persons devote their wealth to public purposes. Especially in America have vast sums been thus used.

CHAPTER XVII

GOVERNMENT

THE terms Government and State need to be clearly distinguished, as do also the questions as to their ethical right to exist. The State is the political entity in which, from a legal point of view, inheres the supreme right or faculty, known as Sovereignty, to determine, for the individuals subject to its authority, what it is legally permissible for them to do, and what affirmative acts in support of public authority and the promotion of the general welfare they may be compelled to perform. The question of the ethical right of a State to exist is, therefore, one as to the ethical legitimacy of political authority itself as an element in the maintenance of social relations. The Government of a State is the machinery or complexus of organs or instrumentalities through or by means of which the State effectuates its purposes, that is, issues its commands and secures their enforcement. The question, therefore, of the ethical right of a particular government to exist is plainly a different one from that of the ethical legitimacy of political authority as an abstract or general proposition.

Thus far in the present inquiry, we have had to deal with this abstract or general proposition. A basis having been found for justifying, upon ethical grounds, the exercise of political coercion, there remains only the problem of determining, in the case of each particular State, the manner in which it is proper that a decision shall be reached as to the character of government that should be established and maintained, and the specific policies it should pursue.

Though different in character, the results reached by the inquiry as to the right of a State to exist throws some light upon the question as to the location of the right to determine what its form of government and policies shall be; for the demonstration of the invalidity of those theories that give to the State a directly divine, mystical, or transcendental character, and the repudiation of the doctrines which, upon divine, historical or patrimonial grounds, assert the inherent and absolute right of particular individuals or families, or classes of individuals to exercise, according to their own judgments and wills, the sovereignty of the State, make it clear that, in the case of each particular State, the form of government that shall exist, and the policies it shall pursue, are matters of expediency. A government being but a means to an end, it necessarily results that its form and its policies depend upon the specific conditions which surround the State in question and which determine the practical problems which it has to meet. It is obvious, therefore, that that type of government is justified which will best determine and most efficiently execute the policies that are required in order that the legitimate ends of the State will be secured. There is thus presented, in the case of each political society, the question as to how the wisest answers to these questions of governmental organization, of policy determination, and of administrative execution, may be solved.

In the history of political speculation it is found that many have reached a comprehensive answer to these problems by asserting that the governed should determine for themselves what form of government shall exist, who shall exercise its powers, and what the policies of the State shall be. The mistake has, however, been made of defending this doctrine, not upon purely utilitarian grounds, but by asserting, as an apodictic proposition, that, without regard to special conditions of time, place, and people, no government can be ethically defended that does not owe its origin and continued existence to this popular consent.

This doctrine, which can be denominated the "governmental compact theory" as distinguished from the "social" or "political" compact theory which has been discussed in earlier chapters, has had, as has been earlier shown, a long history.

The Ethical Basis of Popular Government. The discussion of the social or political compact theory has shown that there is this kernel of truth in it, that each individual has the ethical right, and is, indeed, under the moral obligation, to determine for himself the ethical rightfulness of commands that are addressed to him by his political superiors. From this conclusion it follows that there is the same kernel of truth in the governmental compact theory, namely, that no type of government can properly be spoken of as inherently and necessarily a good one, that is, under all circumstances, but that a government must be justified, if at all, as a means whereby the specific political problems that are presented in a community may be satisfactorily solved, and that each individual who is subjected to its authority has the ethical right and obligation to determine for himself, as a matter of reasoned judgment, based upon the results that are reached, whether the existing government is what it should be, and, if not, how it may be changed either as to its form or as to its policies.

However, this does not mean, either that a government may not justly exercise control over an individual who disapproves of its form or policies, or that all governments, in order to have an ethical basis, must be founded upon, and have their policies determined by, the collective will of the generality of the governed. That these two corollaries do not follow has been shown in the earlier chapter of the present work, and it is but to repeat what has already been said, when it is pointed out that those who fix the policies or exercise the other powers of a government must necessarily themselves determine when political coercion may properly be applied. It does not need to be said, however, that, in reaching this determination, they should take account of the wishes and judgments of those who are to be coerced, just as they should consider and be guided by other objective facts.

The proposition that (to borrow the words of the American Declaration of Independence of 1776), all governments derive their just powers from the consent of the governed, if viewed as an absolute proposition, necessarily assumes two facts, neither of which is true: first, that, as a practical proposition, it is possible to obtain an authentic expression of the will of a people, collectively considered, that is, a veritable "General Will" as distinguished from the sum of the particularistic wills of the individuals constituting the body-politic, and which may therefore be said to voice the public or political will of every individual of the community, and, therefore, according to the principle *volenti non fit injuria*, not to coerce or oppress any one of them when enforced; and second, that this General Will, when secured and followed will lead to the best possible results.

In the discussion already had of the theories of Rousseau it has appeared that he, as well as all those who have been influenced by his theories, have recognized not only that in all communities there are many individuals who, by reason of infancy or other causes, are not competent to form intelligent judgments regarding the problems of social and political life or even to appreciate the nature of agreements to which they may give their assent, and, therefore, that a distinction has to be made between persons who are to have, and those who are not to have, the rights of active citizenship, and that, even as to them, only those commands of the State are to be deemed ethically obligatory which, by reason of their content and the universality of application of their prescriptions, meet the requirements of a truly general will.

It is clear, then, that the doctrine of consent, as applied to the determination of the form of government that is to be maintained, loses its absolute character when it is admitted that, in every community, some persons are not qualified to participate in this consent, and must abide by the decisions made for them by others; and that the general will, even as thus construed, can be obtained in an authentic and purified form only under special conditions and as to a few policies that are general in application and intelligible to all who are to participate, if not in their formulation, at least in their adoption. Aside, however, from these inherent limitations upon the consent-of-the-governed theory, as it is ordinarily understood, there is the further fact that it is an illegitimate assumption to declare that there is an inherent and necessary merit in following, in all cases, and under all circumstances, the political judgments collectively expressed by the governed. Unless one is to return to a divine, or mystical, or instinctive theory of politics and ascribe to the people of a State the status and attributes formerly claimed, under those theories, by the monarch or by the transcendental State person, and assert that, by reason of some inherent or underived quality, the *vox populi* gives utterance to commands that are *ex necessitate* ethically right, and judgments that are necessarily practically expedient, the merits of popular governments,—governments that owe their existence to, and have their policies more or less directed by the consent and will of a considerable portion of their citizens—, must be determined by their actual achievements, by the results reached.

If this be so, then, popular governments, whether directly democratic, or representative in character, or otherwise subjected to the control of the will and opinions of the governed, take their place alongside other and more autocratic types of government, and, in common with them, must have their merits determined by the practical success with which they are able to meet the problems presented by the special conditions of the peoples which they govern and whose welfare they are supposed to advance. And this process of evaluation applies not only to the general character of the government, but to the employment of such special popular features or political processes as qualifications for the exercise of the suffrage or to hold public offices, proportional representation, the use of the initiative and referendum and recall, frequent elections, etc. These same criteria of expediency also apply to such other features of government as the establishment of constitutional restraints upon its action, the vesting of the performance of its functions in different, and more or less mutually independent, branches or departments, the centralization or decentralization of its administrative agencies, and the like.

The Theory of Popular Government as Practically Applied. Surveying the history of political practices it is seen that the demand by the governed for a greater control over their rulers advanced by a series of well defined stages. At first the demand went little further than that the governed should be recognized to have the ethical right, in cases of extreme oppression, to resist the enforcement of a law, or to depose their supreme ruler and select another in his place, or even to get rid of him by assassination.[1] Next came the claim that the supreme ruler

---

[1] The history of the theory of Tyrannicide forms an interesting chapter in the general history of political theory.

should hold himself bound by certain fundamental laws or customs, written or unwritten. This was the demand for constitutional government which found its full satisfaction when these fundamental principles found definite statement in solemnly adopted constitutions or charters, and when courts were created competent to determine when they had been violated and to grant corresponding legal relief or impose appropriate legal penalties upon those adjudged guilty of such legally *ultra vires* acts.

Succeeding to, or contemporaneously with, the demand for constitutional government went, in practically all the civilized States, the demand of the governed that they should have the right of determining for themselves the form of government under which they were to be ruled, and also that they should have the right to participate directly, or through their representatives, in the determination of the policies of the government. This they secured either by establishing, as a constitutional proposition, that policies of State before being enforced or promulgated by the executive should receive the approving vote of a considerable or presumptively representative portion of the whole people or a similar approval by representatives freely chosen by such an electorate, or that the people, acting directly or indirectly through their representatives should have the right to depose from political authority those persons whose policies or administrative acts they might disapprove.

Juristically considered, a State operates wholly within the realm of law; that is, the will of the State can find authentic expression only in law, or, at any rate, in policies which the officials promulgating them have, by law, been authorized to issue.[2] This conclusion follows from the proposition with which the jurist starts that, not only is the State the exclusive source of positive law,

---

[2] For a fuller discussion of this proposition, see the author's *Fundamental Concepts of Public Law*.

but that, being sovereign, whatever the State commands has, *ipso facto,* the force of law, and that those rules of conduct which it enforces or stands ready to enforce, whatever their historical source, the State is deemed to have commanded.

The rules or principles, written or unwritten, which determine its form of government and allot to its several organs their respective powers are spoken of as constitutional in character, and, collectively considered, as providing the State's Constitution. In this sense every State has a Constitution and is, therefore, constitutional in character. Ordinarily, however, when a government is described as constitutional in character it is meant that all those persons to whom are entrusted the determination and execution of state policies have their official powers defined and limited by established and determinate laws, and that, when these limits are overstepped, their acts are illegal, because *ultra vires,* and obedience to them by the citizen need not be given, and, furthermore, that orderly legal means are provided whereby questions of official competence may be determined, and whereby those officials who exceed their jurisdictional powers may be held legally responsible for any damages to the public or to private individuals resulting from such unauthorized acts.

Correlative to this narrower conception of constitutional government is the idea of civil liberty—that there are rights of person or property which are defined by law and which, under existing constitutional law, may not be infringed or ignored by those in official authority. Thus, a government is constitutional in character even though its ruler possesses extensive discretionary powers (that is, powers that he may exercise according to his own personal judgment), provided the extent of this authority, as well as the authority of all inferior officials, is fixed by law, and legal means are provided for preventing or punishing a disregard of the limits to official authority thus set.

Within the broad field of constitutional government, as thus defined, opportunity exists for the greatest variety of governmental structures and of political practices. Some of these varieties are so important as to mark off the governments possessing them into almost definite species, and therefore merit at least brief mention.

One such group or species is represented by the present Government of Japan. In governments of this type the fundamental constitutional principle is that all legal authority is inherent in and exclusively vested in the Crown. From this basic premise important constitutional conclusions are drawn. The first of these is that such legal limits upon the royal power as are recognized to exist are deemed to be founded upon royal grant and are, therefore, in legal theory, formal in character and subject to alteration or abrogation at the will of the reigning sovereign. This means that the written constitutions, if such exist, and whatever may have been the impelling political circumstances leading to their creation, are, in the eyes of the law, octroyed, rather than established by the people, who, in fact, may have forced their promulgation. A second conclusion is that all the organs of government possess only such legal powers as have been expressly or by necessary implication granted to them by the Crown. A third conclusion is that the so-called legislative bodies —the lower Chambers being popularly elected and representative in character,—though participating in the processes of legislation, are not regarded as possessing real law-making power, or as voicing a will that needs to be regarded as decisive in matters either of law or of public policy. The essential law-making power remains exclusively in the monarch, and his is the will which, in constitutional theory, is viewed as embodied in the laws which find a place upon the statute books. In other words, the legislative chambers are considered as participating in the determination of the content or substance of the laws, but not in giving to them legal force.

It follows from this constitutional conception that the part played by the elected representatives of the people in the enactment of laws and in the adoption of public policies is one quite different from that played in countries whose constitutional systems are founded upon a democratic basis. Essentially speaking, the situation is this: The monarch, as a matter of grace and expediency, is pleased to learn, through their elected representatives, the wishes of his people regarding a proposition of law or the adoption of a public policy, and to obtain such information regarding its wisdom as a representative chamber is able to provide; and these wishes and this information he necessarily takes into consideration in determining the exercise of his own sovereign will. But never does he regard these factors as controlling in any affirmative sense. So long as the constitution which he or his predecessor has promulgated exists, he agrees not to act contrary to its provisions with regard to the matters which are therein specified. But not for a moment does he admit himself to be under a legal, or even an impelling moral, obligation to give effect to an expression of the will of the representatives of the people of which he disapproves.[3]

In Great Britain monarchy persists, and the Crown is still regarded as the original historical source of all legal authority, but, using the term constitutional in the sense in which the English employ it in their public law, the king has been brought under the legal as well as the political control of the Parliament and especially of the popularly elected branch of that body.[4]

[3] This paragraph is substantially taken from the author's *Prussian Political Philosophy*, Chapter V, "Prussian Constitutional Theory."
[4] Governmental action is "constitutional," in the British sense of the word, when it conforms to the established conviction of the British

The very right of the British ruler to his throne has been, since 1688, a parliamentary one, and he has no option but to give assent to and conscientiously to enforce his parliament's will. Even as to those so-called prerogative powers which he still may exercise through "orders in council," he is obliged to follow the advice of ministers of State who are held politically responsible to the House of Commons for the advice which they may give. Thus, while it is possible to maintain, as an empty legal proposition, that the king still retains a right to refuse his assent to measures approved by Parliament or, within the field of the royal prerogative, to disregard the advice of his ministers, the substantial or practical fact is that he has no such power. Thus, though still clothed in the trappings of monarchy, and still employing much of the phraseology of the time when the king governed as well as reigned, in its actual operations and in its constitutional theory—again using this term in its English sense—the British Government falls within the class of constitutional governments next to be described.

This class of governments include those which start with the constitutional principle that all public authority is obtained by delegation or grant from the people, or, at any rate from those persons who possess the franchise and are supposed to represent and speak for the entire body of the governed. From this premise it follows that all the organs of government,—the executive as well

people as to what is proper to be done, or rather, in almost all cases, as to the mode in which public action shall be taken. Thus questions of constitutionality seldom arise as to the substance of public acts. When their constitutionality is questioned it is as to whether the procedure has been a proper one—whether this or that organ of government has or has not been justified in participating in their commission. The term constitutional therefore has not in Great Britain the strictly legal connotation that it has in other countries, but, as Dicey in his *Law of the Constitution* first clearly pointed out, it is, in fact, seldom possible for a public official to disregard a constitutional "convention" without being forced to violate provisions that are strictly legal in character.

as the judicial and legislative,—possess only such legal powers as the people, acting in a constituent and corporative capacity, has seen fit to endow them with. This is the doctrine which found statement in the famous Bill of Rights prefixed to the Constitution of the State of Virginia, adopted in 1776, to the effect "that all power is vested in and consequently derived from the people; that magistrates are thus trustees and servants, and at all times amenable to them"; and which, in the first constitution of the State of Massachusetts, is declared in the following words: "All power residing originally in the people, and being derived from them, the several magistrates and officers of government, are thus substitutes and agents, and are at all times accountable to them."

A government is democratic in character when the determination of the major policies of the State, and the selection of the chief executive officials of its government, are vested in the governed, or, at any rate, in a considerable proportion of them, as, for example, in the adult males of the community.[5] In order that this form of government may be clearly distinguished from the representative or republic form, it is often spoken of as a "Direct Democracy."

The line which separates an aristocratic from a democratic government is not a very definite one. The most that can be said of it is that when political rights—the suffrage, eligibility to public office, etc.,—are legally confined to a comparatively small number of persons, the government is aristocratic in character. Especially is this so when the possession of these rights is made dependent upon accident of birth or other quality or status which

[5] How considerable the restrictions upon the rights of suffrage or to hold office, or to participate in law-making, may be without destroying what may fairly be said to be democratic government, and substituting oligarchic or aristocratic government in its place, it is impossible to say. No hard and fast line can be drawn.

it is not within the power of the individual to acquire. Almost synonymous with Aristocracy is the term Oligarchy. Generally, however, this latter term is limited in its application to governments which are within the control of a very few individuals—a smaller number than is connoted by the term Aristocracy—and, not unusually, the designation is one of reproach, the implication being that the persons constituting the oligarchy have obtained possession of or hold their power in ways that are not approved.

A government is said to be representative or republican in character when its policies are determined by a body of persons freely selected by the governed or by a considerable portion of their adult members. Construing the provision of the American Constitution that the United States shall guarantee to the member States of the Union governments republican in form, the eminent jurist, Judge Cooley says: "By a republican form of government was intended a government in which not only would the people's representatives make the laws, and their agents administer them, but the people would also, directly or indirectly, choose the executive. But it would by no means follow that the whole body of people, or even the whole body of adult and competent persons would be admitted to political privileges."

Judge Cooley, having in mind, no doubt, the government of Great Britain, says that a republican government is not inconsistent with monarchical forms, "for a king may be merely an hereditary or elected executive while the powers of legislation are left exclusively to a representative body freely chosen by the people." That such a government may fairly be said to be representative in character, if the popularly elected Chambers have the decisive voice in the fixing of public policies, is certainly true, but it is questionable whether it may properly be described as republican in form. However, this is more a matter of terminology and of no great importance one way or the other.

The term Popular Government refers not so much to a particular form of government as it does to the question of the extent to which any government, whatever its form, or the manner in which the officials are selected, is, in fact, subject to the control of the public opinion of its citizens or subjects. Thus, as in Great Britain, the government may be monarchical in form, but, in operation, popular in character. So, also, conversely, a government may be representative in the sense that political rights are widely diffused among the people, and yet its policies may be determined by a few political leaders with the result that, in fact, the popular will exercises little control.

With regard to this demand that State policies should be dictated or controlled by the will of the governed or of a considerable and representative portion of them, it may be noted that this does not involve the requirements that popular or, as it is also called, political, control should be continuously exercised over public officials other than those who are invested with powers sufficiently discretionary in scope and character to enable them to exert an appreciative influence upon the policies of the government. In other words it is not necessary, in order that popular government may be secured, that those who perform only routine non-discretionary, or as in law they are termed, merely ministerial functions, should be elected by the governed and for comparatively short terms of office, rather than owe their positions to executive appointment and subject to removal from office only because of proved incompetency or dishonesty. Universally, where popular government has existed, the peoples' will has been expressed largely through the instrumentality of political parties, and this has meant partisanship, which partisanship, in so far as it has been intelligent and public spirited, and therefore justifiable, has been due to differences of opinion regarding the policies to be pursued by the government. But if officials have no other function than to carry out efficiently the policies which the other organs or branches of the public service formulate, it is clear that there is no good reason, certainly none based upon the principle of popular government, why the people should retain the power to remove them from office. This conclusion of logic is now generally recognized in all modern States, though the practice as regards administrative officials has been by no means a corresponding one. As for judges, whose assumed function it is to apply the law rather than to determine its policies, the expediency of removing them from possible influence by political partisanship, is very generally admitted.[6]

It is worth noting at this point, though the matter is one of practical rather than of theoretical significance, that, in all political communities, the actual distribution of political influence is only in part, and, in many cases, only in small part, determined by the governmental system as fixed by formal constitutional provisions. The history of nearly all States shows that, without changes in the fundamental law, the location of the decisive voice in the determination of public policies has shifted from point to point. Not only has the pressure of public opinion varied in degree, but, within the government itself, now the executive, and now the legislative body has had the paramount power. And, when the legislature has been bicameral in stucture, now one House and now the other House, has exerted the greater influence. So also in governments organized for the purpose of rendering decisive the voice of the electorate, it has all too often happened that the actual control of the government and of its policies has been in the hands of a very small group

---

[6] As to the distinction between the policy-forming and the mere executing or administrative organs of government, see especially F. J. Goodnow's *Politics and Administration*.

of party leaders or political "bosses." In his *Liberty, Equality, and Fraternity*,[7] Fitzjames Stephen says: "Legislate how you will, establish universal suffrage, if you think proper, as a law which can never be broken. You are still as far as ever from equality. Political power has changed its shape but not its nature. The result of cutting it up into little bits is simply that the man who can sweep the greatest number of them into one heap will govern the rest. The strongest man in some form or other will always rule. If the government is a military one, the qualities which make a man a great soldier will make him a ruler. If the government is a monarchy, the qualities which kings value in counsellors, in generals, in administrators, will give power. In a democracy the ruling men will be the wirepullers and their friends."

Stephen's last statement that, in a pure democracy, the ruling men will always be the wirepullers and their friends is scarcely fair to democracy. However, though this has not been the inevitable result, it has occurred sufficiently often to give point to his assertion.

It is also appropriate at this place to note one general fact which is discoverable in all the countries of the world which have sought to develop popular governmental institutions: This is: that, in every case, the deliberate and successful attempt has been made to place limitations upon the free and unfettered operation, within the political field, of popular government. In some cases this has been with reference to specific matters, in other cases the operations of government in general have been concerned. In other words, in no case have those who have determined the constitutional processes of their respective governments been willing that these governments should be compelled immediately to respond to every form of popular pressure that may be brought to bear upon them.

[7] Edition 1873, p. 240.

This unwillingness has been responsible for many of the "checks" which abound in all modern system of constitutional government. Many of these checks, it is true, have for their purpose the placing of limitations upon the exercise of arbitrary power by executive officials, even by those who have been popularly elected.[8] Other constitutional checks have had for their aim the prevention of a sudden gust of opinion or passion being taken as a deliberate and informed public conviction. Such checks have thus had for their purpose the realization of true popular government as distinguished from an apparent or fictitious one. They have nevertheless involved the admission that it is possible for the people to be moved, for the time being at least, by wishes or desires that they will later regret and repudiate.

But, more fundamental than this, is the connection found embodied in all systems of constitutional law that the rights of active citizenship—to vote and to hold office—shall be possessed by only particular classes of community. Only by slow degrees have these rights been extended to larger and larger portions of the citizen body. Furthermore, in many States, the legislative body is denied the right to legislate with regard to certain subjects, and the process of amending the written constitution, where one exists, is made more difficult than is ordinary law-making. Finally, in nearly all States, there exists an upper legislative Chamber of a more or less aristocratic, or hereditary, that is, non-popular character, whose consent is required for all law-making. In Great Britain we find a popularly elected Lower House with a minimum of limitations upon its power to create law or control the political policies of the executive, but, even there, the Upper House still has a considerable power to retard, if not to veto, acts of the popular representative body.

[8] This last shows a distrust not of the principles of popular government but of the efficiency of representative methods.

Enough has been said to show that nowhere has there been a full acceptance of the doctrine that the whole adult body of the governed should have an untrammelled right to control the actions of their government. Furthermore, there is the fact that nowhere, except in a very few instances, where the popular initiative and referendum are employed, has it been deemed possible to permit the electorates to act directly in the determination or control of public policies. Instead, they have been obliged to act through elected representatives.

Only by the boldest of fictions has it been possible to hold that thus the will of the entire body of the governed finds expression and enforcement.

As a practical proposition, the governed, as a single body, have found it impossible either to control the nomination of those who are to be voted for as their representatives, or to exert a continuous and effective control of their representatives when elected. In other words, it has been found impossible to operate representative institutions except through political parties, the management of which has inevitably fallen into the hands of a few leaders, and thus another barrier to free popular action interposed. And, as regards the representative principle itself, the device is accepted and defended, not simply as a means whereby an expression and enforcement of the General Will may be secured, but as a means of obtaining executive and legislative representatives who will have greater political wisdom than can be expected of the electorate acting directly in its character as the primary possessor of political authority.

So strongly felt is this argument in behalf of representative, as distinguished from direct democratic government, that statesmen, and political scientists the world over, are almost unanimously of the opinion that electorates should not seek, except occasionally and with reference to very specific matters, to bind by pledges their elected representatives, but rather that they should leave their representatives free to exercise their own best judgments as questions of policy arise. It is, however, of course agreed that means should exist whereby the governed may hold their representatives politically responsible for the decisions they make and actions they take.

The foregoing is, for example, the argument of Mill in his *Representative Government*. He says:

"No reader of this treatise can doubt what conclusion, as to this matter, results from the general principles which it professes. We have from the first affirmed, and unvaryingly kept in view, the co-equal importance of two great requisites of government: responsibility to those for whose political benefit political power ought to be, and always professes to be, employed: and jointly therewith to obtain, in the greatest measure possible, for the function of government the benefits of superior intellect, trained by long meditation and practical discipline, to that special task. If this second purpose is worth obtaining, it is worth the necessary price. Superior powers of mind and profound study are of no use if they do not sometimes lead a person to different conclusions from those which are formed by ordinary powers of mind without study: and if it be an object to possess representatives in any intellectual respect superior to average electors, it must be counted upon that the representative will sometimes differ in opinion from the majority of his constituents, and when he does, his opinion will be the oftenest right of the two. It follows that the electors will not do wisely if they insist on absolute conformity to their opinions as the condition of his retaining his seat." [9]

Another way in which this defense of representative government is frequently phrased is the statement, as a fact demonstrated by experience, that an electorate is

[9] *Op. cit.*, Chapter XII.

better able to select able representatives qualified to decide wisely as to public policies, than it is able itself to determine wise policies.

In this connection it is, perhaps, worth while to refer to the distinction between elected representatives viewed simply as agents to embody in laws the opinions of the constituencies, and those same representatives viewed as persons with presumedly better political judgment than their constituents, and, therefore, authorized and expected to exercise their own personal judgments as to what public policies shall be adopted. According to the first of these assumptions, the representative acts as the agent or delegate of those who elect him, and is under an implied mandate to carry out their will; according to the second view, he is regarded as the veritable representative of his electors, so that his will and judgment is to be taken as theirs.

This distinction was excellently brought out by Edmund Burke in his *Thoughts on the Cause of Present Discontents,* and in his speech of November, 1774, at Bristol at the conclusion of the poll. In the Bristol speech, in explanation and defense of his position that an elected representative should deem himself truly a representative rather than an agent of the electors, he said:

"It ought to be the happiness and glory of a representative to live in the strictest union, the closest correspondence, and the most unreserved communication with his constituents. Their wishes ought to have great weight with him; their opinion, high respect; their business, unremitted attention. It is his duty to sacrifice his repose, his pleasures, his satisfactions to theirs; and above all, ever, and in all cases, to prefer their interest to his own. But his unbiased opinion, his mature judgment, his enlightened conscience, he ought not to sacrifice to you, to any man, or to any set of men living. These he does not derive from your pleasures; no, nor from the law and the constitution. They are a trust from Providence for the abuse of which he is deeply answerable. Your representative owes you, not his industry only, but his judgment; and he betrays, instead of serving you, if he sacrifices it to your opinion. . . . Government and legislation are matters of reason and judgment and not of inclination; and what sort of reason is that in which the determination precedes the discussion; in which one set of men deliberates, and another decides; and where those who form the conclusion are perhaps three hundred miles distant from those who hear the arguments?

"To deliver an opinion is the right of all men; that of constituents is a weighty and respectable opinion, which a representative ought always to rejoice to hear; and which he ought always most seriously to consider. But *authoritative* instructions; *mandates* issued, which the member is bound blindly and implicitly to obey, to vote, and to argue for, though contrary to the clearest conviction of his judgment and conscience—these are things utterly unknown to the laws of this land, and which arise from a fundamental mistake of the whole order and tenor of our constitution.

"Parliament is not a congress of ambassadors from different and hostile interests, which interests each must maintain, as an agent and advocate, against other agents and advocates; but parliament is a *deliberative* assembly of *one* nation, with *one* interest—that of the whole; where, not local purposes, not local prejudices, ought to guide, but the general good resulting from the general reason of the whole. You choose a member indeed; but when you have chosen him, he is not a member of Bristol, but he is a member of *parliament*."

CHAPTER XVIII

INTERNATIONAL RELATIONS: NATIONAL STATES AND NATIONALITY

MUCH has been written in discussion of the question whether, within the field of state action, the same principles of morality should apply as apply with regard to acts of private individuals, or whether, indeed, morality, as distinguished from expediency, has any application whatever. The question is not a difficult one, however, if one bears in mind the fact that the State is not in itself a moral person; that those who influence or control its policies are individually responsible for its acts; and that all governments and laws are but instrumentalities which men employ, just as they employ countless other means, to reach the ends which they desire. As thus viewed, all state action is individual action, and, ethically speaking, must be judged as such. It has already been seen that the question of the morality of every act is determined for the actor by the good or bad will or motive with which it is done, and that, objectively viewed by the impartial third person, it is or is not ethically justified according to the sum total of its effects. Thus, all the attending circumstances of each case determine whether or not a certain act should or should not be done. What in one case, is ethically justifiable, is, under other conditions, morally reprehensible. Hence, it often happens that it is right for a person acting in behalf, and with the authority, of his State, to do things which, as a private individual, it would not be morally right for him to do. But this is not because the principles of right and wrong which apply to state actions are different from those that hold good with regard to private action, but because the circumstances are different, and because the results will be different.

It can scarcely be denied that the welfare of the entire family of nations or of all humanity is more important than the welfare of any single political or national group of people. Therefore, it is proper to say that there is an ethical obligation upon the people of each State to adopt public policies which will advance the general welfare of all peoples even though this may, at times, mean the sacrifice of their own immediate interests or the interests of their own State.

Can this proposition be properly pushed to the extreme extent of saying that, when the several interests of a larger group or of the entire family of nations requires it, a people should be willing to surrender its own independent political existence? As to this two observations may be made. In the first place, in determining whether such a state suicide will be desirable, a calculation should be made of the value of maintaining in its integrity the system of independent sovereign States, and, in the second place, that there would be an exceedingly strong presumption as to the need of continuing the national existence of a people so moralized as to be willing to sacrifice themselves upon the altar of humanity's welfare.[1]

[1] Professor W. R. Sorley, in an article entitled "The Morality of Nations" in the *International Journal of Ethics*, Vol. V, p. 427, says: "Sacrifice of his individual life is only a duty for the individual when such loss is the sole means of attaining a greater good than personal life, or avoiding a greater evil than death. It is its function to guard and develop the lives of its citizens, and so to direct the national life, with its powers of limitless continuance and development, as to make it contribute to that greater purpose which can only be realized through the social and political relations of men. How can we even conceive as possible the voluntary sacrifice of its own life by a nation? Is it the act (or idea) of the ruler without the consent of the people? In this case it is not national self-sacrifice at all, but a sacrifice of others,— a betrayal of trust on the part of the person whose duty it was to protect them. If, on the other hand, it is to be conceived as a unanimous act of self-sacrifice on the part of the people, then all that can be said

Inherent Value of a System of Independent States. Surveying, generally, the field of interstate relations with a view to discovering what, if any, fundamental principles of ethics may be laid down upon which to base the rights and obligations of States, it will be necessary to distinguish between the State and the Nation and to determine whether to either may properly be ascribed rights that are inherent and indefeasible and therefore absolute in character. The distinction between the State and the Nation is one that has been earlier mentioned but may, for convenience, be here repeated. A State is a group of individuals politically united under a single sovereign power. A Nation is a group of individuals which, whether politically united or not, constitute, because of common interests and ideals, a psychological unity. As to these national units the chief question is whether they are, because of their national unity, entitled to political self-determination.

Considering first the question whether States, as such, are to be held to possess rights which it is ethically obligatory upon other States to recognize, and which therefore must find embodiment in any system of International Law claiming to be ethical as well as legal, we shall find the problem simplified if, to begin with, we ask whether, in the nature of things, that is, apart from considerations of practical difficulties of organization and operation, there is any final reason why the peoples of the world should be grouped into a number of independent States instead of being organized under a single world authority.

To most persons it would seem that but one answer can be given to this question, namely, that, if the difficulties of organization and operation could be overcome,

is, that any nation, whose citizens are capable of such heroism, must surely be worth preserving on account of their unique moral development."

a World State would be preferable to the maintenance of a number of independent States, each pursuing its own particularistic interests, and, therefore, constantly liable to come into conflict with other States. But this is not the way in which the matter was looked at by those German political philosophers, who, before the Great War, following the teachings of Hegel, saw, in the independent National State, the final and highest product of man's political genius, and the indispensable means whereby the welfare of humanity might continue to be advanced, or, as Hegel would say, Absolute Reason made real and objectified.

Holding this view, these philosophers rejected, as defective and immoral, the idea of a universal State in which sovereign National States would be swallowed up. Also, in effect, they declared that the conception of international laws with more than provisional binding force was a vicious one, since, if accepted, the National States would be deprived of that complete freedom of action which, it was declared, it was necessary that they should have in order that they might play the parts assigned to them in the world process of realizing and objectifying Reason. Different peoples or Nations, they asserted, have their several contributions to make to civilization, and it is only as organized in these wholly independent National States that they can give reality to the special attributes or forms of "Spirit" which are inherent in themselves, and can thus lay upon the altars of civilization the gifts which it has been fore-ordained that they should severally make. "Each particular National genius," said Hegel, "is to be treated as only one individual in the process of Universal History. For that history is the exhibition of the divine, absolute development of Spirit in its highest forms,—that gradation by which it attains its truth and consciousness of itself. The forms which these grades of progress assume are the characteristic

'National Spirits' of History; the peculiar tenor of their moral life, of their Government, their Art, Religion, and Science. To realize these grades is the boundless impulse of the World-Spirit—the goal of its irresistible urging; for this division into organic members, and the full development of each, is its Idea." [2] "In the History of the world the Individuals we have to do with are Peoples; totalities that are States." [3] "The State is the Divine Idea as it exists on Earth." [4] "The general principle which manifests itself and becomes an object of consciousness in the State . . . is the whole of that cycle of phenomena which constitutes the *Culture* of a nation. But the definite substance that receives the form of universality, and exists in that concrete reality which is the State, is the Spirit of the People itself." [5] "A Nation is moral, virtuous, vigorous, while it is engaged in realizing its grand objects, and defends its work against external violence during the process of giving to its purposes an objective existence." [6]

These quotations show us the argumentative process by which, in German philosophy, not only was the State exalted, but the principle of what may not unjustly be termed the divine right of National Groups wedded to it. Not only was the State raised up above the individual, but to it was given the task of carrying into effect the divine mission which each Nation was deemed to be providentially called upon to fulfill in the processes of Universal History. A spiritual significance was thus given to States' rights which rendered them absolute in character.

With such a view of the State and its relation to the Nation which has been described, we are prepared for the view which Hegel and his followers took with re-

[2] *Philosophy of History* (Bohn's Ed.), p. 35.
[3] *Ibid.*, p. 14.   [5] *Ibid.*, p. 52.
[4] *Ibid.*, p. 41.   [6] *Ibid.*, p. 77.

gard to the ethical character of interstate relations and of the rules or laws which regulate these relations. Hegel's doctrines as to these matters are found in the closing paragraphs of his *Grundlinien der Philosophie des Rechts,* and from that work the following quotations are taken.[7]

"A State is not a private person, but in itself a completely independent totality. Hence the relation of States to one another is not merely that of morality and private right. It is often desired that States should be regarded from the standpoint of private right and morality. But the position of private persons is such that they have over them a law court, which realizes what is intrinsically right. A relation between States ought also to be intrinsically right, and in mundane affairs that which is intrinsically right ought to have power. But as against the State there is no power to decide what is intrinsically right and to realize this decision. Hence we must remain by the absolute command. States in their relation to one another are independent and look upon the stipulations which they make one with another as provisional."

In the State, according to Hegel, the interests of individual persons are harmonized and realized, but he was not able to find in a Society of Nations a higher unity in which the interests of the different States might be harmonized. In the international world, according to his view, a régime of conflicting state interests necessarily prevails. "Because the relation of States to one another has sovereignty as its principle, they are, so far, in a condition of nature one to the other. Their rights have reality not in a general will, which is constituted as a superior power, but in their particular wills." "Therefore, when the particular wills of States can come to no agreement, the controversy can be settled only by war." "War is not to be regarded as an absolute evil. It is not a merely

[7] Translated by S. W. Dyde under the title, *Philosophy of Right.*

external accident, having its accidental ground in the passions of powerful individuals or nations, in acts of injustice, or in anything which ought not to be." "As a result of war peoples are strengthened; nations, which are involved in civil quarrels winning repose at home by means of war abroad."

In the writings of men like Bernhardi and Treitschke we find repeated in still balder terms these doctrines of Hegel. Thus, we find Bernhardi saying: "War is a biological necessity of the first importance, a regulative element in the life of man since without it an unhealthy development will follow, which excludes every advancement of the race, and therefore all real civilization." [8] And again: "The acts of the State cannot be judged by the standards of individual morality. If the State wished to conform to this standard it would often find itself at variance with its own particular duties. The morality of a State must be developed out of its own peculiar essence, just as individual morality is rooted in the personality of the man and his duties toward society. . . . The end-all and the be-all of a State is Power." [9]

Bernhardi took his conception of the essential character and mission of the State from Treitschke, who had said: "The idea of one universal empire is odious—the ideal of a State co-extensive with humanity is no ideal at all. In a single State the whole range of culture could never be fully spanned; no single people could unite the virtues of aristocracy and democracy. All nations, like all individuals, have their limitations, but it is exactly in the abundance of these limited qualities that the genius of humanity is exhibited. The rays of the Divine light are manifested, broken by countless facets, among the separate peoples, each one exhibiting another picture and another idea of the whole. Every people has a right

[8] *Germany and the Next War.* Trans. by A. H. Powles, 1924, p. 18.
[9] *Idem*, p. 437.

to believe that certain attributes of the Divine reason are exhibited in it to their fullest perfection." [10]

From this it follows not only that a plurality of States is demanded, but that each of these States has the right to gain, by its might, the most important place that it can in the world of States. "If it, the State, neglects its strength in order to promote the idealistic aspirations of man, it repudiates its own nature and perishes. This is in truth for the State equivalent to the sin against the Holy Ghost, for it is indeed a mortal error in the State to subordinate itself for sentimental reasons to a foreign State." [11] "Every sovereign State has the undoubted right to declare war at its own pleasure, and is consequently entitled to repudiate its treaties. . . . The establishment of a permanent international court is incompatible with the nature of the State. . . . The appeal to arms will be valid until the end of history and therein lies the sacredness of war." [12]

Two American writers who have specially emphasized the transcendental rights of the National State have been Professor John W. Burgess and Elisha Mulford. Professor Burgess in his *Political Science and Comparative Constitutional Law,* published in 1893, under the evident influence of German thought, sees in the Nation, when politically organized, "the most modern and the most complete solution of the whole problem of political organization which the world has yet produced," and adds: "The fact that it is the creation of Teutonic political genius stamps the Teutonic Nations as the political Nations *par excellence,* and authorizes them, in the economy of the world, to assume the leadership in the establishment and administrations of States." [13]

[10] *Polities,* I, p. 19 (The Macmillan Co., 1916).
[11] *Idem,* p. 24.
[12] *Idem,* pp. 28, 29.
[13] *Op. cit.,* Vol. I, p. 39. Within the Teutonic Nations, Professor Burgess included the Anglo-Saxons of Great Britain and the United States, as well as the Germans of Central Europe.

In his chapter on "The Ends of the State," Professor Burgess not only characterizes the National State as "the most perfect organ which has yet been attained in the civilization of the world for the interpretation of the human consciousness of right" and as furnishing "the best vantage ground as yet reached for the contemplation of the purpose of the sojourn of mankind upon earth," but gives to this form an absolute value by declaring it to be one which must be developed before men may approach that final end of political development,—the Universal State. Having thus accepted this form of political organization as essentially, that is, inherently, superior to every other form save the Universal State, and as one that must be developed before that perfect type can be reached, Professor Burgess is able to assert as an apodictic principle, that a National State, or one striving to become such, has at all times, and under all circumstances, the right to preserve and develop its nationality, even though this may entail injury and destruction to other States and peoples. The primary aim of the modern constitutional State, he says, should be to attain proper physical boundaries and to render its population ethnically homogeneous. "When, therefore, a State insists upon the union with it of all States occupying the same geographic unity, and attains this result in last resort by force, the morality of its action cannot be doubted in sound practical politics, especially if the ethnical composition of the population of the different States is the same or nearly the same." [14]

Not only is it thus declared to be an absolute duty of the National State to preserve, in fullest degree, its character as such, but it is also to feel itself called upon by Providence to establish National States in those portions of the world whose populations are not qualified for the task. Thus, what is really a divine character, is given

[14] *Op. cit.*, Vol. I, pp. 40, 41.

to the National State, and to the Teutonic nations is ascribed the divine mission of regenerating the politically heathen world. Lest it be thought that we are unwarrantably interpreting Professor Burgess' doctrine, we will quote his language. "Certainly," he says, "the Providence which created the human race and presides over its development knows best what are the true claims of humanity; and if the history of the world is to be taken as the revelation of Providence in regard to this matter, we are forced to conclude that National States are intended by it as the prime organs of human development; and, therefore, that it is the highest duty of the State to preserve, strengthen and develop its own national character. My . . . conclusion from this . . . is that the Teutonic nations are particularly endowed with the capacity of establishing National States, and are especially called to the work; and, therefore, that they are entrusted, in the general economy of history, with the mission of conducting the political civilization of the modern world." "The Teutonic nations," he continues, "can never regard the exercise of political power as a right of man. With them this power must be based upon capacity to discharge political duty, and they themselves are the best organs which have yet appeared to determine when and where capacity exists."

It is not only over the wholly barbaric peoples that the Teutonic nations are declared to have a "manifest mission." Their right to interfere extends to the affairs of those who have made some progress in political organization, but have manifested an "incapacity to solve the problem of political civilization with any degree of completeness." [15] "But for the sake of the half barbarous State, and in the interest of the world, a State or States, endowed with the capacity of political organization, may righteously assume sovereignty over, and undertake to

[15] *Op. cit.*, Vol. I, p. 47.

create State order for such a politically incompetent population." Professor Burgess is, indeed, careful to say that the civilized States should not act with undue haste, or extend their authority for any other purpose than that of civilizing those upon whom that control is imposed; but, he adds, "they are under no obligation to await invitation from those claiming power and government in the efficient organization or from those subject to the same." [16]

Mulford's *The Nation,* first published in 1870, is en-

[16] In an article entitled "The Political Theories of Professor John W. Burgess," published in the *Yale Review* for May, 1898, the author made the following comment upon the views of Professor Burgess as quoted above:

"The writer of this article is not disposed to deny that the modern national constitutional State, as exemplified in Europe and North America, represents an efficient political type; but to speak of it, as does Professor Burgess, as, short of the unrealizable universal State, a perfect type,—as a final form for the realization of which any political acts are justifiable,—is to indulge in absolutist reasoning which is surely unwarrantable. The history of political speculation shows us that premises and reasoning similar to those of Professor Burgess have been employed in behalf of many forms of political organization which have existed in the past, but which now, by common consent, are recognized to have been fundamentally defective. As a matter of fact, the modern constitutional State possesses defects, from the viewpoint of national strength and efficiency, which seem almost ineradicable. And even its national character, upon which Professor Burgess lays so much stress, can scarcely be held to be an essential element in an ideal polity. The value of an ethnically homogeneous citizen body under present conditions may be admitted, but it requires no great stretch of the imagination to conceive of a time when men will have developed intellectually and morally to an extent that will enable them to rise superior to the ordinary prejudices of race, history and tradition, and successfully to combine, politically, upon the higher planes of community of interests and aims. With the denial that the modern national constitutional State is necessarily, that is to say, inherently, the best form of political government thus far developed by man, and as such to be desired at all times and in all places, there falls to the ground the deduction made by Professor Burgess that, to the national constitutional States which now exist, there belongs the right of taking under their direction, forcibly, if necessary, the political destinies of the entire world. The writer by no means holds that any given State, whatever the character of its organization and administration, has an indefeasible right to be, but he is not prepared to say that any given type of political life is so essentially superior as to warrant the absolute statement that all other types, no matter what the special conditions that environ and condition them, are less desirable forms, and that, if necessary, compulsion may be used upon them, either to establish the national constitutional form or to submit to the control of a national constitutional State until they are prepared to adopt that form."

tirely devoted to an exaltation of the Nation in Hegelian terms, but with the immediately practical purpose of showing that the primary allegiance of American citizens should be given to their National Government rather than to the individual States of the American Union. To him, in the same sense that, as declared by Aristotle, man is by nature a political being, he is also a member of a Nation. "The nature of man, apart from the Nation, is unfulfilled" and "the destination of humanity is unrealized." The Nation, he says, cannot be viewed as a machine or human contrivance, it "has in itself thought and will and power to do or not to do, and capacity to suffer or rejoice"; in it there is an assertion of men's determination and of their free endeavor. The Nation is eternal and the evidence of its continuous life through generations is in the consciousness of the people constituting it. "It has the unity of an organism, not the aggregation of a mass; it is indivisible; its germ lies beyond analysis, and it is enfolded in its whole future. This unity is the postulate of the existence of the people as a Nation, and the condition of its independence." "It has a determinate end, and apprehends in its own conscious purpose its vocation in history." "The conscious life of the people appears in its literature and arts, its manners and laws." It is a moral organism—a moral personality, and in this subsists its independence of other Nations. "The conditions of the realization of personality is the same in the Nation as in the individual." It is not an historical accident or merely a jural society or an economic group; it is not a development out of the family or founded upon might or a social contract, but is the direct creation of the divine or providential power that rules the universe. "The boundaries of the Nation are laid in Nature and in the historical course of the people. This law is universal, and the Nations which have violated it, again have been compelled to acknowledge it. . . . The bounds of the Nation which are written in the courses of the mountains and the lines of the oceans are written also upon the hearts of its children." "In this faith the people will assert them reverently and carefully, will guard them steadily and well. The integral unity of the land will be maintained against all alienation and division." "Political sovereignty is the assertion of the self-determinate will of the organic people, and in this there is the manifestation of its freedom." "The sovereignty of the Nation, or political sovereignty, implies independence." It "primarily presumes the power in the political people to determine the form of its own political life. It cannot be imposed upon it from without." "The Nation is before the Constitution. It precedes and enacts the Constitution as the determinate form of its political life; it establishes the Constitution as the order in which it will realize its determination." The sovereignty of the Nation involves "the right to exclusive legislation in its domain; the right to self-preservation, to independence, to property; the right to exist in a common relation to other nations." "The science of International Law has its foundation in the being of the Nation as a moral person; this is the condition of the rights and obligations which it is to embrace and define."

Thus, throughout more than four hundred pages, Mulford conceives of Nations as persons possessing inherent, individual, inalienable and indefeasible rights, and yet nowhere does he attempt to show by what specific marks the existence of a National personality may be so indubitably shown as to furnish ground upon which, in specific cases, these rights may be conceded. Apparently, he is convinced that divine providence working in history will make this sufficiently evident.[17]

[17] He is, however, indignant that the Southern Confederacy in 1861-1864 should have obtained so much moral support from other Nations, and especially that Gladstone should have said that Jefferson Davis had created a Nation.

Nationality. This matter of Nationality deserves somewhat extended criticism not only because of the fact that, as we have seen, the so-called National State has been given such an exalted value by writers like Hegel, Burgess, Mulford, and others, but because the doctrine is widespread that to groups of individuals which are held to constitute Nations belong certain inherent rights, as, for example, to political independence, to "self-determination," to self-defense, and to development,—rights which correspond very closely to those inalienable, indefeasible rights which, under the old doctrines of Natural Law, were ascribed to individual persons.

Many attempts to indicate the forces which operate to weld into a national unity a group of individuals, have been made. None of them has been successful in the sense of furnishing criteria whereby the existence of a Nation may be shown beyond dispute. This will appear from a consideration of some of the best known attempts that have been made to ascertain the elements of which the attribute of Nationality is compounded.

More often cited than any other attempted analysis is probably that of Ernest Renan. After showing by various references to historical facts that the secret of Nationality is not to be found exclusively in race, language,[18] economic interests, religion, geographical features or military necessities, he says: "A Nation is a soul, a spiritual principle. Two things which, in truth make only one, constitute that soul, that spiritual principle. One is in the past, the other in the present. One is the possession in common of a rich legacy of memories; the other is the actual consent, the desire of living together, the disposition to give value to the undivided inheritance they have received. . . . To have a common glory in the past,

---

[18] For an especially able article dealing with language as one of the more efficient factors in creating the sentiment of Nationality, see the *American Political Science Review*, Vol. X, p. 44, "Language and the Sentiment of Nationality," by C. D. Buck.

a common will in the present; to have done great things together, to desire to do still more; these are the essential conditions of a people. . . . It is never for the real interest of a Nation to annex or to retain a country against the will of that country. The wishes of Nations are, in fact, the only criterion, that to which it must always return. . . . One may say that secessions, and, in the end, the crumbling away of Nations, are the consequence of a system which puts these old organizations at the mercy of wills often little enlightened. It is clear that in such a matter no principle should be pushed to excess. Truths of this kind are applicable only in a very general manner. Humanity desires change; but what does not change? Nations are not eternal. They had a beginning, they will have an end." [19]

Mazzini, the Apostle of Italian nationalism, could come to a no more satisfactory definition of the Nation and of its rights than did Renan. He, like Hegel, saw something divine in the principle of Nationality, and, apparently, left it to Providence to point out when the principle should be applied. "A Nation," he said, "is a living task, her life is not her own, but a force and a function of the universal Providential scheme." But Mazzini was unable to settle upon any one or more factors as the decisive creative elements of Nationality—neither race, geography, language nor literature. His chief reliance was on what the history of the past has indicated as the will of God. "Nationalities," he said, "appear to me to have been traced long ago by the finger of Providence in the map of Europe," and upon Italy (with which, of course, he was primarily concerned) this Providence, he declared, had left its "sublime, irrefutable boundary marks." In final result, however, he came to the conclusion that the

---

[19] *Qu'est-ce qu'une Nation?* The quotations are taken from this address of Renan as translated under the title "Nation" in Lalor's *Cyclopedia of Political Science.*

essence of Nationality consists in the strong desire of a people to live a common and politically independent life. This desire, however, he emphasized, must have in it a deep moral purpose—the purpose to seek, through their own national life, the welfare of Humanity. "National life and international life should be the manifestations of the same principle, of the love of God."

In truth, no one has more emphasized the duties owed by men to all Humanity than did Mazzini. But he was equally insistent upon the idea that this duty can best be performed when men act in and through a National group:

"You are citizens, you have a Country, in order that, in a given and limited sphere of action the concourse and assistance of a given number of men, already related to you by language, tendencies and customs, may enable you to labor more effectually for the good of all men, present and to come; a task in which your solitary effort would be lost, falling powerless and unheeded amid the diverse multitude of your fellow-beings." "Before men can associate with the Nations of which Humanity is composed, they must have a National existence."

Liberty, equality and fraternity, he declared, must be present in order that the Nation should exist, for that which is of its essence is the Spirit that moves and unites its people, and this spirit, he said, can exist only when men are free, equal, and united by bonds of fraternity. "The true Country is a community of free men and equals, bound together in fraternal concord to labor towards a common aim." "So long as a single one amongst your brothers has no vote to represent him in the development of the National life, so long as there is one left to vegetate in ignorance where others are educated, so long as a single man, able and willing to work, languishes in poverty through want of work to do, you have no Country in the sense in which Country ought to exist—the

Country of all and for all. Education, labor, and the franchise are the three main pillars of the Nation."

The volume *The Duties of Man* from which most of the foregoing quotations have been taken was undoubtedly an eloquent sermon, of high moral purpose, addressed by Mazzini to his countrymen. It linked up the ideas of Nationality and Internationality with the rights of the individual, but it threw no clear light upon the problem of determining when a given group of individuals should be recognized as a Nation by other Nations, and what specific rights of political action should be accorded to a Nation as such.[20]

Among the writings of the eminent French publicist, Maurice Block, is to be found an especially earnest attempt to determine the essential attributes of the Nation, and the rights flowing from the quality of Nationality. He, too, is obliged to confess that there are no tests of general applicability. He says: "The sentiment of nationality may have been produced by various causes: It is sometimes the effect of the identity of race and stock; frequently a community of language and religion contributes to create it, as geographical limits also do. But the most powerful cause of all is the identity of political antecedents, the possession of a national history, and consequently the community of tradition, of pride and humiliation, collective pleasure and regret as attached to the same incidents of the past. Nevertheless none of these circumstances is indispensable, nor absolutely sufficient in itself. We find that there is no certain sign by which strictly to characterize a Nation. In one place the bond is made to consist in a common origin; in another, in the community of language (*wo die deutsche Zunge klingt*); in the third, geographical limits (Belgium, Switzerland); in the East, even in reli-

---

[20] M. Bolton King in his *Life of Mazzini*, Chapter XVII, has an excellent discussion of Mazzini's doctrine of Nationality.

gion. The Nation, therefore is not a physical body or unity, but a moral body; it is not always determined by external facts nor by them alone, but by sentiment." [21]

In result, then, we come to the proposition that Nationality is nothing more than a consciousness, due to an indeterminate number of causes, and more or less generally diffused among the members of a group of individuals that have common interests and ideals. How large such a group must be in order that it may claim, upon these grounds, to be treated as a Nation, it seems impossible to say. But, what is still more important, none of those statesmen or political theorists who have most strongly urged the claims of Nationality have been able to lay down any rule or principle in accordance with which may be determined with reasonable certainty when the sentiment of unity is sufficiently general in a given group to warrant the assertion that the group constitutes a Nation and is to be treated as such without regard to the wishes of those of its members who may desire to give their primary allegiance to some

[21] See the article "Nationalities, Principle of" in Lalor's *Cyclopedia of Political Science*. For an excellent discussion of Nationality see Hayes *Essays on Nationalism*. In one of these essays is drawn a striking parallel between contemporary nationalism and medieval Christianity. "Nowadays the individual is born into the State, and the secular registration of birth is the national rite of baptism. With tender solicitude the State follows the individual through life, teaching him in patriotic schools the national catechism and commemorating his vital crises by formal registration not only of his birth but likewise of his marriage, of the birth of his children, and of his death. And the death of national potentates and heroes is celebrated by patriotic pomp and circumstance that make the obsequies of a medieval bishop seem drab. . . . Nationalism's chief symbol of faith and central object of morality is the flag, and curious liturgical forms have been devised for 'saluting' the flag, for 'dipping' the flag, and for 'hoisting' the flag. . . . Nationalism has its parades, processions, and pilgrimages. It has, moreover, its distinctive holy days, and just as the Christian Church adapted certain pagan festivals to its own use, so the National State has naturally borrowed from Christianity. . . . Nationalism, too, has its temples. . . . Every national State has a 'theology,' a more or less systematized body of official doctrines which have been deduced from the precepts of the 'Fathers' and from admonitions of the national scriptures and which reflect the 'genius of the people' and constitute a guide to national behavior."

other political group, or to separate themselves from the given group and themselves form another and different State or Nation. Thus is involved the practical difficulty, in enforcing the alleged rights of a Nation, that, if the right of self-determination as to the sovereignty under which a people is to live is predicated upon the assertion that they constitute a Nation, we find that, if pushed to its logical limits, it will justify the secession of very small as well as larger groups of persons who, in a given State, may be dissatisfied with its rule. It also involves the right of portions of the citizen body to transfer their allegiance to another State, and, indeed, would justify that State in taking steps to compel the first State to consent to this transfer. The principle of Nationality thus, if logically pursued, would tend not only to disrupt most of the now existing States but would, as a continuing principle, make practically impossible the maintenance of political stability. Furthermore, even if the principle should be accepted, it would be impossible to apply it in the very many cases in which, in the world as at present politically constituted, the individuals who desire to escape from their existing bonds of allegiance or subjection do not live in a particular district but are mixed throughout the territory of a State with other individuals who desire to preserve their existing allegiance, or, at any rate, do not feel themselves united by a common Nationality to the individuals first mentioned.

May we not, however, say this much with regard to the practical significance of the sentiment of Nationality, when it has been determined to exist, that there is, in all cases, a *prima facie* case for giving political unity and independence to the group? In his *Considerations on Representative Government,* John Stuart Mill is of opinion that there is this presumption. He, however, is dealing not with States in general, but only with those attempting to maintain representative institutions. In a chapter entitled "Of Nationality as Connected with Representative Government," he says: "Free institutions are next to impossible in a country made up of different nationalities. Among a people without fellow-feeling, especially if they read and speak different languages, the united public opinion, necessary to the working of representative government, cannot exist." For these reasons, he goes on to say, the boundaries of States that wish to maintain republican institutions should coincide in the main with those of nationalities. But, he admits, the application of even this principle of expediency is often precluded by geographical hindrances, that is, where different Nationalities are locally intermingled. In still further modification of the principle of Nationality, Mill asserts that "experience proves that it is possible for one Nationality to merge and be absorbed in another; and when it was originally an inferior and more backward portion of the human race the absorption is greatly to its advantage." Indeed, Mill goes so far as to say that "whatever really tends to the admixture of nationalities, and the blending of their attributes and peculiarities in a common union, is a benefit to the human race." If this be true, then there are affirmative grounds upon which the demand for separate political life upon the part of different peoples who feel themselves to be distinct Nations should be disregarded when it is feasible, as a practical proposition, to bring about their assimilation with other National groups.

In one of the ablest indictments of the principle of Nationality ever penned,[22] Lord Acton, as opposed to Mill, sees distinct advantages to a State in having its body politic made up of distinct national groups; but he is emphatic in his condemnation of the doctrine that

[22] Originally published in the *Home and Foreign Review*, July, 1862, and republished in the volume entitled *History of Freedom and Other Essays*, Chapter IX, "Nationality."

to the bond uniting individuals to their national groups should be ascribed such value that political allegiance should be subordinated to it,—that is, that, because a group of individuals deem themselves to constitute a nation, therefore, other considerations of political expediency and loyalty should be waived in order that this higher demand of national independence may be satisfied. As thus construed, he says, the principle of Nationality "overrules the rights and wishes of the inhabitants, absorbing their interests in a fictitious unity; sacrifices their several inclinations and duties to the higher claim of nationality, and crushes all natural rights and all established liberties, for the purpose of vindicating itself." And, he continues: "Whenever a single definite object is made the supreme end of the State, be it the advantage of a class, the safety or the power of the country, the greatest happiness of the greatest number, or the support of any speculative idea, the State becomes for the time inevitably absolute. . . . In supporting the claims of national unity, governments must be subverted in whose title there is no flaw, and whose policy is beneficent and equitable, and subjects must be compelled to transfer their allegiance to an authority for which they have no attachment, and which may be practically a foreign domination."

The true theory of Nationality, according to Lord Acton, is one which divorces it from the idea that a national group, as of right, should be a politically independent unit; which admits the superior claims of political sovereignty, and asks only that, within the body politic, each national group be allowed to preserve its own customs and culture. When this is done, he says, not only will the "Nation" receive all that it can properly claim, but the State itself will be benefited by the diversities in its own citizen body. The paragraph in which this conviction is stated deserves quotation.

"While the theory of unity makes the Nation a source of despotism and revolution, the theory of liberty regards it as the bulwark of self-government, and the foremost limit to excessive power of the State. Private rights, which are sacrificed to the unity, are preserved by the union of Nations. No power can so efficiently resist the tendencies of centralization, of corruption, and of absolutism, as that community which is the vastest that can be included in a State, which imposes on its members a consistent similarity of character, interest, and opinion, and which arrests the action of the sovereign by the influence of a divided patriotism. . . . That intolerance of social freedom which is natural to absolutism is sure to find a corrective in the national diversities, which no other force can so efficiently provide. The co-existence of several Nations under the same State is a test, as well as the best security of its freedom. It is also one of the chief instruments of civilization; and, as such, it is in the natural and providential order, and indicates a state of greater advancement than the national unity which is the ideal of modern liberalism. The combination of different Nations in one State is as necessary a condition of civilized life as the combination of men in society. Inferior races are raised by living in political union with races intellectually superior. Exhausted and decaying Nations are revived by the contact of a younger vitality. Nations in which the elements of organization and the capacity for government have been lost, either through the demoralizing influence of despotism, or the disintegrating action of democracy, are restored and educated anew under the discipline of a stronger and less corrupted race. This fertilizing and regenerating process can only be obtained by living under one government. It is in the cauldron of the State that the fusion takes place by which the vigor, the knowledge, and the capacity of one portion of mankind may be communicated to another.

Where political and national boundaries coincide, society ceases to advance, and nations relapse into a condition corresponding to that of men who renounce intercourse with their fellow men."

In another place in the same essay, Lord Acton says: "The greatest adversary of the rights of Nationality is the modern theory of Nationality. By making the State and the Nation commensurate with each other in theory, it reduces practically to a subject condition all other Nationalities that may be within the boundary. It cannot admit them to an equality with the ruling Nation which constitutes the State, because the State would then cease to be national, which would be a contradiction of the principles of its existence. According, therefore, to the degree of humanity and civilization in that dominant body which claims all the rights of a community, the inferior races are exterminated or reduced to servitude, or outlawed, or put in a condition of dependence."

In short, according to Lord Acton, the modern theory of Nationality, is, upon the one hand, revolutionary in that it furnishes a basis for resistance upon the part of subject national groups to the political authority to which they happen to be subjected; and, upon the other hand, conservative, in that it justifies the ruthless subjection of these lesser national groups by the dominant national group of a State.

In the statements which have been quoted, Lord Acton possibly pushed too far the probable benefits to the State upon the one hand and to individual national groups upon the other hand, from a coexistence of several nations under a single government. But that he was fundamentally right in refusing to give his adherence to a doctrine of Nationality that would make its claims either absolute in character or so high as to override all the other requirements and exigencies of political jurisdiction, there can be no doubt. Also, we can agree with him that there is political wisdom, if not absolute ethical obligation, in giving to particular national groups within larger political groups, every possible opportunity to maintain, or even to cultivate, their special ideals in art, literature, religion, and modes of life, and even to give to them, if they desire it, autonomous powers with reference to matters of local government. Especially is this last true when a State is dealing with colonies or dependencies inhabited by populations of a civilization different from or inferior to that of its own people. Here is a topic which *deserves* extended treatment were there space for its discussion.

Territorial Inviolability. One principle which has been closely united to that of Nationality, but which is distinct from it, is that which maintains that, upon historical grounds, or as divinely intended (as evidenced by physical geographical features) certain territorial areas should, as of ethical right, belong to particular States. Thus, we have earlier seen in a quoted statement of Mazzini that he held that upon Italy Providence had left its "sublime, irrefutable boundary marks." Other Peoples or States have made the same claim with regard to what they have conceived should be their territorial limits, but, perhaps, in no country has the doctrine of the sanctity of national domains, as delimited by tradition or geographical configuration, been more strongly asserted or stated in more abstract terms than by France. By a unanimous vote, on December 16, 1792, the National Convention decreed death to any one who should propose or attempt to break the unity of the French Republic or to detach one of the integral parts of its territory in order that it might be united to a foreign territory. And, on April 13, 1793, this decree was again made.[23] And it will be remembered that in 1871 Thiers, upon this principle of the essential inviolability of French soil, sought to

[23] Cf. Mattern, *Employment of the Plebescite*, p. 79, note.

obtain aid from neutral nations in preventing the cession to Germany of Alsace-Lorraine.[24]

This theory of territorial inviolability is so obviously artificial in character that it does not deserve criticism. It is upon a par with the theory of "Legitimacy" that played a part in the deliberations of the Congress of Vienna.

Self-Determination. The assertion of a right to "self-determination" upon the part of national groups is not made in the Covenant of the League of Nations, nor declared elsewhere in the treaty of peace with Germany, and, indeed, as is well known, a considerable number of the provisions of that instrument, as well as of the other treaties concluding the Great War, are in open conflict with the doctrine that national feelings of the people concerned should control the political allegiance imposed upon them. Where the political interests of the victorious Powers, or military strategical considerations, or economic needs, or even the prior secret promises of the Allies among themselves, interposed, claims based upon sentiments of nationality were disregarded. Without question, however, the existence of rights of political self-determination was repeatedly asserted during the war by the statesmen of the Allied and Associated Powers, and especially by President Wilson, who, to a very considerable extent, was accepted as the spokesman for them all.

In an address to The League to Enforce Peace, delivered May 27, 1916, President Wilson declared that "every people has a right to choose the sovereignty under which they shall live"; and in his famous "Fourteen Points"

---

[24] With regard to this plea, Morley, in his *Life of Gladstone*, reports that Gladstone "could not understand how the French protests turned more upon the inviolability of French soil than on the attachment of the people of Alsace and North Lorraine to their country. The abstract principle he thought peculiarly awkward in a nation that had made recent annexations of her own." Quoted by Mattern, *op. cit.*, p. 174.

which, on January 8, 1918, he put forward as "the only possible programme" of the world's peace, he declared that the frontiers of Italy should be readjusted "along clearly recognizable lines of nationality"; that the peoples of Austria-Hungary should be accorded "the first opportunity of autonomous nationality"; that the relations of the several Balkan States to one another should be fixed "along historically established lines of allegiance and nationality"; that the other non-Turkish nationalities under Ottoman rule should be given "an absolutely unmolested opportunity of autonomous development"; and that the Polish State should be reconstituted so as to include all territories inhabited by indisputably Polish populations. In concluding the address in which, *inter alia,* these Points were stated, President Wilson said: "One evident principle runs through the whole programme I have uttered. It is the principle of justice to all peoples and nationalities, and their right to live on equal terms of liberty and safety with one another, whether they be strong or weak."

In the foregoing it is seen how prominent was made the principle of rights based upon Nationality. In his address of February 11, 1918, the principle was still more strongly emphasized, the declaration being made that "National aspirations must be respected; peoples may now be dominated and governed only by their own consent. 'Self-Determination' is not a mere phrase. It is an imperative principle of action, which statesmen will henceforth ignore at their peril." In the same address it was asserted that "this war had its roots in the disregard of the rights of small nations and of nationalities which lacked the union and the force to make good their claim to determine their own allegiance and their own forms of political life. Covenants must now be entered into which will render such things impossible for the future."

Elsewhere, however, in this same address of February 11, 1918, President Wilson somewhat qualified the principle which he had so often stated as an absolute one. He demanded that "all well-defined national aspirations shall be accorded the utmost satisfaction that can be accorded them without introducing new or perpetuating old elements of discord and antagonism that would be likely in time to break the peace of Europe and consequently of the world." [25]

Even as thus qualified it is clear the doctrine of national rights was not stated by President Wilson, or

[25] General Smuts in his pamphlet "The League of Nations," used with approval the expression "The self-determination of nations." In the printed draft of his constitution or covenant for the League of Nations, President Wilson included the following article (3):
"The Contracting Powers unite in guaranteeing to each other political independence and territorial integrity; but it is understood between them that such territorial readjustments, if any, as may in the future become necessary by reason of changes in present racial conditions and aspirations or present social and political relationships, pursuant to the principle of self-determination, and also such territorial readjustments as may in the judgment of three-fourths of the Delegates be demanded by the welfare and manifest interest of the peoples concerned, may be effected if agreeable to those peoples; and that territorial changes may in equity involve material compensation. The Contracting Powers accept without reservation that the peace of the world is superior in importance to every question of political jurisdiction or boundary."
As Ex-Secretary of State Lansing has pointed out in his volume *The Peace Negotiations*, and in an article entitled "Self-Determination" (*The Saturday Evening Post*, April 9, 1921), this Article 3, as it appeared as Article 7 of President Wilson's revised draft, lost its modifying clause and provided simply that the Contracting Powers should undertake to respect as against external aggression the territorial integrity and existing political independence of the States which might become parties to the League—an undertaking which found embodiment in the famous Article 10 of the Covenant of the League as finally made a part of the Treaty of Versailles.
Why this modifying clause with its recognition of the right of Self-Determination was thus dropped out by President Wilson, Mr. Lansing says he cannot, from actual personal knowledge, say. However, he says: "There prevailed a general belief that the elimination was due chiefly to the opposition of the statesmen who represented the British Empire in contra-distinction to those who represented the self-governing British Dominions. It was asserted, and I have no reason to doubt the correctness of the assertion, that this opposition was caused by the unwillingness to recognize as a right the principle of self-determination in arranging possible future changes of sovereignty over territories." Whether this be correct or not, it remains true that President Wilson never sought or availed himself of an opportunity to disavow or to qualify it further than he had done in his address of February 11, 1918.

by the statesmen of the Allied Powers, in a sufficiently guarded manner. Throughout their utterances there was the implied assumption that there is attached to the attribute of nationality rights of political self-determination which, if not absolute in character, are nevertheless so sacrosanct that a heavy burden of proof is laid upon those who would disregard them. The true doctrine, however, is that, in itself, the existence among a people of a feeling or sentiment of common nationality, whether based upon race, religion, historical tradition, language or economic interests, should, in determining matters of political allegiance, be given no greater weight than any other fact that would tend to show that, under a given sovereignty or given form of government the best results will be reached for the peoples of the world as well as for those directly concerned. In truth, when the treaties of peace came to be written the rights of nationalities were, without hesitation, disregarded when other considerations were involved which the statesmen of the victorious Powers deemed politically more important. Those statesmen, then, are not to be criticized for not having rigorously applied the so-called doctrine of national rights, but they are open to censure for having originally stated the principle without sufficient qualifications, and for having, in some instances, refused to apply it because of selfish political or military strategic purposes, rather than because the true interests of the world made necessary this disregard.

Summing up, now, by way of conclusion, the objections to the rights of nationality as absolute in character, they are these: First, that the idea of nationality is itself so indefinite that it cannot be clearly defined, with the result that, in many cases, it cannot be determined with certainty whether or not a group of persons is properly entitled to be viewed as constituting a national unit. Even when the elements that constitute or create the sentiment of nationality are clearly seen to exist, there is no rule that can be laid down as to how generally or nearly universally this sentiment must be diffused among the individuals of the group in order that it may claim national unity. Secondly, that, at the best, this psychologically cementing and unifying principle can have no application except in communities which have reached a degree of enlightenment which makes possible the formation of an intelligent public opinion regarding matters of political interest, and, furthermore, in which legally sanctioned instrumentalities exist through which may be formulated and freely enunciated the sincere expression of the desires of the people as to the sovereignty to which they are to give their allegiance. In the third place, the foregoing conditions having been met, the doctrine of national rights, because it makes other rights subordinate to them, is at once a creed of despotism and a platform of political disorder. It justifies the dominant national group in a given State in attempting, by whatever means available, to crush out the dissentient cultures of all other groups which, even if in numerical majority in the community, do not happen to be in possession of corresponding coercive power. Upon the other hand, it furnishes all groups within a political community which claim national unity and corresponding national rights, an apparent justification in refusing to recognize the persuasive force of other considerations in favor of continued political unity, and in attempting, by revolutionary means and civil war, if their demands are not granted, to release themselves from the sovereignty under which they happen to be living.

At best, then, the demand of a people to determine the sovereignty under which they are to live is but one of the factors to be taken into consideration by statesmen in deciding as to the territorial limits of political jurisdictions. Mr. Lansing, in the article to which reference has been made, has stated this doctrine in a manner that deserves quotation. He says:

"In the settlement of territorial rights and of the sovereignty to be exercised over particular regions there are several factors which require consideration. International boundaries may be drawn along ethnic, economic, geographic, historic or strategic lines. One or all of these elements may influence the decision, but whatever argument may be urged in favor of any one of these factors, the chief object in the determination of the sovereignty to be exercised within a certain territory is national safety. National safety is as dominant in the life of a nation as self-preservation is in the life of an individual. Self-preservation is an instinct of human existence; and self-preservation is an even more compelling instinct of national existence, since nations do not respond to the impulse of self-sacrifice. With national safety as the primary object to be attained in territorial settlements the factors of the problem assume generally, though not always, the following order of importance: The strategic, to which is closely allied the geographic and historic; the economic, affecting the commercial and industrial life of a nation; and lastly the ethnic, including in the term such conditions as consanguinity, common language and similar social and religious institutions. In the application or the attempted application of the so-called right of self-determination the chief considerations with individuals are naturally ethnic—the least important factor, as a rule, in the problem of deciding political allegiance. This is not always so, but the exceptions are few. If the right conflicts with national safety, with normal geographic frontiers or with the economic life of a nation, it has been and it will continue to be disregarded; in fact the cases are few in which there has not been this conflict. The attempt then to make self-determination a right fundamental and constant to the exercise of sovereignty over territory is bound to be denied in practice. It cannot be uniformly followed if the territorial integrity and the political stability which are essential to a nation's peace at home and abroad, to its growth and development, are to be preserved." [26]

[26] Cf. the note of Professor Philip M. Brown entitled "Self-Determination," in the *American Journal of International Law*, Vol. XIV, p. 235 (January-April, 1920). With reference to the use of the plebescite in determining sovereignty,—the history of its use as well as the arguments in support of the ethical obligation to resort to it—see Johannes Mattern, *The Employment of the Plebiscite in the Determination of Sovereignty* (Johns Hopkins University Studies in Historical and Political Science, Series XXXVIII, 1920) ; and Sarah Wambaugh, *A Monograph on Plebescites* (Publications of the Carnegie Endowment for International Peace, 1920). For an excellent brief sketch of the "Theory and Practice of Nationalism" see that of Professor W. A. Dunning in the chapter bearing this title in Volume III of his *History of Political Theories.*

CHAPTER XIX

THE RIGHTS ACCORDED TO STATES BY INTERNATIONAL LAW

IN this chapter will be considered the rights accorded by International Law to independent States as such, and without regard to those based upon nationalistic claims, such as have been treated in the preceding chapter.

With the rights of States regarded simply as juristic postulates we are not here concerned. They are dealt with in the author's volume, *The Fundamental Concepts of Public Law,* in which the nature of the State is examined from the strictly juristic point of view. We are here concerned, however, with these rights insofar as their existence is attempted to be justified upon ethical grounds, or upon the assumption that there is something in the very nature of statehood that makes it imperative that certain specific rights should be accorded to the political "Persons" with which international law has to deal.

An inspection of the earlier international law writings shows a very general acceptance of the doctrine that all sovereign States should be conceded to have certain rights which are not deducible from common agreement between States, or based upon considerations of expediency, but which are inherent in them as independent bodies-politic. Thus, in effect, the old doctrine of the natural rights of the individual human being was applied to States as the 'Persons' of International Law. This method of determining the primary State rights which all States should recognize as possessed by each was especially seen in the treatises of Grotius, Pufendorf, Wolff, and Vattell. For example, as typical, we find Vattell saying:

"Nations, or sovereign States, are to be considered as so many free persons living together in the State of Nature. . . . The Nation possesses also the same rights which Nature has conferred upon men in order to enable them to perform their duties. We must, therefore, apply to Nations the rules of the Law of Nature, in order to discover what their obligations are, and what their rights: consequently the Law of Nations is originally no other than the Law of Nature applied to Nations."

Upon this basis, Vattell goes on to deduce the rights of independence, self-defense, territorial jurisdiction, and the like.

It does not need to be said that, since Vattell's time, the general tendency has been, without interruption, to render international law more "positive" in character, and to found its precepts, not upon abstract ethical or *naturrechtliche* principles, but upon the actual practices of nations and upon their express agreements. This is now the accepted doctrine of all modern publicists. It is, therefore, somewhat surprising to find the American Institute of International Law at its first session on January 6, 1916, issuing a "Declaration of Rights and Duties of Nations," of an absolutist or naturalistic character. Because of its source, this Declaration deserves quotation *in extenso*.

"WHEREAS the municipal law of civilized nations recognizes and protects the right to life, the right to liberty, the right to the pursuit of happiness, as added by the Declaration of Independence of the United States of America, the right to legal equality, the right to property, and the right to the enjoyment of the aforesaid rights; and

"WHEREAS these fundamental rights, thus universally

recognized, create a duty on the part of the peoples of all nations to observe them; and

"WHEREAS, according to the political philosophy of the Declaration of Independence of the United States, and the universal practice of the American Republics, nations or governments are regarded as created by the people, deriving their just powers from the consent of the governed, and are instituted among men to promote their safety and happiness and to secure to the people the enjoyment of their fundamental rights; and

"WHEREAS the nation is a moral or juristic person; the creature of law, and subordinated to law as is the natural person in political society; and

"WHEREAS we deem these fundamental rights can be stated in terms of international law and applied to the relations of the members of the society of nations, one with another, just as they have been applied in the relations of the citizens or subjects of the States forming the Society of Nations; and

"WHEREAS these fundamental rights of national jurisprudence, namely, the right of life, the right to liberty, the right to the pursuit of happiness, the right to equality before the law, the right to property, and the right to the observance thereof are, when stated in terms of international law, the right of the nation to exist and to protect and to conserve its existence; the right of independence and the freedom to develop itself without interference or control from other nations; the right of equality in law and before law; the right to territory within defined boundaries and to exclusive jurisdiction therein; and the right to the observance of these fundamental rights; and

"WHEREAS the rights and the duties of nations are, by virtue of membership in the society thereof, to be exercised and performed in accordance with the exigencies of their mutual interdependence expressed in the preamble to the Convention for the Pacific Settlement of International Disputes of the First and Second Hague Peace Conferences, recognizing the solidarity which unites the members of the society of civilized nations;

"THEREFORE, The American Institute of International Law, at its first session, held in the City of Washington, in the United States of America, on the sixth day of January, 1916, adopts the following six articles, together with the Commentary thereon, to be known as its

DECLARATION OF THE RIGHTS AND DUTIES OF NATIONS

"I. Every nation has the right to exist, and to protect and to conserve its existence; but this right neither implies the right nor justifies the act of the State to protect itself or to conserve its existence by the commission of unlawful acts against innocent and unoffending States.

"II. Every nation has the right to independence in the sense that it has a right to the pursuit of happiness and is free to develop itself without interference or control from other States, provided that in so doing it does not interfere with or violate the rights of other States.

"III. Every nation is in law and before law the equal of every other nation belonging to the society of nations, and all nations have the right to claim and, according to the Declaration of Independence of the United States, 'to assume, among the powers of the earth, the separate and equal station to which the laws of nature and of nature's God entitle them.'

"IV. Every nation has the right to territory within defined boundaries and to exercise exclusive jurisdiction over its territory, and all persons whether native or foreign found therein.

"V. Every nation, entitled to a right by the law of nations, is entitled to have that right respected and protected by all other nations, for right and duty are correlative, and the right of one is the duty of all to observe.

"VI. International law is at one and the same time

both national and international: national in the sense that it is the law of the land and applicable as such to the decision of all questions involving its principle; international in the sense that it is the law of the society of nations and applicable as such to all questions between and among the members of the society of nations involving its principles."

Accompanying this Declaration was an *Official Commentary*.

As to existence and self-defense, this Commentary declared that the right of a State is to be deemed similar to that of the individual under municipal law, namely, to take the life of another if necessary in self-defense against an unlawful attack.

As to the rights of independence, the pursuit of happiness and to unimpeded development, to juristic equality, and to exclusive territorial jurisdiction, the Commentary had little to say beyond quoting certain *dicta* of courts and commentators.

As to the correlation between international rights and duties, which make it obligatory upon all States to protect as well as to observe the rights of other States, the only supporting authority which the Commentary was able to produce was a case in the Supreme Court of the United States [1] in which it was held, but only as a matter of American constitutional law, that the National Government of the American Union has the authority to punish the counterfeiting upon American soil of securities of a foreign State. Upon the declaration that international law is to be deemed at the same time both national and international, the Commentary contained what amounted to a brief in support of the position, but made no real attempt to meet the proposition that a principle of international law becomes one of municipal law only when accepted, and because

[1] United States v. Arjona, 120 U. S. Reports, 479.

of that acceptance, by the competent authorities of the several States.

The futility of this attempt upon the part of the American Institute to fix in international jurisprudence a series of absolute rights of States was easily shown by Professor Philip M. Brown in his volume entitled *International Realities* from which the following quotation is taken:

"When it is asserted that a State has the 'right' to exist, it can hardly mean that all existing States have a right: . . . If a State deteriorates in its domestic life, and becomes incapable of maintaining a political organization, it may require something of the nature of a protectorate or an international receivership. . . . If it misbehaves in such a way as to become a menace to the welfare of other nations, it will deserve either restraint of its freedom or actual extinction as a separate nation. Society does not guarantee to the individual any legal or moral right to exist. It protects him from assassination but does not allow him to continue to exist if he is a menace to the community as a whole. His right is not 'absolute', it is a qualified right. And so it must be with nations; they have no 'absolute right' of existence." [2]

The right of a State to existence having been shown to be a relative one, it follows *a fortiori*, that its other alleged rights to independence, territorial sovereignty, and the like, are also ones that are qualified by special conditions of fact. And, even as regards the principle of the juristic equality of States, it is easily shown that it is one of expediency rather than of absolute ethical obligation, and that it is disregarded, without compunction, when put forward by the smaller States, and that it has interposed an obstacle to the better organization of international relations. In such international gatherings as the Hague Peace Conferences, the London Naval Con-

[2] *Op. cit.*, p. 58.

ference of 1909, and the Paris Peace Conference of 1919, no pretense was made of giving to the smaller States an equal voice with the larger States; and, in proposed international organizations, such as the International Prize Court, the Permanent Court of International Justice, and the League of Nations, the larger States are frankly given preferential treatment.

Self-Defense and Development. No definite line can be drawn between the right of self-defense and the right of the State to extend its dominion. Aside from the fact that the right of self-defense, when carried to its full length, often shades off into what, in substance, amounts to offensive action (as, for example, when a State, in order to protect itself against a possible danger from a neighbor, interferes with the internal affairs of that neighbor or even, in extreme cases, brings that neighbor by force wholly under its own sovereignty), the same principle that justifies the State in asserting its ethical right to a continued existence can be used to maintain its right to increase its influence.

The exercise in practice of the doctrine which has been stated is seen in the use which has been made by the United States of the Monroe Doctrine. In its original form this doctrine declared that "as a principle in which the rights and interests of the United States are involved," "the American continents, by the free and independent condition which they have assumed and maintain, are henceforth not to be considered as subjects for future colonization by any European powers." Further, President Monroe declared: "We owe it, therefore, to candor, and to the amicable relations existing between the United States and those powers, to declare that we should consider any attempt on their part to extend their system to any portion of this hemisphere as dangerous to our peace and safety."

In the policy, thus announced, there was apparent

in the minds of those that framed it the doctrine that popular, as opposed to autocratic, government deserved the approval and protection of the United States, and that the United States, so far as concerned the Western Hemisphere at least, was prepared to stand as its protagonist and defender. In addition, however, the United States based its declaration of policy upon a right of self-defense, that is, upon the ground that the increase of European influence or the establishment of monarchical institutions upon its borders would endanger the permanency of its own republican institutions or make it necessary for the United States to maintain a larger military or naval establishment than it otherwise would wish to do.

Another illuminating illustration of the use of the doctrine of self-defense is seen in the policies of Japan since 1894. The purpose avowed by Japan for the Sino-Japanese war of 1894-1895 was to expel foreign influence from Korea which, it was felt, would, if it should become dominant, endanger the peace or even the independence of itself.[3] So, also, the Japanese have claimed, and with undoubted justice, that they fought the Russo-Japanese War of 1904-1905 in order to prevent the establishment at their very doors of a strong and expanding power that would be a continuing danger to themselves. The result was, however, that Japan not only expelled Russia from Korea and South Manchuria, but, within a few years, incorporated Korea in her own Empire, and, in South Manchuria took over the former rights of Russia which, when in Russia's hands had, according to the Japanese, violated the territorial integrity and endangered the autonomy, if not the independence, of the Chinese Empire. Having secured a foothold upon the mainland of

---

[3] The result of that war was not simply to put an end to foreign political influence in Korea but to annex to Japan the great island of Formosa lying off the southern coast of China.

Asia by annexing Korea, leasing the Liaotung peninsula, and obtaining "special interests" in Manchuria, Japan has asserted a right to take such action as may be necessary to protect these new areas of influence and control. Thus it is seen how the mere right of self-defense broadened out into what became, in substance, an imperialistic policy. Similarly, if it were necessary to do so, it could be shown how Great Britain has steadily spread her dominion over new portions of the earth's area, and at the same time interposed vetoes upon the expansion of other powers by calling to her aid the doctrine of self-defense of what she has already possessed. Even the United States, which has reiterated with especial emphasis the pacific and anti-imperialistic character of its policies, has found it necessary or expedient during the last twenty years to extend its political control over the Philippines, the Canal Zone, Porto Rico, Hawaii, the Virgin Islands, and other smaller islands, not to speak of exercising actual military control of Haiti, Santo Domingo, and Nicaragua.

In addition to the right of self-defense, peoples have, at times, asserted the right to extend, by force or by propaganda, those political views which they believe it to be to the interest of other peoples to adopt. Thus, the French during the Revolutionary period preached democracy as a religion and sought in every way possible to induce or compel other peoples to substitute popular for autocratic forms of political rule, and offered their military aid to such peoples as might desire to make the change. So, also, the monarchical powers, after the overthrow of Napoleon, agreed among themselves not only to maintain autocracy but to intervene in other countries to prevent the establishment in them of republican institutions; and, as is well known, it was the fear that this so-called "Holy Alliance" might extend its operations to the New World that led, in large measure, to the service upon them, in the message of President Monroe of 1823, of the notice that the United States would deem it an unfriendly act towards itself should this be attempted to be done in the Americas.

Control of Inferior Peoples. Most extreme of all the assertions on the part of individual States has been their claim of a right to bring, by force if necessary, other nations under their own sovereignty, upon the ground that their own culture or civilization is of such excellence that the welfare of humanity will be promoted by the increase to the greatest possible extent of their own power and political influence.

This claim of right upon the part of a people to compel other peoples to accept its political rule is seen in cases where the so-called civilized powers have sought to defend upon grounds other than of self-defense or of unashamed force their control of peoples whom they deem to be so far uncivilized as to be unable to appreciate the value of civilized life, or who, for any reason, are unable to maintain a reasonably efficient and stable form of political rule.

When justification is sought upon these grounds certain obligations upon the part of the dominant power are necessarily implied. The first of these is that the true welfare of the subject peoples shall be conscientiously sought. This does not mean that the dominant power may not obtain benefits from its dependencies, but that such benefits shall be incidental only. The prime purpose of every such exercise of controlling power should, however, be to promote the welfare of the peoples who are given no option but to obey. The second of the obligations resting upon the dominant State is that it should seek in every way, by education, by commercial and industrial development, and by the grant as rapidly as possible of autonomous powers of administration, to prepare the subject peoples for self-government and for independence should they continue to desire it.[4]

[4] The most recent as well as the most formal statement of the obligations which civilized States owe to peoples less civilized and, at the same time, the assertion of a right possessed by these superior States to take politically less developed peoples under their direction and control, is contained in Article XXII of the Covenant of the League of Nations. Because this is a statement agreed to by so many of the States of the world, it deserves quotation *in extenso:*

"To those colonies and territories which as a consequence of the late war have ceased to be under the sovereignty of the States which formerly governed them and which are inhabited by peoples not yet able to stand by themselves under the strenuous conditions of the modern world, there should be applied the principle that the well-being and development of such peoples form a sacred trust of civilization and that securities for the performance of this trust should be embodied in this Covenant.

"The best method of giving practical effect to this principle is that the tutelage of such peoples should be entrusted to advanced nations who by reason of their resources, their experience or their geographical position can best undertake this responsibility, and who are willing to accept it, and that this tutelage should be exercised by them as Mandatories on behalf of the League.

"The character of the mandate must differ according to the stage of the development of the people, the geographical situation of the territory, its economic conditions, and other similar circumstances.

"Certain communities formerly belonging to the Turkish Empire have reached a stage of development where their existence as independent nations can be provisionally recognized subject to the rendering of administrative advice and assistance by a Mandatory until such time as they are able to stand alone. The wishes of these communities must be a principal consideration in the selection of the Mandatory.

"Other peoples, especially those of Central Africa, are at such a stage that the Mandatory must be responsible for the administration of the territory under conditions which will guarantee freedom of conscience and religion, subject only to the maintenance of public order and morals, the prohibition of abuses such as the slave trade, the arms traffic, and the liquor traffic, and the prevention of the establishment of fortifications or military and naval bases and of military training of the natives for other than police purposes and the defence of territory, and will also secure equal opportunities for the trade and commerce of other Members of the League.

"There are territories, such as South-West Africa and certain of the South Pacific Islands, which, owing to the sparseness of their population, or their small size, or their remoteness from the centers of civilization, or other geographical contiguity to the territory of the Mandatory, and other circumstances, can be best administered under the laws of the Mandatory as integral portions of its territory, subject to the safeguards above mentioned in the interests of the indigenous population. In every case of mandate, the Mandatory shall render to the Council an annual report in reference to the territory committed to its charge.

"The degree of authority, control, or administration to be exercised by the Mandatory shall, if not previously agreed upon by the Members of the League, be explicitly defined in each case by the Council.

"A permanent Commission shall be constituted to receive and examine the annual reports of the Mandatories and to advise the Council on all matters relating to the observance of the mandates."

The obligations resting upon a dominant State with reference to its dependencies have been recognized by the United States in its dealings with its dependencies. In one of the state papers of which the American Government may always be proud, the Instructions of the President, in 1900, to the Commission which was, for the time being, to govern the Philippine Islands, the following, among other, mandatory directions were given:

"In all the forms of government and administrative provisions which they are authorized to prescribe the Commission should bear in mind that the government which they are establishing is designed not for our satisfaction or for the expression of our theoretical views, but for the happiness, peace, and prosperity of the people of the Philippine Islands, and the measures adopted should be conformed to their customs, their habits, and even their prejudices to the fullest extent consistent with the accomplishment of the indispensable requisites of just and efficient government. . . . It will be the duty of the Commission to extend and, as they find occasion, to improve the system of education already inaugurated by the military authorities. . . . The main body of the laws which regulate the rights and obligations of the people should be maintained with as little interference as possible. Changes made should be mainly in procedure, and in the criminal laws to secure speedy and impartial trials, and at the same time effective administration and respect for individual rights."

From time to time since 1900, American Presidents, the Congress and American national political parties in their platforms have promised the Philippines that, when the Filipinos have shown that they are qualified for complete self-government and independence, it will be granted to them. The Act of Congress under which the islands are now governed declares in its Preamble that "it is, as it has always been, the purpose of the people of the

United States to withdraw their sovereignty over the Philippine Islands and to recognize their independence as soon as a stable government can be established therein."

It is to the credit of the American Government that, with comparatively few exceptions, its acts have been in conformity with its professed purposes. It has sought the welfare of the natives and has endeavored to fit them for the time when they may take fully into their own hands the control of their own political destinies. And, in pursuance of this last purpose, the autonomy of the Insular Government has been progressively increased and more and more the natives given control of it. The Filipino leaders now assert that the point has been reached at which the full independence of the Islands should be recognized, and this, as a statement of fact, was accepted by President Wilson who, in his annual message to the American Congress, in December, 1920, said: "The people of the Philippine Islands have succeeded in maintaining a stable government since the last action of Congress in their behalf, and have thus fulfilled the condition set by the Congress as precedent to a consideration of granting independence to the Islands. I respectfully submit that this condition precedent having been fulfilled it is now our liberty and our duty to keep our promises to the people of those Islands by granting them the independence which they so honorably covet."

Objectively viewed, that is, from the standpoint of an impartial observer, the ethical propriety of a dominion over a people in a comparatively low stage of civilization or of political development by a highly civilized and politically developed people is fairly plain if that dominion be in fact exercised in accordance with the principles that have been stated. The question becomes a more difficult one, however, in proportion as the differences in degree of civilization and political development between the dominant and subject peoples become less and less pronounced. The controlling principles, however, do not change, and all that one can say is that where these differences are not considerable, the State claiming an ethical right to rule should make its assurance doubly sure that the welfare of the ruled population, or of humanity in general, will, in truth, as an ultimate as well as a proximate result, be better subserved by their subjection to its own rule than would be the case if the population in question were left to seek their own welfare in their own way, or if they were remitted to the political control of some third State.

Though never an absolutely controlling consideration it may be said that, other things being equal, peoples should be allowed to decide for themselves what sovereignty over themselves they will recognize. That is, the presumption is that they best know what their own interests are and how they may best be secured. But this is only a presumption that may be rebutted. The same is true as to the particular laws and institutions which are to be maintained. In the case of the Philippines, the American Government, as we have seen, directed its commissioners to interfere as little as possible with local customs and laws. Nevertheless, in the Instructions of 1900 which have been quoted from, President McKinley went on to say:

"At the same time the Commission should bear in mind, and the people of the Islands should be made plainly to understand, that there are certain great principles of government which have been made the basis of our [the American] governmental system, which we deem essential to the rule of law and the maintenance of individual freedom and of which they have unfortunately been denied the experience possessed by us; that there are also certain practical rules of government which we have found to be essential to the preservation of these great principles of liberty and law, and that these principles and these rules of government must be established and maintained in their Islands for the sake of their liberty and happiness, however much they may conflict with the customs or laws of procedure with which they are familiar."

The Instructions then went on to enumerate these "inviolable rules." Thus was plainly declared the conviction of the American Government that, as to these rules at least, there was no doubt that it knew better than did the Filipinos what would be best for themselves—a conviction so strong that no option was to be given to those to whom they were to be applied.

Germany's Ante-War Doctrine. Prior to the Great War many Germans, and especially Prussians, appear to have convinced themselves of the fact that the Germans were, as the Kaiser said, "the salt of the earth." As early as 1868, the philosopher Lasson boasted that "we [the Germans] are morally and intellectually superior to all men. We are peerless." William Ostwald, the eminent scientist, after the outbreak of the war, published his persuasion that "Germany has reached a higher type of civilization than other peoples, and the result of the war will be the organization of Europe under German leadership." And Bernhardi, speaking for the military mind, declared: "The proud conviction forces itself upon us with irresistible power that a high, if not the highest, importance for the entire development of the human race is ascribable to the German people." These are but typical of a multitude of statements from German philosophers, poets, scientists, priests, and statesmen, and give evidence that there was in Germany a very widespread conviction that, because of the inherent super-excellence of its *Kultur*, the German State was ethically entitled to spread its dominion as widely as possible, and that, however unwilling the other peoples of Europe or of the world might be to accept this *Kultur,* it would be to their advantage to do so, and that, therefore, German political authority might be exercised over them in order to compel them to receive it. In other words, the ethical right of the German Empire to expand was asserted not merely as a means whereby the German people might themselves be advantaged, but in order that the other and less enlightened peoples might profit by the precious gift of *Deutsche Kultur.*

The argument that a nation has a right to assert itself in so far as it has a conviction of the value of its civilization to the world has found no better statement, so far as the author's reading extends, than that of Professor Max Maurenbrecher, a German divine, published some fourteen years before the outbreak of the Great War.[5] After stating the problem: "What moral and social duties belong to our [German] people in consequence of the development of Germany into a world power?" and defining the phrase "development into a world power" as "the compulsion which a nation feels to unfold the power beyond its own limits because its interests are no longer confined to its own territory," he asks: "Can we reconcile with morality and with the principles of Christianity the conduct of a nation when it subdues another in order to obtain for itself a better place?" Having called attention to the increased and increasing population of Germany he asks: "Have we, on the whole, a right, in the sight of humanity, to defend the indispensable necessity of our increase?" These questions he answers as follows:

"According to my view, we should make substantially this statement: A people which surrenders the belief that its own existence has a significance for humanity in general thereby gives up all claim to a reason for being. It is the characteristic nucleus of the love of fatherland,

[5] *The American Journal of Sociology,* November, 1900 (Vol. VI, pp. 307-315): "The Moral and Social Tasks of World Politics (Imperialism)."

of patriotism, of national feeling, or, as we may designate this fundamental political feeling of every sound, progressive people, its faith in itself, the consciousness that it has a value, an importance in relation to mankind. This faith cannot be proved, as if it were some kind of a theoretical principle; much nearer accuracy would be to call it an axiom, or, better still, in the Kantian phrase, a moral postulate, a fundamental demand of the spirit, which is as really innate in men as nationality, in which it is manifested. To yield this faith would mean to deny reason and purpose in history generally, and to abandon faith in the rational direction of the world. . . . We do not know the final goal of human development, and we cannot know it because we are ourselves only a part of the way toward that goal. But this we believe, that every nation has the duty to pour into the stream of human development as much of its own, its peculiar spiritual possession, as it possibly can. Exactly in this value for humanity which each nation has, and in which we believe, without being able to prove it by experience to the skeptic, lies the moral basis and the moral right of our political aims. Precisely on moral grounds we say: The supreme law for a people (not for an individual) is self-preservation and the deepening and diffusion of its national culture. . . . If the requirements of self-preservation in two peoples are antagonistic, then it is the moral duty of each people to battle for its independence and self-preservation. . . . The solution of this contradiction lies in the realm of religion, that in history after all the conflicts, that will triumph which is best for all. But this faith in the national unity of history should hinder no nation from pushing forward its own interests with all its might. If the requirement of self-preservation is the supreme moral norm for a nation, then we cannot introduce any other standard for judgment. If we require for our political and economic independence expansion, then we must struggle for it with all the means which experience has taught us are most conducive to the end. Thus it is our right and our duty to draw under our dominion other nations, especially the uncivilized, when the interest of our independence requires it. . . . The individual man must live according to the example of the compassionate Samaritan who offered himself for his neighbor who had fallen among robbers. An entire people, however, would act against its primary moral duty if it should hazard its own existence in order to rescue another. . . . As soon as we enter upon the details of the policy of expansion we discover so much oppression of other peoples, so much destruction of lower cultures, so great annihilation of innocent and happy human life, that we should really be compelled to despair of justifying this policy if we did not regard our own national self-interest as the supreme moral norm for our political conduct."

Reasoning such as this, from a Doctor of Divinity, when joined to the conception of the State as "the most supremely real person, in the literal sense of the word, that exists," makes us able to understand the teachings of Treitschke that "the national task of a legally constituted people, conscious of a destiny, is to assert its rank in the world's destiny and its measure to participate in the great civilizing mission of mankind"; that if the State "neglects its strength in order to promote the idealistic aspirations of man, it repudiates its own nature and perishes. This is in truth for the State equivalent to the sin against the Holy Ghost, for it is indeed a mortal error in the State to subordinate itself for sentimental reasons to a foreign power, as we Germans have done to England"; that "every sovereign State has the undoubted right to declare war at its pleasure, and is consequently entitled to repudiate its treaties"; that "the establishment of a permanent international arbitration court is incompatible with the nature of the State"; that "the appeal to arms will be valid until the end of history, and therein lies the sacredness of war"; that "small States, because they are small, and therefore weak, have no right to existence against stronger States"; that "when we apply this standard of deeper and truly Christian ethics to the State, and remember that its very personality is power, we see its highest moral duty is to uphold that power"; that "weakness must always be condemned as the most disastrous and despicable of crimes, the unforgivable sin of politics"; "that moralists must first recognize that the State is not to be judged by the standards which apply to individuals but by those which are set for it by its own nature and ultimate aims." [6]

Wherein lay the error of this German state philosophy? Upon what points of fact or of political ethics did the Allies and the United States join issue with Germany and her allies in the Great War?

In the first place they were convinced that the Germans were not, in truth, actuated by any such high, philosophically founded, ethical purpose as their thinkers had declared, but, rather, that they were moved by sordid desires for material gain supplemented by an eagerness for a prestige in the world that would satisfy the extreme national pride which they had so sedulously cultivated.

In the second place, those who in the war opposed Germany denied the validity of the German conception of the State as a moral personality of so exalted a character that it lives in a realm where the ordinary rules of morality do not apply—that political power is an end that justifies itself.

In the third place, those who opposed Germany were profoundly convinced that *deutsche Kultur* did not pos-

---

[6] The foregoing quotations are taken from Treitschke's *Politics*, Vol. I, Chaps. I, II, and III. The Macmillan Co., 1916.

sess the intrinsic merits that were claimed for it. This was a square issue of fact upon which honest differences of opinion could exist. Convinced as the author of this volume is that there was in the German conceptions of life no such super-excellence as the Germans asserted, he, nevertheless, does not assert that this can be so certainly proved as to render essentially irrational an opinion to the contrary.

In the fourth place, the Allied and Associated Powers were convinced—rightly or wrongly—that the governments of the Central Powers were of a character that made it possible for them to be ruled by military leaders, and that, so long as such a condition should prevail, European or world peace could not be placed upon a firm basis. In his reply of August 27, 1917, to the Pope, President Wilson said:

"The object of this war is to deliver the free peoples of the world from the menace of the actual power of a vast military establishment controlled by an irresponsible government. . . . This power is not the German people. It is the ruthless master of the German people."

And, finally, when we come to the correspondence immediately leading up to the Armistice of November 11, 1918, we find it insisted, as a prerequisite of a consideration of terms of peace, that the rulers of Germany should be deprived of their power, and that the character of the government itself should be so changed that the world might be assured that policies should henceforth be determined by the German people themselves and not by a military or other autocratic establishment.

This condition the Germans accepted, and, in their communication of October 20, 1918, they said: "Hitherto the representation of the people in the German Empire has not been endowed with an influence on the formation of the government. The Constitution did not provide for a concurrence of the representation of the people in decisions on peace or war. These conditions have just now undergone a fundamental change. The new government has been formed in complete accord with the wishes of the representation of the people, based on the equal, universal, secret, direct franchise. The leaders of the great political parties of the Reichstag are members of this government. In future no government can take or continue in office without possessing the confidence of the majority of the Reichstag. The responsibility of the Chancellor of the Empire to the representation of the people is being legally developed and safeguarded. . . . The permanence of the new system is . . . guaranteed not only by constitutional safeguards, but also by the unshakable determination of the German people whose vast majority stands behind these reforms and demands their energetic continuance."

International Right of Eminent Domain. As a matter of practical necessity all systems of constitutional jurisprudence recognize that the State, through its government, may, when occasion demands, take private property for a public use, just as, also, it may, when necessity arises, compel the individual to perform public services, including service in its armed forces. As a matter of justice, when such private property is taken, compensation to the owner is usually made, and, in the United States, express constitutional provisions require that this shall be done. The question, then, arises whether an analogous right should not be recognized in International Law.

If the States of the world were organized into one system with a single organ qualified to speak their common will and to assume their joint responsibility, there can be little question that this organ should be given, or be recognized to have, the inherent power to override the selfish interests or mistaken judgments of individual

INTERNATIONAL RIGHTS

States in order that the more general interests of all the peoples of the world might be advanced. Possibly, with the development of The League of Nations such an ecumenical agency will be provided. But until it is demonstrated that confidence may be placed in the wisdom and catholicity of purpose of this or of some other organ of world government, it is necessary, if the right of international eminent domain is to be recognized, that its exercise should be in the hands and at the discretion of particular States. Hence, in the present stage of development of international morality, and with the emphasis now placed upon national rights as determined by national interests, there is the greatest danger in admitting that, under any circumstances, a particular State may justify its disregard of the recognized international rights of other States upon the ground that the end sought is one that will be generally advantageous to all the world.

The alleged necessity for such a doctrine arose in connection with the attempts made to secure from certain of the Central American States permission to build across their territories a ship canal that would unite the Atlantic and Pacific Oceans. Finally, as is well known, under a very thin veneer of legal procedure, the United States obtained from the State of Panama, which had seceded from the State of Colombia, the right to build the present Panama Canal, and the coercion that, in substance if not in form, was applied to Colombia has, by many, been justified upon the ground that the selfish or mistaken judgment of that State should not have been allowed to prevent the construction of a great public work that would be of undoubted and enormous advantage to all the world.

If, in a given case, it be admitted that an interest more general than that of the particular State which is invaded, is advanced, it is difficult, as a detached proposition, to argue that ethical wrong is done. But it is not possible thus to detach one exercise of such a power from the whole complexus of international rights and obligations. Such an act is in violation of the fundamental principles upon which the whole body of orderly international relations is built. In result, then, in the present state of the world's political development, only an extraordinary international exigency will ethically justify a State, or even a group of States, in overriding the recognized international rights of other States. Commentators, therefore, exercise a very reasonable prudence when they refuse to admit into international jurisprudence a right of international eminent domain.

PART II
ETHICO-JURISTIC THEORIES

CHAPTER XX

INTRODUCTION TO PART II

As indicated in its title, the purpose of this volume is to discuss the ethical basis of the State. It has, therefore, not been necessary, thus far, to give any consideration to the conceptions which jurists employ when dealing with the State or with the exercise of its powers. These conceptions the author has dealt with in his volume entitled *Fundamental Concepts of Public Law.* However, during recent years there have been developed theories regarding the nature and purpose of political authority which, while laying claim to lie within the field of juristic speculation, and, as such, to deal with the conceptions of sovereignty held by jurists and applied by courts, are, in reality, ethical theories. Therefore, an examination of them finds a proper place in the present volume. However, in order to distinguish these pseudo-juristic theories from those which have made no pretense to juristicity—if such a word may be used,—the author has segregated them, and will deal with them in this, the second part, of this volume. In order to prepare the way for the examination of these theories, it will be necessary to summarize, as concisely as possible, the conclusions reached by the jurist as to the nature of the State, and its unique attribute, Sovereignty.

By the jurist, the State is conceived of as an entity or juristic person, possessing, legally speaking, an omnipotent will; and laws, in a strict analytical or 'politive' sense, are regarded as the expression of that sovereign will.

This attribute of legal omnicompetence which is, by publicists, attributed to the State is exercised by the State through various organs which collectively are named its Government. Thus the particular organs of a Government may be of limited legal competence because of the restraints placed upon them by constitutional law, but the State itself, as the source of all the law which it recognizes, is, and must be, itself legally omnipotent. The Government as a whole must be deemed to possess the right to *exercise* all the powers of sovereignty. This is because the State is deemed to be wholly organized in its Government. Hence, where the exercise of certain powers is not vested in any one of the ordinary organs of government but, as it is commonly said, is reserved to the people, it results that the people acting through the modes and instrumentalities for the creation of constitutional law are, *quoad hoc,* an organ of the government, just as the electorate, when electing or recalling public officials or initiating or approving by referendum projects of legislation, is an organ of the Government. In every politically organized community, then, there exists a public authority to which, from the legal standpoint, all interests are potentially subject, and therefore liable to regulation and control by the State when this ruling power decides them to be of public interest.

It is true that there are, and have been since the earliest times, certain subjects that it has seemed just and proper should be left to the free exercise of the individual, and it does not seem reasonable to expect that the time will ever come when this opinion as to many of these subjects will be changed. But this is by no means the same thing as saying that these subjects constitute a domain that can never be entered by the State. The present domain of individual liberty is one that, according to present standards of politics, the *Government* is not allowed to enter. From the power of the *State*, however, it cannot be shielded, and, as regards it, its boundary line will ever depend upon political expediency. As Professor Burgess says: "The individual is defended in this sphere *against* the Government by the power [*i.e.* the State] that makes and maintains and can destroy the Government; and by that same power, *through* the Government, against the encroachments from any other quarter. Against that power itself, however, he has no defence." [1]

It is plain, then, that Sovereignty, thus juristically viewed, has no connection whatever with material or physical power. It is an attribute of the smallest and weakest of States as fully as it is of the mightiest Empire. It carries with it no implication that there exists in a State the ability actually to enforce those expressions of its will which, *ex hypothesi*, it has the juristic competence to utter. For the Sovereign State knows no limit, whether territorial or personal, to its legislative authority, whereas, of course, every State is in fact limited in the extent of its power not only by the existence of other States, but by the temper and disposition of its own subjects. At any one time a State actually exercises through its governmental organization only those powers which it has seen fit to draw to itself. The residue belongs to it only in a potential aspect, and at any one time the amount of this power and the manner in which it is, or may be, actually exercised, depends, of course, upon the character and disposition of its citizens; that is to say, upon their willingness to submit to such exercise without insurrection. As a mere matter of power, every government depends, as Hume long ago pointed out, upon public opinion, but this ultimate might of the people is not juristic in character except as it has received formal recognition in law.

[1] *Political Science and Comparative Constitutional Law*, Vol. I, p. 176.

Simple as is this formalistic juristic conception of Sovereignty there have been many writers who have not been willing to accept it, either because they have feared that, however carefully the term may be defined, the idea of actual omnipotent physical power, or of authority to determine moral as well as legal rights and duties, will be implied, or because they have themselves been unable to keep clearly in their own minds the distinctions between legal right and actual power, and between legal and moral obligations. If this unwillingness to predicate legal omnipotence to the State were found only in the thought of untrained minds it would not be worth while to dwell longer upon this point, but, because we find it present in the writings of distinguished scholars, and even of jurists, it will be necessary to give their views a hearing. Incidentally, also, the result will be, by contrasting these conflicting views, to present in sharper outline the positive or analytical concept.

Of these opposing systems, it will be sufficient if we consider as typical those of Professor H. Krabbe of the University of Leyden, and of the eminent French jurist, Dr. Léon Duguit, Professor of Law at the University of Bordeaux.

CHAPTER XXI

THE THEORIES OF DUGUIT[1]

M. DUGUIT is a realist or positivist in the sense that he absolutely excludes, or at least claims to exclude, from his political or juristic thought all mystical or transcendental elements. It is, indeed, his chief criticism of what may be called the orthodox juristic philosophy that it does not, as he believes, do the same. He refuses the ascription of personality to the State even in its abstract juristic sense because, as he thinks, such a concept carries with it implications that do not correspond with objective facts and leads to conclusions regarding the legitimate

[1] Professor Duguit's theories may be found in his two volume treatise *L'État* (Vol. I, *Le droit objectif et la loi positive*, 1901: Vol. II, *Les gouvernants et les avents*, 1903) : *Le droit social, et le droit individuel et la transformation de l'état*, 2d ed. 1911; *Les transformations du droit public*, 1913; *Les transformations générales du droit privé, depuis le code Napoleon*, 1912: *Traité de droit constitutionnel*, 5 volumes, 1921-1925: *Manuel de droit constitutionnel*, 3rd ed. 1918; *Souveraineté et Liberté*, 1922; and *Law and the State*, Harvard Law Review, vol. XXXI, (November, 1917). Certain chapters from Duguit's *L'état* have been translated and incorporated in Volume VII of the Modern Legal Philosophy Series, entitled *Modern French Legal Philosophy;* while, in the volume of the Continental Legal History Series, entitled *Progress of Continental Law in the Nineteenth Century*, appears a translation of his *Les transformations générales du droit privé*. Duguit's *Les transformations du droit public* has appeared in English dress under the title *Law in the Modern State*. Under the title "Objective Law," Duguit has also published a series of four articles in the *Columbia Law Review* for December, 1920, and January, February and March, 1921 (vol. XX, p. 87, vol. XXI, pp. 17, 126, 242).

Duguit's theories have been much criticized by French jurists, and especially by Esmein in his *Droit Constitutionnel*, Gény in his *Science et Technique en Droit Privé Positif*, and by Charmont (*Modern French Legal Philosophy*, Part I, Chapter XI). For other criticisms see W. Jethro Brown, "The Jurisprudence of M. Duguit," in the *Law Quarterly Review*, April, 1916 (vol. CXXVI, p. 168) ; "The Metaphysics of Duguit's Pragmatic Conception of Law" in the *Political Science Quarterly*, December, 1922 (vol. XXXVII, p. 639) by Professor W. Y. Elliott; "A Recent Development in Political Theory" in the *Political Science Quarterly* (vol. XXIV, p. 284), by Professor J. M. Matthews.

sphere of politicial authority which are unwarranted and unwise. Along with his rejection of juristic personality he repudiates the orthodox conception of sovereignty, and refuses to accept the legal doctrine that law, in any sense of the word, is to be regarded as the creation of the State. It is this rejection by Duguit of the generally prevailing doctrines of sovereignty and law that we shall chiefly consider.

In agreement with positive or analytical jurists, Duguit rejects all theories that ascribe a divine or quasi-divine or mystically transcendental character to the State or to the law. Along with this rejection, is the exclusion from his system of "natural" or "subjective" rights, that is, rights which find their original and abiding source in the individual, and, as such, place limits upon the legitimate sphere or scope of political or legal authority.

A subjective right he defines as "the power residing in a person's will to impose his purpose *as such* upon one or more other wills, so long as he intends something which is not prohibited by law." [2] "The idea of right", he continues, "always implies two wills face to face with one another: one will which can enjoin the other; one will superior to the other. This implies a hierarchy of wills. Now that is an assertion in the highest degree metaphysical. . . . It can be truthfully said that such a metaphysical conception cannot be maintained in an age of realism and positivism such as our own. The great philosopher Auguste Comte declared this truth more than a half century ago, when he so forcefully said: 'The word *right* must be shelved from an exact vocabulary of political thought, just as the word *cause* from an exact vocabulary of philosophy. Of these two theologico-metaphysical conceptions, one, that of right, is immoral and anarchical, while the other, that of cause, is irrational and sophistical.

---

[2] See *Progress of Continental Law in the XIX Century* (Continental Legal History Series), p. 69.

A true right cannot exist except in so far as constituted authority emanates from supernatural will. To contend against this theocratic authority, the philosophy of the last five centuries introduced the so-called rights of man, which supplied simply a negative need. When the attempt was made to give them a truly affirmative rôle, they soon manifested their anti-social nature by their constant tendency to set up the individual. In any positive state of existence which does not admit of the divine origin of authority, the conception of right disappears forever. Each one has duties towards the individual and towards all, but no one possesses a right in a strict sense. In other words, no one possesses any right save that of always doing his duty.'"

The rejection of the conception of the State as a divine or metaphysical being exalted above the individuals ruled by it, and therefore having the subjective right, inhering in itself, to impose its will upon them, removes the foundation from all systems of law of an autocratic or transcendental character. With the denial of subjective rights to the individual man, the basis for individualistic systems of law is destroyed. Therefore, says Duguit, if a valid philosophy of law is to be constructed it must be *realistic* in the sense that it eliminates transcendental and subjective individualistic ideas, and it must be *social* in the sense that it is directly related to, and springs out of, the nature and needs of that human society which alone enables men to live a satisfactory life. The basic idea must therefore be that of *social function*.

"In the individualistic system," says Duguit, "liberty is defined as a right to do all that does not injure another, and hence, *a fortiori*, the right to do nothing. The modern notion of liberty is no longer this. To-day each person is considered as having a social function to fulfil and therefore as under a social duty to perform his function. He is under a duty to develop to the highest possible extent his physical, intellectual, and moral personality in order to perform his function most effectively, and no one may interfere with this development. But man may not remain inactive, he may not be an obstacle in the free development of his own personality; he has no right to inaction, to idleness. The government may intervene to force him to labor; it may even regulate his labor, for in doing so it merely forces him to perform the social function which devolves upon him."

"As to property," Duguit continues, "it is no longer in modern law regarded as an unassailable and absolute right over one's wealth. The right of property exists and must exist. It is the indispensable condition upon which rests the prosperity and greatness of society; collectivism must be a return to barbarism. But property is not a right, it is a social function. The owner, that is to say, the possessor of wealth, by the fact of his possession, has a social function to perform. So long as he fulfils his mission, his acts as owner are protected. If he does not perform his function or performs it ill; if, for example, he leaves his land uncultivated or allows his house to fall into ruin, the intervention of the State is justifiable to oblige him to perform his social function as a property holder. Such intervention consists of procuring at the hands of the owner the employment of his wealth according to its nature." [3]

It is upon this basis that Duguit declares that all systems of law, if they would be valid and of obligatory force, must be developed: "Herein," he says, "appears very clearly the social basis for a specific rule of law or for objective law. It is both realistic and social: realistic, in that it rests upon the fact of social function observed and proved at first hand; social, in that it rests upon the essentials themselves of social life. Specific rules of law,

[3] *Ibid.*, p. 74.

as they are imposed upon men, are not founded upon respect for, and protection of, individual rights that do not exist, nor upon manifestations of individual will which, of itself, can produce no effect upon society. Rather do they rest upon the very foundation of the social structure, the necessity of preserving a cohesion between the different elements that compose society through the accomplishment of the social function which devolves upon each individual and group of individuals."

The elements entering into this social cohesion of which he speaks, Duguit declares, have been definitely determined by sociologists, and are summed up in what he terms Social Interdependence or Social Solidarity.[4] This social solidarity, he asserts, is a fact susceptible of direct proof. The elements of which it is composed are the similarity of needs and the diversity of needs and talents of the persons forming a social group. The similarity of these needs urges men to, and necessitates that they should, live in common. The diversity of their needs and talents makes it necessary that they should render reciprocal services to each other, and resort to that division of labor which is the fundamental element in modern highly civilized life. "Civilization itself has come to be measured by the multiplicity of individual needs and of the means of satisfying them in the shortest possible time. This implies a very complete division of labor and also a very far-reaching division of the functions of individuals, and consequently a very great equality between men to-day. . . . Each individual, each group of individuals, whether

[4] Duguit is greatly influenced by the doctrines of the sociologist Durkheim. For an interesting account of the doctrines of Durkheim, and of the extent to which he furnished the sociological basis not only for Duguit's political theories but also for the Guild Socialists and, in general, for the Political Pluralists, see the article by Professor H. E. Barnes, entitled "Durkheim's Contribution to the Reconstruction of Political Theory," in the *Political Science Quarterly*, vol. XXXV, p. 236.

the supreme dictator of a nation or its humblest subject, whether an all-powerful executive or parliament or a modest association, has a certain task to perform in that vast workshop composing the social body."

It would seem that, thus far, we have been dealing with a system of social or ethical philosophy rather than with one of law or politics, but, in fact, Duguit has been but preparing the way for his theory of law and the State. "We are entirely agreed," he says, "that the designation 'State' be given to a body of men, dwelling on a determined territory, of which the stronger impose their will on the weaker, or that this power of the stronger over the weaker be termed political sovereignty, but to go further is to enter the region of hypothesis. The assertion that the will of those who command is compulsory on individuals only because it is the collective will, is a fiction conceived to justify this power of the strongest, an ingenious fiction invented to legitimize force by those exerting it, but it is nothing more." [5]

The State, Duguit goes on to say, is not the personified entity which it is usually taken to be. It is nothing more than "the group of men who in fact in a society are materially stronger than the others." And whenever we find a society in which there is this distinction between those who have this superior force, and those who are in fact obliged to yield to it, we have a State. This is all there is to this political conception that has played so great a part in political speculation. "The State is no more than that, and that is what it has always been and always is, whatever be its form, whether material power be held by one individual, by several, or by a majority."

This conception of the State leads Duguit on, as we

---

[5] Modern Legal Philosophy Series, Vol. VII, *Modern French Legal Philosophy*, p. 245. This quotation shows how mistakenly Duguit interprets the purely juristic conception of the State's sovereignty.

have already said, to a denial of the legal personality of the State. This portion of his argument is, however, a complete *ignoratio elenchi,* since the juristic conception of the State as a person, with a plenitude of legal competence, carries with it no implication as to the ethical rightfulness or of the physical power to control the actions of persons subject to its authority; it furnishes no basis whatever for an assertion that a command of the State, simply because it is such a command, imposes a moral obligation upon those to whom it is directed. In other words, a command is not necessarily morally obligatory because it is legally obligatory. The most radical of positive or analytical jurists do not assert this.

Still confusing the formal juristic character of positive law with the matter of its substantive content, that is, with the character and purpose of its provisions, Duguit proceeds to a definition of law based upon its purpose and contents, and, relying upon this definition, asserts that law is not a creation of the State, but, upon the contrary, arises independently of it, and limits and controls the State, with the result, of course, that the sovereignty of the State, as connoting legal omnicompetence, is denied.

Having quoted as typical of orthodox juristic doctrine, the assertion of Seydel, that "there is no law without a sovereign, above the sovereign, or besides the sovereign," and that "law exists only through the sovereign," [6] Duguit says: "On the contrary, we think the law exists without the sovereign, and above the sovereign. . . . We firmly believe that there is a rule of law above the individual and the State, above the rulers and the ruled; a rule which is compulsory on the one and on the other; and we hold that if there is such a thing as sovereignty of the State, it is juridically limited by this rule of law. Law, if it is anything, limits individual wills, and that

[6] Seydel, *Gründzüge eines Allgemeinen Staatslehre.*

which is termed the will of the State is at bottom but the will of a certain number of individuals. This limitation of the State is both positive and negative. Some things the State is obliged to do, other things it cannot do. To determine the principle of this double limitation is the province of legal science; to express it in words and to provide it with a practical sanction is that of legal art." [7]

What now is this rule of law which is obligatory upon the State as well as upon individuals? It is, according to Duguit, the rule which the fact of Social Solidarity creates—the rule that only those specific rules of conduct, whether imposed by the State or otherwise, may properly be termed laws which tend to maintain and perfect this Social Solidarity. This rule of law is such because it is a fact, that is, because, taking men and human societies as they are, it must be observed if men's needs are to be satisfied and their desires realized. It is, says Duguit, an objective rule. "It is not, however, Kant's categorical imperative, neither is it the moral rule of the utilitarians or hedonists. It is a rule of fact, a rule which men possess not by virtue of any higher principle whatever—good, interest, or happiness—but by virtue and perforce of facts, because they live in society and can live only in society. In a sense it is the law of social life. This rule does not admonish the individual 'Do this because it is good, because it is useful, because your happiness depends on it'; it says, 'Do this because this is.' It depends not on a higher principle, but solely on reality. It came into being as soon as men began to live in society, and it will exist as long as society continues, unchangeable in its basis, variable in its application. It is the law of the social man, because the facts are as they are. The individual feels it or conceives the rule, the sage formulates it, the positive legislator declares it and guarantees that it be respected, and is himself subject

[7] *Modern French Legal Philosophy*, p. 247.

to it because his statutes are nothing unless they are the expression of this rule applicable to everybody." [8]

It would seem, then, that this rule of law is not otherwise in its application to men than the so-called laws of his own physical being or of the phenomenal world in general. Duguit, however, attempts to distinguish it from the laws of the physical and biological world by reason of the fact that this social law has a purpose and is directed to conscious beings, whereas physical or biological laws are merely relations of cause and effect. This distinction, he declares, does not, however, import a moral quality in the social or juridical law which is lacking in the so-called laws of physics and biology. "The rule of law may be termed a rule of conduct, since it applies to conscious wills, since it determines the relative value of the conscious acts of men. It is not, however, an ethical rule any more than it is a physical law, because it does not determine the value of the individual actions in themselves."

Duguit, it is clear, refuses to draw a clear distinction between legality and morality, or, for that matter, between moral obligation and physical necessity. He asserts that his rule of law, the contents of which are determined by the requirements of social solidarity, is not a moral rule. In fact, he declares, the question whether or not it is a moral rule is uninteresting and unimportant. He says: "If there be found, through the observation of facts, a principle of conduct sufficiently general to be imposed on all, sufficiently fixed to apply in any society, sufficiently supple to bend to all the needs of a period, to all the requirements of a people, what matters it whether this principle be termed moral or legal?" [9]

In another place, Duguit says: "Admitting this distinction [between law and morals] would the rule which we have formulated be a rule of morals and not of law?

[8] *Modern French Legal Philosophy*, p. 251.
[9] *Idem*, p. 305.

We do not think so. To establish a specific difference between law and morals, it must be admitted that ethics may establish a principle according to which the worth of an act taken by itself may be estimated. Either words have no meaning, or that is ethics. Whatever that principle may be, it will be ethical only if it is a criterion which permits us to measure an act and to know whether that act is good in itself.[10] Now the rule whose foundation and formula we have established is not such a criterion. We do not say that man should coöperate in social solidarity because such coöperation is good in itself; but man should coöperate in social solidarity because he is man, and, as such, can exist only through social solidarity."

It is difficult to see what meaning Duguit attaches to the word "should," as used in this last clause, and this obscurity is not cleared up when he goes on to say, "This coöperation does not appear to us a duty, but a fact which, as conceived by man, operates as a spring of action in consequence of his constant aspiration towards life, that is, towards diminution of suffering,"—unless, indeed, Duguit denies not only that there is a distinction between legality and morality, but that there is any such thing as morality at all; unless, in other words, he holds that men instinctively seek their own welfare but that this welfare is determined by no moral considerations, and that there is no moral obligation upon the part of men to seek it: they do seek it, or what they deem to be it, as a matter of fact, but that is all there is to it.

As regards what may be termed the physical sanction for his rule of law, Duguit asserts that the rule contains its sanction within itself by reason of its psychological appeal to the individual. "Even if there is no organized

---

[10] It scarcely needs be said that this is not a fair statement of the meaning of ethical. Few moralists assert that the ethical value of an act can be determined wholly without regard to the circumstances under which, and the purposes for which, it is committed.

means of physical coercion," he says, "it is, by virtue of its own nature, sanctioned by a psychological coercion ... to give it the character of a rule of law. ... In conceiving and in desiring social solidarity, men conceive and desire the rule of conduct which is its consequence, and also respect for every action which conforms to such solidarity and to such a rule; therefore the rule has a sanction, a social sanction, and is consequently a rule of law." Previously to this, Duguit had said: "Even admitting for a moment, with Jhering and Jellinek, that the rule of law cannot be conceived otherwise than as accompanied by social coercion, must we conclude that it cannot exist till after the organization of this social coercion? Organization will give the coercion greater force, but will not create it; it will strengthen the rule of law, it will even assure a definite respect for it. But it will not create this rule of law, which existed not only before the organization of the coercion which is its sanction, but even before men were conscious of the coercion, from the simple fact that men live in society." [11]

In a series of articles entitled "Objective Law," published in the *Columbia Law Review*,[12] in which Duguit has attempted still further to define his conception of positive law, he says: "The acts of men are not, then, the product of a blind and unconscious force, which succeed each other, and cause each other, as physical events appear to us. They are the result of the pursuit of a consciously selected goal, of a spontaneous manipulation producing a certain amount of energy, in one direction or another, according to a consciously made choice. Once this is established, the social law whose existence we have recognized [*le droit objectif*] cannot be a causal law, because it applies to the voluntary and conscious acts of man. It can only be a law of purpose, a rule, a norm

[11] *Idem*, p. 317.
[12] Vol. XX, p. 817; XXI, pp. 17, 126, 242.

which directs and limits the conscious and voluntary activity of man, which establishes the object and goal of his will, which forbids certain acts and imposes certain others."

Previously to this he had said: "The voluntary act of a man remains always a conscious act, determined by some goal consciously chosen;—I do not say freely. Man is conscious that he had the power not to choose the goal which finally determined his course of action. It makes little difference if this be an illusion."

In truth Duguit takes practically the position that men are under an illusion when they deem that they have an ability to fix the goal to be reached by their actions, and to select the means for reaching that goal. In reality, the goal is fixed for them by the facts of social life from which they cannot escape. Not that they cannot possibly act in a way which tends to defeat the attainment of that goal, but that, when they do so act, they are doing violence to their own natures and are acting against their own welfare, and when those other persons who happen to have the power to coerce them take steps to prevent them from so acting, these dominant persons are carrying out the objective law of social solidarity not only as to themselves but as to those who are coerced. "The social norm," Duguit says, "exists by the fact alone that there are human societies composed of conscious beings. Man lives and can live only in society. A society can exist only if the individuals who compose it comply with the law of the social being. As these individuals are conscious and wish certain things which are determined by a goal, the law of society necessarily and solely determines the object of their desire and the goal which determines it. Society and social norm are two inseparable facts. The social norm is a law of object and of purpose, not a causal law; it forbids or commands conscious acts."

It thus appears that when a man is compelled by others

who happen to be able to coerce him, to conform to the law of social solidarity, he is in a position analogous to that of the one who, according to Rousseau, is compelled to be free when he is coerced to obey the "General Will," which, according to Rousseau, is his own true or real will if he but only knew it.

How close is the similarity between the unescapable force of the social law of Duguit and the irresistible operation of so-called physical or biological laws is shown in the following quotation:

"The cells which compose an organism," says Duguit, "are subjected to the law of that organism. Everyone recognizes this, and the law of that organism is the one which presides over its formation and development. In the same way, the individuals who compose a social group are subject to the law of this group, a law which presides over its formation and development. Both these laws are laws of coördination. We do not call the law of the organism a norm, because we cannot affirm that the cells which compose it are conscious; we call the law of a social group a norm, because the individuals who are members act consciously, wish for a thing which they have in mind and because of a motive of which they are conscious. But, aside from this difference, there is no difference between the law of a living organism and that of a human society; and if it be admitted that the biological law is based upon the fact which constitutes this organism, we cannot see why the social norm as well should not be founded upon the fact which is society." [13]

In sum result, this brings Duguit to an almost purely organismic conception of society. Each group, in its life and development, is determined by inherent group processes with practically the same fixity as that exhibited by the processes of growth which control the life and growth of the biological being.

[13] *Columbia Law Review*, Vol. XX, p. 827.

When, according to Duguit, a person is coerced by those who happen to occupy the seat of authority in a social group, the event is practically similar to the instinctive reaction which all living beings exhibit against influences which threaten their well-being. The norm of social life, says Duguit, forbids the individual to commit acts that prejudice the social life, and compels him to perform acts which contribute to it. "The obligation which results is not, properly speaking, moral, but only social. If it is violated, there is no attack upon a superior principle of morality, but only the equilibrium of the social group; there is a certain disorder which results in a more or less energetic reaction against the violator of the norm." [14]

Since the true law-making function is denied by Duguit, not only to the State, but to the will of individuals, it may be asked: Just what parts are played by scientific jurisprudence and the judicial, legislative and executive organs of the State in the matter of determining and applying the rules of conduct which social life supplies to them?

As for jurisprudence, he says that its task is to determine or discover the rules which the social facts create; upon its technical side, its function is to give precise statement to these rules. In this way they can aid in bringing the law into the clear consciousness of the people. "I do not believe," he says, "in the preponderating, exclusive influence of a few directing minds in the formation of the ideas of a social group; but I believe, nevertheless, that their action cannot but be recognized. Incontestably, jurists can form a certain state of consciousness in the group from which will issue a juridical norm. It is in this sense, strictly speaking, that one may use the term 'the law of jurists' (*Juristenrecht*) as the German historical school does. But this influence can be

[14] *Columbia Law Review*, Vol. XX, p. 828.

real only at a period when scientific work has been highly developed and consequently at an advanced period of juridical evolution. On the other hand, it is greatly impeded by legislative codification. Indeed, I cannot repeat too often that the adhesion, even the unanimous adhesion, of jurists, cannot make a rule into a juridical norm. They can only bring to light a rule already existing in the popular consciousness and give it a precise formula." [15]

The rôle of state officials in determining the law, Duguit declares, is strictly analogous to that of the scientific jurists. "Tribunals before which a litigation has been brought should strive to discover the juridical norm according to which the litigation should be decided and to do this they should proceed as do the jurists: examine the facts, seek out the aspirations and tendencies of the time, the needs of social solidarity, and the solution which the sentiment of justice demands. . . . Tribunals discover and give expression to the standardizing rule; they do not create it—it is valid in itself. They help in the formation of certain customary constructive rules; they create an important element in the formation of custom. But customary law so formed does not receive its obligatory force from the decisions of tribunals any more than tribunals consider the law formed by jurists as thus receiving its force." [16]

The more crucial question is, however, as to written, and especially statute, law. Whence does it derive its obligatory character, if it has any, and how may this fact be determined?

State legislation, says Duguit, is but a means of giving more or less precise definitions to law, obedience to which is due not to the law itself but to the juridical norm which it contains. The function of legislation is thus similar

[15] *Columbia Law Review*, Vol. XXI, p. 140.
[16] *Idem*, p. 142.

to that of scientific jurisprudence and custom, although it works more precisely than do they. Also, and this is an important point, it operates, according to modern ideas, to fix limits of competence for public agents "which is a precious guaranty for those amenable to trial and those subject to jurisdiction." [17]

As for the legislative statement of juridical norms, Duguit says: "It emanates from the governors. Their power is the result of a natural and spontaneous differentiation between the strong and the weak. This differentiation has taken place under varying conditions, but it can only be maintained if the mass of minds continue to attribute to the governors certain qualities not belonging to other individuals. Those governing, then, have, necessarily, a special influence on opinion. In the great modern democracies, governmental power belongs to those who represent the majority more or less exactly; and, it can be said, the laws are in a general way the very expression of public opinion. If it can happen and really does happen that there is not a complete agreement between a law and opinion, it is none the less true that the parliament, author of the law, exercises an influence on opinion, and that between the parliament and opinion there is a series of actions and reactions, and that thus the acceptance of the principle of the law by the mass of minds can be hastened." [18]

But there is nothing conclusive regarding a statute. Its binding force is always subject to criticism and denial by the jurist. As for the judge or administrative agent of the State, the condition is somewhat different. Except in extreme and clear cases they are bound by statutes. "When written law has not spoken or when it is obscure, the public agent should be allowed a very wide liberty of judgment; he should seek to discover the rules of cus-

[17] *Columbia Law Review*, Vol. XXI, p. 243.
[18] *Idem*, XXI, p. 244.

tom and jurisprudence, and he should act and decide in conformity with the indications they furnish him. But when legislation is formal, it limits the public agent in his action, and he can do nothing directly contrary to the legal ordinance. The public agent, whoever he may be, is hierarchically subordinate to the legislator. Modern minds have reached this conception, which is that of an incontestable juridical norm, according to which no individual act can be committed by a public agent in contravention of an ordinance passed by due legal process. This fundamental rule springs from conviction that it is the best guaranty for the individual against the arbitrary rule of the governors. But in order that it may apply, there must be a definite prohibition in law." [19] However, "a time may come when even the positive ordinance is so manifestly contrary to the juridical consciousness of a period that it can no longer be claimed that it imposes itself as a limit upon the judges and the administrator. . . . Custom and written law are not rules of law in themselves, and there cannot be a question of the abrogation of one by the other. But when, as a matter of fact, it is certain that it is custom which reveals the true nature of the juridical norm and the text of the positive law is certainly contrary to it, then the question of knowing what the public agent should do arises. It seems to me impossible to deny that he should apply the norm revealed by custom. But, incontestably, he should proceed with many precautions and all legislation characterized by foresight should organize a strong system of judiciary and administrative hierarchy to reduce to a minimum the danger of arbitrary action." [20]

Further describing the nature of statute law, Duguit says: "A statute is a general rule for governing conduct. But because we have to-day eliminated from politics

[19] *Idem*, XXI, p. 245.
[20] *Idem*, p. 246.

the theories of metaphysics, the hypothesis of national sovereignty, that of divine right and of an inheritance from God, a statute can no longer be the formulated command of sovereign power. A statute is simply the expression of the individual will of the men who make it, whether they be the leading statesmen or the private members of a legislative body. Beyond that we are in the realm of fiction. . . . The social environment necessarily gives rise to a rule of social conduct. But this rule is in no sense metaphysical. It does not transcend society. . . . We obey this rule not because it creates a superior duty, but simply because we are, for good or ill, members of society, and therefore necessarily subject to its social discipline. It is, for example, clear that the rule prohibiting murder, pillage, and arson existed as a rule of right before it was formulated into positive statute. It is clear to all of us that it has an obligatory character, not transcendent and abstract, but based on the facts of life. Once that is understood, it becomes clear why a statute compels us to obedience. It is not, technically speaking, a command. It is yet compelling because it formulates a rule of law which is itself the expression of social facts." [21]

Statute law and custom Duguit distinguishes as follows: "Statute is the expression of a rule which social needs are elaborating in individual consciences. Sometimes, of course, the same rule finds its first and imperfect expression in a custom to which statute gives later a more precise and complete expression. It is doubtless true that the compelling power of statute and custom is derived from the same source, but they represent different degrees of the expression of objective law. Often the degree that custom expresses is socially defective and the objective law is first, and directly expressed in statute. . . . It is, of course, true that when there is no

[21] *Law in the Modern State* (transl.), p. 70.

THE THEORIES OF DUGUIT

written statute, or, at least, no formulated custom, there does not exist for that rule of law a definite legal sanction. But that does not involve the absence of obligation in that rule of law understood not as a command but as a way of life derived from the necessities of social existence." [22]

Holding the views that he does regarding the nature of positive law, it is but to be expected that Duguit should apply the same tests to International Laws, or, as he prefers to term them, "Intersocial Juridical Norms." These, like the norms of particular national or social groups, are based upon the solidarity of interests that unite the individuals of different national groups. They are addressed to these individuals and not to the personified groups of which they are members. When the consciousness that a given intersocial norm should be observed has become so clear in the minds of the individuals that they react against a violation of it and take steps to prevent such violation, the norm becomes a veritable objective intersocial or international law. When its essential nature is thus understood, says Duguit, it is clear that the objection to viewing so-called International Law as positive law disappears, for there is involved no necessity for a superior juridical will imposing itself upon an inferior will, no existence of a Super State above subordinate States.

Furthermore, as Duguit goes on to say, just as the distinction between governors and governed arises in the national State, so the same situation tends to arise in the international world,—the peoples of a single State or of

[22] *Idem*, pp. 73-74.

The purposes of the present study do not make it necessary to consider the conclusions to which Duguit is led with reference to the status of autonomous communal and administrative groups or organizations within the State, to the legal character of administrative ordinances as distinguished from statutes, to the province of constitutional law, or to the interpretation which he gives to prevailing doctrines regarding the responsibility of the State, in contract or in tort, for the wrongful acts of its agents.

groups of States obtain the actual power, which they exercise through their respective governments or through common organs to supply a sanction to the intersocial juridical norms which they accept as inherently valid. Thus he declares that the Treaty of Versailles was "a solemn and definite affirmation of an international juridical rule, standardizing and constructive at the same time." [23]

In result, Duguit maintains that the State does not create law but merely formulates it. It does not even enforce it, in any true sense of the word, for that is the function of public opinion without whose approval no rule of action can be effectively carried out.

Criticism. This account of Duguit's theories has occupied more space than their intrinsic merits to the jurist justify. Whatever value they may have to the sociologist or to the moralists, they have, in the judgment of the writer of this volume, little worth to the analytical jurist. The fact, however, that Duguit is a jurist, and professes that he is constructing a philosophy of law and not merely one of sociology, coupled with the fact of the wide notice which these theories have received, has made it appear necessary that they should be stated with some degree of fullness. The conclusions reached in Part One of the present volume, together with those reached in the author's *Fundamental Concepts of Public Law* furnish a sufficient basis for a criticism of Duguit's sociological theories.[24] Here it is sufficient to say that, for the most part, his speculations, notwithstanding his claims for them, lie outside of analytical jurisprudence, and the validity or invalidity of his assumptions or assertions of fact are without significance to the jurist. Furthermore, when he directly attacks cer-

---

[23] *Columbia Law Review*, XXI, p. 255.
[24] The author ventures also to refer, in this connection, to his volume *Social Justice*, published in 1900.

tain of the positions of the analytical jurist, he ascribes to them meanings which the analytical jurist does not give to them, and thus expends his energies in tilting at mere windmills. Thus, Duguit appears unable to appreciate that the predication by the jurist of legal omnicompetence to the sovereign State carries with it no implication whatever either of unlimited actual powers of coercion on the part of those who control the activities of the State or of an ethical right to exercise an arbitrary will as to what commands shall be uttered by the State. Similarly he draws from the ascription of juristic personality to the State the wholly unwarranted conclusion that thereby the State is clothed with mystical and transcendental attributes. But, most fundamental of all, is his failure to appreciate the juristic quality of a positive law as determined by its legislative or political source, and its ethical or utilitarian value as determined by its contents or specific provisions. Thus, one might grant all that Duguit has to say regarding Social Solidarity, and agree with him as to the conduct required of individuals, whether rulers or ruled, in order that the claims of this Solidarity may be realized, and yet insist that only those rules of conduct should be termed laws, in a positive or analytical sense, which can be shown to express the will of some sovereign political power, and which are at least promised enforcement by that power. In other words, the jurist can admit that individuals should, in their conduct, have regard for the Social Solidarity of which Duguit speaks, and that those who are in possession of political power should be equally guided, and yet insist that clearness of thought and exactness of juristic reasoning will be increased by distinguishing clearly between those so-called laws or rules of conduct which are authentic expressions of the State, viewed as a juristic volitional entity or person, and those which cannot be so regarded. The jurist can admit that this fact of Social

Solidarity exercises so profound an influence upon those who formulate and declare the will of the State as well as upon private individuals that it is practically impossible for them to escape from it, and yet be able to insist that juristic thinking will be more coherent and lead to more precise and therefore desirable results, if the distinctions between law and morality, between social and political sanctions, are rigorously maintained. Certainly the doctrines of Duguit, if accepted, would tend to obscure these distinctions, and, as a consequence, render juristic thinking less precise and, therefore, less scientific.

One further criticism of Duguit needs to be made, and this has regard to the logical consistency of his own thought. It has been seen that he has been especially emphatic in his refusal to admit any mystical or transcendental elements into his system, and that the chief merit which he claims for his philosophy is its realistic and objective character. And yet, in result, his *régle de droit* is one that comes into existence independently of human volition and imposes itself upon men by reason of its own inherent character and force. It is thus a veritable "natural law," which differs from the other and earlier conceptions of natural law chiefly in the characteristic that it does not lay the basis for a definite, hard and fast code of commands valid *semper, ubique et ab omnibus,* but, instead, lays down a general purpose to be achieved, the specific acts for the attainment of which depending upon varying conditions of time and place. In other words, instead of deducing the natural rights of individuals from *a priori* convictions as to the essential moral nature of men as rational beings, Duguit deduces a general rule of law from the solidarity of the social group in which men live. "Man living in society," he says, "has rights; but these rights are not prerogatives to which he is entitled as a man; they are powers which are his because, being a social being, he has a social duty to perform and ought to have the right to perform it." And again: "The rule of law (*régle de droit*), as we conceive it, is not an ideal and absolute law to which men should seek each day to approach more nearly; it is a variable and changing rule; and the rôle of the jurist is to determine what rule of law will be exactly adapted to the structure of the given society." [25]

A further difference which distinguishes Duguit's *régle de droit* from the older *jus naturale* is that all moral force is denied to it. Duguit, so far as the writer is aware, nowhere has flatly asserted that there is in the world no such thing as ethical obligation, no such thing as either moral rights or duties, but such an assertion would seem to be a necessary implication from his general social and political philosophy. If this be so, then the only practical guidance which either the state legislator or the individual may gain from Duguit's system is that, as a matter of pure policy of dictated self-interest, it will be to his ultimate if not immediate material advantage to cause others to do and himself to do those things which will promote that social solidarity without which men cannot realize, in any measurable degree, the instinctive desires that spring from their innate needs as living beings of the human species.

But, even this practical guidance, when analyzed, becomes of slight value to the individual, for Duguit sets forth no specific and recognizable tests by means of which either the public or private individual can determine, in concrete and specific instances, what conduct is indicated —one cannot say commanded—by the principles of Social Solidarity. At the most, then, Duguit's principle is of value, even in the fields of public and private conduct, only in so far as it tends to destroy the influence which false transcendental or mystical, or *a priori* individual-

[25] *Manuel de droit constitutionnel*, 7.

istic theories have sought to exert. Upon the affirmative side, it emphasizes the social interests of men, and furnishes them with a general guiding-principle similar in purpose to that of the older utilitarian maxims that each person should count as one and that the greatest good of the greatest number should be sought. But, whereas the Utilitarians ascribed an inherent moral validity to their canon of conduct, Duguit ascribes to his the mere weight of unescapable fact—the fact that men, whether they would or not, must, in their conduct, yield to the requirements of social interdependence. And yet Duguit does not, of course, assert that men do not often differ as to what these requirements are. When these differences do occur, all that remains to be done, Duguit appears to say, is that the stronger shall compel the weaker to conform to the judgments of the stronger.

Duguit does not attempt to meet the problem presented by the deliberate refusal of persons to act according to what they may perceive the fact of Social Solidarity to demand. It would not seem open to him to say that, so great is the pressure exerted by the fact of Social Solidarity, no such deliberately anti-social conduct can occur. All that he can say is, that, when the principle of Social Solidarity is fully appreciated by all, no one will wish to act otherwise than, under the given conditions of time and place, its requirements dictate. Such an assertion would, however, imply not only that all men always do what their judgments tell them it is most advantageous to themselves to do, and that there is an essential consonance between the interests of each individual and those of other individuals: also, that there is a harmony between the interests of different groups of individuals, and, possibly, between the interests of present and future generations.

In truth, of course, if this Social Solidarity were the *fact* which Duguit so unqualifiedly asserts it to be, men could not escape from the pressure it would exert, any more than they could avoid the operation of the so-called physical and biological laws. Duguit himself admits, however, that this is not the case, with the result that his much emphasized Social Solidarity becomes, in truth, an end, if not an ideal, to be realized, a purpose to the fulfilment of which men need to be urged. As to this, one can accept as convincing the argument of Professor W. Y. Elliott in his article "The Metaphysics of Duguit's Pragmatic Conception of Law." [26] "It is evident," he says, "that if society were completely organic in its functioning, Social Solidarity would operate ruthlessly toward the suppression of any disruptive influences operating within it. . . . But an examination of the historical development of our society or of a slice out of any particular period of the past will serve to convince us, I believe, that quite as good a case might be made out for the laws of social disruption as for those of social solidarity. . . . Now it is true that *droit objectif* need not equate the preservation of the *status quo* with social solidarity any more than it need speak of progress. It remains none the less true that though social interdependence may make men realize the need for social solidarity, it does not create that desideratum as a fact. The fact surely is that social solidarity is precisely one of those ideals which at the same time exist as great needs of which men are conscious and as consummations all the more devoutly to be wished because they can never be even approximately realized. In the light of what we know of the nature of such ends, our 'fact' turns out to be one of the most metaphysical order imaginable, leading us straight on to all the moral issues it was claimed we should avoid by its admission." [27]

---

[26] *Political Science Quarterly*, December, 1922 (Vol. XXXVII, p. 639).
[27] For further criticism of the theories of Duguit, see Allen, *Law in the Making*, 336 ff.; and Wilde, *The Ethical Basis of the State*, 74 ff.

CHAPTER XXII

THE THEORIES OF KRABBE [1]

THE political doctrines of H. Krabbe, professor of public law in the University of Leyden, are to be found in his *Die Lehre der Rechtssouveränität,* published in 1906, and his *Die moderne Staatsidee,*[2] the second edition of which appeared in 1919.

The political theory of Krabbe resembles that of Duguit in that it denies law-making power to the state, and recognizes law (as defined by himself) as the ruling power in human society, as sovereign, and, therefore, as above the State. However, as will presently be seen, Krabbe places the State upon a much higher plane than does Duguit. To Duguit, political rulership is nothing more than the bald fact that, in a given community certain persons, for some reason or other, possess and exercise, actual power of control over the actions of the other persons of a group. It is, as it were, an objective fact which cannot, and need not be, ethically justified. To Krabbe, upon the other hand, the State is, in essence, a community of persons unified by the general agreement of its members as to the valuation of public and private interests, and possessing organized instrumentalities for clarifying and formulating these common convictions, and, when necessary, enforcing them. To Krabbe, the State thus plays a necessary part in the declaration and

---

[1] This chapter has appeared as an article in *The American Political Science Review,* August, 1926 (vol. XX, pp. 509-523).

[2] This second work has appeared in English dress under the title, *The Modern Idea of the State.* The translators, Professors George H. Sabine and Walter J. Shepard, have increased the value of the volume by adding an extended and luminous note of introduction.

410

enforcement of law, if not in investing it with essential validity as such.

We find, however, in Krabbe, and also in his translators, as will be later pointed out, that same mistaken idea which is to be discovered in Duguit, that an inquiry into the idealistic or ultilitarian validity of law, as determined by its substantive provisions and the purposes sought to be achieved by its enforcement, has a relevancy to, and that its conclusions can affect, the validity and usefulness of the purely formalistic concepts which the positive or analytical jurist employs.

To Krabbe the creative source of law is the conviction of the people as to the rightfulness of the principles of conduct which the law prescribes. "Thus," he says, "not the will of a sovereign who exists only in the imagination, but the legal conviction of the people, lends binding force to positive law; positive law is valid, therefore, only by virtue of the fact that it incorporates principles of right." [3]

Accordingly, Krabbe goes on to say: "We no longer live under the dominion of persons, either natural persons or fictitious legal persons, but under the dominion of norms, of spiritual forces. In this is revealed the modern idea of the State. . . . Hence we no longer perceive the State as localized in a sovereign, but find it wherever we perceive the power of the law to create obligations. What is now in actual practice adorned with the old name of sovereign is a man or an assemblage of men upon whom the law has laid a task. They are not, therefore, invested with a power to be expressed, through their will, in independence of the law." [4]

"The theory of the sovereignty of law," he says in another place, . . . "takes account only of that basis for authority which it finds in the spiritual life of man, and

[3] *The Modern Idea of the State*, p. 7.
[4] *Idem*, p. 8.

specifically in that part of this spiritual life which operates in us as a feeling or sense of right. The law which is in force, therefore, includes every general or special rule, whether written or unwritten, which springs from men's feeling or sense of right." [5]

A statute, says Krabbe, which is not supported by this sense of right is not law. "It must be recognized, therefore, that there may be provisions of positive law which lack real legal quality. The legislative organ runs the risk of enacting rules which lack the quality of law either because the organization of the legislature is defective or because it mistakes what the people's sense of right demands. On the other hand, it may happen even more easily that what it embodied in a statute ceases to be law and so is no longer valid because it has lost the basis of its binding force. In such a case compulsion—the punishment or legal judgment which disobedience to the statute entails—is irrelevant. Constraint is justified by the necessity of maintaining the law, but it can never bestow legal quality upon a rule which lacks it. Mere force, whether organized as in the State or unorganized as in an insurrection or revolution, can never give to a rule that *ethical* element which belongs essentially to a rule of law." [6]

Though Krabbe states so emphatically, and without qualification, that a statute or other formal command of the State is not valid if its contents are not in consonance with the convictions of right of the persons to whom they are directed, he does not clearly declare that the individual who deems that this test has not been met should, as a practical proposition, refuse obedience to it, or that as an ethical proposition, he would be justified in so doing. One may, however, possibly infer that Krabbe asserts that the courts or executive organs of the govern-

[5] *The Modern Idea of the State*, p. 39.
[6] *Idem*, pp. 47-48.

ment would be justified in refusing to apply or enforce statutes or other commands claiming to be law, whose contents do not conform to popular convictions of right. Or, possibly, his meaning is that the control of governments by the convictions of the people regarding what is right is an ideal end to be realized, as rapidly as possible—that, until this ideal is realized, and to the degree that it is not realized, existing governments and their systems of law are not ethically justified, without, however, going to the extent of declaring the essentially rebellious or insurrectionary doctrine that, from a legal as well as an ethical point of view, individuals are justified in refusing to support such governments or obedience to their laws.

It is, however, clear that, according to Krabbe, a rule of law is essentially valid when springing from, and supported by, men's feelings of right, even though those feelings or convictions may be improper or erroneous when judged from the standpoint of abstract justice as determined by the ethical philosopher. For he says: "The sense of right as it actually reveals itself, with all its defects, is recognized as the original source of authority." In another place he says: "To a philosopher or to any outsider the law thus declared (by the people's sense of right) may not appear to be just. . . . It is of course possible, owing to the influence of numerous factors both material and ideal, and because of an imperfect insight into the nature of the interests to be evaluated by law, that this sense of right may be different now from what it formerly was, just as it may vary in different individuals under the pressure of divergent experiences and interests. We have to deal with this more or less imperfect sense of right. Its activity produces rules and imparts to them the character of positive rules of law. . . . Practice must content itself with a legal system whose rules are based upon a defective sense of right. . . . If a higher justice is to be evolved, the legal instruction of the people must be undertaken." [7]

Krabbe then goes on to make the interesting assertion that the sense of right of only those individuals who are in a position to share in the spiritual life of the time is to be considered. And, even as to these individuals, they may properly participate in determining and formulating this sense only as to interests about which they are qualified to form an intelligent judgment. "If they are required to decide upon the legal value of interests about which they have no knowledge, their minds are compelled to react upon phenomena from which they have experienced no effects. The exclusion of such persons from law-making cannot be taken as denying that the sense of right is the basis of law." [8]

The theories of Rousseau, says Krabbe, first made it possible to view political authority other than as inhering in specific persons, but this had only the effect of placing legislative authority in the people—a conception which jurists have since developed to the extent of transferring this law-making power to the abstract State of their own conceptual creation. The further and necessary step which needs to be taken, says Krabbe, is to locate this ultimate and decisive law-creating power in the common conviction of the people as to what is right, and to view popular or representative assemblies as merely the mouthpieces through which the people's convictions find utterance. "The sole rulership of the law," he says, "emerges only where law-making rests exclusively in the hands of the popular assembly, since the popular assembly gets its significance from what it represents, namely, the nation's sense of right. It is therefore the bearer of that spiritual power from which is derived the rulership and the imperative nature of law." [9]

[7] *The Modern Idea of the State*, pp. 50-51.
[8] *Idem*, p. 51.   [9] *Idem*, p. 34.

The explanation which Krabbe gives of the origin of, and ethical basis for, law would seem closely to resemble that of the historical school of jurists, especially as voiced by Savigny, according to whom law is a product of the national consciousness or spirit of a people. But there is, says Krabbe, this important difference between his own view and that of Savigny and his school. According to them, there exists, as it were, a superconsciousness or national spirit which finds expression in custom and a body of laws which are binding upon all the individuals of the community or nation. According to his own view, says Krabbe, there is no such superpersonal or national consciousness, and law is created, not by communal convictions, but by an identity or consonance of individual convictions or sentiments of right.

Krabbe's political and legal philosophy also undoubtedly exhibits some close resemblances to that of Rousseau. In result, it locates sovereignty in the governed rather than in a monarch or ruling class. It views governments as but instrumentalities for carrying out the popular will or judgment. It defends the right of majorities. It asserts that political or legal control cannot be ethically justified by reason solely of its source—that it must be justified, if justified at all, by the intrinsic merits of the substantive provisions of the commands that are enforced. But here the resemblances cease. Krabbe does not, as does Rousseau, start with the conception of men as endowed by their very nature with certain inalienable rights which the law must respect. His political philosophy is clearly a social rather than an individualistic one. Hence he sees no necessity for founding the social and political community upon a contract to which all the individual members are voluntary parties. Nor is he led by any other route to the acceptance of that absolute sovereignty of the State which Rousseau asserts—that sublimation of the individual will into the general will, that complete surrender of individual liberty which results from the contract according to which, to use Rousseau's words, "each of us puts his person and all his power in common under the supreme direction of the General Will; and, in our corporate capacity, we receive each member as an individual part of the whole." [10]

Though Krabbe, in his search for ethically valid principles of law, does not recognize that men, apart from social life, have inalienable rights or indestructible interests to which value should be attached, and which, therefore, should find recognition and embodiment in all systems of law, he nevertheless asserts that law derives its validity as to each individual from the fact that its provisions are in consonance with the individual's feeling or conviction of the rightfulness of the conduct which it prescribes.

This position makes it necessary for Krabbe to determine the validity of laws, in their application to those particular individuals who do not happen to agree with their fellow citizens as to the laws' rightfulness. Where there are such differences, says Krabbe, the majority should govern. This right of the majority he defends upon the following grounds:

Law, he says, is a rule of a community, and the purposes of that community cannot be realized unless its rules are general in operation and not virtually contradictory. "Hence our sense of right attaches the highest value to having a single rule, and sacrifices, if necessary, a particular content which might otherwise be preferred." [11] The fact that a rule is accepted as right by

---

[10] *Social Contract*, Bk. I, Chap. VI. Krabbe says: "If Rousseau's political theory had been regarded only in the light of its main principles and had not been criticized exclusively with reference to what he borrowed from earlier theories, viz., the explanation of the community and the establishment of its sovereignty by the social contract, there might have been seen in it, what it doubtless contains, the principle of the modern idea of the State" (p. 29).

[11] *Idem*, p. 74.

a majority of the individuals of a community shows that it has a higher value than any contradictory rule. Even by those who prefer the contradictory rule, this fact is perceived. "Even according to their own sense of right, it is more important to have a single rule in the community to which they belong than to have the rule which they prefer. Consequently, for those whose convictions accord with the rule, the obligation to obey the customary rule rests upon the value of the *content* of the rule; for all others it is based upon the value of having the single rule." [12]

Krabbe holds so strictly to this majority principle that he will not admit the validity of provisions, even though embodied in written constitutions, which require more than a majority vote for the legitimization of particular state actions. "Such provisions have no legal value"; he declares, "they are not rules of law, and are not binding," because they prevent the operation of the simple majority principle. Rules thus retained, though opposed by a majority of the individuals of the community, may continue to be obeyed, but they are not really rules of law and therefore *ought* not to be enforced.

This majority principle is also applied by Krabbe in determining the action of legislative or other collegiate political bodies. He emphasizes the fact that the representatives of the people should hold themselves bound by the known judgments of their electorates as to the rules of law to be adopted. So far as this is not known the representatives must, of course, act according to their own sense of right. The problem of political science is to perfect the organization of societies so that the sense of right of the individuals may find modes of authentic expression and enforcement when so expressed. That, according to Krabbe, unwritten law, voicing the popular sense of right, may abrogate and modify statutory law, or

[12] *Idem*, p. 75.

even written constitutional provisions, goes without saying.

As can now be seen, Krabbe, though agreeing with Duguit as to the sovereignty of law rather than of the State, attaches to the State a greater importance than does Duguit. He does not regard the control exercised by state officials as a bald matter of fact, of superior power or force which neither can nor needs to be ethically justified.[13] Upon the contrary, he declares that political rulership is one of law—that it is essentially *legal* in character, and justified as such. The State exists, in other words, as a legal institution and has for its purpose the clarifying, and, when necessary, the enforcing of the rules of right which the people hold, whether or not, from the philosophic point of view, those rules are wholly just. "It may be admitted," he says, "that the positive law does not yet correspond to our ideal of it and that the sense of right which gave rise to it was defective; it may be admitted that the persons entrusted with law-making are not sufficiently impartial in their attitude toward social interests of a material, moral, religious, and intellectual kind. Still this does not alter the fact that the title of the rulers is a *legal* title founded upon positive law. This is the point which deserves all the emphasis." [14]

"A people is a State," says Krabbe, "because of the body of legal relations (*Rechtsleben*) existing in it. And one State differs from another State because of the particular standard of legal value applied in the valuation of interests." [15] It is barely possible, he says, to imagine a

[13] Duguit says: "La vérité est que la puissance politique est un fait quin n'a en soi aucun caractère de légitimité ou d'illégitimité." *Manuel de Droit Constitutionnel* (1907), p. 36.

[14] P. 207. Krabbe, furthermore, does not accept Duguit's doctrine of "solidarity" as an adequate basis for law. He says: "It cannot even be shown as yet that the law can be deduced from solidarity, for solidarity is an abstraction and cannot be recognized as an active principle unless it can be shown that the sense of right is inspired throughout by it."

[15] *Idem*, p. 209.

State, thus defined, as existing without some organization of its body of legal relations, but in all civilized States there is this organization involving the existence and operation of governmental organs. These organs owe their origin and competence to the law, that is, to the sense of right of the people, and this decisive law-making power of the people is never vested in these organs or limited by their action, for, independently of these organized methods of law-making, the unorganized sense of right continues to operate legislatively, whether to annul the legality of the statutes or ordinances which these organs have declared, or to modify the constitutional provisions which provide for the existence and functioning of these organs themselves.

The doctrine which Krabbe declares with regard to law makes it easy for him to bridge the gap which analytical jurisprudence is compelled to recognize between municipal and international law, and to assert the possibility of a world state which will not do violence to the sovereignty of the State of analytical or positive jurisprudence.

Just as national or municipal law springs from, and is created by, the sense of right felt by members of a given people or national group, so international law, says Krabbe, is born of a cosmopolitan conviction as to the principles that should be applied in the dealings of national States with one another. To the extent, then, to which international law exists, its validity is exactly the same as that of municipal law. "International law is distinguished from national law not in respect to its origin and foundation, but in respect to the extent of the community to which its commands apply. And the incomplete and less perfect character of international law does not lie in the fact that it rules over 'sovereign' States, and is therefore rooted in the will of these States. It lies rather in the defective organization of the sense of right which tends to regulate the community of civilized nations."[16]

Furthermore, to the extent that international law exists, that is, to the extent that there are cosmopolitan convictions regarding rules of right applicable to groups of individuals irrespective of national boundaries or affiliations, an international State already exists, and, with the development of its organized modes of declaring and executing these rules, the importance of this international State will increase until the now existing national States will find their proper places as parts or local organizations of the greater whole.

With regard to Krabbe's conception of the nature of international law, it is furthermore to be pointed out that, according to it, the subjects of international law are not the States, as held by the doctrine of orthodox international jurisprudence, but private individuals. It is their sense of right which creates and sustains it. Therefore, says Krabbe, it is unfortunate that the term "international law" should be employed. "There is no interposition of a hypothetical state authority. The name international law is really a misnomer. The name is suitable only to the theory which regards States as subjects of this law and which consequently regards it as a law *between* States. It would be better, therefore, to speak of a *Supernational Law,* since this expresses the idea that we are dealing with a law which regulates a community of men embracing several States and which possesses a correspondingly higher validity than that attaching to national law."[17]

Whether or not one accepts Professor Krabbe's philosophy of law and of the State, one cannot but agree with him as to the need which he urges that better pro-

---
[16] *Idem,* p. 236.
[17] *Idem,* p. 245. Krabbe says: "What is usually called the law of nations is really international constitutional law" (p. 246).

vision should be made in the several States of the world for organs or instrumentalities by means of which the peoples of these States will be enabled to obtain a better knowledge of, and to express more clearly their convictions of right regarding, international interests. At present it is chiefly the legal conceptions of central governments that are influential, and, even as to them, it is the judgments of executive rather than of the more truly representative legislative organs that are decisive. "Only when the vital interests of the nation are at stake does the national [popular] sense of right exert a powerful influence, and when this happens the government is frequently subject to pressure from convictions and conceptions which have been formed without a complete knowledge of the relationships. Consequently, one of the greatest defects in the making of international law lies precisely in the lack of an organization in the different States such as would insure the existence of a popular organ which, like the government [the executive], would be in constant touch with international interests. This might be either a special organ or the one already existing for law-making within the State. The sense of right represented by this organ, being supported by a knowledge of the interests concerned, could make itself effective in the field of international law. Such an organization is the first object to be striven for in the immediate future and pacivism ought to devote all its energy to this end." [18]

It has been seen that Krabbe definitely states that positive law owes its force as such to the consonance of its substantive provisions with the feelings or convictions of right held by the people to which its commands are addressed, and not to the fiat of the State which enforces it. And, therefore, he is obliged to hold that rules or commands issued by the legislative organs of a State the contents of which do not voice this popular conviction of

[18] *Idem*, p. 250.

right are not valid—are not, in fact, law, except in a formal sense. In truth, he appears to deny the quality of law to any such legislative products that have not been the utterances of governmental organs so constituted as to be able to express the ethical judgments of the governed. He nowhere, as has been said, expressly asserts, however, that commands of the State whose contents do not conform to the convictions of right of the majority of the persons to whom they are addressed and who are qualified to form such judgments should be disobeyed. If, then, Krabbe may be held to assert that such laws are valid in a formal sense, even if not intrinsically valid from an ethical point of view, his system becomes a purely ethical one; that is, his argument is addressed wholly to the matter of the ethical validity of the State's commands, and his conclusions, even if accepted, do not affect or invalidate the assumptions of the analytical jurist. In short, it can be conceded that, ethically viewed, law, as an expression of the people's convictions of right, gains nothing, as to its validity, from the State, and as thus viewed is sovereign, and controls the State; and yet it can be asserted that, juristically viewed, that is, as *juristisches Recht*, law is a creation of the State, an expression of its juristically sovereign will.

Krabbe asserts that the orthodox juristic theory, though predicating sovereignty or omnicompetence in the matter of law-making, nevertheless, and inconsistently with this fundamental premise, has, in fact, been forced to subordinate the State to its own law,—that this is involved in the conception of what has been termed the *Rechtsstaat*, according to which the State can act only in and through law, and also according to which all governmental agencies have their legal competences determined by law. Thus, after quoting the statement of Laband that "the State can require no performances and impose no restraint, can command its subjects in nothing and forbid them in nothing, except on the basis of a legal prescription," Krabbe says: "The modern idea of the State [i.e., his own idea] recognizes the impersonal authority of law as the ruling power. In this respect it accepts the standpoint of the theory of the legal State as this was formulated by Laband. But . . . it no longer holds that the State subordinate itself to the law, but insists that the authority of the State is nothing other than the authority of law. Hence there is only one ruling power, the power of law. According to this view, the State is not coerced by law, but is rather endowed with the authority of law. The law is not a superior and the State a subordinate power, but the authority inherent in the State and the authority of the law are identical, so that the basis of the rulership of the State is coincident with the binding force of law."

In this statement of the orthodox juristic conception of the state as a *Rechtsstaat,* Krabbe is scarcely fair when he asserts that the State, according to the orthodox juristic view, is subordinated to law. The fact, of course, is that the jurist regards the State as the creator of all law which, as to itself, is deemed to be legally valid. It has been earlier pointed out that a State may be regarded from a variety of points of view, and as thus variously regarded—sociologically, ethically, psychologically, or juristically—it may be differently defined and clothed with different essential attributes. When it is analyzed by the jurist solely from the legal point of view, it is necessarily considered as a *Rechtsstaat,* that is, as living and having its being in law and functioning solely through law. But surely this is not to conceive of the State as subordinated to law. In this respect is evidenced the failure of Krabbe to distinguish between the State, in which legal sovereignty inheres, and the governmental organs through which it operates. Laws, and especially constitutional laws, determine the competences of these organs, but they do not, and *ex hypothesi* cannot, control their creator, the State.

Krabbe's essential errors, then, would seem to be his failure to keep sufficiently sharp the distinction between ethical and legal validity, and his conviction, of which he does not appear to be able to rid himself, that when the jurist asserts the legal validity of a law there is implied a claim as to its ethical validity, that is, as to the intrinsic worth of its substantive provisions.

Professors Sabine and Shepard in their Introduction seem to appreciate clearly enough the strictly limited field within which the analytical jurist confines the application of his concepts, for they correctly say: "The theory of sovereignty says nothing about the content of the command. The only question is whether it issues from a proper source: an imperative arising from an authoritative source is law." But then they immediately go on to declare: "The only question concerns the means by which a given will can be designated as authoritative. Accordingly theories of sovereignty differ only with reference to the method of determining the source from which imperatives may rightly issue. Or, to state the question somewhat differently, if law is the will of the State, how is the State given the right to express its will in commands binding upon its subjects?" Now, if by this it were intended to say that, in the case of every State, the analytical jurist is confronted with the constitutional or public law problem of determining the juristic origin of the State, or of ascertaining the organs through which, or the legal processes by means of which, the State's legislative will may be authentically declared and enforced, no objection could be raised. But this is evidently not what is meant, for Professors Sabine and Shepard at once go on to discuss what they conceive to have been the unsuccessful attempted answers to the questions which they have stated; namely, the theories of divine right, of political contract, etc. Thus, from a matter of formalistic juristic envisagement the leap is made to the question of the ethical basis upon which political authority may be justified.

Confusion of ethical and formal legalistic conceptions of the validity of the law recognized by the States is still more evident in the section of the translators' Introduction in which they discuss "The Authority of Law".[19] They say: "We have argued that the law deals with the manifold human interests which exist within a community, that it represents a system of relatively stable judgments of value concerning these interests and that its end is to safeguard as wide a range of interests as possible, due regard being given not only to the number of interests but to their intrinsic importance. If this be correct, it is obviously meaningless to ask further why law in general has authority. It has authority because of its very nature. . . . Like any other problem the evaluation of interests is settled when it is settled correctly. In other words, the correctness of the solution cannot be judged according to its content, that is, according to the correctness of its practical success in making effective the valuation it expresses. It is clear, therefore, why this conception of law gives a radically different view of authority from that implicit in the doctrine of sovereignty. The latter is purely a formal conception of authority. The law is authoritative because of the source whence it comes. It is the voice of a superperson, either of an individual in some way designated as a superior, or the collective person or State. This view neglects the fact that, as an evaluation of interests, a law has to demonstrate its correctness in a way fundamentally like that by which any other decision is justified. Verification is in terms of content and not of form. To urge formal correctness exclusively is nothing

[19] Pp. lxx *et seq.*

but a way of withdrawing a favored solution from criticism."

It has been worth while to make this extended quotation because it states so clearly the distinction between the jurist's conception of validity and that of the moralist. At the same time, it is to be observed that it is unfair to the jurist, in so far as it seems to imply that he sets up his conception as a substitute for that of the moralist, or, at any rate, as a device for escaping from the necessity of meeting the ethical problem. Of course neither of these implications is true. The jurist does not claim that his doctrine of legality is an alternative to that of the moralist; it has a wholly different purpose, and, therefore, it is not an attempt to avoid the problem as to ethical justification of law in general or of special laws in particular. It simply leaves that question unconsidered, and, accordingly, one which the moralist may freely solve as seems to him right.

CHAPTER XXIII

POLITICAL PLURALISM [1]

IN the writings of Duguit and Krabbe we have examined doctrines which deny the legal personality and sovereignty of the State. There is another modern school of writers who, while recognizing the sovereignty of the State and conceding, and even emphasizing, the *reality* of its personality, assert that these are attributes in the possession of which the State is not unique, but that, upon the contrary, these qualities are exhibited by other than political associations of men, and, therefore, that such other organization should be placed upon a plane of juristic equality and independence with the political State.

As in so many other cases, this new political theory of "Political Pluralism," though stated in abstract and philosophical form, has been born of practical considerations. Upon the one hand there has been the conviction that in most modern States the number of distinct interests that need to be represented, if their governments are to be really representative in character, has become so great, and the functions of control and regulation that need to be exercised, have become so many that single legislatures have become inadequate for the task, and that, for reasons presently to be stated, this defect cannot be corrected by a devolution upon other and subordinate bodies of some of the work now attempted to be directly performed by these central legislatures.

[1] This chapter appeared as an article in *The Chinese Social and Political Science Review*, July, 1926.

Upon the other hand, closely related to this belief, is the special desire that certain of these interests should escape from the control over them now exercised by the political authority, and their regulation be provided for by the creation of separate and distinct representative bodies of their own establishment. This demand upon the part of those who advance this doctrine, which has received the name of political pluralism, goes beyond the claim for those interests of an autonomous administration subordinate to the sovereign jurisdiction of the political State, and amounts, practically, to an assertion of a status for their respective governmental organs and laws equal to and coördinate with that of the political organs and laws.

In his volume *Churches in the Modern State*, Figgis has made for churches in general, and especially for such ecclesiastical organizations as the Church of England, a claim that they possess a "real personality" similar to that possessed by the political State. As a corollary to this assumption, he argues that such ecclesiastical institutions should have a status or power coördinate with the political State. We shall now see how the same arguments which Figgis and his school have employed have been seized upon to support the policy urged for adoption by the so-called Guild Socialists. Without considering further than we have already done the question as to the reality of the personality of either political or other groups or associations of men, we can examine the social phenomena from which these pluralists deduce the propriety of the practical measures which they propose.

The fact is, these writers say, that in all societies there is not a single allegiance and patriotism, namely, to the political State, but a plurality of such allegiances and patriotisms growing out of the various groups of which almost every individual is a member and to which he is united by the special interests which constitute the cementing factor of those groups. Furthermore, these writers do not content themselves with complaining that these group interests are not sufficiently represented and given sufficient weight in the determination of the regulatory and other activities of the political State, but assert that it is not practicable or possible to give to these interests this sufficient representation and consideration. In other words, the facts demand, they say, that, in the case of at least the more important of them, these interests should have their own governmental organizations which should be allowed to operate as fully within their respective spheres as does the State within its special and appropriate sphere. In short, the program is that there should be established what would amount to a federation or confederation of governments, organized functionally along the line of special interests, in a manner similar to that of the governmental organizations of ordinary confederations of States which are established upon a territorial basis.

"More and more," says Figgis, "it is clear that the mere individual's freedom against an omnipotent State may be no better than slavery; more and more it is evident that the real question of freedom in our day is the freedom of smaller unions to live within the whole." [2] Again, he says: "What we actually see in the world is not on the one hand the State, and on the other a mass of unrelated individuals; but a vast complex of gathered unions, in which alone we find individuals, families, clubs, trade-unions, colleges, professions, and so forth; and, further, that there are exercised functions within these groups which are of the nature of government, including its three aspects, legislative, executive, and judicial; though, of course, only with reference to their

[2] *Op. cit.*, p. 52.

own members. So far as the people who actually belong to it are concerned, such a body is every whit as communal in its character as a municipal corporation or a provincial parliament." [3]

"The theory of government which is at the root of all the trouble," Figgis says in another place, "is briefly this. All and every right is the creation of the one and indivisible sovereign; whether the sovereign be a monarch or an assembly is not material." [4] "But the truth is that this State in a sense of absolute superhuman unity has never really existed and cannot exist. . . . What do we find as a fact? Not, surely, a sand-heap of individuals, all equal and undifferentiated, unrelated except to the State, but an ascending hierarchy of groups, family, school, town, county, union, Church, etc., etc." [5] "Between these groups will be relations, and not merely between the individuals composing them. To prevent injustice between them and to secure their rights, a strong power above them is needed. It is largely to regulate such groups and to ensure that they do not outstep the bounds of justice that the coercive force of the State exists." [6]

It is apparent from this last statement that Figgis does, after all, admit the superior power of the State in the matter of maintaining peace and order between the groups. Even as to the Church, as he grants that the State "may or must require certain marks, such as proofs of registration, permanence, constitution, before it recognizes the personality of societies." He therefore founds upon the predicated real personality and extra-state origin of the ecclesiastical and other groups, only a right inhering in them to operate freely according to their own rules, and in consonance with their own special interests, so long as they keep themselves within their own respective spheres. His doctrine thus becomes, in effect, one of

[3] *Op. cit.*, p. 70.
[4] *Idem*, p. 85.
[5] *Idem*, pp. 86-87.
[6] *Idem*, p. 89.

group rights as distinguished from the individual rights of the old natural rights theory.[7]

Laski. Professor Harold J. Laski deserves a prominent place among Political Pluralists.[8]

Laski's political thought would appear to have been especially influenced by Duguit and Figgis, and, of course, by Maitland, who so strongly influenced Figgis. Duguit's influence has been especially with reference to his attack upon the monopoly of the legal authority of the State, but, in opposition to Duguit, Laski has emphasized the reality of the State's personality, though, at the same time, recognizing an equally real personality in other than political groups. It is in this latter respect that the influence of Figgis and Maitland has operated.

Laski recognizes the logical necessity to the jurist of the conception of sovereignty, but declares it to be a worthless one to the politician. "Juristically," he says, in an Introduction to a translation of one of Duguit's works, "the argument does not seem answerable; for, in the legal theory of the State there must be some one authority beyond appeal. But while the [jurist's] criticism [of Duguit] has legal validity, it is, in other part, politically worthless," [9] Holding this opinion regarding the jurist's sovereignty, we are not surprised to find Laski developing his political theories along practical or ethical rather than juristic lines.

---

[7] "Advocating a federalistic view alike of the Catholic Church and of the State, Dr. Figgis ingeminates the phrase 'inherent rights of associations.' He returns, in a word, to the old idea of natural rights, but he resucitates that ghost by giving it blood to drink—the red blood of real corporate personality." Ernest Barker, *The Political Quarterly*, February, 1915, p. 110 (Article: "The Discredited State").

[8] The quotations in the paragraphs which follow are taken from Professor Laski's two volumes, *The Problem of Sovereignty* (published in 1917) and *Authority in the Modern State* (published in 1919). Professor Laski has since published (1925) a general political treatise under the title *A Grammar of Politics*. However, the views expressed in the later volume, so far as they are pertinent to the theory of political pluralism, do not vary substantially from those expressed in his earlier works.

[9] *Law in the Modern State*, Translator's Introduction, p. xxv.

In his *Problem of Sovereignty* Laski speaks of the monistic doctrine of sovereignty as asserting the existence of "a legally determinate superior whose will is certain of acceptance," which statement, it does not need to be said, though couched in language similar to that of Austin, is not Austin's conception of Sovereignty any more than it is that of other consistent analytical jurists. "Certainty of acceptance" is not an element of the jurist's conception of Sovereignty. Starting, however, with this quality or attribute which he has himself attached to it, Laski has no difficulty in declaring that, in no State does such an instrument or political person exist.[10] "We have," he says, "nowhere the assurance that any rule of conduct can be enforced. For that rule will depend for its validity upon the opinion of the members of the State and they belong to other groups to which such rule may be obnoxious." "The will of the State obtains pre-eminence over the wills of other groups exactly to the point that it is interpreted with sufficient wisdom to obtain general acceptance, and no further." If it be objected, he says, that this view of sovereignty makes it mean nothing more than power, that is, the ability to secure assent, he can only reply by admitting it. "There is no sanction for law other than the consent of the human mind." A little later on he says: "We have only to look at the realities of social existence to see quite clearly that the State does not enjoy any necessary preeminence for its demands. That must depend entirely upon the nature of the demand it makes. I shall find again and again that my allegiance is divided between the different groups to which I belong."

Laski cannot, of course, be justly criticized for preferring to discuss practical problems of power rather than those of legal or juristic competence, but it is scarcely fair that he should imply that, because no political sov-

[10] *Op. cit.*, pp. 12-14.

ereignty is all powerful in the matter of the enforcement of its will, it cannot properly be deemed to be legally omnicompetent. And yet this is exactly what he does when he says: "When you come to think of it, the sovereignty of legal theory is far too simple to admit of acceptance. The sovereign is the person in the State who can get his will accepted, who so dominates over his fellows as to blend their wills with his. Clearly there is nothing absolute and unqualified about it."

From the contradiction, which is wholly his own creation, between the legal absolutism of the jurist's conception of the State, and its actually limited powers of coercion, Laski asserts that the pluralistic theory of the State is free. "It denies," he says, "the rightness of force [which, of course, the monistic theory does not assert]. It dissolves—what the facts themselves dissolve—[and which the jurist does not deny] the inherent claim of the State to obedience. It insists that the State, like every other association, shall prove itself by what it achieves. It sets groups competing against groups in a ceaseless striving of progressive expansion." [11]

Near the close of the same book from which we have been quoting, and still confusing legal competence with actual or physical power, Laski commits himself even more definitely to the pluralistic theory of the State in the sense that whatever sovereignty the State may lay claim to is equally possessed by other groups. He says: "Now it does not seem valuable to urge that a certain group, the State, can theoretically secure obedience to all its acts, because we know that practically to be absurd. This granted, it is clear that the sovereignty of the State does not in reality differ from the power exercised by a Church or a trade-union." [12]

In his volume *Authority in the Modern State,* published two years later than the work from which we have

[11] *Op. cit.,* p. 23.   [12] *Op. cit.,* p. 270.

been quoting, Laski frankly says that what he desires to know is, "not what has a legal right to prevail, but what does in actual fact prevail, and the reasons that explain its dominance," and, as to these questions, he adds, "the legal theory is worthless." This last statement would have been improved if he had said irrelevant rather than worthless. However, Laski, though thus apparently appreciating the significance of the juristic conception of Sovereignty, at once goes on, as he had done in his earlier work, to treat the conception as though it implied either ethical right of rulership, or actual power of coercion, or both.

Defining the pluralistic theory of society, Laski says: "The State is only one among many forms of association. It is not necessarily any more in harmony with the end of society than a church or a trade-union, or a freemason's lodge. They have, it is true, relations which the State controls; but that does not make them inferior to the State . . . legal inferiority is either an illegitimate postulation of Austinian sovereignty [13] or else the result of a false identification of State and Society. . . . When we insist that the State is a society of governors and governed, it is obvious that its superiority can have logical reference only to the sphere that it has marked out for its own and then only to the extent to which that sphere is not successfully challenged." [14]

Later on he says: "What we have thus far denied is the claim of the State [upon ethical or utilitarian grounds, Laski must mean] to represent in any dominant and exclusive fashion the will of society as a whole. It is true that it does in fact absorb the vital part of social power; but it is yet in no way obvious that it ought to do so. It is in no way obvious immediately it is admitted

---

[13] One queries as to the sense in which the word illegitimate is here used. It would seem that the only reference can be to logical inconsistency.

[14] *Op. cit.*, p. 66.

that each individual himself is in fact a centre of diverse and possibly conflicting loyalties, and that in any sane political ethic, the real direction of his allegiance ought to point to where, as he thinks, the social end is most likely to be achieved. Clearly there are many forms of association competing for his allegiance." [15]

Aside from the general proposition that social interests in the modern civilized State are so many and diverse as to make impracticable their adequate representation in governments as at present organized, the political pluralists further assert that modern industrial society is composed of two great economic classes whose interests are, to a considerable extent, essentially and incurably antagonistic to each other, and that the political State, as we now know it, adequately represents the interests of but one of these classes, and, therefore, that its policies almost necessarily favor these represented interests. For this reason the political pluralists urge that the situation cannot be corrected either by proportional representation in present parliaments along functional lines or by a devolution upon subordinate legislative or administrative bodies of some of the work which the central legislatures are now attempting to perform. The only solution of the problem, they assert, is that this unrepresented or inadequately represented class, which, generally speaking, is declared to be the economic producers as distinguished from the consumers and those living upon invested capital—*les rentiers*—should have a parliament and other governmental organs of their own creation and, as such, be qualified to legislate regarding, and otherwise to regulate, the interests of the producers. Thus we find Laski writing as follows:

"In the main, it is reasonably clear that political good is today for the most part defined in economic terms. It mirrors within itself, that is to say, the economic struc-

[15] *Op. cit.*, p. 81.

ture of society. It is relatively unimportant in what fashion we organize the institutions of the State. Practically they will reflect the prevailing economic system; practically, also, they will protect it. The opinion of the State, at least in its legislative expression, will largely reproduce the opinion of those who hold the keys of economic power." [16]

Here we find two assertions. First, that social interests are predominantly economic in character; and, second, that those who are in economic power control the government and dictate its legislative policies. Now, Laski continues, an examination of present conditions in modern industrial States shows, "that the aspect upon which they concentrate their work is the use by the community of industrial resources. It is not interested in the processes of production as such; it concerns itself in securing due provision from industry for the needs of society. It deals with men in the capacity that is common to them all. It regards them as users of certain goods. It is uninterested in men engaged in any function save that of consumption, except, of course, in so far as the performance of their duties hinders the achievement of its own basic effort. Clearly, for instance, the State, through its government, would be vitally interested in a railway strike; for it is vitally interested in securing to the members of the State the uninterrupted use of railway facilities. But an analysis of the part played by the Government in settlements of industrial disputes can hardly fail to suggest that the primary concern of the State is not in the cause of the dislocation, but in the dislocation itself. Causes are important only in so far as they seem to imply a renewal of disturbance. In that aspect the relation of the State to a member of the railway unions is very different from its relation to the ordinary member of the public. For its main concern with the trade-unionist

[16] *Authority in the Modern State*, p. 83.

is to get him back to work; whereas that at which he aims is some redistribution of economic power within a group only the results of whose functionings concern the State as a whole." [17]

The foregoing, says Laski, furnishes the reason "why it is impossible to regard the State as capable, in any general view, of absorbing the whole loyalty of the individual." In other words, as a consumer he can give his loyalty to the State, but, as a producer, his loyalty must be given to his trade-union, or other trade association. As a practical proposition, therefore, provision must be made for some controlling authority representing production as a whole just as the State, as now organized, represents its citizen body viewed as consumers.

In connection with this argument in behalf of trade-unions is of course to be remembered Laski's envisagement of political and other associations or groups as "real" persons.

Guild Socialism.—Seizing upon the theory of political pluralism, emphasizing the diversity of interests of consumers and producers, and alleging the impracticability of securing their adequate representation and influence in the parliaments of the political State as now organized, the so-called Guild Socialists of England have furnished themselves with what they consider to be a political philosophy as well as a basis for practical action.

In the present volume we are of course concerned only with the political side of Guild Socialism, and can probably find this best stated in the writings of G. D. H. Cole, and especially in his volumes *Self Government in Industry*, first published in 1917, and *Social Theory* published in 1920.

In the first of these volumes Cole devotes a special chapter to "The Nature of the State," and a series of

[17] *Idem*, p. 83. We are not here concerned with the correctness of Professor Laski's analysis of modern economic and political conditions.

quotations from this chapter will serve to present both his theory and the constructive proposals he founds upon them.

Up till now, he says, the State has claimed to be the supreme and comprehensive representative of the community, and, in fact, monopolizes the right to exercise coercion through law and government. There is, however, no inherent reason why this should be so. "The fact that the State claims to be the community, and in fact exercises the greatest part of the community's power, does nothing to prove that the State is rightfully the community, or its sole representative, or that it has an absolute claim upon the individual's loyalty and service." As in Laski, we find the declaration that "However the State may be organized, and whatever parliamentary system may exist, economic dominance will find its expression in political dominance." "In modern society, as it is now industrially organized, capitalism controls in the economic field, and, therefore, it necessarily controls, predominantly, if not autocratically, in the political field. The fact that these political institutions are largely democratic in form [the reference is to Great Britain] does not make them democratic in practice, because the power of capitalism stands behind the State." "State sovereignty, if the phrase has any meaning at all, implies, not indeed that the State ought to interfere in every sphere of human action, but that the State has ultimately a right to do so. . . . It regards the State as the full and complete representative of the individual, . . . whereas our whole view is that the person of the community cannot truly be sustained by any single form of organization." "Trade unions are associations based on the 'vocational' principle. They seek to group together in one association all those persons who are coöperating in making a particular kind of thing or rendering a particular kind of service. In the common phrase, they are associations of 'producers,' using 'production' in the widest sense. The State, on the other hand, we have decided to regard as an association of 'users' or 'enjoyers' or 'consumers' in the common phrase."

"Collectivism . . . is the practical equivalent of State Sovereignty. . . . Syndicalism is an inversion of Collectivism. The one asserts the absolute sovereignty of the consumers, . . . the other the sovereignty, no less absolute, of the producers, of the professional association. . . . Guild Socialists recognize that neither the territorial nor the professional grouping is by itself enough; that certain common requirements are best fulfilled by the former and certain others by the latter; in short, that each grouping has its function and that neither is completely and universally sovereign."

"I conceive that the various guilds will be unified in a central Guild Congress, which will be the supreme industrial body, standing to the people as producers in the same relation as Parliament will stand to the people as consumers. . . . Neither Parliament nor the Guild Congress can claim to be ultimately sovereign: the one is the supreme territorial association, the other the supreme professional association. . . . The ultimate sovereignty in matters industrial would seem to belong to some joint body representative equally of Parliament and of the Guild Congress."

"Every individual under the Guilds will not be a member of a Guild; but every individual, one may expect, will be a member of some form of association based on social service rendered,—a productive association in the widest sense of the word. Similarly, it goes without saying that every individual will be a member of the State, and probably of other associations of 'users,' 'consumers,' or 'enjoyers'." "The Guildsman must claim for the Guilds, not only administrative, but also legislative functions. Their law must be as sovereign in the industrial sphere, exercised through the Guild Congress, as the law of the State must be sovereign within the political sphere."

"What, then, will be the position of the judiciary under the Guilds? It will have two sets of laws to administer—State law and Guild law, each valid within its sphere, and coördinated, where need arises, by the Joint Congress of the Guilds and the State. It is not desirable to divide the judiciary as it is to divide legislation and administration, because the judiciary is concerned, not with policy, but with interpretation of policy already decided. Guild theory . . . preserves the integrity of the judiciary, making it an appendage neither of the State nor of the Guilds but of the two combined."

In his *Social Theory*, Cole goes deeper into social and political philosophy than he had done in his earlier writings, but makes no substantial addition to the ideas he had previously developed. He is, however, somewhat more explicit upon some points. Especially is this true as to the position he would assign to Churches in his reconstructed economic and political system. He concedes that they should receive recognition as distinct and integral parts of the social and political structure, at least when considerable proportions of the people are concerned with them. But, he says, the function of the Churches is one that differs radically from that of economic and political associations, and their powers and function should correspond. Their appeal is to the spiritual side of men, and their power should be exercisable upon their minds rather than their bodies: their relations to the political and economic forms of association should be one of coöperation without formal coördination. Therefore, they should not participate in the organ of government which coördinates the powers and activities of the governmental agencies of the other associations.

This coördinating power, he says, must be a combination not of all associations but only of the essential associations, "a Joint Council or Congress of the supreme bodies representing each of the main functions in Society." [18] It will be "less an administrative or legislative body, though it cannot help partaking in some degree of both these characters, than a court of appeal. It does not in the normal case initiate; it decides. It is not so much a legislature as a constitutional judiciary or democratic Supreme Court of Functional Equity." [19]

But, Cole concedes, this coördinating tribunal must have more than the power to decide; it must have the right to coerce. Coercion and coördination, he says, go hand in hand. "If the supreme power of coördination rests in the hands of this joint body compounded from the essential functional associations, it seems clear that the supreme power of coercion must rest in the same hands. This involves that the judiciary and the whole paraphernalia of law and police must be under the control of the coördinating body." [20] This right and possession of the means of coercion, Cole declares, should extend to matters of external or international affairs as well as to those of internal or national concern.

It will have been observed that, using Cole as their spokesman, the Guild Socialists, under their general scheme of organizing society along functional lines, give to the terms "State" and "political" meanings much more limited than those assigned to them by monistic political scientists. Under their scheme the "State" refers simply to that governmental organization whose function it is to represent and care for the interests of the citizen body regarded as consumers, which interests are termed "political." No serious attempt, however, appears to have

[18] *Social Theory*, p. 135.
[19] *Idem*, p. 137.
[20] *Idem*, p. 137. Cole is, however, so optimistic of the results to be obtained from society reorganized upon the lines suggested by the Guild Socialists, that he thinks the necessity for coercion will speedily and progressively disappear (p. 140).

been made to determine exactly and comprehensively just what these interests are, and, therefore, what specific powers the State should exercise. In fact, the inference would seem to be justified that the Guild Socialist would assign to the State the protection and regulation of all those interests which, on the one hand, concern all the members of the given community, and, on the other hand, do not arise out of the specific activities of the other organized groups or associations.[21] Thus the State, as distinguished from these other groups has a territorial basis, and its membership or citizenship—if the term may be used—is all-inclusive.

To the entire community organization, viewed as a whole, that is, as embracing all the governmental organs of the several groups, including those of the State— as defined above—and also the coördinating instrumentalities, Cole suggests that the name "Society" should be given. As thus employed the term is distinguished from that of "Community." This latter term he uses to designate "a complex of social life, a complex including a number of human beings living together under conditions of social relationship." When this social complex becomes organized it becomes a "Society." "I mean to use the term Society," he says, "to denote the complex of organized associations and institutions within the community."[22]

S. G. Hobson in his *National Guilds,* published in 1919, does not regard the State as primarily the representative of the interests of its citizens viewed as consumers, but,

[21] But, it would appear, not including those interests which are so individualistic or personal in character as to defy organization or general regulation. Thus Cole says in his *Social Theory* (p. 31) : "Society, as a complex of organizations, cannot stand for, or express, all human life of any single human being. Indeed, it is probably true that what is best and most human in men and women escapes almost entirely from the net of Society because it is incapable of being organized." For Cole's definition of the term "Society," see the next paragraph of the text.
[22] *Social Theory,* p. 29.

upon the contrary, seems inclined to rest the regulation of all economic interests in the guild organizations. However, in other respects, he concedes political control and legal sovereignty to the State much more clearly and fully than does Cole. Two quotations will sufficiently indicate that his position with regard to the State is such that, though a Guild Socialist, he cannot be classed as a political pluralist. He says (p. 132): "The active principle of the Guild is industrial democracy. Herein it differs from State Socialism or Collectivism. In the one case control comes from without and is essentially bureaucratic; in the other, the Guild manages its own affairs, appoints its own officers from the general manager to the office boy, and deals with the other Guilds and with the State as a self-contained unit. It rejects State bureaucracy; but, on the other hand, it rejects Syndicalism, because it accepts co-management with the State, always, however, subject to the principle of industrial democracy. Co-management must not be held to imply the right of any outside body to interfere in the detailed administration of the Guild, but it rightly implies formal and effective coöperation with the State in regard to large policy, for the simple reason that the policy of a Guild is a public matter, about which the public, as represented by the State, has an indefeasible right to be consulted and considered. It is not easy to understand precisely how far the Syndicalist disregards the State, as such; nor is it necessary for our task that we should make any such inquiry. For ourselves we are clear that the Guilds ought not and must not be the absolute possessors of their land, houses, and machinery. We remain Socialists because we believe that in the final analysis the State, as representing the community at large, must be the final arbiter."

In a later chapter, entitled "The State and the Guilds," Hobson says: "Whilst the separation of the political and economic functions gives equipoise and stability to the State, nevertheless the policy and the destiny of the State, in the final analysis, depend upon its economic processes being healthy and equitable. For this reason amongst others, the State, acting in the interests of citizenship as distinct from Guild membership, must be adequately represented upon the governing bodies of the Guilds. . . . Let us, then, after allocating every economic activity to the Guilds, consider what remains in the political sphere. Its problems will hinge upon one or the other of the following: (1) Law, (2) Medicine, (3) The Army, Navy and Police, (4) Foreign Relations, (5) Education, (6) Central and Local Governments and Administration. To these we might add the Church, which, by the way, is a guild." After showing why these enumerated functions should be left in the hands of the State, Hobson says: "Broadly stated, these are the reasons for our belief that the State, with its Government, its Parliament, and its civil and military machinery must remain independent of the Guild Congress. Certainly independent; probably even supreme. That will ultimately depend upon the moral powers and cultural capacity of the nation's citizens. Having solved the problem of wealth production, exchange and distribution, we may rest assured that a people thus materially emancipated will move up the spiral of human progress, and that out of that part of this movement will grow a purified political system, in which great statesmanship will play its part."

Criticism. In view of the powers which the Guild Socialists, even as represented by Cole, have been obliged to concede to the coördinating agency of their reconstructed society, can it not be said that they have in part returned to practically that same conception of sovereignty which, at the start, they rejected? In other words, is not their theory, after all, one which would provide a scheme of governmental organization radically different from that exhibited by States now existing, but which, none the less, does not render impossible the conception now held of the State by orthodox political scientists? These questions must be answered in the affirmative.

Any one who stops for a moment to consider the disputes of jurisdiction which necessarily arise in federated governments, such, for example, as those that have presented themselves in the course of United States history since the adoption of the Constitution, must be advised of the fact that the government which possesses the organ with final and decisive legal competency to determine these conflicts is the legally sovereign governing body in the community, and that when, as conceded by Cole, that organ also has at its disposal adequate rights and powers for coercing obedience to its decrees and protecting the international interests and enforcing the international polices of the community taken as a whole, it becomes the political sovereign. In other words, if a community were governmentally organized according to the scheme of the Guild Socialists, the State—using that term in the orthodox and not the Guild Socialist's sense—would be the politically organized people and territory of that community. The juristic sovereignty would be in that entity viewed as a single legal person. The possession of that sovereignty would be especially manifested in the powers of the coördinating organ, but all the organs—legislative, executive and judicial—of the several guilds—industrial, ecclesiastical and others—would, together with the coördinating organ or organs, constitute parts of the governmental organization, comprehensively considered, of that State, just as the governmental organs of the member commonwealths and of their local subdivisions constitute parts of the governmental organization of the sovereign, but federally organized American State. The only difference between the two would be that whereas, under the American federal system, separate governmental organizations are provided for the territorial subdivisions of the Union, under the Guild Socialistic scheme, separate governmental organizations with defined spheres of authority, would be provided for different economic or other interests or functions.

The only way in which one who would carry Political Pluralism to its fullest logical extent can avoid the foregoing reasoning is to assert that, according to their plan, the organ which is empowered to determine disputes between the several governmental systems as to jurisdictional powers, and to enforce the decrees rendered thereupon, is to be regarded not as an organ of the community viewed as a unity, or, to use Cole's phraseology, as a "Society" or "complex of organized associations and institutions within the community," [23] but as the creation of the several organized associations acting severally, but by identic act, according to which each of them agrees that this coördinating organ shall act, as to the powers vested in it, as its own organ. This is substantially the view of a composite form of government when deemed a confederacy of sovereign States and not the national government of a single, national, federally organized sovereign State. If, leaving aside all questions of practicability of operation, a community or "Society" could be conceived of as thus organized, there would be presented the example of a politically organized group subject to the legal control of two or more authorities, each of them sovereign in the sense that they would be independent of legal control by each other, or, for that matter, by any other political authority.

But would they be sovereign in the sense that each of them would or could be conceived to have an unlimited legal competence to bring under the control of its law whatever matters it might deem fit? Certainly none

[23] *Social Theory*, p. 29.

of them could extend its control to matters unrelated to those interests with which it was specially concerned without doing violence to the fundamental economic or other principle upon which it was founded, and for the protection and regulation of which it justified its existence. Yet, if it were granted that each of these political entities was not subordinated to legal control by any other political body whatsoever, the jurist would have to concede that, simply as a legal proposition, it would be competent, that is, without illegal action upon its part, to extend its authority over all other interests of the community. Each of these predicated political bodies would, therefore, be sovereign entities and entitled to be termed States by the jurist. Of course, the citizen bodies of these entities being largely the same, and their territorial basis exactly the same, there would arise conflicts between them as soon as one attempted to regulate interests belonging to, or conceived to belong to, one of the other entities. This would, however, be merely a practical difficulty, and, in fact, the situation would be not dissimilar from that which now confronts the sovereign States of the world. In their case, they have, each of them, the legal power to determine over what areas their several claims to territorial jurisdiction shall extend, and, for that matter, what control they will exercise outside of such territorial limits, and constant conflict between these States, due to such potential overlapping of claims of authority, is only avoided by the voluntary foregoing by each of them of the exercise of rights which, from a legal point of view, they are competent to exercise.

Professor George H. Sabine, in an extremely interesting article entitled "Pluralism: A Point of View," [24] raises a point that is closely allied to one we have been discussing. He queries whether the monistic jurist has

[24] *American Political Science Review*, February, 1923 (Vol. XVII, p. 34).

not laid too much emphasis upon the logical necessity of predicating unity and juristic completeness to systems of municipal law. Defining the implications of the orthodox juristic theory, he says that it asserts that "in the case of any two authorities, legislative or otherwise, the relative competence of the two must be capable of determination in such a way that conflicts of authority can be adjudicated and authoritatively set aside. On the other hand, it is also implied that legal authority must have no gaps or holes in it; there must be no case that can escape through the meshes of the net. Some organ of the States must be competent to handle every case that can arise. In short, the law is a system. This is, indeed, the only definite meaning that is conveyed by the assertion that the State is a juristic personality."

Political pluralism he defines as a theory "which denies that there is any rigid necessity about the demand for a unified legal and political system. It insists, on the other hand, that an amount of loose-endedness is possible and under some circumstances inevitable and even desirable. It asserts that, at least at any given time, a community may be living under two systems of law and that a government may be organized in such a way as to include two or more authorities that are juristically coordinate, in the sense that their respective jurisdictions are not fixed by a third and higher authority competent to coerce them. This does not mean, as sometimes is supposed, that the different authorities would be without relation to one another. . . . The pluralist merely insists that such relations could not be brought under the conception of a delegation of authority. Neither would have the legal power to fix the competence of the other; relations between them would take the form of what Mr. Laski calls negotiation."

To Professor Sabine there appears no logical difficulty in accepting the pluralistic idea. The unescapable presumption of logical consistency in juristic relations he declares to be "reminiscent of a time when a rational law of nature was supposed to be behind the obligations created by positive law. . . . The objections to a two-fold [or manifold] legal authority are not logical but practical, for when there are coördinate authorities there may be conflicts of authority and such conflicts may be disastrous. . . . The demand for administrative unity is a guiding principle and as such its importance should not be underrated, but that is not a good reason for magnifying it into a universal form of human thought." Professor Sabine concludes his article with the statement: "For my own part, then, I must reserve the right to be a monist when I can and a pluralist when I must."

It must be admitted, as we have seen, that, *in conceptu,* as a mere intellectual feat, there is no impossibility in conceiving of political pluralism as thus defined. It is, however, to be observed that no political pluralist, neither Figgis, nor Cole, nor Laski, nor, least of all, Hobson, so far as the writer is aware, has urged the adoption of a scheme of political or social organization which would apply the pluralistic theory in the pure and consistently undefiled form in which it is stated by Sabine. Each of them, as we have seen, has felt the practical, if not the logical, necessity of making provision for organs with not only judicial but legislative and administrative powers and rights of military or police coercion extending over the whole community, and, as to international relations, exercising practically complete and exclusive control. Thus, as has been already said, they have, in effect, brought back that juristically sovereign and monistic State of which they have sought to rid themselves. Their schemes of political reconstruction have reduced themselves to governmental reorganizations the novelty of which has consisted in the emphasis which, in apportioning jurisdictional powers, has been laid upon functional interests—upon the governmental representation of economic, ecclesiastical and other interests, and the provision of autonomous self-governing agencies for these interests analogous to or in substitution for the territorial local or self-governing bodies found in modern States as now organized.

Before leaving this subject it is proper to point out that, in the modern monistic State, it is not always the case that there is some one supreme judicial governmental organ for the final and authoritative settlement of all questions of legal right and authority that may arise. For example, in Great Britain, the House of Lords is the final court of appeal from the English, Scotch and Irish Courts of Appeal, and, in some cases, from the Criminal Appeal Court; while the Judicial Committee of the Privy Council is the highest tribunal for the determination of ecclesiastical concerns and for appeals from the colonies, India and the overseas Dominions.[25]

In the United States in the matter of what are called "political questions," the acts of the officials or organs in whom or in which the exercise of these acts is vested by the Constitution are not subject to judicial control as regards their wisdom or the correctness of the findings of fact upon which they are predicated, but, and this is the important fact, the courts, and, in last resort, the Supreme Court of the United States has jurisdiction to determine whether or not a given act is or is not within the constitutional competence of the official or organ committing it. The treaty-making power under the United States Constitution is vested in organs different from those in which the general legislative power is vested, and, in each case, the resulting treaty or statute is equally the law of the land, with the result that either

[25] In actual practice the personnel of these two bodies is practically the same. The House of Lords gives its judgments as a part of its regular business. The judgments of the Judicial Committee are in form advices to the King which are sanctioned by orders in Council.

may operate to amend or repeal the other. But, here again, each of these organs derives its constitutional powers from the same legal source, the Constitution, and the Supreme Court of the United States has jurisdiction in every case to declare null and void *ultra vires* action. Back of the Supreme Court, as well as of all the other organs of government, and binding them into a single legal system is, of course, the constituent or constitutional law-making power as provided for in the Constitution. It is by the acquiescence of this ultimate source of legal authority in the United States that the terms of the Constitution remain unchanged, and, by its affirmative action, it has a legal competence which knows no legal limits, to alter as it sees fit the form of government that shall exist and the manner in which legal powers or jurisdiction shall be allotted to its various organs.[26]

Follett's *The New State*. The political philosophy developed by Miss M. P. Follett in her interesting volume *The New State: Group Organization the Solution of Popular Government,* published in 1918, is allied to political pluralism is so far as it emphasizes the failure of democratic governments, as at present organized, to give adequate representation to the diverse interests of

[26] Under existing practice there is at least one group of instances in which it is possible to have in the United States contradictory propositions of valid law. Under the American judicial system the federal courts have a jurisdiction based upon the diversity of citizenship of the parties to a suit and without reference to the subject matters involved. This has meant that a federal jurisdiction exists concurrent with that of the courts of the States in suits with reference to the same matters between parties who are citizens of the same State, with the result that there has not been an agreement between the federal and state courts as to the law governing certain subjects. Thus litigants now have applied to them certain legal principles if they happen to be in the federal courts, when, if they should carry exactly the same facts into the state courts, other principles would be applied. The same thing happens in the different inferior federal courts in cases in which no appeal or writ of error lies to the Supreme Court. That court has, however, been granted by Congress the right, when it deems it desirable, to obtain jurisdiction of causes by writ of *certiorari*, in order to give a final and unifying determination upon points of law regarding which there is a diversity of opinion in the lower federal courts.

modern society, and in so far as it stresses the value of group wills, and the advantages to be obtained from group organizations. However, there is no claim by Miss Follett that these organizations should be severally sovereign, and coördinate in legal status and authority with the political State. Her argument is that the true public will is not a composite or sublimation of the wills of separate individuals, but of the group wills in terms of which individual wills, so far at least as social or political matters are concerned, find their true expression. The practical purpose she has in view is, as is suggested by the sub-title of her work, to describe a form of state organization through which the popular will, as thus analyzed, can find authentic and controlling expression. Miss Follett does, indeed, speak with some contempt of the State, and does declare that it has been very generally discredited, but it would appear that she has reference only to the State as at present governmentally organized, and that she would not have political sovereignty itself abolished. In other words, she does not oppose sovereignty *per se*. "All thinking men," she says, "are demanding a new State. The question is—What form shall 'that State take?" [27]

In fact, Miss Follett devotes several chapters to a criticism of political pluralism. In one of them (XXIX) entitled "Political Pluralism and Sovereignty," she says that she wants to revivify local life "not for the purpose of breaking up sovereignty, but for the purpose of creating a real sovereignty."

Syndicalism. In the preceding pages the term Syndicalism has been several times used, and it remains here to add only a few words with regard to its general theory.

Syndicalism as a distinct body of social and political philosophy is French in origin. The name comes from the French word *Syndicat* meaning a union or combination.

[27] *Op. cit.*, p. 22.

So far as it may claim to be founded upon a philosophy it is chiefly that which has been developed by Georges Sorel, especially in his work *Réflexions sur la Violence*. It asserts the inherent iniquity of the wages system; alleges that the interests of capital and labor are irreconcilable; and declares that the State is an instrument for defending the unjust claims of property and capital. The State, the Syndicalist declares, cannot be reformed, but must be abolished. In the place of politically and capitalistically organized society, it urges the establishment of a régime under which the laborers will control not only the operations of all industrial plants, but, through their unions, exercise such general or political control as may be necessary. The means advocated for bringing this about is the abandonment upon the part of the laborers of all political or parliamentary action, that is, of all effort to secure the desired ends through existing political parties or parliamentary representation and state legislation, and the adoption in its place of direct action in the form of "sabotage" and strikes and especially the "general strike."

A critical examination of the theory and purpose of Syndicalism shows that though it is closely allied to Anarchism, in that it seeks the overthrow of existing governments, it does not propose permanently to abolish political rule itself. Syndicalists may believe, as do other economic or political reformers having great confidence in the humanizing and moralizing effects of their several schemes of social reconstruction, that, under the régimes proposed by them, the need for political coercion will decrease, and, possibly, ultimately disappear altogether, but, until this perfect result is reached, political authority is to be exercised by and through the syndicats or trade unions. In final result, there will be but a substitution of an industrial or proletarian for what is now alleged to be a capitalistic government.

The close relation of the Syndicalist philosophy in France to that of the Industrial Workers of the World (the I. W. W.) in America, to Guild Socialism in Great Britain, and to Sovietism in Russia, so far as self-government in industry is concerned, is very clear.[28]

As regards this matter of self-government in industry it is interesting to note that legal or constitutional provision has been made both in Great Britain and in Germany for instrumentalities through which, to an extent at least, trade or labor unions may settle their problems and disputes among themselves without state action, and, furthermore, may have organs through which they may express their policies and thus directly exercise a more enlightening and pursuasive influence upon the political authorities than they have been able to do in the past. In Great Britain this has been done by the establishment of the so-called "Whitley Councils" as a result of the recommendations made in 1916 by the Whitley Parliamentary Commission.[29] In Germany we have Section V of the republican Constitution, devoted to the economic interests of the people, which, while authorizing collectivism when deemed advisable, that is, the state ownership and operation of business enterprises now under private ownership and operation, nevertheless recognizes the propriety and desirability, when possible, of giving to the laborers a share in the operation of the industries in which they are employed.[30] The most important Article

[28] For a brief statement, with references to authorities, of what is known in France as "Administrative Syndicalism," see the article by F. W. Coker, "The Technique of the Pluralistic State," in the *American Political Science Review*, May, 1921 (Vol. XV, p. 186).

[29] Parliamentary Command Paper, 9099 (1918), October, 1916.

[30] Article 156 of the Constitution reads: "The Reich may by law, without impairment of the right to compensation, and with a proper application of the regulations relating to expropriation, transfer to public ownership private business enterprises adapted for socialization. The Reich itself, the States or the municipalities may take part in the management of business enterprises and associations, or secure a dominating influence therein in any other way.

"Furthermore, in case of urgent necessity the Reich, if it is in the interest of collectivism, may combine by law business enterprises and

of the Constitution in this respect is No. 165, which reads as follows:

"The wage-earners and salaried employés are entitled to be represented in local workers' councils, organized for each establishment in the locality, as well as in district workers' councils, organized for each economic area, and in a National Workers' Council, for the purpose of looking after their social and economic interests.

"The district workers' councils and the National Workers' Council meet together with the representatives of the employers and with other interested classes of people in district economic councils and in a National Economic Council for the purpose of performing joint economic tasks and coöperating in the execution of the laws of socialization. The district economic councils and the National Economic Council shall be so constituted that all substantial vocational groups are represented therein according to their economic and social importance.

"Drafts of laws of fundamental importance relating to social and economic policy before introduction [into the National Assembly] shall be submitted by the National Cabinet to the National Economic Council for consideration. The National Economic Council has the right itself to propose such measures for enactment into law. If the National Cabinet does not approve them, it shall, nevertheless, introduce them into the National Assembly together with a statement of its own position. The National Economic Council may have its bill presented by one of its own members before the National Assembly.

associations on the basis of administrative autonomy, in order to insure the cooperation of all producing elements of the people, to give to employers and employés a share in the management, and to regulate the production, preparation, distribution, utilization and pecuniary valuation, as well as the import and export, of economic goods upon collectivist principles.

"The cooperative societies of producers and consumers and associations thereof shall be incorporated, at their request and after consideration of their form of organization and peculiarities, into the system of collectivism."

"Supervisory and administrative functions may be delegated to the workers' councils and to the economic councils within their respective areas.

"The regulation of the organization and duties of the workers' councils and of the economic councils, as well as their relation to other social bodies endowed with administrative autonomy, is exclusively a function of the Reich."

INDEX

Acton, Lord, views of, as to nationalism, 344.
American Institute of International Law, declaration of, as to rights and duties of nations, 357.
Analytical Jurisprudence, Hobbes prepares the way for, 184.
Anarchy, theories of, 42 *seq.*; 260.
Aristotle, political doctrines of, 7.

Barnes, his exposition of Fascist theory, 136, 144.
Bernhardi, views of, 331.
Block, Maurice, views of, as to nationalism, 341.
Bolshevism, 70 *seq.*
Bluntschli, organismic theory of, 28; views of, as to divine right, 100.
Brown, Professor Philip M., quoted as to rights of nations, 361.
Burgess, Professor John W., views of, 21; as to national States, 332.
Burke, quoted as to representative government, 323.

China, theocratic theories in, 94 *seq.*
Church and State, 84 *seq.*
Coercion, true basis of, 236 *seq.*; distinction between political and other forms of, 256; legitimate ends of, 270; doctrine of Stephen, 284.
Cole, G. D. H., doctrines of, as to Guild Socialism, 437 *seq.*
Communism, theories of, 59 *seq.*; see "Socialism."
Communist Manifesto, 69.
Competitive Process, and State authority, 286.
Conscience, as an ethical guide, 274.

Constitutional Government, defined, 310 *seq.*
Contract Theory, 149 *seq.*; truth and error of, 221 *seq.*; See "Hobbes," "Locke," "Rousseau," "Natural Law."
Cynics, 161.

Declaration of Rights and Duties of Nations, 357.
Democratic Government, defined, 315.
Dewey, John, quoted, 241.
Dickinson, Professor Edwin, quoted, 246.
Divine Right, theories of, 83 *seq.*
Duguit, theories of, 385 *seq.*
Durkheim, influence of, upon Duguit, 389.

Elliott, quoted, 409.
Eminent Domain, international right of, 370.
Engels, theories of, 63 *seq.*
Equality of States, 246.
Essential Functions, of the State, 299.
Ethics, relation of, to final political philosophy, 4.
Evolutionary Process, and sphere of State action, 286.

Fascism, theory of, 131 *seq.*
Figgis, cited, 428; quoted, 429, 103.
Final Political Philosophy, distinguished from juristic political philosophy, 3; relation of, to ethics, 4; relation of, to metaphysics, 6; relation of, to theology, 8; importance of, 11; alleged dangers of, 14.
First International, 71.
Follett, M. P., doctrines of, 451.
Force Theory, 33 *seq.*; see "Anarchy."

457

INDEX

Gandhi, theories of, 57.
General Will, Rousseau's doctrine of, 208 *seq.*
Germany, divine right theories in, 98 *seq.*; ante-war doctrines of, 370; workers' councils in, 455.
Gini, Professor, his exposition of Fascist theory, 135, 141, 143, 147.
Gladstone, Morley's Life of, quoted, 115.
Godwin, William, theories of, 43 *seq.*
Government, defined, 304 *seq.*; popular, 306 *seq.*; distinguished from State, 382.
Governmental Compact, history of theory of, 150 *seq.*
Great Britain, constitutional government of, 313.
Grotius, and the social compact theory, 152, 153, 156, 165.
Guild Socialism, doctrine of, 437 *seq.*

Hayes, Professor Carlton, quoted as to nationalism, 342 (n)
Hegel, political theories of, 117 *seq.*; as to value of independent States, 328 *seq.*
Historical Theory, 20.
Hobbes, political doctrines of, 166 *seq.*; precursor of Bentham and Austin, 184; views of, compared with those of Locke and Rousseau, 219 *seq.*
Hobhouse, L. T., quoted, 274.
Hobson, S. G., views of, as to Guild Socialism, 442.
Hooker, and the social compact theory, 155.

Independent States, value of a system of, 327.
Inferior Peoples, control of, 365 *seq.*
International, first, second and third communist, 71 *seq.*
International Law, Duguit's conception of nature of, 403; Krabbe's conception of, 420.

International Relations, 325 *seq.*
International Rights of States, 356 *seq.*

Japan, theocratic constitutional theory in, 90 *seq.*; international interests of, 145; constitutional government of, 312; doctrine of, as to vital interests, 363.
Juristic Political Philosophy and final political philosophy distinguished, 3.
Justice, definition of, 250.

Kant, views of, 116, 238, 263.
Krabbe, theories of, 410 *seq.*
Kropotkin, theories of. 49 *seq.*

Lansing, Robert, views of, as to doctrine of self-determination, 353.
Laski, political pluralism of, 431 *seq.*
Lenin, theories of, 70 *seq.*; 74 *seq.*
Locke, political theories of, 188 *seq.*; 219 *seq.*
Lovejoy, Professor A. O., cited, 199.

Machiavelli, Fascist admiration for, 147.
Majorities, rights of, 226 *seq.*; according to Krabbe, 417; according to Rousseau, 210.
Marx, theories of, see "Socialism" and "Communism," 65 *seq.*
Maurenbrecker, Professor Max, quoted as to German Kultur, 371.
Mazzini, views of, as to nationalism, 339.
Mentally Incompetent Persons, rights of, 265.
Metaphysics, relation of, to final political philosophy, 6.
Mill, J. S., formula of, as to State control, 292; quoted as to representative government, 322; view of, as to nationalism, 343.
Minorities, rights of, 226 *seq.*
Moral Obligation, basis of, 252 *seq.*

INDEX

Motive, ethical significance of, 241.
Mulford, transcendentalism of, 129, 335.
Mussolini, declarations of, regarding Fascism, 131 (n); 138, 141, 142.
Mystical Theories of the State, 114 seq.

National States, views of Hegel, Treitschke, Burgess and Mulford, as to, 331 seq.
Nationality, principle of, discussed, 338 seq.
Natural Law, 8; development of different definitions of, 157 seq., 246, 244 seq.; Duguit's acceptance of, 406.
Nietzsche, theories of, 39 seq.

Organismic Theory of the State, 25 seq.; Duguit's view, 397.

Patrimonial Theory, 110 seq.
Personality, of the State, views as to, of Political Pluralists, 428 seq.
Philippines, American control of, and right to independence, 367.
Philosophy, see "Political Philosophy."
Plato, political doctrines of, 7, 17, 34, 160.
Pluralism, political, 427 seq.
Police Power, defined, 292.
Political Coercion, reality of problem of, 18; analysis of problem of, 19.
Political Compact, and the social compact distinguished, 154.
Political Pluralism, see Pluralism.
Popular Government, ethical basis of, 306 seq.; theory of, as practically applied, 309 seq.; defined, 317.
Proudhon, theories of, 45.
Prussia, constitutional doctrines of prior to 1914, 104.

Renan, views of, as to nationality, 338.
Representative Government, 316.

Rights, equality of, 246; no absolute, 248; see "National Rights," "Natural Law."
Rocco, Signor, his exposition of Fascist theory, 132 seq.
Romans, and doctrines of natural law, 162.
Rousseau, political theories of, 199 seq.; 219 seq.; influence of, upon Krabbe, 414 seq.

Sabine, Professor, quoted, 424, 447.
Second International, 71.
Self-Defense, international right of, 362.
Self-Determination, doctrine of, examined, 349 seq.
Shepard, Professor, quoted, 424.
Shintoism, 91.
Smuts, General Jan, and doctrine of self-determination, 351 (n).
Social Contract, see "Contract Theory."
Socialism, theories of, 59 seq.; state, and social reform distinguished, 60; and syndicalism distinguished, 61; and communism distinguished, 62; Marxian, 65.
Socialistic Functions of the State, 300.
Sophists, 160.
Sovereignty, juristic concept of, 381 seq.; Krabbe's definition of, 422; Laski's treatment of, 431 seq.
Spencer, Herbert, organismic theory of, 27; theory as to anarchy, 55 seq.; views of, as to sphere of political control, 287.
Spinoza, political theories of, 186 seq.
State, right to exist, 18 seq.; historical theory as to, 20; organismic theory, 25; force theory, 33; independent system of, 327; international rights of, 356; inherent limits to authority of, 283; classification of functions of, 299.

Stephen, Sir James Fitzjames, doctrine of as to when coercion justified, 284, 297.
Stirner, Max, theories of, 36 *seq.*
Stoics, 161, 162.
Suarez, political theories of, 152.
Suicide of a State, 326.
Syndicalism, theory of, 61; 452 *seq.*

Territorial Inviolability, 348.
Theology, relation of, to final political philosophy, 8.
Thiers, doctrine of, as to territorial inviolability, 348.

Third International, 71.
Transcendental Theories of the State, 114 *seq.*
Treitschke, political theories of, 123 *seq.;* 331, 373.

Utopian Socialism, 64.

Whitley Councils, 454.
William II, divine right theories of, 98 *seq.*
Wilson, Woodrow, quoted as to self-determination, 349, 351.
Workers' Councils, of Germany, 455.